APPLE IN CHINA

APPLE IN CHINA

THE CAPTURE OF THE WORLD'S GREATEST COMPANY

PATRICK McGEE

SIMON & SCHUSTER

London · New York · Amsterdam/Antwerp · Sydney/Melbourne · Toronto · New Delhi

First published in Great Britain by Simon & Schuster UK Ltd, 2025

7 9 10 8 6

Simon & Schuster UK Ltd
1st Floor
222 Gray's Inn Road
London WC1X 8HB

www.simonandschuster.co.uk
www.simonandschuster.com.au
www.simonandschuster.co.in

Simon & Schuster Australia, Sydney
Simon & Schuster India, New Delhi

The authorised representative in the EEA is Simon & Schuster Netherlands BV, Herculesplein 96, 3584 AA Utrecht, Netherlands. info@simonandschuster.nl

A CIP catalogue record for this book is available from the British Library

Hardback ISBN: 978-1-3985-3436-0
Paperback ISBN: 978-1-3985-3437-7
eBook ISBN: 978-1-3985-3438-4

Book text design by Kathryn A. Kenney-Peterson

Typeset in Arno Pro

Printed and Bound in India by Thomson Press India Ltd.

For my family

Building on a long-forgotten or neglected legacy of technique from classical antiquity, with additions imported by the so-called barbarians, or acquired from more advanced cultures to the east, they succeeded in developing by the fourteenth century—certainly by the fifteenth—a corpus of knowledge and skills that not only put them far ahead of their teachers, but conferred on them a decisive superiority of power. It is on this basis that Europe changed from a hapless victim to global aggressor, from a poor backwater, obliged to make its balance of payments in slaves for want of marketable exports, to the affluent workshop of the world.

—David Landes (1924–2013), Harvard economic historian

Without a strong manufacturing industry, there will be no country and no nation.

—Made in China 2025, Beijing policy document, 2015

Contents

PROLOGUE

"INCOMPARABLE" ARROGANCE

Xi Jinping wasted no time making it known to the world's biggest tech company that things would be different. On March 15, 2013, just one day after he was inaugurated as China's new president, Beijing's state broadcaster aired its annual *Consumer Day* show, a segment watched by millions that dated back to 1991. Every March, China Central Television would call out various corporate players that hadn't been treating customers well. In the 1990s, Chinese companies were savagely criticized. By the 2000s, foreign companies came under scrutiny, with McDonald's and French grocery chain Carrefour called out for food violations in 2012. And in 2013, the target was Apple. The CCTV charged that Apple treated Chinese customers poorly and unequally. In foreign markets, CCTV said, broken iPhones were wholly replaced or restored with new parts, but Chinese customers' phones were fixed with refurbished parts.

In Cupertino, Apple executives were perplexed by the allegations. Initially, there was no worry, just confusion. It looked like a simple misunderstanding. Apple's warranties were near identical around the globe, whether the consumer was in China or Canada. The gap between the negative coverage and the apparent problems—warranty differences, of all things—was jarring. So the iPhone maker reacted the way any company might: It matter-of-factly denied the claims, clarifying that its warranties in China were "more or less the same as in the U.S. and all over the world." For good measure, Apple added that it provided an "*incomparable* user experience."

Wrong answer! Cupertino was soon victim to a digital blitzkrieg as state-backed media engaged in a coordinated multi-week attack on Apple. Some newspapers called the company "dishonest" and said Apple's customer service was poor. China's quality inspection bureau warned Apple of "severe repercussions" if it didn't improve its warranties. *The People's Daily,* a Beijing mouthpiece, scolded the "empty and self-praising" statement in an editorial printed on its front page. Millions of Chinese subscribers woke up to a paper whose chief headline read: "Strike Down Apple's '*Incomparable*' Arrogance." The editorial accused the company of greed and "throwing its weight around," portraying it as just the latest foreign company to exploit the Chinese consumer. "Here we have the Western person's sense of superiority making mischief," the editorial said. "If there's no risk in offending the Chinese consumer, and it also makes for lower overheads, then why not?" The editorial had a menacing "or else . . . " tone to it, pointing out that Chinese consumers had "propped up the brand's remarkable results." *It'd be a shame if something happened to it,* was implied.

For Apple, the stakes were enormous. From its founding in a garage in 1976 through its incredible growth in the 1980s to its near bankruptcy in 1996, Apple largely manufactured its own computers. It operated major factories in California and Colorado, Ireland, and Singapore. Shortly before Steve Jobs returned to the company in 1997, Apple began to abandon this strategy, though, in favor of offshoring its production to contract manufacturers. Production initially moved to South Korea and Taiwan, and then Mexico, Wales, the Czech Republic, and China. It was a period of experimentation before the armies of flexible, affordable, and hardworking laborers in China prevailed, aided by government policies meant to lure multinational corporations by offering depressed salaries, a suppressed currency, and a relaxed take on labor laws. As the Chinese scholar Qin Hui puts it, the country's competitiveness was based on "low wages, low welfare, and low human rights."

These operations played such a salient role in Apple's success that by 2011 the unassuming character behind them, chief operating officer Tim Cook, was handpicked by Steve Jobs to succeed him as CEO. Cook, unlike Jobs, wasn't a charismatic leader or a product visionary, but his appointment was a recognition that he'd established unparalleled efficiencies that had become a decisive factor in Apple's ascent. The selection signaled that Apple's goal for the coming decade was less about breakthrough products and more about distributing, at scale, the hit products it had already conceived.

The vitriolic commentary directed at Apple following the CCTV episode, coupled with a sharp decline in China sales, underscored that Apple's gargantuan operations in the country had created the company's biggest vulnerability: its newfound dependence on a single country, China. For the prior decade this risk had felt remote. China was opening to the world, embracing capitalism and marching toward democracy. But in 2013, Xi took China in a radically different direction. The years of being a multinational haven were over. Prizing "indigenous innovation," Xi hardened conditions in the country and twisted the arms of corporations to "give back" to China, part of a goal to turn the country into the unquestioned leader in technology.

At the time of the digital blitzkrieg, Apple's business in China had been soaring—a development that, harkening back to the way things had looked at the time of the 2008 Beijing Olympics, was wholly unexpected. Back then, Apple had opened its first China store. That year, its China revenues were far less than $1 billion; by 2012, they'd ballooned to almost $23 billion. But with the negative publicity, sales abruptly declined: Greater China revenues had experienced 67 percent growth in the December quarter, but growth plummeted to just 8 percent in 2013's March quarter, and in the June quarter they shrank 14 percent. An internal document from Apple later said the decline was "likely influenced by the Chinese Government's decision to target Apple on Consumer Day." Apple, in a matter of weeks, went from feeling untouchable to fearing its products would be blacklisted.

Eighteen days after the CCTV episode, Tim Cook personally apologized with a letter, translated into Mandarin and posted on Apple's China website. He offered "sincere apologies," said he had "immense respect" for China, and acknowledged that a "lack of communication" had led to Apple appearing arrogant or signaling that it didn't value feedback. He declared a new replacement policy that was superior to what American customers would receive.

In the years since, two narratives within Apple have developed regarding what happened in those eighteen days. One is that CEO Tim Cook underwent something of a twenty-first-century show trial: Beijing had deliberately accused Apple of something it knew wasn't true, to demonstrate its power. The whole episode was a spectacle designed to make Cupertino understand its junior position in the partnership and then publicly kowtow. Some hard-liners in China certainly saw Cook's apology this way: On social media one rejoiced that Apple had been compelled to "bow its arrogant head."

But there is a competing, more nuanced narrative that points to real setbacks experienced by Chinese consumers. The problem here wasn't with Apple per se, but rather with a series of challenges that had emerged from counterfeit iPhones being sold around the country. In some cases, bad actors and duped customers were bringing fake iPhones to the Apple Store, saying they were defective and asking for a replacement. Employees would determine the products were knockoffs and reject them. These difficulties were exacerbated by dozens of sham stores emerging in cities where Apple hadn't built a retail presence. These stores could appear so genuine that the employees themselves thought they were real. The phony stores often sold real goods, but it was a grift—they had no interest in replacing defective or broken hardware. The experience of customers going to these stores for help created misinformation, fueling anger and complaints to government officials. The situation was confounding: Beijing's concerns were valid, in that there was real consumer anger, and yet its critiques were technically wrong, as Apple warranties were virtually identical across the world.

Neither of these narratives, however, represents the full story, revealed later in this book. In any case, the Consumer Day incident and its aftermath was a watershed episode for Apple. Cupertino realized just how deeply exposed it was in China and how ill-equipped it was to understand the situation and respond. Apple's top brass abruptly came to understand that they had no answers to basic questions like *What's our government strategy in China?* or *What's our political strategy in China?* For years the company had relied on partners, led by Taiwanese assembly giant Foxconn, to engage with provincial governments on labor issues and supply chain challenges. Apple had no broader, coordinated strategy. It employed around 1,000 engineers in China at the time, but none were senior. The company was orchestrating vast production networks but doing so under the radar. Not a single manufacturing site bore the Apple name or displayed a bitten fruit outside, yet by 2012 the value of Apple-owned machinery in the country had soared to $7.3 billion—more than Apple's US buildings and retail stores put together. Apple had essentially cracked the code on how to manufacture the world's best products without doing any of the manufacturing itself. It wasn't really "outsourcing" in the normal sense—that would imply it was sending blueprints to companies capable of taking the orders and executing. Instead, Apple was routinely sending its top engineers, designers, procurement specialists, and lawyers from the United States into hundreds of factories across the country, where they'd import machinery, train armies of workers, coordinate the delivery of intermediate goods, and scrutinize suppliers to ensure compliance. Apple's influence was enormous, but no senior executives lived in China or understood the politics, nor had Apple appointed anyone to oversee the business or manage government affairs.

The thinness of its team on the ground might have been unremarkable in 2009, when Apple was primarily just an operator that used China as a base for building products and exporting them around the world. But by 2012 the iPhone had become a massively sought-after device by Chinese consumers, boosting Apple's regional revenues by 2,830 percent. That growth testified to the dual potency of Apple's remarkable product designs and world-leading production. But its particular success in China was totally unforeseen and not the result of some well-thought-out strategy. In just a few years the Greater China region had progressed from delivering minimal revenue to generating almost 15 percent of Apple's global total. This wild success was as surprising to Cupertino as to everyone else—even Tim Cook called it "mind-boggling." When *Time* published a cover story called "The Cult of Apple in China" in mid-2012, writer Hannah Beech had correctly mused: "much of Apple's growth in China has been a lesson in how to prosper without really trying."

The Age of Apple

Apple in China tells a huge untold story—how Apple used China as a base from which to become the world's most valuable company, and in doing so, bound its future inextricably to a ruthless authoritarian state. It's the story of how Apple convinced Beijing it was not merely a merchant in China, but a kind of patron and mentor, financing, training, supervising, and supplying Chinese manufacturers. This isn't a story about the globalization of electronics, but rather, about its Chinafication.

The prevailing Western narrative about Apple in China is remarkably narrow. The go-to story of the past two decades has been about the tedium of assembling Apple products—a tale of low wages, underage employees, sixteen-hour workdays, suicides at Foxconn, and accusations of forced Uighur labor. This narrative isn't wrong, but it misses the biggest piece of the puzzle: It's not merely that Apple has exploited Chinese workers, it's that Beijing has *allowed* Apple to exploit its workers, so that China can in turn exploit Apple.

It would be banal to say that Apple wouldn't be Apple today without China. There is no other place on earth that could have provided similar cost, efficiency, and scale. What this book contends is more intriguing—that China wouldn't be China today without Apple. Its investments in the country have been spectacular, rivaling nation-building efforts in cost, man-hours, and impact. Apple itself estimates that since 2008 it has trained at least 28 million workers—more people than the entire labor force of California. China brilliantly played its long-term interests against Apple's short-term needs. In 1999, none of Apple's products were made in mainland China; by 2009, virtually all were. This rapid consolidation reflects a transfer of technology and know-how so consequential as to constitute a geopolitical event, like the fall of the Berlin Wall—but it's an event that played out over many years, hidden by the twin threats of strict nondisclosure agreements and a censored media landscape where all the action was.

Internal documents obtained for this book reveal that Apple's investments in China reached $55 billion *per year* by 2015, an astronomical figure that doesn't include the costs of components in Apple hardware—the so-called Bill of Materials, which would more than double the figure. Compare that to the CHIPS and Science Act, the flagship policy of the Biden administration that then–Commerce Secretary Gina Raimondo called "a once-in-a-generation investment"—one that would "usher in a new era of American leadership in advanced semiconductor manufacturing." The CHIPS and Science Act, which is designed to stimulate computer chip fabrication in America, will cost the US government $52 billion over four years—$3 billion shy of what Apple invested annually in China nearly a decade earlier. Let me underscore this point: Apple's investments in China, every year for the past decade, are at least quadruple the amount the US commerce secretary considered a once-in-a-generation investment.

Although it's far from secret that Apple manufactures its products in China, the seminal role the tech giant has played there is largely unheralded and unknown. By contrast, Taiwan's critical, multi-decade role industrializing China through investment and worker training is widely recognized. At least three major books have been written on the subject in English since 2017. Even Xi Jinping, who seeks to annex Taiwan and has little reason to flatter its citizens, has acknowledged that China's forty years of opening and reform "has to be chalked up to our Taiwan compatriots and Taiwan companies." Taipei calculates that between 1991 and 2022, total business investment from the corporate sector exceeded $203 billion, a huge number by any standard—barring Cupertino's.

The size and influence of Apple aren't properly understood, in part because they are so difficult to fathom. How can it be, for instance, that demand from China's 1.4 billion people indirectly supports, across all industries, between 1 million and 2.6 million jobs in America; whereas, by Tim Cook's estimate, Apple alone supports 5 million jobs in China—3 million in manufacturing and another 1.8 million in app development? That upside-down contrast boggles the mind: one super-corporation has more of an impact on job creation in China than all of China has on America.

As I write this, Apple is expected to pull in $414 billion of global revenue in 2025, a company record. Since 2007, the iPhone alone has already earned a cumulative $2 trillion in sales. Apple's business is so large and lucrative that in 2024 its $94 billion of net profit exceeded all revenue at NVIDIA—the chips architect worth $3 trillion that rivals Apple for world's most valuable company. It's common to hear that Apple is now stagnating, either because innovation has slowed or its hardware has reached commercial saturation. But the ubiquity of the iPhone has allowed Apple to wring huge profit from a new business in the last few years: services. The number of Apple devices in active use surpassed 2.35 billion in 2025, led by 1.4 billion iPhone users who spend more than four hours a day immersed in their glowing screens. These users represent the richest quintile of people in the world, and Apple can advertise or promote features to them—wireless payment, television shows, music streaming, fitness offerings—for free. In fact, Google pays Apple close to $20 billion a year just to be the default search engine on the iPhone.

The control Apple has over its ecosystem is extraordinary: When in 2021 Apple changed how third parties like Instagram and Facebook could "track users"—ostensibly a move to protect the privacy of iPhone owners—Meta estimated the new policy diminished its annual earnings by $10 billion. Meanwhile, revenue from Apple's own privacy-first ad business was on a path to grow from $1 billion in 2020 to $30 billion by 2026. One advertising executive characterized the change as going "from playing in the minor leagues to winning the World Series in the span of half a year." On average, Apple's Services business earns margins north of 70 percent, double that of its hardware, and the business has been growing at nearly 20 percent a year for six years—all before potentially being supercharged by new artificial intelligence features. In short, the notion that Apple is at its peak is patent nonsense. But there is one Achilles' heel: The fate of all the company's hardware production relies on the good graces of America's largest rival.

One of the narrative arcs of this book is how Apple, a company that built the world's most sophisticated supply chain, ended up making the rookie and calamitous mistake of concentrating the vast bulk of its operations in a single area. As tech analyst Horace Dediu puts it: "It's hard to reconcile the fact that the greatest American company, the most capitalist thing in the world, survives on the basis of a country that has Communist in its title." In the years after Steve Jobs's death, Dediu argued that maintaining Apple's team, its culture, was paramount. "But today, what keeps Tim Cook up at night is China," he says. "The China thing is existential."

This book details how the Taiwanese manufacturer Foxconn refined an idea developed in America in the 1960s—electronics contract manufacturing—and took it to unprecedented heights using cheap and readily available labor in mainland China to develop cutting-edge expertise on a scale unknown anywhere else. At a time when China was severely lacking in manufacturing skill, Taiwanese entrepreneurs played a vital role in building operations and transferring skills to the mainland. None was more influential than Foxconn, whose revenues today are greater than Facebook parent Meta and NVIDIA combined. Its ascent to become the world's largest maker of electronic components was driven by Apple's sending troops of engineers en masse to mainland China to teach automation, engineering, and manufacturing.

But after years of Apple seemingly calling the shots, with Chinese provincial governments and suppliers bending over backward to win orders, the power dynamics have shifted. Since 2017, Beijing has made increasing demands of Apple's China business, applying greater control over the content on the iPhone, forcing customer data to be housed in Chinese data centers, and pressuring Apple to partner with more local businesses. Cupertino has chosen not to expend political capital to fight Beijing's more draconian demands; it has banned thousands of apps in the country, including *The New York Times,* encrypted messaging tools such as WhatsApp, and virtual private networks (VPNs) that had enabled users to bypass the Great Firewall. It has also supported companies such as Yangtze Memory Technologies Corp (YMTC)—a Beijing-sponsored chipmaker that a bipartisan group of US senators believe is a national security risk. When Apple shifted production to China in the early 2000s, Washington believed that free trade would help develop a middle class and inculcate democracy in what was then the world's most populous country. Instead, economic success empowered China's rulers, reinforcing their once-tenuous hold on the country and enabling Beijing to weaponize its manufacturing might. As one former Apple engineer puts it: "We've trained a whole country, and now that country is using it against us."

Apple, having invested billions of dollars on infrastructure and training to make Chinese factories unparalleled world leaders, has had little choice but to comply with Beijing. So the "real estate" within the iPhone is increasingly Chinese, as state-subsidized companies known as "the Red Supply Chain" win more orders at the expense of Apple's longtime American, Taiwanese, and Japanese partners.

As the first major history of Apple in the twenty-first century, this book focuses less on product appearance and software features, and more on how the hardware gets made. It's a perspective shift that places the company's five-decade lifespan into its proper geopolitical context. Multinational corporations weren't calling the shots in the early 2000s, as they believed; they were actively being lured by the siren call of an emerging superpower.

Today, Apple works with more than 1,500 suppliers in fifty countries. But all roads lead through China: 90 percent of all production occurs in the country, and its much-vaunted assembly operations in Vietnam and India are no less dependent on the China-centric supply chain.

Operations for the iPhone alone span 200 production lines in China, each making an average 3,330 units a day—nearly a quarter billion per year. From 2007 through 2019, *all* iPhones were assembled by Taiwanese groups working in China, but their influence is rapidly waning; mainland Chinese groups with political backing have been taught the necessary skills and are taking over. How strategic this all was on the part of Beijing is difficult to surmise. But if hindsight is twenty-twenty, a former senior designer at Apple says it looks like Beijing's strategy was to "brain drain" Taiwan, learn everything that is needed, then "cash them out," and take over. Where Taiwan remains strongest is in semiconductors. Every notable Apple product relies on chips sourced from a single company in Taiwan, TSMC, by far the world's most advanced chipmaker and the crux of Taipei's "Silicon Shield" against possible invasion by Beijing.

Washington has reconciled itself to China's authoritarian turn, but America's biggest company has not—and probably cannot. The iPhone maker's relationship with China has become politically untenable, yet the business ties are unbreakable. No other country comes remotely close to offering the right combination of quality, scale, and flexibility needed to ship close to half a billion luxury products each year. Nor does Cupertino want to stop selling into a country with the world's largest middle class. Only a dozen multinationals earn more than $10 billion a year in China, and Apple tops the list with around $70 billion. Never mind conceiving "the next big thing." Apple's China Problem is the company's biggest risk, the most consequential unknown for Tim Cook's legacy, and an urgent challenge for Washington.

This is the story of how Apple got here.

PART ONE

SAVING APPLE

CHAPTER 1

THE BRINK OF BANKRUPTCY

Joe O'Sullivan needed to sell Apple's Macintosh factory in Fountain, Colorado, and fast. The week before, in late March 1996, Apple stunned observers by announcing it would lose $700 million that quarter, the biggest financial setback in its history. Debts were coming due, and Apple needed cash. But the Fountain deal was no ordinary asset sale. It was a capitulation.

The personal computer (PC) industry had undergone an enormous shift over the previous fifteen years, from companies building their own computers to outsourcing as much production as possible. Apple was the last holdout. Since its founding by two college dropouts named Steve in 1976, manufacturing had been part of the company's culture. But now it was failing. The rest of the industry had off-loaded most of their production to contract manufacturers that had proved far nimbler and more cost-effective.

O'Sullivan, a self-deprecating, straight-talking Irishman who would spend fifteen years working in Apple operations on three continents and rise to the level of vice president, was in talks to sell the Fountain factory to SCI Systems, a contract manufacturer with little brand-name resonance relative to the profound role it played in the early history of personal computers.

Founded as Space Craft Inc, SCI was born in 1961 to help America compete with the Soviets after the launch of Sputnik. Its CEO, Olin B. King, had been a young engineer and brash entrepreneur when he co-founded SCI in the basement of his home in Huntsville, Alabama, known as "Rocket City." King and his staff earned their technical chops building satellites for the US government, near NASA's Marshall Space Flight Center. By the 1970s, SCI had switched tactics to build missile components for the superpower arms race and, eventually, instruments for NASA's Saturn V, the rocket that launched astronauts to the moon.

SCI had emerged as the ideal buyer in part because it could take over the manufacturing of Apple's products and retain much of the 1,100-person workforce. O'Sullivan was adamant that Apple get a good deal on the 340,000-square-foot factory, but the talks had reached an impasse. The Apple crew were thirty-somethings from California sporting T-shirts and a disdain for custom. They referred to their suit-wearing counterparts as "the grumpy old men from Huntsville," and irked them by critiquing the bagels that were served. But Apple also wanted SCI to be liable in the event that a sizable number of assembled products failed once they were in customers' hands, even if it was months later. SCI wouldn't sign, considering this an onerous risk—which it was.

King was no pushover. He was a cantankerous and difficult man who relished being known as "the Godfather of Huntsville." He enjoyed money and the social life it enabled, driving a large BMW at a time when imported luxury cars were virtually nonexistent in Alabama. More than anyone else, King brought into being what is now known as electronics manufacturing services, the stealth manufacturing industry now worth half a trillion dollars in annual revenue.

O'Sullivan had been negotiating all through the night, lawyers from Apple by his side. He was a savvy dealmaker and was happy being patient to get the best possible offer. Until, that is, he got a late-night call from Fred Forsyth, senior vice president of Worldwide Operations. "Joe, you need to sign this week," his superior said.

When O'Sullivan started to recount the standoff and stressed the wisdom of taking his time, Forsyth interjected and spoke over him.

O'Sullivan, tired from late-night bargaining, didn't immediately grasp the urgency in Forsyth's voice. Casually he replied: "It's not going to be done quickly, if we want the terms in our favor." Forsyth answered with a cadence and pitch that immediately unnerved the Irishman: "The deal has to be done quickly," he said, "or you don't get paid on Thursday."

The discussion had gone from casual to job-threatening in a matter of seconds. O'Sullivan shot back: "Come on, there is no need to threaten that!" What Forsyth said in return was relieving, personally, but only heightened the alarm. "No, you don't understand," he said, "if the deal doesn't get done, *none of us* will get paid on Thursday."

Death Spiral

Apple's corporate death was such a real possibility that it sought bankruptcy counsel. It hired a leading lawyer, Harvey Miller, of the law firm Weil, Gotshal & Manges. The company wasn't quite at the point of telling Miller to draw up the necessary papers, but it explored options to understand what a Chapter 11 filing could offer. Fred Anderson, who joined Apple as chief financial officer in March 1996, would later say: "This company was in a death spiral."

Months earlier, Apple's treasurer had warned the board of directors that Apple "would be out of money somewhere around May." Cash reserves had shrunk to $500 million, dangerously low for a company with 13,000 employees and $150 million of loans coming due in April. The holiday quarter of 1995 should have brought in reams of cash, but Apple's sales team had panicked over the launch of Microsoft Windows 95. Desperate to maintain market share and move inventory, they cut prices by as much as 30 percent, to below cost. Apple revenues soared to a record high $3.15 billion, but—losing money on each sale—the company stunned Wall Street with a $69 million loss, rather than the predicted $150 million profit.

The terrible results had cost German-born Michael Spindler his job as CEO. It had been Spindler's idea to flood the market with affordable Macs to compete with PCs. Apple warehouses were filled with nearly $1 billion of unsold inventory, a greater sum than the combined profits of the previous three years. Apple's board concluded that the best way out of the crisis was to sell the company. They'd already spent months scouting IBM, Sun Microsystems, and the Dutch electronics group Philips as possible buyers. Nothing much came from the talks, but a good offer almost certainly would have been accepted. Unfortunately, Apple's trajectory toward oblivion was so clear that when Sun CEO Scott McNealy pitched a merger, in late January 1996, he wouldn't even pay the stock market price. Apple was trading at around $28 a share, but McNealy's "best offer" was $23—valuing the company at just $2.8 billion. Apple considered the bid ridiculous and insulting. Yet McNealy was correct in his assessment. If anything, he was too generous. In six weeks, Apple shares would slide below $23. Within a year, they'd trade under $15.

Shortly after the Sun-Apple talks broke down, Apple's rainbow-color logo graced the cover of *BusinessWeek,* set against an all-black background. In bold gray letters was the headline: "The Fall of an American Icon." The article accurately portrayed Apple as "in near-meltdown" and in need of "a radical overhaul." It resonated widely. Another senior vice president of Apple, Guerrino De Luca, was in talks to buy a house in San Francisco the week the issue was published. He'd secured a mortgage and put in an offer. Everything was a go. But the owner of the home subscribed to *BusinessWeek* and got nervous. "This guy works for Apple!" he protested. De Luca's banker tried to explain it wasn't a problem, that De Luca had already secured a loan, but the owner wouldn't listen. His offer was denied.

The Threat from Boca Raton—and Huntsville

In a way, it was amazing Apple had made it this far against a field of rivals who could achieve lower cost and better distribution for every computer they sold. Apple's survival was testament to the twin and somewhat contradictory forces of its founders. The Steve Wozniak–led Apple II computer, released in 1977, was the first personal computer to define a standard for others to follow, and it would be Apple's number one revenue driver for an entire decade. The second force was the advanced nature of the Macintosh operating system (OS). It really was a decade ahead of its time when, in 1984, a boyish and handsome Steve Jobs, then just twenty-eight, unveiled the Mac with dramatic flair to a packed auditorium. When Jobs clicked the mouse—itself a novelty at the time—the computer took the air out of the room by *speaking*. "Hello. I'm Macintosh," it said in an unnatural, synthetic voice, like it was Siri's grandfather. "It sure is great to get out of that bag."

But after Jobs was ousted the following year, time had caught up with Apple. Or rather, Microsoft had. The small software start-up had been a critical partner in the late 1970s, writing a programming language for the Apple II. But Microsoft spent a decade mimicking the Macintosh OS for IBM and other PCs, culminating in Windows 95. It hardly mattered that Windows was less elegant; whatever Microsoft did became industry standard, since every one of Apple's rivals, led by Dell, IBM, HP, and Compaq, ran on Windows. The PC boom of the 1990s fed an ever-greater need for applications made by third-party developers, and those developers prioritized the Windows community, who made up more than 90 percent of the market.

The hardware side of things mirrored this. Apple opened a factory in Fountain in 1991 to make laptop and desktop computers after an earthquake caused it to question whether all its North American production should be centered in the Bay Area. Apple wanted resiliency, as well as lower costs. But as PC leaders Dell and Compaq vastly improved distribution, logistics, and manufacturing efficiency, Fountain just wasn't competitive on price or scale. The PC industry could rely on commoditized parts and intense competition between third-party suppliers, whereas Apple used many custom parts made in lower volumes. That entailed higher costs and often required oversight on the part of Apple to make sure things fit.

By 1996 Apple had devolved into a has-been, a company making more expensive computers for a dwindling user base upset with being ignored by developers and furious with Apple for losing its innovative edge. In a desperate attempt to stay relevant, the Cupertino-based company was selling all manner of electronics—printers, scanners, cameras, and even the Newton "personal digital assistant." It lacked direction or strategy, and was sitting on mountains of unsold inventory.

The list of what had gone wrong at Apple was long, the missteps many. One venture capitalist said, "Apple's management ought to be tried for war crimes." Steve Jobs would pin the blame on John Sculley, his handpicked CEO who, after a feud, ousted Jobs in 1985 and led the company for more than a decade. Sculley, in Jobs's view, was unfocused and diminished the culture of innovation that Jobs had fostered. But part of the failure dates back to August 1981, the first time then twenty-six-year-old Jobs peered into the just-released IBM PC and completely misunderstood what he saw.

In the months before, at just five years old, Apple was an early leader in the nascent personal computer market. The Apple II desktop had carved out a sizable market share and had a reputation for simplicity and elegance. IBM, forty times larger than Apple, didn't make personal computers, but it was the world's most valuable company thanks to its near monopoly in the much larger business of building, selling, and servicing mainframes. A young Steve Ballmer would remember thinking IBM was "the sun, the moon, the stars of the computer industry."

Jobs had for months been anxious about IBM's potential entry into the market. His fear was that IBM—nicknamed Big Blue—would feature some breakthrough technology. His hope was that IBM would announce a solid computer, but one that was priced beyond the reach of the masses. That would bring validation to the very idea of the personal computer and help the whole industry.

Big Blue did neither. Recognizing problems with its own bureaucracy,

IBM took a radical decision: it commissioned a twelve-member task force in Boca Raton to build a desktop computer from scratch and get it to market in just a year. Speed and scale were the priorities, and they succeeded wildly. In the world of mainframes, IBM was known for making virtually everything itself. But the Boca Raton team took the opposite route and forced IBM's other divisions to bid for contracts like any other supplier. The small crew outsourced just about everything, piecing together a computer from already-existing parts. And for the operating system, they found a tiny crew of geeks few people had heard of—a start-up in Albuquerque then calling itself Micro-Soft, led by twenty-five-year-old Bill Gates.

The IBM PC wasn't at all special in how it worked, but rather in how it was put together. But Jobs failed to grasp the brilliance of what IBM had done. In August 1981, he bought an IBM PC, dissected it, then dismissed it as a piece of junk. Overly confident, he took out full-page newspaper ads saying: "Welcome, IBM. Seriously." His folly became clear quickly. IBM had, in 1980, zero revenues in PCs, but by 1982 it had taken 16 percent of the market, outselling Apple two to one. By 1984, IBM had achieved sales of more than $6 billion—nearly triple that of Apple. Big Blue's strategy hadn't just worked; the firm had blown Apple out of the water. Unfortunately for IBM's PC division, the brilliance of the Boca Raton strategy also contained the seeds of its eventual demise. IBM had allowed Microsoft to license its OS to others, and once companies like Compaq and Phoenix Technologies figured out how to "clone" the PC, IBM found itself in a series of furious battles over cost, branding, manufacturing, and logistics. By the early 1990s it was losing out on multiple fronts. The impact of this error had existence-threatening consequences not just for IBM, but for Apple as well.

Within a few years every other computer maker either adopted the PC standard or died. Apple was the sole survivor. If it had continued to be an innovation juggernaut, perhaps it could have thrived. But that didn't happen. Once the Windows world caught up with the Mac's superior OS, Apple's higher prices ceased to make sense and its market share fell apart. This series of events played out over fifteen years—but it all went back to Jobs dismissing the first PC.

Jobs's error was presuming the battle was on Apple's terms: usability and design. IBM instead launched an open architecture, which drove down costs, spurred competition, and enabled economies of scale. IBM might have been a new player in PCs, but its branding was beyond reproach. Millions of Americans could name only one tech company, and it was IBM. And now it was aided by an army of third-party entrepreneurs in both software and hardware.

Apple itself could have played this dominant role; in fact, it *had* played this role. At the behest of Steve Wozniak—overruling Jobs—the Apple II featured an open architecture with eight expansion slots and a floppy drive. This allowed third-party software and hardware companies to build applications for it, widening its appeal beyond hobbyists and gamers to the workplace. That openness gave rise, in October 1979, to a breakthrough digital spreadsheet tool, VisiCalc, the first "killer app" for personal computers. Along with EasyWriter, an early word processor, VisiCalc helped transform the Apple II from a plaything to a workhorse.

The openness of the Apple II was a unique feature and proved critical to its success. Big Blue wouldn't release its first home computer, the IBM PC, until 1981. By that time, Apple had already fostered a community of developers creating business apps and peripheral devices—at little cost to Apple itself. By contrast, rivals such as Atari, inventor of the popular video game Pong, wouldn't give programmers the source code for their computers, while RadioShack, a retail leader, barred developers from selling competitors' software in its stores. As historian Laine Nooney puts it in *The Apple II Age,* "Apple's robust system and hands-off approach" created a market "for the very nontechnical customers Apple would need in order to dominate the industry." By the end of 1983, the Apple II "had the largest library of programs of any microcomputer on the market—just over two thousand—meaning that its users could interact with the fullest range of possibilities in the microcomputing world."

But Jobs resented third-party developers as freeloaders. In early 1980, he had a conversation with Mike Markkula, Apple's chairman, where the two expressed their frustration at the rise of hardware and software groups building businesses around the Apple II. They asked each other: "Why should we allow people to make money off of us? Off of *our* innovations?" An attendee of the meeting would recount, years later, that Apple began to "fight" all third-party development. "Over time it got worse, and it became not just about money but ego," this person said, according to *Infinite Loop,* Michael Malone's history of Apple. "This attitude developed at Apple that nobody could do anything better than Apple could. That's why the company kept building its own keyboards and everything else—and why Apple computers became so much more expensive than [those of its rivals]."

Board-stuffing

SCI, the company O'Sullivan was trying to sell the Fountain factory to in 1996, played a massive but largely forgotten role in IBM's success. When IBM launched its PC, it relied on SCI's military experience in precision engineering to build circuit boards—a core part of the computer that gives electronics their functionality. The first Apple "computer," the Apple I in 1976, was nothing more than a "fully assembled" circuit board designed by Wozniak.

Apple's pioneering strategy to build circuit boards was to employ Jobs's younger, pregnant sister Patty, paying her a dollar for every board she assembled. Patty "settled on the living-room couch of her apartment, the boards on the coffee table before her, the soaps on TV and a phone cradled on her shoulder talking to friends, jamming the rows of little caterpillar-shaped integrated circuits into the holes on the surface of the green placemat-sized fiberglass printed circuit boards," writes Malone. "She wasn't very good at it, with a tendency to jam the chips down when they didn't fit just right—thus bending their little gold legs and setting the stage for future short circuits—but she was cheap, methodical and, most of all, available."

For the more popular Apple II, a small team took all the parts and separated them into little kits. Every few days they gave the kits to a Los Altos housewife, who coordinated a fragmented network of assembly operations spanning houses and apartments crowded with immigrant women from Southeast Asia and undocumented Mexicans. "No one ever mentioned minimum wage, or Social Security, or workplace safety laws," Malone writes. "And thus, for more than a year, the Apple II, promoted as the machine to liberate people from the slavery of bureaucracies and office work, was in fact being partially assembled in sweatshops."

IBM, by contrast, had turned to SCI because in its work building rockets it had pioneered an automated method for reliably assembling circuit boards, known as surface mount technology. As computers were miniaturized and became popular, advances in "board stuffing," as it was called, were a competitive edge that allowed IBM to build its PCs at high volume and low cost. Apple, thanks to Wozniak, had built a pioneering computer with the clever *design* of a circuit board; but IBM achieved market dominance through innovation of circuit board *production*. "SCI really is what made it operate—it was really the essence, the glue, of what made the computer run," says Jay Elliot, who worked at both IBM and Apple in the 1980s. "They really introduced automated manufacturing."

SCI's founder CEO Olin B. King then did something that would set a template for an entire industry. Adding to his knowledge of circuit boards, he had SCI take on adjacent tasks: it learned more about assembly operations, caught up with the latest methods in distribution, and started to win orders for subassembly and, later, to build entire computers—including for the PC clones that mimicked IBM. When SCI was building only circuit boards, it was just a supplier; when it started making another company's designs, it gave birth to a new industry: electronics contract manufacturing.

In the early days, King met all kinds of resistance. America really cared about manufacturing in the early 1980s. His idea wasn't just new, it was offensive. "I've been thrown out of a lot of places," King once recalled. "It was not socially acceptable to tell a manufacturer to give up his manufacturing." But the economics of what he offered were deeply alluring. It was costly to run your own factory. Full-time workers are a fixed cost, paid for year-round even when product demand is low and the workers are idle. King offered manufacturing as a service. His clients had to pay for only what they needed, when they needed it. The more clients he had, the more efficiently he could allocate resources, and the more his team would acquire manufacturing know-how. He could unburden companies of fixed costs, and—depending on the contract—take on the liabilities of product defects.

The idea gained traction quickly. SCI sales jumped from $45 million in 1981 to $500 million by 1985, with IBM as its biggest client. In short order, SCI was joined by the likes of Solectron, Flextronics, Celestica, and Jabil—all North America–based contract manufacturers who collectively killed off the entire concept of the do-it-yourself, vertically integrated computer company. By the mid-1990s, the PC industry still hadn't caught up with the elegance of the Macintosh operating system. But Windows 95 was good enough, and with the production innovations originally spearheaded by SCI, PCs became increasingly commoditized and affordable. As Apple struggled to keep up, SCI joined the Fortune 500 and became the world's largest assembler of electronics, with operations in seventeen countries and a head count north of 30,000.

A Balanced Manufacturing Strategy

This is why Apple's sale to SCI was a capitulation. Offloading the factory in Fountain underscored that Apple was being forced to give up the control-your-own-destiny-through-manufacturing strategy that had guided it from the days Jobs and Wozniak were tinkering in a garage. And it was selling the factory to SCI, no less of an enemy than Microsoft. SCI had pioneered the very strategy that doomed Apple, and now O'Sullivan, recognizing the depths of Apple's financial situation, was having to forgo any leverage to accelerate the deal. The Grumpy Old Men from Huntsville bought the plant for around $200 million, and Apple staff got paid the next Thursday. Soon Apple was pulling off similar deals to save on costs, adopting a new strategic direction that involved slashing 4,200 full-time jobs and downsizing operations globally.

O'Sullivan formed an Outsourcing Group, the first in Apple's history. The goal was to create a "balanced manufacturing strategy." But as inventories piled up, balance wasn't a luxury Apple could afford. Realizing it was in a race for survival, the company committed to outsource virtually everything. Product assembly soon shifted to Asia, primarily Taiwan, while the manufacturing of circuit boards—something Apple had done in Ireland and Singapore since the early 1980s— was offloaded to suppliers such as Singapore-based NatSteel. O'Sullivan remembers two Boeing 747s parked near the runway of the Shannon Airport one weekend. Then all of the printed circuit board assembly lines from Apple's factory in Cork were loaded on and flown away. The same thing happened in Singapore. Apple, the last vertically integrated computer company, was changing tack.

CHAPTER 2

ADVENTURES IN OUTSOURCING—JAPAN AND TAIWAN

Outsourcing had never been part of Apple's strategy before, but it had long been a tactic—something done in one-off cases or with products where Apple lacked proficient manufacturing skill. So the company wasn't ignorant of how outsourcing functioned. In fact, more than a decade earlier, its relationship with one Japanese company had saved the Macintosh from what might have been an embarrassing failure.

When Apple launched what it viewed as Apple II's successor, the Mac, on January 24, 1984, its graphical user interface—a way of interacting with visual icons, windows, and drag and drop rather than typing in arcane commands—was ahead of its time. But the Mac didn't have enough memory to run any serious programs. The computer that introduced itself by speaking was—surreptitiously—a souped-up version with 512 kilobytes of memory, not the 128 kilobytes the consumer got. Worse, so few developers had built programs for the Mac that the buyers who did splurge found there was precious little they could actually do with it. Apple had tried to get developers on board, but the Mac required such a different approach to writing software that programmers were given three-dictionary-size volumes for help. "We, the design team, expected everyone to say, 'Wow, this is fantastic,' but they didn't—no one understood it," says Bill Fernandez, Apple's first full-time employee.

The Mac was positioned as "the computer for the rest of us." But it wasn't. The Mac design team had aimed to make a computer that would cost $1,000, but development proved expensive, and John Sculley, the CEO whom Jobs had lured from Pepsi, raised the price to $2,500. Mishaps in Jobs's manufacturing strategy were part of the failure. He'd overseen the building of a $20 million state-of-the-art factory in Fremont to produce one Mac every twenty-seven seconds—versus six minutes for the Apple II. But when components didn't come in on time, production shut down for weeks. And Mac volumes didn't reach the levels needed for the plant to be efficient.

The combination of poor memory, few apps, a high price tag, and a flawed manufacturing strategy doomed the original Mac. But it took Apple nearly a year to realize this, and longer to accept it. There was little understanding at the time of early adopters—that class of buyers eager to be first and have the latest products. So when sales started out well and the Mac was profitable in its first quarter, Jobs predicted Apple would be selling 80,000 Macs per month by September. When sales petered out to as low as 5,000 a month, Apple launched an expensive marketing campaign and ramped up production for the Christmas quarter. By the second week of January 1985, early signs indicated that Apple revenue had soared to $700 million, more than double the prior Christmas. But Apple didn't have anything like real-time sales information, and it took some weeks to realize that Macs were piling up across retail channels, unsold. Customers had instead purchased half a billion dollars' worth of the Apple II. Demand for the Mac was so underwhelming that Jobs and Sculley declined to break out sales by product line when they delivered earnings to Wall Street. "Nobody wanted to let the world know that the Macintosh was doing so poorly," says Jay Elliot, who ran corporate operations.

Woz, the champion of the Apple II, was furious. For years he'd dealt with Jobs's antics that treated anyone working on the Apple II as a "bozo." So when the company kept secret the dominant role the Apple II was now playing in its earnings, Woz called up Sculley and accused him of deceiving shareholders.

If the Mac was going to be saved, it needed a core consumer group. It needed a killer app. And that's what led it to Japan.

LaserWriter

In the summer of 1984, Jobs, Elliot, and half a dozen engineers boarded a Boeing 747 and took their place in the first-class section, preparing for a ten-hour flight. They'd bought out the entire area for privacy, then laid out cardboard schematics of the controller board they were drawing up on a big round table. It was all part of an unlikely project that would ultimately save the Macintosh.

Back in Cupertino, Apple's documentation team had purchased an expensive Xerox-branded laser printer that was the size of a three-drawer file cabinet. The Mac, at Jobs's demand, could produce all range of beautiful fonts, but unless you had such a printer, they never left your monitor. Since 1982 Apple had been making dot matrix printers in-house, but their pixelated images failed to do justice to what was possible on the Mac. Someone caught wind that Canon, in Japan, was working on a low-cost laser copier and got inspired. "They make good stuff, reliable products; we could use that as the engine for a Macintosh-compatible laser printer," Fernandez recounts the company thinking. Apple started work designing a computer board to be bolted on the Canon machine and quickly determined that it could work. So the team flew to Japan, working on the schematic mid-flight.

Apple commissioned frogdesign—a consultancy that helped mock-up the first Mac—to conceive an attractive white plastic for the shell. It asked Canon to take care of the manufacturing and to make the computer board. Apple had already worked intimately with Japanese suppliers, including Sony, to create disk drives, and certainly it relied on components coming from Asia, but the LaserWriter was the first major Apple-designed, Apple-branded product that was made by a third party.

Apple priced it at $7,000, way too high for a consumer, but appropriate for the publishing industry. Laser printers cost $30,000 or more at the time. Not only had Apple designed a masterpiece, but it had created a whole package—Mac and printer—costing around $10,000. The Mac was previously considered overpriced. Now, in combination with an even pricier printer, it was a total bargain. The LaserWriter took off with help from a small start-up called Adobe, whose Postscript software allowed users to play with typefaces of all kinds, in high quality and in complex layouts, something totally unthinkable on a PC. And the Mac got its first "killer app" in the form of PageMaker, which provided a simple user interface for designing layouts. What the combination of Mac, LaserWriter, and PageMaker made possible was desktop publishing. For years, anyone involved in the business of printing books and magazines wanted to own a Mac. And soon so did anyone else seeking to print brochures and newsletters. "So solid was this business that during the dark months of mid-1985 one could have made a strong case for Apple being not a computer, but a printer company," writes Malone.

The LaserWriter helped to reinforce Apple's identity as the computer company for students, visionaries, and change-the-world types. Its success was a bit too late to save Jobs, however. Tension between him and Sculley was building, in large part because the Mac's failure to live up to expectations brought out Jobs's worst instincts. After he lost a boardroom showdown with Sculley, Jobs was relieved of most of his duties, and he quit on September 16, 1985. But his resignation letter looked beautiful. He'd printed it on the new LaserWriter.

PowerBook 100

By the time Jobs had left, Apple had already started building strong ties in Japan. Jobs had visited Tokyo frequently in the early 1980s, enamored with the Sony Walkman and the emergence of automated manufacturing capabilities. Jay Elliot recalls being with Jobs at a traditional kaiseki multicourse dinner with executives from Sony at an over-the-top restaurant that hosted only one group per night. The start was inauspicious. Elliot, six-four and wearing size 14 shoes, couldn't fit into the ceremonial attire. "They didn't know what to do about it—they were so upset," Elliot recalls. He and Jobs sat on tatami mats and wore ritualistic masks between courses. The highlight, he says, was being given an ornate wooden hammer to break open a clay pot, revealing a delicately cooked dish inside.

At first the Japanese, formal and fond of order, had a hard time dealing with the young, brash millionaire. In one account, when Apple was visiting factories to have a disk drive assembled, "rafts of engineers would come out to show them their drives and Steve would pick one and examine it for a minute with a look of extreme distaste and cry, 'What are you showing me *this* for? This is a piece of crap! *Anybody* could build a better drive than this.'" So it was the older Elliot who'd meet a vendor's CEO; Jobs stayed back with the engineers. After Jobs left the company, executives might have had fewer reasons to visit Japan, but the LaserWriter had become wildly lucrative. As more Apple executives flew in and out of Tokyo, they formed new relationships and got to witness firsthand the manufacturing advances under way.

Among those executives was Jean-Louis Gassée, who in 1986 started work on Apple's first take-anywhere computer, a sixteen-pound beast called the Macintosh Portable. Gassée says the battery-powered computer was cutting-edge at the time, but Apple had so much difficulty assembling it in-house that it met repeated delays. By the time it was ready for the market in 1989, it had lost its edge. And Apple doomed its commercial chances by pricing it at $7,499.

Frustrated by Apple's in-house manufacturing deficiencies, Gassée advocated for the Portable's laptop successor, the PowerBook, to be outsourced to contract manufacturers in Japan. This ignited a contentious debate in Cupertino, and Gassée, a Frenchman, was branded "anti-American." But he won the debate, partially. Apple designed three PowerBooks—the 100, the 140 and the 160, in order of price—and had the 100 assembled in Japan. Sony canceled other projects to take on the challenge and freed up seven of its top engineers. Working from a half-page document of Apple specifications, Sony crammed the innards of a $4,500 Mac desktop into the form factor of a five-pound laptop. The whole project went from drawing board to production in just thirteen months, wowing Apple. It was priced at $2,300.

"That's how it all started—our relationship with contract manufacturing," Gassée says. "As opposed to just getting the pieces like a disk drive and then assembling it ourselves. It started a culture of relying on, mostly, Japanese manufacturers." The cost and quality of what Sony did, he says, awakened many to the capabilities of the Japanese in particular and outsourcers in general. "They were very good, and it was clear to me that we—the Americans—had no way to compete with what they did."

Robert Brunner, who at the time was heading Industrial Design, the Apple unit that conceives the look and feel of products, recalls that the first outsourcing efforts were in areas "where Apple didn't have any manufacturing competency—in printers and displays." The decision to have Sony make the PowerBook 100, he says, followed "a big fucking debate," because for the first time Apple was allowing another company into its road map at the CPU level. "That was a big shift," he says. The teams were astounded by the quality and care of Japanese manufacturing. "The 100 was a better product from a mechanical and electrical point of view than the 140 and 160, which were done by Apple," Brunner says. "Sony had so much depth of experience in building small things."

As Apple established more of a presence in the country, Joe O'Sullivan from operations moved to Tokyo in 1993 to head up supplier quality—meaning he was to oversee production and ensure it was up to snuff. "I was in Japan about five minutes, and it was like, 'Apple can teach the Japanese nothing,'" he says.

Newton

Apple's outsourcing strategy evolved when the first Apple Newton shipped in August 1993. The Newton was a proto-BlackBerry that allowed the user to take notes with a pen, read email, send faxes, and manage their calendar. But its key feature—handwriting recognition—was relentlessly mocked as unworkable. And production in Japan by Sharp was its own disaster.

Cost was one reason. Japan was rapidly losing its edge as an affordable manufacturing base due to labor shortages, climbing wages, and a soaring currency. In 1994, a dollar was worth less than 100 yen, half the value of the late 1970s. The yen's strengthening made exports more expensive and "drove us to look into other areas," says a former Apple executive. "Japan lost out as being the center in Asia for manufacturing and development." Apple also learned that the Japanese companies were masterful at taking an Apple design and manufacturing it, but they were less good at collaborating. "They, perhaps deservedly, had almost a condescending view of Apple engineering," says one product manager. When Sharp took what it learned from Apple and came out with its own rival PDA, Apple felt burned.

The head of the Newton division, a Belgian named Gaston Bastiaens, looked for alternatives. He turned to Phil Baker, a product development expert with fifteen years at Polaroid and earlier work bringing projects to life at Atari, Seiko, and a few start-ups making handheld products. Baker's familiarity with miniature electronics was rare, and just what Apple needed for the second-generation Newton. Bastiaens told Baker: "Look, you've had experience developing handheld products. We need to do it cheaply. I need you to go do it." Baker responded: "Okay, where do you want to do it?" Bastiaens looked up at him blankly. "I have no idea."

The Newton group had been shunned by the rest of the company, like it was a spin-off. But this curse was partly a blessing. Asking to have the Mac assembled in Asia would be fraught with politics, but nobody really cared where the Newton was built. Baker had freedom. The United States, he says, was bureaucratic and already falling well behind Asia in cost and quality. "If you decided you wanted to contract companies in Asia or in the US, you would hear back from the Asian companies within a day or two," he says. "Then you'd hear back from the US companies two weeks later."

Baker had some experience in Taiwan and knew it could be far more affordable than Japan. Indeed, the rise of Taiwan as an industrial center had been facilitated by large Japanese manufacturers and trading companies. From the 1960s onward, Japanese businesses had invested in the island, importing machines and training their workforces to avoid rising costs at home. Taiwan had been a Japanese colony for sixty years until World War II, so there was a shared language between teacher and—if the worker was older than thirty-five—student. By the time Baker flew to the island in 1994 to interview manufacturers, the export-oriented economy was booming. He developed a relationship with Richard Lee, CEO of Inventec. Lee treated his employees well and had experience assembling calculators. Baker soon learned that the Taiwanese were more flexible and speedier than the Japanese factories he was familiar with. Japan had decades of experience and wanted to do things their way, whereas the Taiwanese were eager to learn and open to collaboration. What they didn't have was the right skill sets, so Apple began sending over its engineers to assist in bringing up quality at the factories.

Cupertino executives were "pretty oblivious of what was going on in Asia" at the time, Baker says. Even the Japanese were ignorant of how quickly Taiwan was becoming an electronics powerhouse. Inventec soon proved itself. Baker says it "turned upside down" to accommodate Apple, showing unusual initiative. Apple's Newton design had required expensive equipment that no one in Taiwan had. But Lee said, "No problem," and invested north of $800,000 to buy it. "They just were so forward thinking," Baker says. "It started with the Newton, and then they ended up understanding what was needed for other products."

Back in Cupertino, Baker called on a young creative with a boyish face, a strong jawline, and neatly styled hair to reconceive the look and feel of the Newton. The young man, newly hired by Robert Brunner, had a meticulous eye for detail and favored minimalist concepts with an understated flair. He was passionate, though he didn't exude excitement. He was soft-spoken, carefully pausing to communicate each word clearly. The second-generation Newton he designed would earn him accolades, even with the product itself failing in the market. And that would just be the start of a storied career. Much later, Brunner would quip that no matter what contributions he, Brunner, would make in the rest of his life, his tombstone was likely to say: "Here lies the guy who hired Jonathan Ive."

CHAPTER 3

AN "OUTRAGEOUS" ACQUISITION

Apple's killer combo—the Macintosh and LaserWriter—didn't last. Once Microsoft proliferated the use of Windows 95, every PC could offer similar features, but more affordably, with a better range of software and peripherals, and more customization and compatibility. Meanwhile, Apple's successes in outsourcing were largely experimental and confined to certain products, while PC rivals were taking full advantage of their lower cost and more efficient manufacturing. Michael Spindler, the German-born executive who succeeded John Sculley in 1993, spent two and a half years trying but failing to fend off an onslaught of competition from the PC world, culminating in the disastrous Christmas quarter of 1995, which cost him his job. Spindler had all but given up by then, focusing his efforts on finding a buyer for the company rather than managing its day-to-day operations. When Apple's board of directors appointed Gil Amelio to take over from Spindler in February 1996, it swung too far in the other direction. Here was someone all about day-to-day operations, but with no grand vision.

Amelio looked like an unlikely savior from the day he was appointed. He'd been widely touted as a "turnaround artist" but almost immediately found himself way in over his head. Even by his own account he was overwhelmed by the "range and caliber" of Apple's problems. Later, he would compare joining Apple to boarding the *Titanic*.

Amelio declared that he needed a hundred days of reflection before he'd lay out his plan. That left an already-distressed company, which had recently cut 1,200 jobs, rudderless for fourteen weeks. The hundred days came and went without any brilliant ideas emerging from the CEO's office. Amelio cut Apple's dividend and took other actions to improve finances, but he failed to steer the company in a clear direction. Desperate for a plan, Amelio hosted what he called "coffee klatch" meetings on Fridays, to which he'd invite employees at random in the hopes that someone, somewhere, had an idea.

Amelio's hapless reputation was constantly reinforced visually. His lack of charisma might have been acceptable but for the fact that he didn't seem aware of it. Exuding detachment from Silicon Valley culture, he dressed in a shirt and tie and ate lunch in his office on fine china with silverware. Even when Amelio seemed to get it right, like showing leadership when he pinned Apple's future on the internet and multimedia, the criticism was unsparing. "The dogs of the press were scribbling furiously," Malone recounts. "This might be it! The Apple Messiah, disguised as the head of the paint department at Orchard Supply Hardware."

But the real problem stemmed from the board of directors misdiagnosing what problem Apple needed to solve. Only a few months earlier, Apple had recorded its highest annual revenue ever—$11.1 billion in the twelve months leading to September 1995, up from $7.1 billion three years earlier. Profits had dwindled in that period, and this led the board members to their error. Products and revenues weren't the problem, they thought; efficiency was.

Amelio had been an Apple board member since late 1994; he was an engineer and the CEO of National Semiconductor, whose fortunes he'd revived by streamlining operations. So if Apple's problem, too, was inefficiency, then Amelio was a great fit. In his view, the truth of this diagnosis was everywhere. The computers Apple was making were so "dreadful" that, Amelio later recounted in his memoir, he worried about a backlash if he promoted them. Manufacturing techniques, he wrote, were "ten years out of date"; distribution was such a mess that customers often waited months to receive their computer; and forecasting was such a nightmare that "the company was consistently short of the products in demand, while leaving the channels crammed with too many of everything else."

Amelio set out an ambitious plan to optimize operations. He wanted to share components across Apple's portfolio to drive volumes and rival the PC supply chain. These ideas weren't wrong per se. It was undeniable that Apple was less efficient than the likes of Compaq and Dell. But the PC industry had strengths Apple wasn't going to match by fiat. PCs could rely on a global industry of standardized, interchangeable parts, and they didn't have to spend a dime on software R&D—that was handled by Microsoft. Amelio was starting a battle on terms Apple was never going to win. "Gil was heading Apple toward standardization, which would've just gotten us out of business faster," recalls David Hoenig, an engineer at the time. What Apple needed, he says, was *differentiation*.

In the post–Windows 95 world, Apple was facing an existential crisis. It was quickly losing its raison d'être, but Amelio didn't get the urgency of the moment. Apple was in such free fall that between 1995 and 1998, revenues nearly halved, from $11.1 billion to $5.9 billion, meaning Apple needed to cut $1.7 billion of costs *per year* just to tread water. Amelio was focused on secondary, even tertiary issues, apparently blind to the iceberg risk that could sink the entire company: Apple didn't have a hit product. The company was sinking fast and the new CEO had no clear idea why. "I remember looking at his résumé and thinking, *Oh, this isn't a product guy at all. He's not a visionary,*" recalls Hoenig. "My career had always been in innovative new products, doing creative things. So when Gil came on board, I remember just feeling it as a low point for me. It was like, 'This isn't gonna solve the problem.'"

But Amelio deserves credit for three major actions—in hardware, finances, and software. The sale of the Fountain factory was the first. It gave Apple critically needed cash and would later spur a whole new strategy in how to build computers. Then Amelio and finance chief Fred Anderson orchestrated two deals to stave off bankruptcy: a week before Apple owed Japanese lenders $150 million, in April 1996, they got a six-month extension. Then in June, they raised $661 million in an oversubscribed bond sale. But Amelio will always be remembered for the third action. He realized that a multiyear effort to improve the Mac's operating system was hopeless, and that Apple needed to acquire a new OS altogether. That insight set into motion the action that would get him sacked, even as it saved the company. He brought back Steve Jobs.

The Wilderness Years

That Jobs would end up back at Apple and orchestrate the greatest corporate turnaround ever looks fantastical from the perspective of just four years earlier, in 1993. In the eight years since leaving Apple, Jobs had immediately set out to launch another company to prove the haters wrong. Instead, he substantiated their criticisms.

With around $100 million to his name, Jobs launched NeXT Computer and lavished the start-up with fancy furniture and high-priced talent. NeXT built a sleek all-black computer released in October 1988 that Jobs called "the first computer of the 1990s." But it was as if he'd learned nothing from the Mac's mistakes. The magnesium cube of a computer retailed for $6,500, plus $2,000 for the printer. It lacked much third-party support, so it was even more isolated than the Mac. Jobs had commissioned an expensive, inefficient factory capable of handling 10,000 units per month—far more capacity than it would ever need. The poor decisions highlight the difficult-to-grasp nature of his peculiar genius. Whereas the brilliance of Apple cofounder Steve Wozniak was tangible—he could disassemble a computer, then rebuild it to work faster and with fewer parts—Jobs lacked such practical skills. But through instinct, passion, and an uncompromising vision, he could lead a team to build "insanely great" products. When things weren't going well, however, his idiosyncratic traits felt overbearing and his taste could seem arbitrary. His perfectionist tendencies could lead to breakdowns rather than breakthroughs. Jobs's biographers would later call NeXT "the full, unfortunate blooming of Steve Jobs's worst tendencies at Apple."

By February 1993 it was a conspicuous flop. NeXT had released five versions of its computer, but after almost eight years it was selling fewer units in a month than Apple sold in a day. Jobs was forced to kill off its hardware business and lay off 300 people. He auctioned off NeXT's assets, and four of his five cofounders left the company. Jobs had failed; he was no longer the wunderkind featured on magazine covers. But NeXT wasn't entirely dead. Its proprietary operating system, NeXTStep, might not have wide adoption, but it was a sophisticated, brilliant system that Tim Berners-Lee used to invent the World Wide Web. Jobs and his team changed focus to evolve the software into OPENSTEP, an operating system that could work on multiple platforms.

Meanwhile, the industry had largely failed to notice that Steve was the CEO of yet another company. In 1986, he'd acquired a digital graphics group from *Star Wars* maker George Lucas for $5 million. It was soon renamed Pixar. Jobs sank tens of millions of dollars into turning its high-end $135,000 "image computer" into something more widely accessible. This, too, was aborted. By 1988, Pixar had created only 120 computers and was burning through $10 million a year. But within Pixar was a five-person animation group led by John Lasseter, and in 1989 the team won an Oscar for their 90-second short film.

Previewing the action he would take at NeXT in 1993, Jobs took Pixar out of the hardware business. He cut staff by two-thirds and narrowed their efforts to storytelling. The result was a major deal with Disney, and out of that came *Toy Story*, the first feature-length computer-animated film and a smash hit at the box office. Jobs, who owned 80 percent of the company, took it public, and instantly became a billionaire. Its success reframed the public perception of Jobs.

Back at NeXT, the team had undergone another transition. In early 1996, its focus shifted from building an OS to making a tool for building dynamic internet-based applications. WebObjects worked like Lego building blocks, enabling developers to assemble components together and do so visually, with tools like drag and drop, rather than writing code.

By late 1996, NeXT had all but abandoned its goal of building an OS. Steve Jobs had told his staff "the ships are burning," a metaphor signaling there was no turning back, in announcing WebObjects as the company's new direction. But then a young staffer learned something intriguing: Apple needed a new operating system.

The Deal

When Apple came calling, Jobs entranced Amelio and Apple's board in a private presentation. "It was just mind-blowing to watch," recalls a participant. "The heads started to nod affirmatively. They were very much taken with what he had to say, and taken with him—as people were—with his persona. It was obvious the board was going to approve it."

Apple paid more than $400 million for NeXT, absorbing into Apple everything Jobs had built, including an operating system and WebObjects. The deal, announced in late December 1996, was widely considered desperate and costly. Even Apple's board believed the price tag to be "outrageous." After a decade in business, it was losing money on just $50 million in revenue. But Apple's board had few alternatives. The deal went ahead.

It turned out to be a perfect match. NeXT might have been a flop, but its operating system was excellent—"between five and seven years ahead of everyone else," according to Eric Schmidt, a Sun Microsystems executive and future CEO of Google. The problem was, it had no market fit. The PC world was built on Windows, and NeXT couldn't break in. But Apple, the only viable alternative, offered a way. Plus, as Amelio understood, he was also getting "300 talented people."

As the details were being worked out, a group of NeXT employees sat in a room together, chatting. They'd all worked with Steve, and they just didn't understand what Amelio was thinking. None believed Jobs would ever be a number two. Not anywhere, probably, but certainly not at the company he cofounded as a twenty-one-year-old.

Their premonition was hastened by Gil Amelio hosting MacWorld in San Francisco, in January 1997—"the presentation from Hell," according to Michael Markman, Apple's director of advertising. Amelio hadn't prepared or rehearsed, and his body language said, *I don't want to be here.* But "like a guilty kid who can't stop talking," Markman recalls, Amelio just went on and on, to the point of Apple nearly running out of satellite time as it broadcast the event to thousands of people.

In the months that followed, Jobs studied the failing organization and began to offer the clearest vision of what the company should do. In May 1997, he held a Q&A with developers at one of Apple's annual conferences and told them of a tentative idea: a network computer, or NC. Jobs, in faded blue jeans and signature black turtleneck, sporting long hair that swept across his forehead, said he wanted Apple to ship a computer that did away with a hard drive and instead stored everything on a server—a precursor to cloud computing. "I have computers at Apple, at NeXT, at Pixar, and at home," he told the auditorium. "I walk up to any of them and log in as myself. It goes over the network, finds my home directory on the server, and I've got my stuff, wherever I am. And none of that is on a local hard disk." The internet was becoming much faster, and Jobs envisioned laypeople all working on network computers. "I don't need a hard disk in my computer if I can get to the server faster," he said.

He was an envisioning a plug-and-play computer for the internet age, competitive on cost because less complexity meant less hardware—and software updates would be handled centrally. "I can't communicate to you how awesome this is unless you use it," he said. But Jobs wasn't yet wholly convinced by his own vision. He was just spitballing with developers.

Still, with Jobs looking more like the leader Apple needed, a joke emerged: NeXT had acquired Apple for negative $400 million. The extent to which Jobs actively pushed for Amelio's departure is debated, but he made his feelings eminently clear in mid-1997 when he sold all but one of the 1.5 million Apple shares he'd been given as part of the NeXT deal. By July 1997, Amelio, who'd grown bitter at being asked to do that which he was incapable of, was let go, with a big pay package worth millions to soften the blow. Jobs called his exit "a cashectomy."

Jobs was offered the role of CEO. It was a position he'd never officially held at Apple, yet he demurred. First, he needed to be convinced Apple could be saved.

CHAPTER 4

COLUMBUS—A NEW WORLD OF COMPUTING

Jobs was torn to the point of agony throughout the summer of 1997. "Apple was his baby. It had significant emotional appeal," a staffer from the time says. "The one thing he said to me once, which signaled to me his ambivalence, was, 'I don't know if Apple can be saved.'" Jobs's earlier removal from the company had inflicted a deep wound, and for several years the repeated failures at NeXT had recast his image as an overhyped salesman. Returning to Apple only to oversee its demise was a clear risk. "He didn't want to be the person who let Apple die," the staffer says. So instead, chief financial officer Fred Anderson became interim CEO while Jobs investigated different facets of the business. "He wanted to know what the beast was about, by looking inside it," De Luca says.

In the following weeks, Jobs held meetings with senior executives as he tried to conjure a turnaround plan. The evolution of his thinking is captured in a variety of internal meeting notes from that summer, obtained for this book and quoted here for the first time:

July 22, R&D hardware meeting: Jobs says he is worried that Apple staff are getting demoralized by the perception that Apple is slow. His own diagnosis is that Apple is just unfocused: "[The] outside world thinks that Apple runs slower than the rest of the world. In reality, Apple runs fast on projects that don't matter."

July 25, software review meeting: Jobs expresses his frustration with the company's lack of direction. "Everyone said Apple culture is anarchy, can't be managed, and can't execute," he says. "Rather, people have wanted to fall into line, but there has been no line. There was no coherence." He reminds everyone how dire the situation is. "Declining sales volume is serious, the company will go broke, and we need to act. We have lost relevance."

July 26, MacWorld planning meeting: Jobs believes there are many fanatics who love Mac, the product—but they hate Apple, the company. "Many users feel like they have an alcoholic parent in Apple," he says. "They don't want their friends coming over." Talking points for the upcoming conference include being honest and self-aware, calling for "drastic change." Apple, Jobs will say, has the confidence to fix things and it is "not alone." Plans for the August 6, 1997 MacWorld include a major reshuffle of the executive board and the revelation that longtime nemesis Microsoft will invest $150 million.

July 29, desktop and display review: "We have a big problem," Jobs proclaims. He expresses optimism about the company's prospects if it can make it five years down the road, saying, "The road map does not look like the road map of a company that's at risk of going out of business." But he was less sure Apple could get through the next twelve months. "We won't really have the desktop products we need for one year. This might not be good enough to survive. We are in real danger." The way out of this mess is the network computer. He adds it to the road map. "Plan to have two models of NCs, at $799 and then $999 or maybe $1,099."

August 1, software review: Jobs conveys uncertainty over how the NC will look and feel. "We can't have this seem like a toy," he says. "Best way is to have a big screen. But can't make it look like a cheap TV even though it's the same cheap CRT. Needs to look a little different, too." His hope is to announce an entry-level NC in January 1998 and have it shipping by March. "Need for speed before others do this."

August 11, advertising meeting: "Over the next few months, we need to take advantage of the modest—and elusive—momentum we have," Jobs says. "We must rekindle the feeling that Apple is on the move. The ads are not about selling product, because it is the company [that] needs selling now."

A few days later, Jobs decided to visit the Industrial Design studio, where a team of artists led by Jony Ive were working on Apple's next products.

A Matterhorn of Products

In a twisted, comical sort of way, Steve Jobs and Jony Ive were on the same wavelength the first time they met one-on-one. As Jobs left Apple's main campus and crossed the road to visit the ID studio in mid-August 1997, he intended to fire Apple's lead designer. Prior to Ive welcoming Jobs, the thirty-year-old British designer laid out brochures demonstrating the breadth of the team's capabilities. Expecting the meeting to go poorly, Ive had a resignation letter already tucked into his pocket.

Jobs had little reason to know what Ive was capable of, and even less reason to care. Three weeks earlier, on July 9, 1997, Jobs stood before several dozen Apple staffers in shorts and sneakers, displaying an unkempt beard. "Tell me what's wrong with this place," he stated firmly. Without waiting for an answer, he exclaimed: "It's the *products!* The products suck!" Then he offered remarkable clarity of vision, scribbling out a two-by-two chart on a whiteboard. Apple, he declared, would make desktop and portable computers, each coming in consumer and professional versions. Everything else was dead. In an instant, the number of Apple products in development was cut from forty to four. Reception to the strategy was mixed, but at least, finally, there *was* a strategy. "It felt like we may have all been driving off a cliff," says product designer David Hoenig. "But at least we were all going together in the same direction for once."

Ive was in the room and must have squirmed in his seat a little. He was, at least on paper, the chief designer of those forty products, which made his future at Apple questionable if not doomed, especially given Jobs's propensity for firing people. Steve was letting so many people go that a Frenchwoman from Human Resources often trailed behind him with a suitcase filled with prewritten exit contracts. When Jobs abruptly sent someone packing, she'd take out a crisp contract, fill in the blanks, and catch up to Jobs before the next layoff.

The current lineup of Apple products offered no obvious evidence that Apple had a team of designers brimming with brilliance. Among the computers in development was the Power Macintosh G3, nicknamed the "Molar Mac" because of its toothlike shape. Leadership couldn't agree on its core features, so it came with everything: a CD drive, a zip drive, and a floppy disk drive—all on the front beneath the display, rendering the whole thing ugly. It weighed sixty pounds. "A horse designed by committee will be a camel, and that's what the G3 all-in-one was," says Hoenig. In addition to a variety of computers with overlapping features that confused customers, Apple had also been making cameras, displays, scanners, and printers. Jobs piled all variety of such prototypes like "a Matterhorn of products" in the cafeteria, a veteran engineer recalls. It was like, 'If you want a prototype, grab it. It's all going to be scrapped.'"

What Jobs didn't know was that the bulk of Ive's designs had never made it to production. There'd been no real audience for his team's work. Apple was controlled by engineers who considered the design studio an irritant. And the broader PC industry was so indifferent to design that some Asian manufacturers had started to produce pick-and-choose catalogues for big computer brands to select designs from. Ive, it seemed, was in the wrong industry. He'd been considering quitting Apple for weeks, sometimes wondering if it might go bankrupt while he waffled. Guerrino De Luca, senior vice president of marketing, remembers Ive in these days as "the most frustrated person I'd ever met." De Luca says Ive had prototyped a variety of elegant products whose simplicity masked the enormous complexity that went into their design, but engineers would only scoff, "We can't put the electronics into this!"

Jobs had intended to hire a new lead designer from outside Apple, but nothing had come of it. So he went to visit Ive, whose ID team was ready to put on a show of detailed etchings and prototypes. "The studio was full of eye-catching mock-ups that the previous regime had been too timid to consider," recounted Leander Kahney in a biography of Jony. Jobs "was bowled over by the creativity and rigor he saw." Among the most enticing designs was the team's work on translucent plastic. Ive's team had been experimenting with clear plastic for months, and earlier that year Apple had begun shipping the eMate 300, a rugged and curvy laptop in a child-friendly clamshell case made of translucent green plastic. The electronics were so neatly packed inside that one technophile admired how it resembled "a butt in tight green spandex."

Jobs quickly understood that Apple had great talent, but that Amelio hadn't taken advantage of them. Taking in all that he saw, then looking at Ive, Jobs said, "Fuck, you've not been very effective, have you?" In the world of Steve Jobs, this was a compliment. He was recognizing them, surmising that their problem was an inability to communicate their own worth. According to Ive, the two started collaborating that day on an all-in-one computer code-named Columbus, because it represented the New World. At a software review meeting afterward, Jobs beamed about what a "great group" ID was, then told them about Columbus. He was still thinking it would be a "network computer," but now, after exchanging ideas with Ive, he was suddenly convinced in Apple's comeback. "We are betting our company on NCs. They will be big," Jobs told the group. The network computer had the potential, he said, to create a "halo effect" for the whole company. Jobs was spinning with ideas, a whole new narrative forming in his head: "The company that invented [the] PC is reinventing it!" he told them. "We will be first and [a] bull's-eye will be drawn around what we are doing."

"Something That Will Change This Company"

Within weeks Jobs was wandering around the Apple campus with a bowling ball bag carrying a secret prototype inside. The idea that this product would be a stripped-down network computer soon died; instead, it was upgraded to have a hard drive and a CD-ROM drive. This made the hoped-for price point of $799 unrealistic, but that no longer mattered. Jobs was setting out to create a product that would redefine computer aesthetics.

The first people outside of Apple to get a glimpse of the product were executives in higher education who might buy them in the thousands. In late August, Apple's education division hosted a meeting with decision-makers for multiple universities. It was a high-stakes meeting. "You've potentially got billions of dollars of sales walking through the door," says one participant. Jobs came in late, wearing a jogging suit, while the university people were dressed formally. He immediately started yelling at two staffers who were setting up the room. It was an unsettling start, says José-Marie Griffiths, then the chief investment officer at the University of Michigan. "I almost waited for him to stamp his foot," she says.

Then Jobs started talking about what a disaster Apple was and how much had to change. It was all a lead-up to a pregnant pause. "I want to show you something that will change this company," he told them. His hands moved toward the bowling ball bag, but then he stopped. "I don't trust the Apple people in the room," Jobs said curtly. "So, all of you Apple people—get out of here."

Jobs's newfound enthusiasm brought out the best parts of his character: curiosity, leadership, and an ability to articulate a product path. But it brought out his worst traits, too: arrogance and a habit of belittling others. De Luca, the head of Apple marketing, recalls his embarrassment. The "Apple people" Jobs was referring to were account managers for some of Apple's biggest clients, and their boss was humiliating them. Griffiths felt bad for them. A third person present says: "Even the account manager, who is going to pay their mortgage based on whether Michigan buys this stuff or not, was told to leave."

Then Jobs unveiled what was hiding in the bag: a shiny, smooth, and curvaceous computer, painted in a bright hue. It was just a prototype—a lightweight model made of foam core and containing no electronics—but it was stunning. "It looked like something from outer space," says Griffiths. De Luca recalls how masterfully Jobs got the room of executives excited, himself included. "Steve was spectacular in that," he says. "He was absolutely the best that I have ever met." But the juxtaposition between this "magic moment" and what had transpired just a few minutes earlier before troubled him. After Jobs left, De Luca stayed with Griffiths, uncomfortable and not sure what to say. He apologized, the meeting soon ended, and he returned to his office.

A few minutes later Jobs stopped by. "I've gone a little far, haven't I?" he asked. "Yes, you've gone far—way too far," De Luca scolded. "It's just completely ridiculous that you did that. It serves no purpose." Jobs acknowledged the point. "But," he explained, "I don't trust these people."

De Luca struggled to relate. He'd been working eighteen-hour days and was exhausted. A few days after this meeting, uncertain whether Visionary Steve would pull Apple back from the brink or Bad Steve would steer Apple into the ground, De Luca quit. The same week, on September 16, 1997, Jobs demonstrated how convinced he was of the new computer's future: Anderson stepped aside and Jobs, for the first time, became CEO. It was supposed to be a temporary role, but soon proved permanent. It had been twelve years, to the day, since he'd first quit Apple.

Think Different

Later that month Apple launched what might be the most memorable ad campaign of the 1990s: Think Different. It was an audacious series of monochrome photographs of the century's greatest artists and creative eccentrics. If Apple had lost its identity over the prior decade, this homage to contrarians, outcasts, and geniuses demonstrated that the company's spirit was back, at least in embryo. "Here's to the crazy ones," the TV version of the ad began. "The misfits. The rebels. The trouble-makers. The round pegs in the square holes. The ones who see things differently."

The ads took Apple's humiliatingly small market share and recast it as an advantage, as if being in this minority put you in a class of misunderstood mavericks. It ignited a conversation about Apple at a time when the company had nothing particularly "different" to sell. The campaign was brilliant, but for one snag. Among the people highlighted was the Dalai Lama, the Buddhist spiritual leader in exile from Tibet ever since China crushed an uprising in 1959, killing thousands. The ad campaign was global, but the Tibetan leader was "conspicuously absent" in Asia, having been removed "for fear of offending China," *The New York Times* reported. There was a minor uproar that Apple, in an ad campaign meant to showcase its values, was instead hiding them. One newspaper columnist said if Apple was really brave, Think Different would have included "Tank Man," the unarmed protester who stood defiantly before a formation of armored tanks amid the Tiananmen Square crackdown less than a decade earlier. Now *there* was a rebel. A troublemaker.

Apple, of course, played down the decision. A spokesman implied the Dalai Lama just wasn't well known enough in Asia. But it was an obvious fib. The Asia campaign had instead gone with Amelia Earhart. The removal of the Dalai Lama from the campaign was soon forgotten. But a precedent was set. It's the first known instance of Apple kowtowing to China. There would be many more to come.

CHAPTER 5

"UNMANUFACTURABLE"—THE iMAC

Chris Novak, recently married and just back from vacation, was getting settled into Apple's Product Design office on a rainy morning in November 1997 when two of his direct reports walked over. They looked flummoxed. "Chris, have you seen the new model?" asked Ken Jenks. He hadn't. Jenks told him that he and colleague Glen Walters had visited the Industrial Design studio while Novak was on vacation, and they suggested he go look immediately. "We can't make it," Jenks added, "and they're gonna be pissed!"

It was uncharacteristic of either engineer to be unimaginative or stubborn, so Novak stealthily crossed the two-lane street from his office in Valley Green Six to the Industrial Design studio—the den of creative designers who'd been empowered by Jobs to think radically about the look and feel of Apple products. Laid out before him was a model of the Columbus prototype, soon to be named iMac. It looked like nothing he or anyone else had built before. "Make it lickable," Jobs had told Jony Ive. And Ive had delivered. The prototype, machined from a durable cast plastic and painted a bright color, was see-through along the sides and around its exterior, and shaped more like an egg than the boxy, angular form of every computer made before it.

Novak eyed the iMac up and down. The plastic casing around the display featured horizontal grooves acting like decorative accent lines.

In the back was a recessed handle placed just so, but, curiously, lacking any support structure. "Undercut city" is how Walters described the design, referring to the myriad recesses, cavities, and other cuts to the plastic structure that would necessitate all sorts of complex tooling. Novak was impressed, no doubt; ID was defying all conventions of what was possible in design. But he was scared, too; his team had to transform the pretty prototype into a functioning product—to ensure a computer could be housed inside and then be manufactured at scale. "Oh. My. God!" Novak muttered to himself, realizing Jenks was right. "We can't make this."

Novak had been a veteran of Product Design at Apple since 1981, but given all the leadership changes the organization had undergone, he felt like he'd worked for three different companies. Product Design had once been a boundary-breaking innovation hub, but quality deteriorated substantially when Apple had come under pressure from the PC industry. Leadership responded by making faster, cheaper computers that could be assembled easily. "All the designs I was doing at the time were idiot proof," Novak says. "They snapped together, with giant snaps. You could do it blindly."

Novak now expected that designs would get more ambitious. He was enthused about the good ol' days making a comeback, about saving a company following months of existential crisis. But until that rainy morning, nobody had yet experienced what "saving Apple" would mean in practice. Novak stared at the prototype, then shook his head. It was unmanufacturable. Maybe it didn't defy physics, but it defied the tools they had.

Standstill

The technique Apple would use to build the iMac enclosure dates back to a shortage of billiard balls in the late nineteenth century. The balls were typically made of ivory sourced from tusks, but the game's popularity was growing faster than hunters could kill elephants. When a billiard equipment maker offered a $10,000 prize—more than $3 million today—for someone to come up with an alternative, an American inventor took up the challenge. He melted plastic, then injected it into a casing—a metal mold in the shape of a small sphere—and let it cool. Once the plastic solidified, he removed the casing and out popped a billiard ball. A patent for plastic injection molding was granted in 1872, and over the next 125 years the process became more intricate, automated, and repeatable. There was nothing unique about plastic injection molding the case of a computer, but Apple's Industrial Design studio was intent on pushing the boundaries of what was possible.

Novak liked a challenge, but as he squinted at the horizontal lines on the front cover that wrapped around the display, he concluded the design just wasn't possible. When molding plastic, the steel moves in one direction, but the horizontal texture lines ID had drawn up ran in perpendicular fashion. Technically you could mold one—but just one, because it was never going to come out of the mold. Novak experimented. Failed. Then experimented again.

He took the issue directly to Danny Coster, the New Zealand–born industrial designer who was leading the iMac project. It was Coster, a surfer, who among other things had come up with the computer's Bondi Blue color, naming it after a beach in Sydney. "Chris, you're gonna have to do this," Coster said. "This is what we want. And we know it can be done." Novak, humbled, gathered every senior tooling engineer at Apple into a single conference room. He showed them the design and asked for ideas on how to pull it off. "And every one of 'em said: 'No, can't do it.'"

The recessed handle, Novak believed, was another challenge verging on impossible. Referring to ID, he says, "They wanted to make it so you couldn't tell how it was attached. It wasn't even visible. And I'm like, 'This thing's gonna weigh forty pounds! The handle is gonna come right out when the customer picks it up.'" But ID was standing firm. They knew it was going to be difficult. It was *supposed* to be difficult. Ive and Coster told the engineers: "This will be a world-class design, and we need world-class mechanical engineers and world-class manufacturing engineers." Anyone who wasn't up for the challenge could leave.

The stakes were enormous. Steve Jobs knew that Apple couldn't compete with PCs on price and distribution, so instead he'd developed a hardware strategy to cultivate desire through breathtaking design. Apple's comeback was premised on this single hit product, the hope being that it would establish a new design language for all Apple hardware. Every talented engineer on the project understood that "this is it, or it's game over." But in the very month Jobs originally wanted the computer to be shipping—March 1998—the project had stalled. "We can't do anything," an increasingly frustrated Novak told a meeting of engineers. "ID wants it this way. We can't make it that way. And we're at a dead stop." The back-and-forth with ID had lasted months until the standstill. Eventually ID concluded: "Well, Chris is not the world-class engineer we need. Let's get someone who is."

Novak, pissed off and offended, was demoted, and replaced by David Hoenig, a thirty-three-year-old mechanical engineer who'd been with Apple since 1994. Hoenig brought new energy to the team but was no less mystified by what ID was trying to accomplish. "The product could not be built," he says. The problem wasn't just that you couldn't *mass*-manufacture it. "It was as fundamental as you couldn't build one *in the lab*," he says.

Hoenig describes the difficulty of the eggshell shape like this: "Imagine you have an egg that's horizontal," he says. "If you cut it at the center, right in half, then there's a core side and a cavity side, and I can mold that. But the iMac design was like, 'We wanna go below the halfway point.' So you have this thing called the undercut. Like, there's steel that has to be inside of that egg to build a form. How am I gonna pull that inner steel out when I've got this egg curving back around? You literally can't. So we literally couldn't make it the shape because of the way the curvature was." Two specialty contractors were brought in to focus on the problem. They tried molding the part so it wasn't undercut, then forming it into the right shape afterward. Two months went by before they abandoned the effort.

The stress got to the team. "Everything was driven by ID," Hoenig says, "and they weren't taking no for an answer." They demanded constant experimentation. A whole wave of senior engineers who wouldn't get with the program were let go. Others quit. "They wanted 'can do—we'll figure it out' attitudes," Hoenig says. "It probably took about six months to a year for them to kinda weed out those more seasoned engineers who said, 'No, you can't do that.'

"One Fucking Share of Apple Stock"

Somehow Steve Jobs hadn't been fully plugged in on just how many problems the manufacturing engineers were having until he showed up for a meeting at Infinite Loop 6, on the fourth floor of Apple's campus. The iMac team was having a meeting scheduled as a "tooling review," but once Jobs arrived, the nature of the meeting changed drastically. "Tooling review, my ass," says one participant, "it was an entire product review."

Jobs went on a tirade. "Ninety-five fucking hundred jobs are depending on you, and you've failed!" Jobs fumed to Jony Ive, hardware chief Jon Rubinstein, technology chief Glen Miranker, director of engineering Josef Friedman, and a few others. "You've screwed the pooch," Jobs continued. "I'm going to sell my one fucking share of Apple stock!"

Jobs, his face red, yelled about their failure, their incapabilities as engineers, their *unseriousness*. One participant characterized the episode as "explosive rage-fueled profanity," reminiscent of a mob-run fish market in New Jersey. Brian Berkeley, one of the original engineers on the first Macintosh, arrived late to the meeting just as Jobs was laying into the executives. "I naïvely didn't fully understand the significance of the iMac until the product design reset meeting," he said in 2021. "Steve vigorously informed the senior staff present . . . that we had blown it. I quickly grasped that Apple's survival really did depend on our project success, and if the team wasn't focused prior to that time, we surely were afterward."

Jobs's biographer Walter Isaacson briefly recounted the event, with Jony Ive calling the rant one of Jobs's "displays of awesome fury." In Isaacson's telling, quoting Jobs, Apple's manufacturing engineers "came up with thirty-eight reasons they couldn't do it. And I said, 'No, no, we're doing this.' And they said, 'Well, why?' And I said, 'Because I'm the CEO, and I think it can be done.' And so they kind of grudgingly did it." But Jobs's recollections of events were often simplified if not fabricated, and this was no exception. The reality was that Jobs told the engineers he would send the blueprints to Acorn, his favorite design consultancy, then located in south Fremont. "I'm gonna send them all of our design files and ask them if they can make this," Jobs warned, "and if they tell us they can do what you say you can't do, you guys are all outta here."

The threat was harsh, but it was a sound strategy. Jobs had inherited Apple's Product Design team, a ragtag crew of veterans who had survived three CEOs. When they couldn't make what ID had envisioned, he needed to figure out whether the problem was their incompetence or something else. The two men running Acorn, Ken Haven and Tim Lau, had founded the group in 1993 after building hardware for NeXT. "Ken was a spectacular mechanical problem-solver, of 'What if we did this?' kind of ideas," says an Apple engineer who worked with both. "And Tim was a world-class injection mold tooling debugger of what's possible. So you put those two together, and they were an unstoppable duo. So if these two couldn't figure it out, nobody could."

The duo had proved themselves making the cube-shaped computer at NeXT, when Steve wanted "no draft angles, no parting lines," meaning that the sides of the cast part would be perfectly parallel to the direction the part was ejected from in the mold. "Tim and Ken figured it out," this person says. "And it was absurdly expensive, but that was a defining experience. So if Jobs was having a hard problem and these guys say, 'It cannot be done,' then it really can't. But if these guys say, 'It can,' then it's just really hard. Acorn was almost his brain trust or sounding board for, is this *possible* or is this *crazy*?"

Tim Lau recalls when he took the phone call and agreed to a meeting. "We were like a 911 design house for them," he says. "They'd call us if there's a fire." So a team of Apple engineers showed up at Acorn with multiple rolls of blueprints and spread them across the table. The group went over the whole design in detail. Lau took a deep look and spotted the same challenges Novak and Hoenig had been stuck on for months. "The biggest issue we saw was there was no structure," Lau says. The handle wasn't anchored to anything, nor was there a place it could anchor because the printed circuit board sat directly under it. His conclusion was unequivocal. "You don't have a quality product," he told them.

Hard Reset

Getting that message to Jobs wasn't easy. He would fume about it, and for good reason. "This incident was earthshaking," says Lau. "This was the first product that Steve was doing after his comeback. If he couldn't launch it, it was basically the end of Apple."

Jobs was calmed down by Brian Berkeley and David Lundgren, an MIT-trained engineer who worked with Jobs at Pixar before joining Apple's Product Design group in 1989. Both had attended the Acorn meeting and had to break the news to him. Jobs then implemented a "hard reset," with a new goal to ship by August.

Lundgren hadn't been working on the iMac until now, but he joined the project in a leadership role to manage Product Design. Before he came in, there wasn't much structure in how the project was scheduled. An engineer would say something would take two weeks, and they'd go off for two weeks, maybe longer, with little communication to the team. Lundgren brought in a top-down view, giving everyone a sense of what was progressing well, what needed work. He also staffed up the project and liaised with ID to improve discussion. "He was our General Patton," says Bob Olson, a PD veteran who also joined the iMac project.

Several changes were made to get the project over the line, beginning with tweaks from Industrial Design. Jony Ive realized he'd pushed engineering too far. He oversaw changes that made the iMac easier to manufacture and offered more room inside for the logic board. The horizontal pinstripes that were so difficult to make became vertical instead, aligning with the movement of the plastic injection tools. The transparent blue plastic case was redesigned to give only a foggy view into the interior. Tweaks allowed for screws, bolts, and mounts to be carefully hidden below the surface so the recessed handle was structurally robust.

The team created bonds and really started working together. "We didn't have any trust in that first [attempt] because everything was new to everybody," says a person from ID. Afterward, "everyone knew that we were absolutely dedicated to making the best possible end result, in quality and volume, of a beautiful unimagined object." This person emphasizes that the essence of ID's original vision was maintained. Some things were tradable, but the big idea was never compromised.

Within a few months, ID's original work didn't look like a flawed design so much as a leadership exercise. They'd weeded out engineers who weren't willing to try the impossible. In driving too far with plastic injection molding, they'd found limits that would've otherwise been undiscovered. Or, as someone from ID put it, in skiing terms: "You gotta do a triple diamond to do a blue slope easily, don't you?"

Jony Ive emerged from the hard reset with newfound powers and influence. Jobs had made it crystal clear that ID's zero tolerance for defects was integral to a new culture that would cascade across product development and then throughout the organization. The new approach hit Apple in waves. "I remember these other groups being like, 'I'm glad I'm not in your shoes!'" Hoenig says. "But sure enough, it just literally rippled through the organization over the course of a year, and every group eventually suffered."

Engineers in other departments gained a respect for Ive because of his diplomatic skill. "What Jony did was—he understood that Steve's cruelty, his savagery, his impatience would cause people to split and just quit the company," says a senior person on the project. "That happened a lot. And he would run interference with them. He was a Steve handler as much as he was a visionary, detail obsessed, brilliant designer."

After the first team was pushed aside, the second crew ended up looking like saviors. But Hoenig says he and others were given too much credit. It's not as though they solved something where the previous team had failed; they were just given a task that wasn't impossible. As for Novak, he thrived under Lundgren, who later named him an "iMac hero" along with ten others. Jony Ive recognized it too. Late in the project, Ive invited Novak into his conference room in ID. Novak walked over, worried he was going to be taken to task for having said the original design wasn't manufacturable. "And he sat me down, just him and me, and he apologized," Novak recalls, describing Ive as a pure gentleman. "He said, 'I'm sorry for what happened. You went through a lot of grief on this. It won't happen again.'" From that point on, Ive and his team got way more involved in the production process, getting educated on materials, tooling, and more of the engineering so as to never make the same mistake again.

Years later, Novak was working in Japan with aluminum forging and machining, finding it difficult. "I would say, 'Hey, Jony, I'm not sure you can do that. 'He goes, 'Well, we are.'" Ive's team had already been to Japan, worked with the supplier, and made damn sure their vision was achievable.

PART TWO

APPLE'S LONG MARCH TO CHINA

CHAPTER 6

OUT OF THE ASIAN FINANCIAL CRISIS—SOUTH KOREA

Steve Jobs was convinced the iMac was going to be a hit product. But who would manufacture it, and where? Jobs's preference was Apple, which despite a nascent push toward outsourcing still had factories in California, Ireland, and Singapore. The iMac design was so intricate that he didn't trust any supplier to have the necessary skills to build it. During his years in exile, Jobs held firm to his original belief that controlling the hardware meant building it. At NeXT, he once said his favorite thing about the computer was that "it's not made in Osaka." But Apple was strapped for cash, operations had been significantly downsized, and the company lacked the capability or expertise to build a cathode ray tube, or CRT, the monitor the computer was built around.

A practical compromise was reached. Apple took care of the guts inside the computer—basically the same circuit boards that were in its G3 desktop—but it would rely on a supplier to build the CRT. Then units would be sent to an Apple site for final assembly, test, and pack out, or FATP. That way, Apple had the last look before any computer was shipped, giving Jobs the level of control he desired. "Steve was adamant that we would manufacture the iMac internally," says Joe O'Sullivan, who was by then leading operations in Singapore. Jobs asked O'Sullivan to kill the partnership with SCI in Colorado, a cancellation that cost Apple $5 million and infuriated SCI. Instead, Jobs asked O'Sullivan to turn Singapore into a pilot plant for iMac manufacturing. "It was our best, our cheapest manufacturing plant," the Irishman says. "And I was running it. So he had a throat to grasp."

LG in South Korea was already Apple's supplier of monitors. And the iMac was basically a CRT monitor with a computer stuffed inside, so it was a natural choice. Jobs wasn't so sure; he knew little about Korea and wanted to work with the Japanese, but they were more expensive. South Korea was a solid second choice. Like Taiwan, it was a former colony that had received significant investment and training from the Japanese since the 1970s. LG won the bid with an enticing offer: It would pay for the up-front tooling and the cost to make prototypes. "All the project expenses were wiped off—that kept us going until July 1998," a senior person on the project says.

LG was desperate to win the order because the Korean economy had been rocked by the Asian financial crisis, in which currency turmoil in Southeast Asia spread to the rest of the continent and brought South Korea to the brink of default. The Korean currency lost roughly half its value amid the upheaval, with numerous banks facing insolvency because of their high exposure to dollar-denominated debts. One Apple engineer recalls that inside the LG factory was a large banner the workers walked past multiple times per day. It was two feet tall, twelve feet wide, and had just one word in big letters: SURVIVE.

The team in Cupertino worked in close collaboration with LG's engineers. David Lundgren, the Product Design manager, created the "Man on Mir" program, named after the Mir space station established by the Soviets in 1986. It meant that someone from Apple was in the LG factory twenty-four hours a day, keeping tabs on all that was going on and exchanging information back to headquarters. "There was always someone from Cupertino there, managing everything, every step," says a PD engineer. "Every aspect—the sampling, the mold map, the cosmetic finish, the texture. And to make sure the tools don't get broken."

Danny Coster, the ID lead, practically lived in Korea as the project came into being, ensuring that the vision of the ID studio wasn't just aesthetically pleasing but also "designed for manufacturing." One person recalls Coster telling Cupertino that the post-reset redesign was "coming up trumps," meaning it was succeeding. Apple's Product Design team had played a critical role figuring out how to manufacture the computer, but they leveraged LG's capabilities extensively for mass production. The same zero-tolerance-for-defects culture that ID had inculcated in Cupertino made its way over to Korea, with Apple engineers routinely descending on the country to fix things at a frequency they'd never experienced.

"It wasn't that way before," says David Hoenig, who recalls flying to Korea more than twenty times in a three-year period. "There was some of that, like if something really bad blew up. But this was even the minutiae, like we had these speaker balls that were not sealing properly. We weren't getting the right bass frequency response. So it was 'Who's getting on a plane?'"

The Apple team kept pushing LG to try different things, to experiment using tools in novel ways—anything to make assembly work, but all attempts were failing. "We were doing tooling on things that just had never been done before—for injection molding parts," Hoenig says. "I mean, just never." He was worried about pushing too hard, creating even greater risks of production. "We were doing a lot of things called hydraulics," he says. "If the hydraulics aren't synced properly, the tool will crash and it will break. And then [the production line would be down] for like two months." That risk never materialized, but it was a constant worry.

"We were fighting for things with our manufacturing partner, LG, and they're just looking at us sideways," Hoenig adds. "All of the suppliers thought we were nuts—always. But for some reason they just saw—they believed in—the bigger vision. I think part of LG was always about like, 'How do we become better?'"

The LG factory was in an industrial center called Gumi, an inland city 140 miles southeast of Seoul. The engineers didn't find it a pleasant place to visit, and getting there was arduous. The bigwigs visiting from Cupertino would fly in via helicopter from Seoul, but the engineers going regularly had to take a circuitous three-hour train journey. "You had to know how to read the schedules and the train numbers, and they were not obvious," says Chris Novak. Gumi established itself as a tech center when Samsung created a major electronics complex there in the 1970s. Seoul had named the area a key industrial complex, attracting other companies, including LG. But Apple employees found little to do in the city. The Rio Tourist Hotel they stayed in was quaint but grimy—a "pigsty," in the words of one engineer—and it had a designated floor that doubled as a "room salon," or brothel. Engineers said the sheets were so over-starched they likened them to sheet metal.

One time, when a newly hired senior operations executive named Tim Cook visited to see iMac development, Apple's engineers made sure he had the best room available, knowing full well that it was still subpar. The next morning at breakfast, Cook wasn't looking great and someone asked, "What did you think of the room, Tim?" Cook replied that he hadn't slept well. "Why's that?" someone asked. "Because I stayed standing up all night," Cook said.

The factory itself was bare-bones and scrappy. Just to save on electricity costs, LG had every other light unplugged. It was also small and cramped, the space between the production lines was tight, and the overhead conveyor system carrying the plastic iMac enclosures could hit you in the face if you didn't duck. "Korea was still very, very crude and very kind of heavy-handed," says one senior Apple engineer. "It was amazing what they did, but there were no high-quality manufacturing processes or systems or automation at all. It was all bodies on a line just putting shit together." Building the iMac at scale to meet demand was such an enormous challenge that another senior executive on the project recalls having nightmares in the weeks leading up to it going on sale. "I had sacrificed so much—my marriage had nearly died," this person says. "And I was dreaming that nobody wanted it, and we were building tents for the unsold inventory."

By the time Steve Jobs was ready to unveil the iMac to the world, the factory in Gumi was not at all production-ready. So the first models Jobs had shown on stage were handcrafted by Apple's ID team in Korea. "There was only two or three of them," says Jon Rubinstein, the head of hardware whom ID reported into at the time. "One of the guys sat in the bathtub and hand-did the surface because it's a disgusting mess—you just get plastic everywhere."

Hello (Again)

On May 6, 1998, Steve Jobs wore a dark formal suit. After a lengthy warm-up in which he declared that other computers were "u-u-u-gly," Jobs matter of-factly removed a black cloth on a nearby tabletop and declared, "This is iMac." Engineers on the project recall a sense of great relief when the cloth was removed and the iMac was intact, beautiful, and functional. "We were scared to death it would melt onstage and we'd all get fired," Novak says. The fear was unfounded and hyperbolic, reflecting the stress of the whirlwind eight-month project. But it's not like they had working models for weeks ahead of the unveiling. They had only a few units, carried back from Korea as personal luggage, and they hadn't yet built models in a way that would meet the quality levels of a consumer product. Jobs, wanting to underscore the Bondi Blue translucence, had placed a light source underneath the computer to make it glow, and the PD team worried what the heat might do to the plastic.

The response of the audience was curiously tepid, with little applause. But then, as in 1984, Jobs turned the machine on, revealing a montage of graphics ending with "Hello (again)." As a cameraman panned around the computer and gave a 360-degree view of the translucent plastic, the crowd roared. "It looks like it's from another planet," Jobs exclaimed. "And a good planet! A planet with better designers."

Ian Parker of *The New Yorker* would later write that the iMac's design "had the giddiness of a pardoned prisoner." Consumers immediately loved it. Beyond the design, the iMac reflected Jobs's focus and drive, his ability to take uncompromising stances. The iMac did away with a floppy drive and shunned serial ports in favor of USB, then just an emerging technology. Plus, it had two powerful built-in speakers and could connect quickly to the web. It cost $1,199, a reasonable entry point and one that would come down over the next three years. An enormous $100 million marketing campaign was all about the design, reinforcing the Think Different slogan with an actual product this time. "Sorry," said one ad prominently displaying the blue enclosure, "no beige."

When the first iMacs started shipping in August 1998, Jobs held a celebratory, all-hands meeting in the atrium of Infinite Loop. Some of the same people he'd reamed out half a year earlier were there, and Jobs thanked them. Standing next to a blow-up iMac the size of a kids' air castle, Jobs said, "I came here a year and a half ago, and people were laughing at us. They aren't laughing at us now."

Within six weeks, Apple sold 278,000 units, making it Apple's fastest-selling Mac to date. By Christmas, Apple had sold 800,000 units. It was America's bestselling computer. Apple revenues in the holiday quarter rose 8 percent to $1.7 billion, and profits were $152 million—a fifth straight quarterly profit since Jobs was named interim CEO, and more than triple that of a year earlier. Apple doubled down on the success and prepared for a wider ramp-up. In January 1999, it replaced Bondi Blue with five Life Saver colors, and the computer got a speed bump. By February 1999, Apple's stock had hit $39, up from $12.75 a year earlier. More radical than the new iMac design, though, were the changes Apple made in how and where its new computer would be manufactured.

CHAPTER 7

LG GOES GLOBAL—WALES AND MEXICO

The success of the iMac gave Apple a problem it hadn't experienced in years: overwhelming demand. It now sought to pay more attention to the efficiency of its production and day-to-day operations. These were the things that Gil Amelio had tried to improve, but he'd had the sequence backward: First Apple needed a hit product; only then could it focus on how to manufacture more efficiently.

Apple responded by doubling down on the outsourcing model. Over a multiyear period, Apple gutted its own factories and commissioned suppliers to mirror the triple-continent strategy it had deployed since the early 1980s. Instead of having LG build the CRT and ship it to Apple—which by late 1998 was assembling iMacs in Singapore, Sacramento, and Ireland—Apple began to take its own factories out of the equation. It cut 350 manufacturing jobs in California and slashed 450 positions in Ireland. In one sense, that shift wasn't itself massive, as LG's work making the CRT already represented close to 90 percent of the iMac's assembly. But it was a milestone shift in strategy. Apple, for its most successful Mac ever, was fully committing to managing outsourcers rather than building anything itself.

LG agreed to set up iMac operations in Wales and Mexico. It was a well-thought-out strategy, designed to smooth production issues, ramp up scale, avoid tariffs, and globalize distribution. Instead, disaster ensued.

The "Toaster Line" in Wales

When LG announced it would produce 6,000 jobs in Newport, Wales, with a massive project costing £1.7 billion, the UK's Welsh secretary William Hague called it "the biggest vote of confidence the Welsh economy has ever had." On the day the factory broke ground in January 1997, Prime Minister John Major attended the ceremony. It was the high point of a project now remembered as a debacle.

The ambitious plan called for LG to "produce semiconductors, monitors, color picture tubes, color display tubes, and other television and monitor components, to be sold in Britain, Europe and North America." LG wanted to rival Samsung, and international expansion was core to the effort. Carol Hughes, a Welsh electronics technician in her twenties, joined the LG Wales project as a "training officer" to guide a team of younger apprentices. Apple was among the first clients. Hughes recalls feeling a bit sheepish the first time executives from Cupertino visited because the site was far from complete. The area looked like it had tram lines running through concrete, with troughs in the ground and wires hanging from the ceiling. The concrete floor hadn't yet been prepared for production.

But after LG Wales won the contract to make iMacs, before Christmas of 1998, Hughes and a team of about twenty flew out to Singapore. Their mission was to learn the ins and outs of how Apple was assembling the iMacs after importing the CRT monitors from LG Korea, so they could replicate the operations. They learned how to install motherboards into the housing and perform a software test. Dozens of Apple employees from Cork were also brought to Wales to train the new team, unaware that once their Welsh apprentices got up to speed, they'd be out of a job.

The hours were long. "It wasn't five days a week, and sometimes it wasn't just the six," Hughes says. "You'd get called in for all sorts of reasons. We'd gone from doing an eight-hour day, to a ten-hour day, up to twelve hours and then to fifteen. There was no leeway with Apple. They said, 'Jump!' and you said, 'How high?'" The training in Singapore was also tough, and the Welsh team experienced burnout. They were picked up at seven a.m. each morning, brought back around eight p.m. The team of apprentices would want to decompress with dinner and drinks, so they'd end up at the bar together. On more than one occasion the time went by so quickly that the waitress would say, "Do you want some toast with your beer?" Deep in the cavern of the bar, they hadn't realized it was sunrise and the waitress was offering them breakfast.

Back in Wales, LG struggled to hire enough people, and turnover was high. LG was so rushed to begin production on Apple's schedule that when iMac assembly started, the factory walls weren't finished. It was cold out and the building lacked heating, so the Welsh workers wore jackets, scarves, and fingerless gloves. "At one end there was a production line, and on the other end they were still pouring in concrete for a new floor," Hughes says.

LG's game plan was hugely ambitious. The site took up nearly thirty American football fields and included multiple factories to build cathode ray tubes, motherboards, and the housing—the aesthetic enclosure of electronic hardware. LG had a specific spot in the warehouse purely for Apple inventories. This was part of a significant shift from Apple assembling its computers to adopting a technique called vendor-managed inventory. A yellow line was painted down the factory, demarcating when Apple took "ownership" of the hardware. Until a finished product crossed the line, it was LG's—a critical step to reduce inventory.

Steven Paterson, who did quality control for LG Wales, says the factory had two production lines manned by roughly 150 people. At its peak, LG Wales was shipping 500 iMacs per line per day. So it was successful in some regards, but he recalls multiple problems. Hard drives were being stolen, which caused delays in production, and there was tension between LG's focus on shipments and Apple's slowing things down to ensure quality. The copy-and-paste-from-Singapore approach hadn't taken UK weather into account, resulting in wet pallets and ruined cardboard packaging.

At its worst point, LG workers took to calling the iMac production area "the toaster line," for the propensity of the computers to catch fire. The problem was caused by faulty capacitors, and it upset LG because—in their view—the challenge stemmed from Apple's design, not their configuration. "We were contracted to build, not to design, so there was a little bit of an argy-bargy over that," says a Welsh worker, using local slang for "squabble."

Meanwhile, LG's broader experience in Wales was proving disastrous. LG abandoned efforts to fabricate semiconductors after chip prices fell, and its long-term hopes for CRT monitors fell into disarray as flat-panel TVs appeared in the market, causing the price of CRTs to collapse. After just a year, iMac production was halted entirely, never to resume.

Mexicali Blues

LG's foray into Mexico wasn't much better. Almost immediately the plans went awry, beginning with a fire in April 1999 that halted shipments of iMacs for nearly a month. Meanwhile, cultural differences between Korea and Mexico were hard to grapple with, making life difficult for all participants.

It didn't help that the Korean executives were scared and refused to stay overnight in Mexicali, where LG was assembling iMacs. News reports at the time told lurid stories of kidnappings and ransoms in Tijuana-based maquiladoras—manufacturing plants—so the LG engineers stayed in Calexico, six miles north across the border in California. "They were concerned about getting targeted for ransom," says an Apple project manager. "We were all nervous driving into Mexico. They would pick me up in these beat-up cars and drive me over the border."

LG's game plan was for the Gumi factory in Korea to build the generic base unit of the iMacs, then ship them to Mexicali, where employees would do rework, put the correct color shell on the unit, and ship it out to North American customers. But the Mexicali plant struggled with demand forecasting, as Apple lacked any good ways of knowing which of the five iMac colors would be popular. The company often found itself guessing—ending up with too many of one color and not enough of another. Tangerine, unexpectedly, was a dud.

Daniel Vidaña, a director of iMac supply management, says the scale Cupertino required was "insane." On average, Apple was selling 5,000 iMacs per day. The operations team had to be ultra-efficient to avoid hemorrhaging cash, as the iMac was meant to be a low-cost product that families would buy. The multiple color options, he adds, amplified complexity and uncertainty. "I was in charge of the planning side of things," Vidaña says. "I was telling the factories every week which colors, which models, had to be built. That was sent to our logistics teams and the manufacturers, but they weren't doing it. Every day we got a report saying, 'This is what we built.' They were not adhering to our plan. They were not building what we wanted; they were building what was easiest for them. And they were only building in quantities they could manage or handle in the supply chain."

Vidaña says LG just wasn't prepared for the sort of fast-paced changes Apple was trying to establish. "Look, they built TVs. And you can imagine: TVs don't change a lot," he says. "There's not a lot of configuration aspects to them, at least not then. They were not a high-volume, rapid-change type of organization, and that's why it was a difficult situation for us."

Another Apple project manager says meetings with LG management in Mexicali were often tense, and the executives could be rude. "I was leading one meeting where I had to call out LG for not meeting a contractual agreement or failing to supply units," this person says. The LG executive was dismissive and instead asked to tell a joke. "What do you call a person who speaks two languages?" he asked. "I answered, "Bilingual," the Apple manager says. "Then he replied, "What do you call a person who speaks one language?" The Apple manager waited for the punch line. "An American."

"I Can Fix This"

LG had taken a high-and-mighty attitude at exactly the wrong time. As the sole manufacturer for America's bestselling computer, LG believed it had leverage to exert against Apple. But its factory in Wales never left the hand-holding stage, and though Mexicali was better, it certainly wasn't living up to Cupertino's demands. So as Apple tried to get lower prices as volumes ramped up, LG stood firm.

The Korean group had been intimately involved not just in building the iMac at scale, but also in working with Apple's engineers on the design. And because Apple was in such a rush to get the first version of iMac out, it was LG—not Apple—that had much of the documentation on how to actually build the computer. But LG forgot the first rule of contract manufacturing: The client comes first. Instead, it tried to use its position as a strength. "They sunk their own grave with the negotiation piece, trying to leverage it," says an Apple engineer, calling negotiations at the time challenging. "It was horrifically documented—the product itself was coming out of LG. So LG had all the specs, all the schematics, all the part files, everything." LG had played such a role creating the computer that a senior executive in Korea publicly said his company had basically designed it. Steve Jobs, deeply protective of the ID team, demanded a retraction.

But LG didn't know two things. One is that Apple's Industrial Design studio had, by March 1999, revamped every aspect of the iMac design to lower the cost, beautify the design, and take greater ownership of the intellectual property. The first-generation iMac had used textured plastic to create only a semi-translucent shell—deliberately obscuring some of the uglier aspects of the guts inside. It had big and awkward vertically printed circuit boards on both sides of the CRT, and three rows of perforated holes above the handle. It also had a fan, which created some acoustic noise. The second generation had a much cleaner look. The colored plastic was fully transparent, giving a detailed look into a far better design inside. The circuit board was smaller and tightly packed into the bottom. The perforated holes now circled around the handle, resulting in such improved ventilation that Apple could remove the fan, making it silent. "Not a single component, not a single fastener, carried over," says an engineer from Product Design. "It's an entirely different product," adds a subordinate to Jony Ive. Another executive says the bill of materials—the cost of all the components in each iMac—nearly halved from the first generation to the second, saving Apple hundreds of dollars per unit. LG was still Apple's supplier for this revamped iMac, and they worked together to figure out how to build it at scale. But whatever leverage LG had in the design and schematics of the first iMac was gone.

The second thing LG didn't know is that a little-known Taiwanese company called Hon Hai Precision was already reverse-engineering LG's capabilities in building a CRT and was being "brought up" by Apple as a secondary supplier to build the iMac in China. The founder of Hon Hai had heard of LG's twin fiascoes in Wales and Mexico and called up Apple with a simple message: "I can fix this." That phone call would have enormous consequences and reverberate for decades, turning Hon Hai Precision into one of the world's largest companies by revenue and a household name the world over. Most people would know it by its trade name: Foxconn.

CHAPTER 8

THE TAISHANG—TAIWANESE ON THE MAINLAND

No country was more important to Apple than Taiwan in the first five years of Steve Jobs's comeback. While the iMac was built out of Korea by LG and the lower-volume PowerMac G3 and G4 desktop computers were assembled by Apple in California and Singapore, the other two product lines in the "quadrant strategy"—the entry-level iBook and the PowerBook—were assembled in Taiwan.

The island nation had undergone an enormous transformation since the late 1940s, when the Communists under Mao won a ruthless civil war and took power in China. The defeated Nationalists under Chiang Kai-shek fled to the island and established the Republic of China in exile, claiming sovereignty over both Taiwan and the mainland—a claim recognized by the United Nations until 1971. The island, once a backwater province of China, had modernized under fifty years of Japanese rule that ended with World War II. Then, with the United States acting as both a military shield and a significant importer, Taiwan experienced a postwar economic miracle. Its economy shifted away from agriculture and toward manufacturing and exports, first in low-tech electronics and textiles, and later in high-tech industries. Political reform followed. Taiwan had been under martial law since 1949, but the strict rules were lifted in 1987, giving way to wider liberalization and, in 1996, the island's first democratic presidential elections.

Apple's offshoring to the island nation began when Phil Baker had the Newton manufactured by Inventec in the mid-1990s. And when Baker moved over to the Portables division, he pushed for laptops, too, to be made there. But Inventec was building notebooks for Compaq, an Apple rival, and its CEO, Richard Lee, didn't feel right taking the order. He connected Baker with a friend he went to school with, Barry Lam, who had founded Quanta in 1988. "So they ended up doing the notebook, and that was the beginning of Taiwan building products for Apple," says Baker, referring to "core" products beyond the Newton. "There was never any attempt to do it before. It was kind of accidental."

Apple was making PowerBooks in Ireland at the time, but as part of its manufacturing overhaul it started second-sourcing to Quanta. At first the quality and capabilities Apple found were subpar. "Treachery, ineptitude, sloppy, negligence on every level," are the words used by one senior engineer to describe Taiwan at the time. "Quanta was not a very good development partner whatsoever," says another. "The talent to take on manufacturing, part fabrication, assembly, design challenges—the talent to do that with Quanta in Taiwan was not there."

The role of Apple engineers was to change all that through extensive training. This strategy soon proved to have a profound impact on the country and its neighbors, where Apple sourced many of the components. Apple wasn't, by any stretch, the largest computer maker working in Taiwan, but its penchant for complex designs and intolerance for defects was unique and over-the-top, necessitating a form of intellectual investment shared by none of its rivals. Apple veterans from the time can't stress enough that nobody else was embedding dozens of engineers into Taiwanese suppliers, then consistently pushing the envelope on what was possible. "Apple is single-handedly responsible for bringing quality into Southeast Asia," says Robert Brunner, the director of the ID studio from 1990 to 1997. "If you look at the capability they brought up in that region, from a manufacturing standpoint, it's solely on their presence and their demands on these organizations that caused them to build that competency of being able to make quality things." For the biggest computer makers at the time, design and R&D were such secondary considerations to logistics and efficiency that Sun Microsystems CEO Scott McNealy once likened Dell to a grocery store: "They're not in the PC business any more than Safeway is in the food manufacturing business."

Apple selected Taiwan again when Steve Jobs commissioned the iBook, an almost neon-bright laptop marketed as the "iMac to go" upon its July 1999 release. To manufacture it, Apple turned to Taipei-based AlphaTop, a failing contract manufacturer that offered all kinds of assistance to win the order. Chris Novak, the early iMac Product Design lead, had moved over to laptops in the late nineties and was sent to Taiwan to help "bring up" their quality. "When we started, it was a pretty deplorable factory," Novak says. "As they got money in, they started to fix the factory, but it was quite an experience, 'cause you could tell these guys were low on cash. They didn't have a lot of anything."

An AlphaTop engineer who worked sleepless nights on the project says the work was so difficult that if he had to do it over again, he wouldn't. "If I had to keep working for Apple, it would kill me," he says. "I wouldn't survive." A large part of the difficulty involved overmolding—a multistep process where two or more components are molded on top of one another. The engineers had to work this out to place bright rubber directly on the polycarbonate iBook case, making sure it sealed the perimeter. It was a novel technique that kept creating microcracks, day after day. To ready some prototypes for the official unveiling, Apple engineers had donned AlphaTop factory smocks, took out X-ACTO knives, and sat with about fifty laborers to manually cut the "flash"—excess material seeping out of the mold cavity—around the perimeter of the laptop.

The iBook was a big success upon its July 1999 release. It was the first laptop with built-in Wi-Fi—such a novelty at the time that Jobs, ever the showman, surfed the internet onstage while waving a Hula-Hoop around the computer to prove there were no hidden wires. When the Reese Witherspoon character in *Legally Blonde* stood in line wearing her pink bunny ears to buy a laptop and study for the LSATs, an iBook was the obvious choice.

Two years later, Apple went in a distinctly noncute direction with the Titanium PowerBook. Workhorse laptops were typically bulky, had square monitors, and were constructed of cheap plastic. The TiBook, by contrast, was just an inch thick and featured a 15.2-inch widescreen. It was a notoriously difficult product to manufacture, causing eighteen of the twenty PD people on the project to quit. The loss of talent was a major blow. "It was a shit show. The whole thing was awful," says one of the engineers. "Everybody got burned out from the Titanium PowerBook because the Product Design team was doing all these roles," says another PD engineer. "They were designers, they were material scientists, they were process engineers, they were manufacturing engineers, they were supplier quality audits. They had twenty hats. Because there was no one else they could rely on to take this risk that came from the ID goals and turn it into a manufacturing product."

But the difficulties in manufacturing were a boon to Apple's assembly partner and the factories around it. The Taiwanese were learning fast, evolving from taking orders to commanding respect as a genuine partner. Taiwan's rapid growth led to soaring labor costs and capacity constraints. Like Japanese groups in the 1960s, which set up shop in labor-abundant countries and used the shared colonial language of Japanese to teach Korea and Taiwan how to manufacture, Taiwanese entrepreneurs in turn had begun to deploy the same tactic in the mother of all developing countries. Taipei had ended a thirty-eight-year ban on traveling to China in 1987, opening the mainland for commerce and trade. Within a decade Taiwanese entrepreneurs were building major factories on the mainland, teaching their apprentices in Mandarin and attracting some of the world's biggest PC brands.

Uncle Terry

Michael Dell couldn't understand why the phone reception at Foxconn was so bad until one day in the mid-1990s he visited its Longhua campus, just north of the Chinese coastal city Shenzhen, during monsoon season. Heavy rain struck a roof made of corrugated metal sheets, sounding like a chaotic symphony of tiny hammers drowning out everything else. Dell realized this was why, when dialing from the United States, he could barely hear Foxconn CEO Terry Gou.

"Dell couldn't hear Terry because everything was inexpensive," a former Foxconn official says, adding that the landline phones were old and battered, and the place was painted a drab gray. "The roof was tin roof. And everything was cheap, cheap, cheap."

The tin roof of Terry Gou's cramped and cluttered, cement-floored office served a subtle purpose. Foxconn, a Taiwanese contract manufacturer taking advantage of cheap labor on the Chinese mainland, was all about the client. The shabby quarters at Gou's office indicated that Gou's clients were getting the best deal. Every dollar he earned was going to the production line, not to marble floors in the reception area.

This especially appealed to Michael Dell, who launched one of the world's biggest computer companies out of his college dorm with a relentless focus on logistics, distribution, and manufacturing. He was even known for getting angry when Dell Computer was earning too much, since it indicated his customers could be getting even lower prices.

Gou's austere strategy was directly opposed to what Steve Jobs had tried to do in the 1980s both at Apple and NeXT. At Apple's Fremont factory, Jobs obsessed over trivial things, asking that the machines be painted in bright hues to match the rainbow-colored Apple logo. He wanted the walls to be a very specific, pure white. He told one manager the factory should be so clean you could eat off the floor. Jobs envisioned consumers visiting Fremont and watching their computer get built. As regards the NeXT circuit board, he once said, "It's built completely untouched by human hands!" By contrast, Gou's factories were not to be seen at all. Workers lived and slept within a gated community cordoned off from the public and patrolled by guards. And later, when it became the biggest maker of Apple hardware, the hands of thousands of people were involved, sometimes performing tasks nine to eleven seconds long, hour after hour, with few breaks and penalties for mistakes.

In 1999, when Apple and Foxconn started working together closely for the first time, Apple executives saw what Dell saw—but more. Cupertino realized it could take advantage of the conditions in China in very different ways. For Dell, ever focused on efficiency, China's advantages were all about cost and scale—that is to say, they were about *margin*. But Apple looked at the armies of affordable, available labor and saw a different potential: *unconstrained design*. Or to put it differently: Western PC companies were shifting to China because of what was *available*; Apple shifted because of what was *possible*. Before the return of Jobs, Apple computers were manufactured in a fashion called *poka-yoke,* a Japanese term meaning "mistake-proofing." The idea was that products should be designed for easy assembly. And a desire for more automation amplified the trend: From the sketching stage on forward, blueprints for hardware were constrained so machines could put them together without error. But what Apple was realizing was that thousands of laborers cheaply handcrafting Apple hardware on a conveyor-belt production line allowed its designs to be maddeningly intricate, complex, and automation-unfriendly.

The labor force on China's mainland was unskilled, but they were also hardworking and determined. Taiwanese entrepreneurs like Gou were pouring in capital and resources, importing a managerial class of experienced manufacturing executives to the mainland to train staff and run the production lines. These Taiwanese executives—known as Taishang—played an essential role on the mainland ushering in capitalism. Working with local government officials, they brought into being "the Guangdong Model," an export-driven template for growth focused on low-cost manufacturing, named after the province where Shenzhen and neighboring cities were given free rein to attract foreign investment and experiment with Western business concepts. Local officials, earning fees from factory growth, were incentivized to work hand in glove with the Taiwanese entrepreneurs. They were empowered to subsidize land and machinery, to build infrastructure to aid logistics, and to facilitate the flow of migrant workers from China's rural areas. At an institutional level, rural migrants were exploited as second-class citizens, earning lower wages and receiving few social welfare benefits. The Guangdong Model is what made China the workshop of the world, particularly once Beijing took the blueprint and established it across the country.

Thanks to this alliance of private and state interests, Foxconn didn't just command low-cost labor, but also cutting-edge equipment. One Apple executive recalls, in 1999, being stunned by the dichotomy between the world-class machines in the Foxconn factory and the "shithole" conditions around them. "Terry's office was, like, a trailer, with a plastic table-desk," this person says. A photographer who visited a decade later described it as an "old, single-story, metal-roofed building that more resembles a landscape maintenance shed than a typical executive suite."

Another Apple executive recalls visiting the Longhua campus during the summer, when the air can feel thick and heavy from all the humidity. "It was hotter than hell," he says. On a tour of the facilities, he observed that only some of the buildings had air-conditioning units, but he was stumped trying to figure out why. He asked his guide, "How do you decide which facilities to put air-conditioning in?' And they go, 'Well, whichever facilities have the equipment that needs air-conditioning.'" Requesting the anecdote be anonymous, the executive underscores the point: "They cared more about the machines than the people."

One attribute that made Foxconn distinct from other Taiwanese contract manufacturers operating on the mainland was not its quality or expertise, but its political savvy. An electronics client didn't necessarily understand this, but the reason Terry Gou's factories had world-class machinery is that the local government had subsidized them, if not outright purchased them. This was part of a quid pro quo with government officials who were judged by, and desperate for, growth. "Uncle Terry," as Apple would come to know Gou, was more adept than any of his rivals in convincing government officials to provide land and machinery and introduce a spate of policies tailor-made to promote exports. "China invested an enormous amount of money," says a senior Apple executive at the time. "Uncle Terry—they subsidized the shit out of him—but he doesn't talk about that . . . They paid for a lot. I mean, I'd walk into a factory, and it'd be all brand-new machine tools—and the Chinese government paid for all of it."

Dirt City

Foxconn had the humblest of origins. In 1974, two years before Apple was started out of a garage, twenty-three-year-old Terry Gou founded Hon Hai Plastics out of a shed. Gou, who'd just completed his duty in the Taiwanese army, founded the company with $7,500. Part of the funds came from his mother, who along with Terry's father had fled to Taiwan from the mainland during the Chinese Civil War. Its operations at first were run out of a Taiwanese town whose name translates to "Dirt City." Gou began by molding plastic knobs for TV sets, dropping off finished products by bicycle. Then he learned what they connected to and how, so he could make those parts, too. Instead of buying the components that made up a part, he would manufacture them; the more components he could make himself, the less he would have to buy. That let him cut costs, which enabled him to undermine competitors on price, especially competitors in higher-cost countries like the United States. When he won more orders, scale let him cut prices further, creating a self-reinforcing cycle.

As the PC revolution took off in the early 1980s, Gou got in on the ground floor and created a name for himself making reliable sockets and connectors—small components that facilitate communication between different parts of a computer. The *conn* in Foxconn—Hon Hai's international name—refers to connectors. "Fox" is just an animal he likes.

Gou had incredible grit, charisma, and an insatiable appetite for practical knowledge. He deployed these qualities to build formidable long-term relationships. Despite speaking little English, he toured more than thirty US states in the 1980s, spending enough time there to memorize the menu at Denny's. Along the way he convinced all manner of electronics companies to try out his components, offering razor-thin margins.

Gou wore a beaded bracelet he received from a temple dedicated to Genghis Khan. The thirteenth-century Mongolian conqueror was a personal hero, and Gou ran his facilities with a similar, military-like efficiency. Workers on the production line often performed the minutest of tasks to the hum of nearby machines, taking Adam Smith's "division of labor" idea to an extreme. Talking was forbidden and could result in docked pay. Managers watched over the production line, and every defect was counted. Shifts were often twelve hours, and day-shift workers periodically moved to the night shift and then back. Employees were given a Little Red Book featuring the sayings of Terry Gou, some of which were also plastered on the otherwise bare walls. The aphorisms ranged from inspirational to threatening. "Work hard on the job today or work hard to find a job tomorrow," said one. "Value efficiency every minute, every second," said another. "Achieve goals or the sun will no longer rise," said a third.

Ask Gou's colleagues, subordinates, and rivals to describe him and there is often a pause. They hesitate to encapsulate such a figure in ordinary language. One rival executive praises Gou as "one of the world's greatest entrepreneurs" and "absolutely charismatic," but also "scary," "demanding," and an "asshole." He was so multifaceted that any adjective would be true; it just depended on the circumstance. "Any word you need to throw at him—it fits," this executive says. "Any word."

His knack for austere efficiency was legendary. "I always joke I didn't work for Foxconn, I worked for the Taiwanese military. It was spartan," a former executive says. "Every day was 'take the hill!'" This frugality was applied down to the smallest thing. During one directive to cut costs, the soap-to-water ratio in the dispensers of the Foxconn bathroom was cut noticeably enough for the color to keep changing: "Instead of putting in two tablespoons, they might put in a quarter, and sooner or later you get down to only one molecule of soap in there," an executive says. Another colleague joked, in the early 2000s, that Gou was "worth about $2 billion in nickels and dimes."

Gou's understanding of electronics grew extensive enough that he created a structured method to break down any product into ten levels, then established a plan to master them all. "Level one would just be a component, let's just say a knob on an old-style television," a former Foxconn executive says. "Level two might be the metal stamp part that goes into the knob to turn the channels. So two mechanical interfaces, no electrical complexity. Level three might be where you add some electrical connections. Level four and five is more complex subassemblies. Level six was PCBAs [printed circuit board assembly]. Then we'd start getting to assembly—level seven and level eight—like putting together a Dell computer or a notebook. And level ten is a finished good ready for shipment." The point of this vertical integration, the executive explains, is that the customer would grow to depend on Foxconn: "If you're fully vertically integrated, where else are they going to go?"

CHAPTER 9

THE SILICON VALLEY OF HARDWARE— "FOXCONN ISN'T CALLED 'FOX-CON' FOR NOTHING"

From the founding of Communist China in 1949 until 1978, mainland China was largely shut off from outsiders as it underwent multiple upheavals. Mao might have been proficient as a military commander, but as a national leader he was paranoid and domineering, driven by a bastardized form of Marxism. Before Mao became head of state, the country had just undergone what the Chinese call their "century of humiliation," a humbling period when the world's top economy for countless generations suffered repeated military defeats by British, French, and Japanese forces. In centuries past, China had been a technological powerhouse that had invented gunpowder, the printing press, the compass, and paper. Mao wanted to catch up to industrialized countries, but his Great Leap Forward was a catastrophe, resulting in famine that killed 30 million to 45 million people. Mao's next act was the Cultural Revolution, a whirlwind decade beginning in 1966 meant to purify Communism. Students organized as Red Guards were encouraged to attack "the four olds": old customs, old culture, old habits, and old ways. By the time Mao died in 1976, China was poorer than sub-Saharan Africa.

In the final years of the 1970s, as Terry Gou was developing a real technical expertise with electronics, China's economy entered a transformative phase initiated by Mao's successor, Deng Xiaoping. As part of his "reform and opening up" policies, Deng established several special economic zones on the eastern coast—areas open to capitalist experimentation—which flourished by drawing in foreign investment and millions of rural workers from inland China. Entrepreneurs in Hong Kong, a British colony at the time, were the first to invest heavily, combining "Third World costs" with "First World caliber management, infrastructure, and market knowledge."

The result was a remarkable boom unprecedented in world history: the Middle Kingdom, a country of more than a billion people, opened to the world, modernized at a frenetic pace, and grew some 10 percent a year for three decades. Hundreds of millions of people were lifted from poverty. As early as 1984, President Reagan was calling China "a so-called Communist country," suggesting that as the country planted the seeds of economic reform, the flower of political reform would bloom.

In 1980, Shenzhen was a fishing village of fewer than 70,000 people. But as a special economic zone just across the harbor from Hong Kong, Shenzhen and the area around it underwent a metamorphosis. "By the late 1980s, the entire 104-mile route from Hong Kong to Guangzhou was lined on both sides with factories," according to the late Ezra Vogel, a Harvard scholar and the biographer of Deng Xiaoping. By 1990 the city of Shenzhen had a population of 1.7 million; in the early 2000s, it had grown to around 7 million. In just twenty-five years, Shenzhen's population grew a hundredfold.

Quality was often horrendous by Western standards. A manufacturing design engineer at Apple recalls visiting Shenzhen-based suppliers in buildings that would fail a regulatory test on a mere glance, let alone a deep audit. "There weren't elevators, so you'd walk the stairs," this person says. "And I'd count the stairs. There might be twelve between the first and second story, then eighteen stairs to the next floor, then sixteen, and then twenty-four." The stairs themselves were sometimes ten inches in height, sometimes seven, and so on. "My point is those buildings were handmade," he says. Everything was done in a slapdash manner. Speed and scale were the only priorities. Apple engineers sent to Shenzhen describe the city as a rough place back then. When one engineer, six-four, tried walking out of the hotel to go for an evening stroll, the concierge stopped him and warned it was too dangerous. "I'm a big guy," he said, dismissing their worries. "A dozen monkeys can kill a gorilla," the concierge responded.

More than any area in China, the province of Guangdong transformed the fortunes of the world's most populous country. Shenzhen in particular became a hub for electronics, earning it the nickname the Silicon Valley of Hardware. The journalist James Fallows, who lived in China in the late 2000s, has argued that Terry Gou ranks second only to Deng Xiaoping in transforming China into an industrial behemoth over the previous fifty years. That's an extraordinary claim, but one backed up even by Gou's rivals. "The reason Shenzhen is Shenzhen is Terry Gou," says a high-ranking contract manufacturing executive. "Without his ambition, Shenzhen wouldn't be the manufacturing power it is."

Yet it's worth highlighting how recently Foxconn developed this reputation. In 1999, it was a company with $1.8 billion of revenue, far smaller than Solectron, SCI, or Flextronics, its US rivals. By 2010, Foxconn revenues were $98 billion, more than those of its five biggest competitors combined. And Foxconn's extraordinary growth in those eleven years is the consequence of one client more than any other: Apple.

A Second iMac Supplier

The Apple-Foxconn relationship goes back to at least the early 1990s, but in a limited way. Foxconn had been championed by H. L. Cheung, a Singaporean Apple executive from 1981 to 1997, who would later join Foxconn. But Terry Gou's company was mostly just a supplier of affordable components, like those connecting printed circuit boards to the housing. Apple engineers from the mid-1990s remember it as "the connector company." But Foxconn quickly expanded its skill set, and approaching the year 2000, it was demonstrating its prowess as a jack-of-all-trades with a model different from the other Taiwanese companies expanding to the mainland.

The business of assembling electronics for Western brands was cutthroat, so the big trend at the time was to hire expensive engineers and designers, invest in R&D, and take on more responsibility for the client. This got to the point where an IBM clone brand could pick its PC designs out of a catalogue produced by groups like ASUS, Inventec, and Acer. These original design manufacturers, or ODMs, would design the model, build it, badge it with a Western logo, and ship it. This work was higher margin than mere assembly, so it worked nicely for the Taiwanese companies. And it offered Western PC brands the distinct advantage of offloading even more of their fixed costs—not just manufacturing, but design and R&D. However, it involved a distinct risk. It didn't take much for ASUS and Acer to expand into branding and marketing themselves. Soon they were selling computers under their own name and competing with their clients. It was a logical step, but one that irked the Western PC brands. They'd ask, "How can I trust you if I'm competing with you?" says Willy Shih, who teaches at Harvard Business School. Their concerns were aggravated in times of component shortages, because a group like Acer would be incentivized to allocate parts to its own PC division.

Gou took a different tack. He shunned being an ODM, not liking the costs of hiring expensive talent to design products. Instead, he touted a vertical integration strategy, in which Foxconn would aim to control the bill of materials as much as possible, either by building the key components itself or sourcing them in bulk. Then it would focus on the client, not just on one particular product, one particular design, but by investing in long-term partnerships. Foxconn championed being an original equipment manufacturer, a model widely derided as second class. Unlike the ODMs, a good OEM makes no effort in design or branding, but it will move heaven and earth to respond to the client's manufacturing needs. This narrow focus allowed Foxconn to go several layers deep in the supply chain and achieve greater scale. More scale required a bigger footprint and more laborers—the key ingredients for a successful relationship with local bureaucrats.

Terry Gou wasn't any more enthused about low-margin assembly than his ODM rivals. Assembly was just a power grab. It offered him the chance to take care of sourcing components, from his own subdivisions and from third parties, which opened further opportunities. "One of the ways Foxconn can make money is PPV, or purchase price variance," says David Johnson, an Apple tooling engineer from the time. "If they can control your supply chain for you—if they take that off your hands—then they can make more money. They'll sell a cable to you for a dollar, but they will buy it for thirty-five cents. So they can make money through all the channels. And the more parts they control for you, the more opportunity there is to make money."

Foxconn began offering final assembly on the cheap for the same reason Costco sells hot dogs: It gets people in the door. Foxconn then upended the world of tooling by giving it away for free. That is, Gou would offer to pay the up-front costs of establishing the custom molds, dies, fixtures, and other equipment necessary to start building a product at scale. "That can be half a million or a million dollars," says a former Apple engineer. "And that was absorbed by the manufacturer—by Foxconn. So Apple just paid for the production parts." Then Foxconn would work to integrate all procurement, manufacturing, and logistics into a one-stop shop. It made its money back the same way a mobile carrier might—giving customers a free phone but earning fees in a two-year contract. This Apple engineer describes Gou's approach as a wily bet to lure in Western companies, getting them hooked on the drug of cheap production, and creating a sticky relationship based on Foxconn's choice of components. "Once they get you in the door, that's it—they control you," he says. "Foxconn isn't called 'Fox-con' for nothing. Terry Gou was a gambler, and the real name of the company is Hon Hai. That was changed to Foxconn because he's a fox, and he's a con artist."

By having a role in so many areas, across several products and down multiple tiers to the sourcing of raw materials, Foxconn was putting itself in a position to scale much faster than its rivals. Longer-term projects allowed it to hire thousands of laborers, then shuffle them around to wherever work was needed. To retain workers and deploy them to different lines on a whim, Gou built the Longhua campus into a dense city within a city, replete with restaurants, markets, entertainment venues, basketball courts, and subsidized dorms. This approach gave rise to a major industrial cluster north of Shenzhen, bulking up his reputation among government officials. Upon scoring political points, Gou could redeem them for better access to land, migrant labor, and cutting-edge machinery.

In 1999, Foxconn won an order to build the enclosure—the external housing—for Apple's Power Mac G4 desktop, a dazzling white-and-graphite computer featuring a semi-translucent, frosted plastic shell and integrated, curved handles. The enclosure was already being made by Singapore Shinei Sangyo, known as "triple S." It had been a trusted supplier to Apple for a decade, building tools Apple would import to its manufacturing facilities in Ireland and California. As demand for the Power Mac increased and Apple sought to cut costs, Foxconn was brought in as a second supplier. There was nothing unusual about this; it was a common move for diversification and resiliency. What was unusual was how well Hon Hai performed. "Foxconn kicked our rice bowl," recalls a mechanical engineer at SSS. It was the first instance that Gou demonstrated to Apple not just his eagerness and commitment, but also his talent.

So as LG struggled with its strategy to build iMacs on three continents, Gou recognized an opportunity for an even larger order with Apple. That's when he made the historic phone call, telling an Apple executive, "I can fix this." The call he made wasn't to just anyone, but to the senior vice president Steve Jobs had hired less than a year earlier to overhaul operations. His name was Tim Cook.

CHAPTER 10

IBM WEST—THE RISE OF TIM COOK

Quitting time at IBM's offices in Raleigh, North Carolina, was 4:12 p.m., and within a few minutes the parking lot looked like the start of a Grand Prix race. IBM, famously bureaucratic and regimented, had developed an Air Force culture under the leadership of Thomas J. Watson, and that culture carried forward well past his retirement in 1971. After the dust settled from the exiting cars, there was only one vehicle left in the parking lot, and it remained there well into the evening, usually past nine or ten. It would be in the parking lot on Saturdays and Sundays, too, often by itself, a testament to the single-minded work ethic of its owner.

Tall, with resolute eyes, exhibiting a stiff posture and exuding a quiet confidence, Tim Cook looked like an IBM executive right out of central casting. He was a small-town Alabama boy, born in 1960 as the second of three sons. Cook had no obviously discernible genius, but he made up for it with an industriousness more suited to characters of fiction. After years of being voted "Most Studious" by his high school classmates, he went off to Auburn University to study industrial engineering.

He took the conventional path to the world of computers, joining IBM in 1982 just as the PC set a standard for the whole industry save for Apple. Cook's specialty lacked any of the glamour or revolutionary change-the-world zeal that typified Cupertino. Certainly no one ever thought to raise a pirate flag at Research Triangle Park, where he worked in the Personal

Computer division. But the twelve years Cook spent at IBM were a period of massive strategic shift, when it went from manufacturing virtually everything itself to outsourcing to Asia. And Cook's ruthless efficiency in materials management was one of those mundane areas that, while lacking flourish, helped IBM and the PC clones nearly send Apple into bankruptcy.

Cook's work discipline put him in good stead, and within just a few years he was selected for a nighttime MBA at Duke University's Fuqua School of Business, a program designed to groom up-and-coming executives who might run an IBM division someday. In 1992, Cook was promoted to director of North America fulfillment. It was an enormous vote of confidence for the thirty-one-year-old, who was developing a reputation for shrewd negotiating and executing just-in-time manufacturing, a method of procuring what's needed when it's needed, and thus doing away with inventories. IBM, though, was foundering. The company that had been the most valuable for decades abruptly lost that title and posted cumulative losses of $15 billion between 1991 and 1994, forcing a restructure toward services.

Cook departed into a senior position at PC wholesaler Intelligent Electronics, bringing order to a distressed business with bloated costs and wasted assets. In 1997 he graduated into a vice president position at Compaq—a dream role. Compaq, whose origins trace back to three friends scribbling their business plans on a napkin in a Houston pie shop, was the first company to clone the IBM PC in 1982. By 1997 it was King of the Clones, with $34 billion of revenue. Cook had been there only a matter of months when recruiters from Apple began calling. He demurred, so they delivered what was quickly becoming a signature move: They offered a personal interview with Steve Jobs.

Round Peg

That Jobs wanted to meet Cook at all illustrated just how much he'd learned in his twelve-year sabbatical from Apple. The young Steve Jobs detested IBM and everything it stood for. Apple's most famous TV ad, introducing the Macintosh at the 1984 Super Bowl, portrayed IBM as an Orwellian Big Brother, stifling innovation. But IBM had also outmaneuvered Apple in consistently and profitably getting affordable products to the masses before losing the battle to companies that did these mundane things even more efficiently.

The older Steve Jobs understood this. Upon his return to Apple, he sought to hire a figure who embodied all the things he wasn't good at and didn't care to think about. Cook, by then thirty-seven, was a no-nonsense operations executive tailor-made for the role. Although Cook has a reputation for being cold, calm, and calculating, Jobs managed to lure him on inspiration and hope. Cook would later describe his decision in almost mystical terms: "You have this voice in your ear that says, 'Go west, young man, go west,'" he once recounted. "It didn't make sense. And yet, my gut said, 'go for it!' And I listened to my gut."

Cook's character was so out of sync with Apple's image of itself that when *Bloomberg Businessweek* profiled him for its cover, it cast his smiling face underneath the enormous text of Apple's Think Different campaign—an homage to "the crazy ones"—with the words reworked to inverse the message: "Here's to the sensible ones, the team players, the problem solvers, the round pegs in the round holes." An executive who joined Apple a little before Cook says of him: "I remember him being very, very cautious and organized about not only work, but about his fitness, about what he ate. It seemed like everything in his life that I could perceive was just very meticulously organized."

Cook's spirit is kindred to that of Immanuel Kant, the eighteenth-century German philosopher whose daily routine was so consistent that residents could set their watch to when he strolled by. His zeal for order is exactly what Apple operations needed. Compaq was a well-run business, but Apple was an absolute mess. Cook could make his mark immediately. Joe O'Sullivan, by then the acting head of operations, was tasked with teaching Cook the ropes. His goal was to distill his eleven years of experience into eight weeks of on-the-job training, beginning around April 1998. After just two weeks, the two men agreed no more time was necessary. "By the time I left him, he knew more than I did about Apple," O'Sullivan says. "That man has a fast mind. And a grasp. And a memory—honestly, it's borderline photographic."

Cook established exceedingly high expectations the first time he held an operations meeting of worldwide managers. In the weekly review, attendees went over what had gone wrong in the prior days, what needed to be fixed immediately, and what was coming up. These meetings were typically ninety minutes; sometimes they could stretch beyond two hours. On the day Cook took over, the weekly review went nearly thirteen hours. He insisted on a granular level of understanding and demanded fluency in the intricacies of every project. If a manager one week, in a lengthy presentation, projected that their team would ship 200,050 of something by Friday, Cook would remember. So the next week, if the manager said, "Yep, we met our numbers. We did two hundred thousand," Cook would look at them and ask, with deadly seriousness: "And fifty?"

Not prepping for a meeting with Cook was a surefire way to embarrass yourself. If a manager was explaining a situation, saying, "Look, if we can charter a 747, our problem will be solved," Cook would reply icily: "If?" A deafening silence would follow. The manager who thought they'd be getting a pat on the back at this point would stumble into an attempted answer. "Well, there's demand worldwide for 747s, and we're looking for one at the moment." Cook would interject: "So you don't have the 747 chartered?" The manager would look down, mumble something until Cook would follow up: "You didn't know you were going to produce a hundred thousand units that week? Why wouldn't you know that?"

By expecting precision, he was basically teaching it, instilling its importance in all of his colleagues so that his underlings would teach their underlings. As exceptional as that first thirteen-hour meeting was, the Friday meeting Cook held with top executives routinely became a four-hour review, a deep dive of spectacular detail into more than 120 pages of Excel numbers related to supply and demand across the global organization. There were so many rows and columns of numbers that the text was printed on special larger paper. Not everyone in these meetings wore glasses when Cook was hired; after a few years, they all did.

However tedious his expectations might feel, Cook himself was the living example of the very demands he expected. He'd arrive each day at six a.m., having already been to the gym. And he'd work so long and so consistently that Apple assigned him two administrative assistants who split the day: one worked from six a.m. to two p.m.; the other worked from two p.m. until whenever Cook went home. Several of Cook's colleagues also had two assistants, an early indication that Cook had found a culture where he belonged. Even at the annual Top 100 meeting—Steve Jobs's retreat in Santa Cruz for a rotating group of his favorite lieutenants—Cook's routine was unvarying. One person recalls going to the hotel gym at five a.m. for an early morning workout and finding a perspiring Tim Cook already midway through his routine.

Numerous executives who worked with both Jobs and Cook can't help but contrast them. One executive says Steve Jobs was difficult because his emotions could abruptly go from zero to a hundred. "Tim," this person adds, "goes from thirty-five to thirty-six." And yet somehow that would be more disconcerting, because it was so unusual. A former vice president at Apple says the way you knew Tim Cook was upset was when he would say, "I just don't understand." This person adds: "When he'd say that, you'd see little puddles on the floor—the sweat coming off of people."

Cook's disdain for mediocrity was similar to that of Jobs, but it manifested itself in an entirely different way. He would persistently ask his managers for layer upon layer of information that flummoxed poor performers and exposed bullshitters. Parents know it takes only a few rounds of a toddler asking, "Why?" before their knowledge is exhausted, leading to frustration and made-up answers. Cook's questioning was like that. He exhibited a memory and an understanding for data and planning that nobody in Cupertino had experienced before. A lower-level executive recalls Cook stopping people in the hallway ahead of a meeting to glance at their spreadsheets. Within a minute he might spot an error. "And if one number was wrong, he wouldn't trust the whole spreadsheet," this person says. "We just knew him as this Terminator machine. Like, he could tell if you were lying. . . . My boss would say: 'If he calls on you and you get the number wrong, he'll try again the next week. If that's wrong, he'll never call on you again.'"

Cook didn't capture everything, of course, but in principle no item was too small to escape his notice—even a rivet costing fractions of a penny per device. Yet he was able to put all the puzzle pieces together and grasp the big picture. "If you send him a pitch, he'll go into page 30, paragraph 7, and ask to talk in more detail," says a person who reported to him. "It's amazing how he can go from high-level to the very details and back."

Cook could make grown men and women cry. A few screamed at him, leaving the room, never to come back. He was unapologetic about these episodes. Like Jobs, Cook wanted only A-list players. No hard feelings if you didn't fit in. Those who stayed, adapted. It might not have been fun. But it was effective.

Foxconn's First Bet

Cook's reputation quickly extended beyond the Apple campus. When Jon Rubinstein, Apple's head of hardware, invited Cook to the Netherlands to negotiate with a company called Lucent as they were trying to help make Wi-Fi a standard, Cook demonstrated a skill in negotiating that awed him. Apple wasn't even a big company at the time, but Cook managed to grasp every facet of Lucent's business to understand what the real costs were, so he could low-ball an offer and convince them they'd still earn profit at scale. "Tim hammered home the prices," Rubinstein says. "It was basically a proctology exam."

Meanwhile, Cook brought in allies with similar experience,

solidifying his style across operational divisions. He hired Bill Frederick to run Logistics, Jeff Williams to lead Procurement, and Jacky Haynes to manage Business Processes. All three had spent more than a decade at IBM, and each completed an MBA at Duke. And they were merely the tip of the iceberg. So many people with IBM experience moved to Cupertino that Big Blue executives would jokingly call Apple "IBM West."

Cook was fond of teaching colleagues to "be aggressive and unreasonable" when negotiating with suppliers. Max Paley, a vice president of graphics at the time, recalls not really knowing what this meant. Cook would say in a calm, deliberative cadence: "Don't . . . ever . . . be . . . afraid . . . to . . . be . . . unreasonable." What did that mean? Was Cook saying to be a jerk? Paley wasn't sure, but he later grew to understand and respect it. "What he was really saying was that it's a typical thing for people—even in business negotiations with a supplier—to try to figure out: What's a reasonable thing to ask them? What are they likely to be able to do?" Paley says. "Whereas he was kinda saying, 'You have no clue! You have no idea what the supplier might actually be capable of. So don't be afraid to ask for the moon. Ask for everything you want. Ask for everything you need. If they can't do it, they'll say no.'"

Foxconn was an early test case for this approach. In Cook's attempt to lessen the risk to iMac operations from LG by getting a second assembler, in late 1999, Apple did ask for the moon—and Foxconn, hoping to play the long game, demonstrated a willingness to do anything to get the order. "Terry Gou was relentlessly focused on doing whatever it took to make Apple succeed," says a senior engineer on the first iMac. "Terry already had a long-term view. And he was willing to sacrifice whatever it took in the rough early days—be it margin or his employees' personal lives—to make that thing succeed. He had a vision. He saw Apple's long-term success, I think, even before Apple did."

CHAPTER 11

FOXCONN GOES GLOBAL—CHINA, CALIFORNIA, AND THE CZECH REPUBLIC

Whereas Foxconn's rivals saw Apple's complex designs as a challenge, Terry Gou saw them as an opportunity. Apple was a low-volume computer maker in 1999, widely seen as difficult to work with and arrogant in the perceived superiority of its products. They were often seen as not worth the trouble. But Gou grasped earlier than anyone that the value of working with Apple wasn't the profits, it was the *learning.* Foxconn might not win much profit from Apple—it might even lose money at times—but the work itself, as well as the lessons Cupertino offered by having its engineers work side by side with locals in the factories, gave his team a deep education. Foxconn's goal was to absorb these lessons and apply the skills to its other, more lucrative clients. "His people used to hate us, because they used to make no money out of us," says an Apple operations executive. "The Compaq guys"—the Foxconn team building for Compaq—"were making a fortune on bonuses, and no one wanted to come work on the Apple account because there were no bonuses." But Gou answered to no one. He took a long-term view, knowing that if his team could please Apple, they could please any client.

Gou saw himself as a visionary. He admired Steve Jobs and sought to be in that sort of company. Jobs had rebuffed him, uninterested in what was a pretty small company in the late 1990s. But the hiring of Tim Cook opened the door. Although Cook had been at Compaq only half a year, the PC behemoth was Foxconn's biggest client, and the two executives had gotten to know each other. So Gou made a big commitment. He offered to build iMacs for Apple at $40 less per unit than LG—big savings for a computer that was shipping in the thousands per day—and, in a bid to replace the Korean company's relationship with Apple entirely, he pledged that Foxconn would establish operations on three continents just like LG. "When Hon Hai goes for something, they go for it all," says an Apple engineer. Apple executives who considered Foxconn "the connector company" were skeptical it had this capability. Cook, astutely, agreed they didn't. Be he argued that they could be taught.

It was the start of a relationship that would transform both companies. The meeting of the minds between Steve Jobs and Jony Ive had made Apple products unique, but it was Terry Gou and Tim Cook who would ensure they were ubiquitous.

Uncle Terry's Vision

Terry Gou gestured animatedly into the distance. He talked square footage and new buildings, how he was going to expand the business and hire hundreds of thousands of workers to live on a bustling campus. The vision was so real, he could almost touch it. Wayne Miller, a senior manager in Product Design sitting next to him, followed the traces of Gou's hand but saw only empty farmland. They were touring the Longhua campus together in a sort of golf cart, in 1999, a time when Foxconn had around 20,000 employees. It was a sizable company, but not particularly special. Miller just nodded, uncertain how to respond. Clearly these weren't the rantings of a madman—Terry Gou was an impressive figure—but normal people didn't have this kind of ambition. "The vision he laid out was quite grand. I was definitely skeptical," Miller says. As they drove around the emerging campus, Miller noticed that workers reacted to Uncle Terry as if he were the mayor or the governor. In a way, in this gated community, he was. "They didn't quite salute, but there was an air of respect when he passed by," Miller says. "People would stop and straighten up."

In 1999, Foxconn was already building the enclosure for the G4 desktop and supplying components for other Apple computers. Miller recalls Foxconn "just crushing it" in terms of production, cost, and speed, a combination nobody could really compete with. "It was mind-blowing how much manufacturing and tooling capability they had," he says. "Terry Gou invested a lot of money, setting that place up to be fast and cheap."

Shenzhen was a sea of cranes in every direction. "They were building everywhere," says another Apple engineer who frequented the area. Foxconn's Longhua campus north of Shenzhen wasn't leading the charge in this respect. "It was a bunch of farmland," this person says. "I remember this one hill—a bulldozer on the top, scraping the hill and removing all the dirt, pushing it down so they can get rid of the hill and just level it. And there was another big hole in the ground where they had pushed a farmhouse into it and they were backfilling it with dirt." Foxconn had been in China for more than a decade at this point, but Longhua was "just four or five, maybe six buildings at the time," says the Apple engineer. "This was the very beginning."

The Pyramid

The fact that it was Cook, in Operations, who developed the relationship with Foxconn is important in understanding Apple's product development cycle. The shape is a pyramid, with Jony Ive's Industrial Design team at the top. ID would conceive how a product would look and feel, with an exactitude that drove fear into the rest of the organization. Their creation goes to Product Design, whose role is to figure out the mechanical engineering and make the product functional. Then it moves to manufacturing engineers—a small team back then, and later a distinct unit called Manufacturing Design, or MD—who work with component makers and final assembly partners to actually build the product. Finally, the Operations team comes in. They work with vendors that their colleagues have already selected, and then optimize everything to help the product scale. But crucially, Ops also has a prerogative to find other component makers, other final assembly partners, to build resiliency, cut prices, and to instill competition.

This model evolved over the course of more than a decade following the return of Jobs. When it worked well, it created discipline and pride. Each domain knew their role, their place in the hierarchy. Jony Ive's group was put into an elevated position often described as godlike. Unless what ID asked for defied the laws of physics, whatever ID said was the way it would be. Saying no to ID was possible, but only if you had reams of experimentation behind you and the data to make your point. A common saying was: "You'd have to drive the car off the cliff to prove the brakes don't work."

But it's not as though other divisions were simply taking marching orders. The respect went both ways. ID's job was pushing the limits while conceiving only of products that were feasible to build. How they would be built was the role of PD and MD, where the ideal employees loved the steepness of the learning curve on every product. "It's loads of hard work," says a veteran of Ive's ID studio. "But the engineer that you want to talk to is just like, 'I have no fucking idea how to make that, but I'll figure it out.'"

By empowering ID, Jobs had created a design-first organization that had zero tolerance for imperfection from the earliest stages of product creation. That approach cascaded down the pyramid, so the Ops team couldn't accept imperfection, either. Mike Bell, a vice president in the 2000s, recalls that for the Titanium PowerBook, an especially difficult-to-engineer laptop released in 2001, Product Design engineers "had to come up with methods of production nobody had ever done before." He characterizes this whole time period as "designing the impossible, then manufacturing the impossible." Engineers would joke that Jobs had asked for "anti-gravity" or wanted them to make the next product out of "unobtanium."

If something was too easy, ID would push the envelope even further. In the making of the Mac Mini desktop around 2004, one engineer recalls Ive asking if he could make the computer such and such a size. The engineer said he could. Ive narrowed the dimensions and asked if he could build that. The engineer said he could. So Ive minimized the dimensions again. This time the engineer said, "No, no, that would be really difficult." And Ive said, "Great, those are the dimensions."

The tricky thing about understanding the pyramid structure is that there were not firm barriers between the four divisions. It's emphatically not the case that ID conceived of a product, threw it over the fence for PD to fit in the electronics, who then threw it over the fence for others to build the machinery and deliver the product at scale. Something like that was happening, but it was *concurrent*. The teams were in constant communication, so operational breakthroughs would feed back into design excellence.

But the pyramid structure could cause problems due to the inherent tension between teams, or their differing incentive structures. Operations was rewarded for low price and high volume, whereas the other teams were focused on quality. In its drive to push scale, the Ops team risked working with second-rate vendors. So when Cook chose to partner with Foxconn, a less experienced company just beginning to prove itself in the late nineties, he was going out on a limb. The project was initially kept secret from the ID and PD Apple engineers working with LG, as Ops first needed to bring Foxconn up to snuff. One engineer from PD recalls being aghast at the decision. "Foxconn had a bad reputation as a second-source copycat who stole other manufacturers' designs and undercut them in price after production started to take over a chunk of production volume," this person says. Engineers in PD complained that Foxconn didn't understand Apple's long development design cycle, but Ops loved Foxconn's low pricing.

And this is where Foxconn made a big impression. Without any interaction with ID, Terry Gou's team deconstructed an LG-made iMac into its constituent parts, worked out how it was assembled, then created or found parts and built their own version, including the CRT monitor. "Every part in that product was reverse-engineered and reverse-sourced by Hon Hai, to replace LG," says an engineer on the iMac project. It was far from perfect, but it was good enough to demonstrate Foxconn's competence. "When you build a tool, the moving parts have to come together, and ID had crafted those to be beautiful," this engineer says. "Foxconn didn't know about that, so they made something where the outside shape was right, but none of it matched what ID wanted." At this point ID and PD were brought in to help, with teams sent to Longhua to give extensive training. "PD practically lived in Foxconn for a year," says an Operations executive.

An Apple engineer recalls telling Foxconn: "If you guys want this business, you have to earn the business. You need to do all the same hard work that LG did to ensure that the tools meet the part quality, interchangeability, and everything, such that the final cosmetic fit and finish is consistent across each and every product, no matter how you mix them or where you ship them across the world." It was a giant effort.

The Hub Model

Once Foxconn started to work on building the iMac at scale, Apple engineers were astonished at what became known as "China speed"—an ability to get things done at a rapid pace beyond the comprehension of Western visitors. It started with Terry Gou pledging that he would build the iMac tooling in just twenty-five days. "It was unprecedented. We're used to twelve weeks for building tooling," says Wayne Miller. "And sure enough, twenty-five days later, everything was there. The quality was amazing. They really impressed the hell out of us."

At the time, Dell was the industry leader in manufacturing and efficiency, particularly with custom build-to-order models. When a Dell customer purchased a computer with a bunch of idiosyncratic options, Dell would take a standard unit off its production line, then place it on a separate line for rework. Foxconn quickly proved itself as an innovative force by managing to work out how to handle both types of orders on the same line—a significant improvement in efficiency. This innovation was born out of necessity. Apple's design of the iMac in five colors was something no computer maker had ever done before. It would have been a mess to produce defined batches of, say, 100 Blueberry computers followed by 100 Strawberry variants. So Foxconn built an automated system. As orders for a particular color iMac came in, the information would be sent to a next-door molding factory—where Foxconn had huge machines to do the entire casing. Once completed, those shells were sent to the production line for final assembly, in the order they were needed.

Foxconn's system could handle other tweaks to the configuration as well, such as different processor speeds and memory upgrades, so regardless of what the customer ordered, Foxconn could put it together without delay. The production lines Foxconn built were just for Apple, and around each assembly line, it formed a hub of sites to build everything else that was needed: the molding factory, plus production lines for the logic boards, keyboards, mice, and language kits. "The whole supply chain was built around the assembly line," says an Apple employee who worked on setting it up. "Only when the order is triggered [would Foxconn] start to pull all the different components from the hub out and into the assembly line." And once an iMac was assembled, it went immediately into Apple's sales division. The system was designed so that Apple's inventory was virtually zero—as soon as Foxconn delivered a finished iMac to Apple, it was placed en route to a customer. If there was no order, there was no inventory. Of course, Foxconn had to buy the necessary components in advance, but that was its problem, not Apple's.

Foxconn Expansion

Once the Shenzhen line for iMacs was up and running, Foxconn established sites on two other continents. In Europe, Foxconn executive Jim Chang found a Soviet-era electronics site in Pardubice, a city of 100,000 people sixty miles east of Prague. The site had previously been run by a state-owned company called Tesla, whose specialty was radar systems and whose biggest client had been the government of Iran. The site had an eerie feel to it, like it had been hit by a neutron bomb. Forklifts stood motionless on the floor and cups of tea, their contents long gone cold, had been left on the tables. In May 2000, Foxconn was able to buy the plant for just 102 million CSK (€2.9 million), a fire-sale price because it was bringing in jobs. Foxconn also won from the government a ten-year tax holiday.

The company once again established its hub model for iMac production, bearing the up-front costs. "Apple didn't own any of the inventory parts that were there. Everything was borne by Foxconn," says a Czech-based Apple worker. "Apple had zero capital expense or investment." More than 300 people were hired to run multiple assembly lines, and Foxconn established a giant molding site for the plastic enclosures. Apple teams from Singapore were sent in to train the workers and ensure quality. Apparently smitten with the country, Terry Gou purchased a twelve-bedroom castle near the Czech factory in 2002, for a reported $30 million, and began spending his summers there. The fabulously rich CEO no longer had to worry about tin roofs.

In California, Apple found Foxconn an old Compaq service center in Fullerton, twenty-five miles southeast of Los Angeles. One of Terry Gou's two younger brothers, Tony, ran the site. It was less ambitious in scale than the other two factories, but it was an important location for build-to-order Power Macs, and Apple engineers could go there and work intimately with Foxconn to build prototypes. Later, in 2004, Apple laid off 235 workers in Sacramento, closed its plant there, and shifted all production to the new Foxconn site.

Strike Emergency

The experience in the Czech Republic was an important proving ground for Foxconn and its hub model, but what it really demonstrated was that producing hardware in China was cheaper, more efficient, and less subject to media scrutiny. In China, assembly got done at incredible speed and with few complaints. Workers did twelve-hour shifts and lived nearby in dorms. At the Czech site, workers put in fewer hours and were represented by a trade union; they protested conditions and spoke to the press. Plans to build dormitories met local criticism and were abandoned. Over the course of a decade, Foxconn expanded its work in the Czech Republic, continuing to build for Apple, adding another location, and taking on production for Hewlett-Packard, Sony, and Cisco. For Compaq alone, it was making 10,000 PCs a day in 2001. But Apple's more complex designs caused problems. One Foxconn employee from the late 2000s calls the whole experience "a disaster," even as the plant was given simpler products to assemble, including the Mac Mini.

At one point, according to an ex-worker named Andrea, workers making Apple products didn't receive an annual bonus as they were promised, so they threatened a "strike emergency" just before the ramp-up ahead of Christmas. "Afraid," the Foxconn managers deposited the bonuses within a week. The incident triggered an audit by Apple, which interviewed workers about their experience. Apple, Andrea said, advocated for better conditions, but "instead Foxconn closed the division within half a year and 330 people were dismissed." Around the same time, in August 2009, Foxconn shut its Fullerton site, too.

How Foxconn laid the Czech workers off is worth highlighting. Mass dismissals—defined as laying off more than thirty people—need to be reported to the Labor Office, but it was important for Foxconn to avoid scrutiny. "What Foxconn did is they dismissed twenty-nine workers every month," Andrea said. "Each month, regularly, they fired twenty-nine people." The threat of a single strike ended all large-scale Apple assembly in Europe. But that was later. In the summer of 2000,

Apple was still in a stage of experimentation. For the first time, Apple was overseeing major manufacturing operations in China. But it was one country of several. Apple products were also being assembled in America, Mexico, Wales, Ireland, the Czech Republic, Singapore, South Korea, and Taiwan. Within a decade, virtually all production would shift to China, with much of the final assembly done by a single partner, Foxconn. But the rapid consolidation was just beginning, and it didn't yet feel inevitable.

CHAPTER 12

A FAREWELL TO MACTORIES

Steve Jobs held on to a hope that Apple could play a bigger role in manufacturing. In 2000, more than eighteen months after hiring Tim Cook to run operations, Jobs distributed T-shirts to staff emblazoned with the word *Mactories.* Apple had already significantly downsized its assembly operations in Singapore, Ireland, and Sacramento, but Jobs contemplated expanding them.

Tim Cook gradually persuaded Jobs on the merits of outsourcing—that it was cheaper, faster, nimbler, and most critically of all, could meet Apple's quality expectations. But this wasn't some overnight decision; the global outsourcing strategy dated back to 1996, preceding Cook's arrival by nearly two years. The nail in the coffin was in late 2000, though Apple continued playing a role in assembly through 2003. Had the first three years of Steve Jobs's comeback been smooth and lucrative, it's possible he would have clamored more for Apple to retake direct control of its manufacturing. Instead, the late-1990s speculative mania in tech stocks abruptly reversed itself in March 2000, threatening the whole industry and causing the entire market to lose trillions of dollars in value.

Apple's comeback story was dramatically rewritten when, on a single day in late September 2000, the company's stock fell by more than half after it issued a profit warning. It was the second such warning in two years. In September 1999, the problem was too few computers: Apple didn't have enough G4 chips from Motorola to meet demand. Now the problem was too few customers, since nobody was buying the G4 Cube, a brilliantly designed but expensive desktop computer ill-suited for the mass market. "We've clearly hit a speed bump," Jobs told the public. The stock's one-day collapse wiped out nearly all the gains made since Gil Amelio's departure. A story called "Apple R.I.P." in *Forbes* demonstrated how tenuous Apple's future felt. "Even after all the successes of the last two years, Apple is still where it was during the Spindler era," *Forbes* wrote. "It is a niche player, with an anomalous operating system, trying to survive in a market dominated by giant corporations like Compaq, Dell and IBM." Gateway, another PC clone, even explored acquiring Apple. "The shit hit the fan, and our sales dropped off a cliff," according to Rubinstein. "Before Gateway had gone off the cliff—but we had—Gateway came in and tried to acquire us."

In that year's holiday quarter—the fiscal first quarter of 2001—Apple posted a loss of $195 million. For all of 2001, total sales dropped by a third to $5.4 billion, the lowest revenues for Apple since 1989. With a US computer market share of 4 percent and a global share of 3 percent, Apple, declared *Fortune,* risked becoming "as inconsequential as Liechtenstein." Whatever hopes Jobs may have had to bulk up Apple's manufacturing capabilities, the company had no cash for such endeavors. The Singapore and Sacramento factories were soon shuttered. (Cork was about to be closed, too, until Apple learned it would receive major tax advantages for maintaining the facility.)

Hollowing Out

The dotcom crisis reshaped tech manufacturing for years to come. In the prior decade, leading contract manufacturers had begun to purchase factories from major brands including IBM, Texas Instruments, Ericsson, Siemens, and Lucent. The deals were often seen as a win-win, with the big brands saving on costs. Negative media headlines could be avoided, since factories were not being shuttered so much as being put under new management. When Apple sold its Fountain, Colorado, factory in 1996, most of its 1,100 employees simply got a new uniform. But the result was a huge transfer in practical knowledge from the computer brands to the contract manufacturers. In the 1990s, when these deals were happening within America or within Europe, they caused few alarms. But as the internet went mainstream, the idea was promulgated that borders didn't matter. As companies competed on cost and scale, their search expanded internationally.

The 1990s had seen an incredible stock-market boom among US-headquartered contract manufacturers that had followed in the wake of SCI. There was massive consolidation as companies few people had ever heard of merged in a battle for scale. Solectron alone acquired some twenty companies in the decade, and in the five years leading up to 1999 its market value grew tenfold. Revenue at Flextronics, a rival, experienced average annual growth of 78 percent in the late nineties, aided by mergers.

Then the dotcom crisis triggered the tech industry's biggest-ever recession. It caused bankruptcies, forced people to question the sustainability of the tech sector, and compelled organizations to rethink the value of in-house manufacturing. Producers of components were left holding huge inventories amid a sudden dip in demand. SCI became an attractive target amid the downturn and was acquired for $6 billion by Sanmina, a smaller San Jose–based rival.

As more manufacturing work was off-loaded overseas, the transfer of knowledge intrinsic to outsourcing underwent an important shift. It was no longer just company to company, it was country to country. At the start of the 2000s, the world's four largest contract manufacturers were headquartered in the United States; the fifth was Canadian. At the time, it looked as though these companies' rapid growth would continue to soar. The share of the circuit board and consumer electronics manufacturing sectors penetrated by contract manufacturers had grown only to 13 percent, "leaving a great deal of room for continued growth," as one widely cited study forecast.

But these forecasts were shortsighted and had ignored the wider societal interests of the West. If electronics assembly was now primarily based on low-wage labor and scale, why stay in the United States or Europe? The logic of the low-cost strategy had a natural end: More work would shift to Asia. By 2010, four of the top five contract manufacturers were still based in North America, but the number one spot was taken by Foxconn—and it earned more revenue than the other four combined. Quite abruptly there was a jarring gap between the interests of corporate America and those of Washington. The contract manufacturers, enabled by the entire computer industry, had waged a battle that America—and Americans—were never going to win.

With no regulatory oversight of what was happening, a shift in where all this work was being performed was inevitable. The cofounder of Intel, Andy Grove, would later diagnose the problem as "a general undervaluing of manufacturing—the idea that as long as 'knowledge work' stays in the US, it doesn't matter what happens to factory jobs." But as Grove warned: "our pursuit of our individual businesses, which often involves transferring manufacturing and a great deal of engineering out of the country, has hindered our ability to bring innovations to scale at home. Without scaling, we don't just lose jobs—we lose our hold on new technologies. Losing the ability to scale will ultimately damage our capacity to innovate."

In the mainframe era of the 1970s, this shift wasn't really possible. It was never going to be economical to build garage-size computers in Asia and ship them over the high seas. But Moore's law—the doubling of chip speed every two years—meant that mainframes were displaced by desktop computers, which in turn were displaced by computers that could fit into a backpack. And by the 2000s, into a pocket. With more companies outsourcing their manufacturing and wanting the lowest cost possible, the stage was set for a country with a large and dense population, low wages, favorable export laws, a depressed currency, and low human rights to take advantage of the situation. At the corporate level, conditions were ripe for a company to release a handheld device that millions of people might desire.

And then, in the final months of 2001, two things happened. China joined the World Trade Organization, integrating the country with much of the world. And Steve Jobs stood onstage in a black turtleneck, held up a pure white product with a chrome back, and said, "This amazing little device holds one thousand songs. And it goes right in my pocket."

PART THREE

SIREN SONG—CONSOLIDATION

CHAPTER 13

1,000 SONGS—MAKING THE iPOD IN TAIWAN

Tony Blevins walked into the room holding an inch-thick stack of papers, which landed with a thud when he dropped them on the table. "Sign it," he said, "and the business is yours."

It was the spring of 2001, and Blevins, an Apple procurement specialist with a reputation for negotiating absurdly good deals across the supply chain, was speaking to several Taiwanese lawyers from Inventec, a contract manufacturer thoroughly unprepared for what was about to happen.

Blevins explained that he was in a hurry. He needed Inventec to sign the papers right away—there was no time for them to even read the contract. They balked in disbelief. Multiple lawyers would need to read the document; they'd need to go through it with a fine-tooth comb, making amendments where necessary. "They said, 'Well, we have to *read* it,'" says a person familiar with the episode. "And Tony says, 'If you don't sign it, I've got another contract manufacturer that we're going to give it to.'" It was a risky tactic. He was there to negotiate a deal to manufacture a new handheld product, something Apple had never made before. It was an MP3 player conceived of only a few weeks earlier, between February and April of 2001. He didn't tell them that, though; he only told them time was running out. Steve Jobs had approved the product on the condition that it would ship by the Christmas season.

Inventec, which had assembled the Jony Ive redesign of the Newton half a decade earlier, was Apple's first choice; if they didn't sign the document, Blevins would just walk out and choose a rival. Except, strictly speaking, there was no rival. But Inventec didn't know that. Blevins would avoid drawing red lines or bluffing—which carried the risk of being exposed—but he had an uncanny ability to shape perception by edging close to that line and making his adversaries feel the precariousness of their own situation. His tactics had the effect of redirecting his counterparts' attention. What Inventec might've focused on was that Apple had a weak hand. It had recently reported a $195 million loss for the holiday quarter, and now it wanted to make a product with which it had no experience.

Blevins had grown up in the rural South, in an area of the Blue Ridge Mountains in North Carolina that he once described as "possibly one of the least affluent places in the United States." Poor but intellectually gifted, he used his smarts as a kid to play elaborate pranks. One time he recorded the sound of the school bell; then he changed the classroom clock back by fifteen minutes. When the time was just right, he played the chime, startling his teacher. She took a look at the clock, "confirmed" class was over just as he'd devised, and let everyone leave. The whole class—in on the prank from the beginning—gleefully lay out in the field chatting and soaking up the sun, all courtesy of Tony. His father, a general contractor in the 8,000-person town of Jefferson, recognized his son's intelligence but was also concerned by his arrogance and tendency to be stubborn; if Tony was going to survive, his father said, he'd need skills. The lesson was reinforced when Tony spent a sweltering summer working in his home state's tobacco fields, "the hardest, most back-breaking work I've ever done," he'd later say. It wasn't an experience he ever wanted to replicate, and he became determined to get an education. The tobacco fields also taught him that not a single penny "should EVER be wasted or conceded in negotiation."

But Blevins wasn't just frugal; he was competitive about it. Getting the best deal was imprinted on his psyche, and he'd turned it into a game. His father had a side hustle running a used car lot, where Tony and his brother worked as teenagers. Each month they'd hold a competition: "Whoever could sell the shittiest car for the most profit would win," is how one colleague remembers him describing it.

The gifted prankster managed to get a full academic scholarship to North Carolina State University to study industrial engineering. Then he spent twelve years at IBM, working out of the United States, Tokyo, Seoul, and Scotland, developing a keen understanding of the electronics supply chain while using his smarts to negotiate for the best deals. Like Tim Cook and Jeff Williams, Blevins had been recognized as a future leader by IBM and was sent off to a higher education program. But whereas Cook and Williams each completed an MBA, Big Blue saw Blevins as more technical in nature and enrolled him at MIT. During his time at IBM, he studied negotiation like it was both an art and a science. Later, describing tricks of the trade, he likened negotiations to "verbal jujitsu" and reflected on his ability to convince adversaries that his ideas were their own. He understood the power of emotion and could feign anger, disbelief, or frustration at will. One time he even took his shoe off and threw it against the wall. Sometimes he'd just quietly peer at an opponent, comfortable in the silence as they grew awkward. "If you just stare someone directly in the eye, with a very concerned look, sometimes their imagination runs wild on what you're thinking, and they'll migrate to what might be the worst possible outcomes for themselves," he recounted in 2024.

Cook and Williams handpicked Blevins to join Apple in mid-2000. "Undoubtedly," a manager at IBM told him, this is "the stupidest decision you're going to make in your life." Apple was a small company, barely making money. "There were strong theories that the company was on the verge of bankruptcy," he'd later recount. What convinced him was a visit to Cupertino where he absorbed the "infectious passion" of the place. "Everyone there had this mindset, 'We're going to change the world,'" he'd later say. "Instead of wing tips and suits, what I saw was people in shorts, flip-flops, T-shirts, including the late Steve Jobs. People rode around on skateboards." The master negotiator was so taken that he accepted a lower salary and moved to California against the advice of his father.

His first role was director of corporate procurement, responsible for buying all the things Apple needed to run the day-to-day business, including toilet paper. In Blevins's own words, he bought "everything from our mainframe computers we needed, to our lab equipment, to the avocados that we needed to stock the cafeteria. And as it turns out, Californians eat a lot of avocado toast." The team he joined was in shambles. Blevins compared them to *F Troop,* referencing a 1960s sitcom about a chronically inept group of soldiers. He'd sometimes find himself burying his face in his hands, asking what he'd gotten himself into. Over the next eighteen months, not one of the thirty-three-member team would stay at Apple. In one instance, Blevins found someone on the payroll who hadn't been to the office in two years but was still collecting a check. His predecessor simply hadn't noticed.

Colleagues called Tony "the Blevinator" for being ruthless and stopping at nothing to get a good deal. He deployed tactics so detailed, aggressive, and consequential that a supplier ostensibly winning an Apple order might later regret it given the scale of investment required, the demands Apple would place on them, and the fact that the company could turn on a dime to another supplier if needed. "Apple has a trail of dead bodies miles long," says a high-ranking executive at a contract manufacturer that worked with the company for decades. "When business is great, everybody wins. And when it's not, they go under." Blevins had a particular ability to read other people. One says it was "a mind-blowing thrill" just to watch him negotiate. "You could see where he was going, and you knew that he was going to get what he wanted, because he was so much smarter than the person he was talking to," the colleague says. "He just steered the conversation to the ultimate ending of what he wanted.

It was absolutely brilliant." Another recounts how, the night before a negotiation, Blevins talked through his reasoning and foretold where his opponent would end up. The following day, after hours of psychological warfare and tit for tat over the smallest details, the opponent proposed the very thing that Blevins had predicted. Then Blevins acted like it wasn't necessarily in Apple's best interests to agree and signed the deal. The Apple team walked out, awed by what had transpired as Blevins chuckled about it.

Bending suppliers to his will wasn't a reflection of business logic, but some combination of charm, fearlessness, and cunning. He served as model for the poker maxim "You don't play the hand, you play the player," a third former colleague says. "Tony was good at sizing up a situation." Blevins speaks with a southern accent that some colleagues can't help but imitate when they recount Blevinator stories. His voice had a bit of southern charm to it, inviting and gracious, masking how unsparing he could be. "An iron fist in a velvet glove," says a former Apple VP. His quick mind is reflected in his unnervingly fast speech. One time in court a judge told him: "You are very fast in your answers, and if we don't give the answers so the jury can hear and comprehend them, we're all just wasting our time. So if you think you've slowed down, multiply it by ten and try and do it that way, okay?"

Colleagues with legal training would find themselves uncomfortable in Blevins-led negotiations, shifting in their seats as he arranged a deal. "As a lawyer, you have certain ethical obligations when you're representing a client," one says. "You're not allowed to lie, because it's a violation. But there are no ethical rules of conduct for businesspeople." Another compared Blevins to a sociopath—someone who saw the negotiation as a prize to be won, the real-world consequences be damned. Blevins's admirers don't dispute that he was a shark, but they say Apple needed sharks if it was going to survive. Certainly there were other companies that didn't deploy these tactics back then, but most don't exist anymore, recounts a former Apple executive. "I always tell people: I worked with two kinds of suppliers when I was at Apple," this person says. "I worked with complete asshole suppliers, and I worked with suppliers who today are out of business. That's the reality."

In Blevins's own words, the consumer electronics supply chain "is more ruthless and cutthroat than most Americans can imagine." He'd later recoil a bit when stories of his tactics were relayed back to him. He'd protest and say that he liked to find a balanced deal, good for everyone. But just minutes later he'd say that his "worst nightmare" would be discovering a counterpart celebrating in a fancy club somewhere, having gotten something past him. "That would just keep me awake at night," he said.

This is the spirit Blevins brought to the meeting with the unsuspecting Taiwanese lawyers. The Blevinator would develop his reputation over the course of a twenty-two-year career at Apple. But the earliest instance of his securing a major deal on fantastic terms was in the spring of 2001, when Inventec signed a deal to make an MP3 player without having read the contract.

Digital Hub

Apple got into the MP3 player market for a simple reason: All other music players sucked. Portable CD players had been all the rage in the 1990s, but by 2000 they felt quaint. Consumers were building up massive libraries of digital music files on their computers, often illegally through services like Napster. In January 2001, Apple launched iTunes for the Mac, a sleek interface for managing those libraries. But there was no good way to take your music with you.

Jobs started speaking about a "digital hub," positioning the Mac as the centerpiece for digital music, photos, and videos. Apple had already launched iMovie, a simplified editing suite for making family films as digital camcorders became affordable. It didn't feel the need to make its own camcorders, because those on the market were reasonably good. But

MP3 players were undesirable—they were slow and bulky, with small screens and awful navigation. Apple executives were already thinking about taking matters into their own hands when, just a month after the launch of iTunes, hardware chief Jon Rubinstein—aka Ruby—and procurement head Jeff Williams were in Japan and stopped by Toshiba. The Japanese supplier showed them a new hard drive, just 1.8 inches in diameter, with a massive 5 gigabytes of capacity. Toshiba didn't really know what to do with it, but to Ruby, the implications were "obvious" immediately: this thing could hold a thousand MP3s! It was *the* enabling technology they needed. "Jeff," Ruby quietly said, "we need to get all of these." Williams negotiated an exclusive supply agreement as Ruby made sure the $10 million check they drew up wouldn't bounce.

The project came together with remarkable speed. Ruby and Williams searched for other components including cellphone displays and lithium-ion batteries. Ruby has said "the form factor was self-evident," describing how the electronics needed were the size of a pack of cards. Apple was still a small ship, and employees were tied up on other projects. So Ruby looked outside for someone to lead the project and determine if it was really feasible. That led him to Tony Fadell, a brash, quick-minded entrepreneur from Detroit with an engineering mind and a knack for punchy storytelling. He'd founded three companies by the time he graduated from the University of Michigan, and then developed an expertise working on mobile devices for General Magic, a pioneering Apple spinout that never made it commercially but garnered respect in Silicon Valley. Fadell, who often dyed his hair in the bleached style of the 1990s, could be consumed by work, as if it anchored him from darker pursuits. Once asked where he'd be if computers weren't invented, he responded: "In jail." A few weeks from his thirty-second birthday, Fadell was out on a ski slope in Colorado when he got the call. He agreed to join as a consultant and in just a few weeks had mocked up several versions of the product.

Rubinstein and Fadell would later dispute who the key figure was behind the hit MP3 player, but the truth is that its brilliance had multiple authors, reflecting how each domain in the pyramid structure (ID, PD, MD, and Ops) worked on their specialty simultaneously. Ruby had found Toshiba's disk drive and realized its potential. Phil Schiller, of marketing, introduced the idea of the scroll wheel—probably the feature most loved by consumers, as it reacted to the velocity of each turn and enabled them to race through hundreds of songs in a matter of seconds. Fadell was the overall architect. He presented to Jobs a prototype made from foam core and stuffed with old fishing weights to give it some heft. Jony Ive's team made it unapologetically white, with a polished, chrome-like stainless steel back, a remarkably sharp turn from the childlike colors of the iMac. It was an unusually high-end material for a mass-market product, giving it a feel unlike any other handheld device. It was also durable and could dissipate heat more effectively than plastic.

Other teams contributed, too. At the Consumer Electronics Show someone chanced upon PortalPlayer, a nascent semiconductor company capable of making chips combining audio processing and power management. And the software group created an interface that, responding to a demand from Jobs, allowed the user to navigate from one song or function to another in just three clicks. Songs would be transferred from the Mac using FireWire, a blazingly fast standard developed by Apple before Jobs had returned.

By April 2001, all the pieces for a hit product were there. Fadell, after some arm-twisting, agreed to join Apple full time, beginning a nine-year run in which he'd climb the ladder from contractor to senior vice president, eventually gaining so much power that a trio of senior executives turned on him and he quit. Fadell officially began the same week that Tony Blevins was brought onto the project. It was a fateful move for Blevins, too: The buyer of toilet paper and avocados was soon heading procurement for the fastest-growing division at the company. Eventually 1,300 people would report to him. Almost immediately, the two Tonys hopped on a flight together. They were off to Taiwan, Japan, and South Korea—a three-week trip to locate the right suppliers and do a rush job for the late October unveiling.

Troubadour

The MP3 player would remain nameless for months, until four people in branding tossed ideas back and forth with Jobs. Vinnie Chieco, a creative director, recalls how the team would write down every permutation and then sort them into three piles: the worst, the ones that suck, and the not horrible. He'd come up with one: Troubadour, named after French poets who went from town to town playing music. This thing, too, was mobile, could travel and play music. The metaphor worked. The name didn't.

Jobs had his own preferred moniker, which Chieco remembers but won't share. Like MacMan—what Steve wanted to call the iMac—his idea wasn't very good, and Chieco is hesitant to share something now that Jobs can't defend. The other three people in the room told Jobs they loved his name for the device, perhaps trying to avoid his infamous wrath. But when Jobs asked Chieco for his opinion, the creative director said, "Well, I understand your name is novel, but . . . " Feeling as if he were putting his head in a guillotine, Chieco told Jobs the reasons he didn't like it. Meanwhile, he kept thinking in metaphors. He was struck by the all-white design, which looked space-like. Riffing on Jobs's idea that a Mac computer was the "hub for your digital life," he considered how in the future, the ultimate hub would be the mother ship. The only way to escape would be in a pod that flies away for temporary adventures, returning to replenish and recharge. He got the idea from *2001: A Space Odyssey,* and hey—now it was 2001! It felt serendipitous, like when the Macintosh emerged in the Orwellian year, 1984. He proposed Pod. Jobs didn't hate it, and over a few meetings it grew on him until it became the obvious name. It just needed one tweak, one letter, and then it was perfect: iPod.

CHAPTER 14

FLAT-OUT COOL!—MAKING THE iMAC G4 ACROSS ASIA

Amid the neon lights and pulsating pop music of the Taiwanese karaoke bar was another group of exhausted and frustrated Apple engineers working on the new, all-white and flat-screen iMac, a product that would help cement Apple as a world-class design leader. It was early 2001; they were behind schedule, and things weren't getting better. They'd spent the last few days visiting suppliers to improve product tooling, part quality, and the processing and finish of components. But the suppliers were painfully incompetent. "We were like, 'There's no way this is gonna happen to the quality we want, the precision we want, the time frame we want,'" recounts Michael Hillman, the senior manager in Product Design overseeing the project. The club they were in wasn't exactly the best place to think. It was a labyrinth of private singing rooms, each glowing with colorful strobe lights from large screens that flashed the lyrics to pop tunes sung by inebriated locals.

This KTV bar was the Taiwanese equivalent of an American golf course—a casual place to relax and discuss business. The dimly lit air was thick with smoke, and as the Apple engineers observed the supplier partners they'd spent the day with, they noticed that some of the men, whose sharp suits distinguished them from the rest, exhibited an understated menace. "The telltale signs were in the way they dressed, the way they acted, the way they spoke," says Hillman. It was the first tip-off of something that would become increasingly clear in the weeks ahead: A portion of the sub-suppliers working with Apple were tied up with the Taiwanese mafia. This was surely something previous teams had grasped, but word hadn't gotten back to Cupertino. Maybe people were just turning a blind eye to it. Or maybe the gangsters were just easier to spot for Hillman, who was new to Apple but old to Asia. He'd grown up in Japan and become wise to spotting yakuza operating openly.

Organized crime was a major problem in Taiwan, with underworld gangs dating back to Japanese occupation in the early twentieth century. By the early 1980s they'd penetrated the legitimate business sector. When the government launched a series of harsh crackdowns, some gangsters responded by running for office and winning elections. By the early 2000s, business, politics, and organized crime were so intertwined that the lines separating legitimacy from illegitimacy were blurry at best. Apple had been paying its contract manufacturer directly, which in turn was supposed to pay these sub-suppliers—vendors a tier or two down in the supply chain. Apple engineers had been, as one of them put it, "beating up on" vendors the past few days, pressuring them to work harder, work smarter, and now they were realizing these vendors hadn't even been compensated. "Apple writes a check, the supplier is supposed to have the vendor make the change, and you go to the vendor as an engineer to see the effects," Hillman says. "And you find out they haven't even been paid a dime because it all went to the mafia."

For Apple, still in the earliest years of transitioning from manufacturing computers itself to relying on production networks abroad, the trouble reinforced the need to take greater control of these networks, down multiple tiers. At the time, Apple had only dozens of people involved in its Asia operations, but the team would expand wildly over the next decade, exerting such a degree of control that the term *outsourcing* would become misleading if not wholly incorrect.

The Apple Swarm Effect

Michael Hillman brought with him a degree in bioengineering and twelve years' experience in the medical device industry, where standards are much higher than in consumer electronics. "If I made a mistake in the engineering, someone could die and I could go to jail," Hillman says of his prior role. As when the first iMac underwent a "hard reset," Hillman introduced another level of rigor to the team "because the functionality we were trying to achieve was way beyond anything Apple had done to date."

Advancements in LCD technology had allowed Jony Ive and the ID studio to reconceive from the ground up what a twenty-first-century computer should look like. The form factor of the original iMac was that of a television, but for the iMac G4—Apple's next major desktop computer—the advent of flat-panel technology allowed the ID studio to think more boldly. Ive drew inspiration from the sunflowers planted by Laurene Powell Jobs, coming up with a variety of designs in which a flat monitor floated toward the user like the face of a flower, held by a stem stuffed with wires connecting to a mound housing the computer's key components and ports. Hillman had been directed to work with Quanta, the Taiwanese assembler of Apple laptops. Quanta had never done an Apple desktop before, but Cupertino was keen to leverage its expertise in the miniature architecture of laptop designs and relocate them into a dazzling all-in-one form factor.

It was a mess from day one. Hillman traveled to Taipei to study the supply chain and quickly concluded that Taiwan alone wouldn't be capable of pulling off the project. Instead, Apple would need to rely on vendors in Singapore, China, Japan, Thailand, and Malaysia. The team Hillman led was also too small for the task. He'd inherited only fifteen engineers who'd worked on the previous iMac, and the experts who would have been most helpful—those who'd just worked with Quanta on Titanium PowerBooks—had quit. Apple went through nineteen prototypes before this final design was formalized, and every few weeks the small team would present updates to Steve Jobs, letting him interact with the latest version to get his feedback. The team building the cables meant to be stuffed through the computer's neck consistently had trouble keeping up with these builds, underscoring the complexity of fragmented assembly operations sprawled across multiple countries. They'd start with 500 extruded cables—wires coated with protective sheathing and insulation—that were cut to length in China, then hand-carry them in a suitcase to a factory in Malaysia. There, extension metal parts would be assembled around the cables, then hand-carried in multiple suitcases back to China, where the cables would be reassembled. From there, they'd be flown to Taiwan for final assembly. Only then could a prototype be sent to California for Jobs's feedback. "I cannot begin to explain how illogical the preproduction extension supply chain was," says an engineer involved in the process. In a few instances, the prototypes were confiscated at the China border. "Claiming to be Apple was useless when appealing to the Chinese government," this person says. Mainland partners with more political clout could, however, usually retrieve them within three days.

No computer supplier had any experience building a computer meant to look like a sunflower. So Apple's PD engineers leveraged specialists from adjacent sectors and taught them new skills. Taiwan's esteemed bicycle manufacturing industry helped with the chrome neck, while metal stamping was done in Japan by a supplier making camera bodies. Apple's engineers found precision machining capabilities at hard-drive makers in Thailand and even visited a turbine blade fabrication facility run by Singapore Airlines. Some of these trials worked; others failed. "The start of Apple applying manufacturing processes from other industries was filled with mistakes and learning curves," says one PD engineer. Even when the skill sets were found, Taiwan was short of labor, so vendors recruited staff from the Philippines.

Some of the extension metal components were assembled in a VCR factory on a palm oil plantation in Malaysia. It was a hot and humid factory, with bees buzzing around. Inside, young women would form three to four assembly lines, with around twenty people on each, and with their small hands they would thread all the wires through the four metal parts of the gooseneck. It took eight to ten minutes per neck, a terribly inefficient process. The VCR factory was near a small, traditional Muslim community, and the locals were wary of these tall engineers from California, with their long hair and shorts. At the end of each shift, men from the town would park their vehicles outside and shine their high beams at the factory. It was an unnerving practice, meant to ensure the factory girls came home rather than stay out late romping around with the Californians.

The design was so complex that it called for all hands on deck, with senior executives moving down a peg or two in the usual hierarchy to get things done. For the chrome neck, Jon Rubinstein recalls telling procurement head Jeff Williams not to come back to California until it had been proven that the computer could be built. Williams, he says, "basically tied up almost every machine shop on the entire island." Sabih Khan, an operations executive who joined Apple in 1995 and would later oversee the company's entire global supply chain, basically lived at the Grand Hyatt until the iMac G4 was completed. He seemed to know everyone, greeting the hotel staff to the factory workers the way a politician might. Colleagues teased him: "Are you running for the mayor of Taipei?"

Apple kept close tabs on its suppliers, moving from one facility to another to ensure they could meet the caliber and scale it needed. One operations manager refers to "the Apple swarm effect" to describe how they'd descend on factories to teach the suppliers. "It was literally Engineering 101, showing them how to do everything," says another person involved.

"Really Fucking Stupid"

For one of the late prototypes, Hillman presented what the manufacturing and assembly would look like to a roomful of VIPs, including Jony Ive and iMac lead Chris Stringer from ID, hardware chief Jon Rubinstein, PD vice president Dan Riccio, and Steve Jobs. At the time, around

March 2001, the base of the computer was shaped more like a Hershey's Kiss, while the connecting neck was a series of aluminum ball and socket joints resembling vertebrae. Running through them was a tension tool that provided the floating sensation for the monitor. There were little tactile switches on the display, and at the press of a button, it would go limp so the user could reposition it. Once the button was released, the display would stiffen within milliseconds. It was a bit of magic, and both Ive and Jobs were delighted with it.

The prototype was impressive, but the mechanisms behind it all were ridiculous. It required aircraft cables and up to 600 watts of power, all driven by an external power brick that marred the all-in-one nature of the product. Servicing the machine would've been a nightmare, requiring a technical expert to access the computer by taking the vertebrae apart. "It wasn't my design, and it's not what I wanted our team to do," Hillman says.

Rubinstein says it was about to be approved for production. But when Hillman presented the process matter-of-factly, describing how the vertebrae would first attach to the base, and then be moved to the next line for the internal computer components to be stuffed inside, the challenges of the complicated design became clear. The process was in opposition to standard procedures, because usually you'd want to build each component and then, as a last step, bring them all together in the enclosure. But Hillman, responding to the demands of ID, was instead beginning with the enclosure, introducing the possibility of scratches and dings that could result in expensive manual rework. Jobs was listening and watching intently. He leaned over the table, pointed at parts, and picked a few up as he digested the process. Then he stood up abruptly and was right in Hillman's face. "Are you telling me *that's* the assembly method?" Jobs asked. As Hillman started to answer, Jobs interjected: "That's so fucking stupid!"

Hillman describes being sworn at by the Apple CEO like Neo's being shot at in *The Matrix*. "I felt like it was ten seconds before I responded to him," he says. Jobs spoke with such ferocity that the *st* in *stupid* propelled spit onto Hillman's glasses. With Jobs so close to his face, Hillman could no longer see his boss or the ID guys and Rubinstein, so he relied on instinct. "I actually responded in a second: 'I agree with you. It is really fucking stupid.'"

He was indicting Jony Ive and the designers—a big no-no, in most every other circumstance—but Jobs, the only power above ID, had given him license. Jobs turned away, looked back toward the assembly process, and became quiet and contemplative. Hillman looked at Ive and Riccio, who offered him sympathetic, accepting glances. Then and there the design was scrapped, Rubinstein says. ID went back to the drawing board, eventually finding a way to get a similar experience but without the need for the complex vertebrae components or a motor.

The final design that emerged was wild, like seeing a Ferrari in a land of station wagons. It was the first computer that looked anthropomorphic, its flat screen of a face elegantly suspended in the air by a chrome neck comprised of metal used in aerospace. "They had to be forged, machined, heat treated, polished, and chrome plated, because their walls are so skinny to fit all the cables in, to flex and move, and support the bearings," says a senior engineer on the project.

The extension cables within the neck included multiple bundles of wires for the LCD screen, the power, the analogue microphone, and the mechanical tension. There were more than forty wires in total, and they had to be funneled manually through a narrowly designed envelope, in a delicate manner so as not to rip them. All told, the bill of materials for the neck alone approached $120 per unit—a comically high figure, nearly 10 percent of the retail price for the entire computer. The neck allowed the user to adjust, tilt, and swivel the screen with a weightless ease. The effect was so smooth it was like the computer was ready to breakdance.

Good, Better, Best

About six months after Hillman's awkward presentation to Jobs, he woke up in Asia to an email from Dan Riccio saying to call him back in the

United States. Riccio, who has a reputation for belittling subordinates, started out diplomatically, so as to not freak Hillman out. He explained that Jobs *loved* the new design and had approved it for production. "It's really exciting, but it's gonna be an enormous challenge," Riccio said. Then he dropped the hammer. For the past few years, Apple had been selling computers in a "good, better, best" lineup, offering customers three ranges of specs and prices. Until this moment, Hillman had been told that the sunflower-inspired, flat-panel iMac G4 was only supposed to be the "best" model; "good" and "better" were revamped CRTs akin to the candy-colored iMac—and, crucially, someone else's problem. But now Riccio was saying the CRT project was dead.

The news was equal parts gratifying and terrifying. It validated all of Hillman's efforts over the prior eighteen months, but it would also be a source of sleepless nights and anxiety for his team. It's not that Riccio's announcement implied that Hillman had to come up with wholly new designs, one more each for the "good" and "better" models; but his team would have to go to every supplier they'd been working with, in multiple countries, and get them to produce way more of whatever they'd been planning. Then they'd have to spec these units into three models with varying computer processors, memory, and other features.

Instead of making just 1,500 units a day, Hillman's vendors needed to produce nearly ten times as many, beginning in just three months. Ramping up manufacturing of the chrome neck alone was an enormous task, since the grade of steel Apple demanded was confined to specialty areas like making rockets and high-vacuum semiconductor processing. "We basically cornered the world market on precipitously hardened 17-4 stainless steel," Hillman says.

When Steve Jobs announced the iMac G4 on January 7, 2002, he hailed "the official death of the CRT." The design was a major hit, making the cover of *Time* magazine the same day—"FLAT-OUT COOL!" the headline blared. But the decision to go all in on the flat panel had created a problem: "Good" started at $1,299—45 percent more expensive than the base model it was replacing. And it wouldn't be available for two months as Apple struggled to ramp. The "best" models that shipped first would cost $1,799, way out of reach for the masses they were intended for.* After a Herculean effort to bring the G4 to production, demand was underwhelming. Component shortages forced Apple to bump up prices on all three models by $100. Jobs had spoken of the computer like it was going to propel Apple into the big leagues, saying it had "a beauty and a grace that will last the next decade." Instead, just six months later Jobs had to announce that Apple would "miss our revenue projections by around 10 percent." The radical design was replaced after just thirty-two months.

The experience building the iMac G4 had big consequences, not only for Apple but also for China. With critical assembly and supply chain teams scattered across six countries, manufacturing had been inefficient, time-consuming, and costly. Apple wasn't about to tone down its design choices or reduce complexity to ease the manufacturing challenge; instead, it sought to consolidate component and subassembly closer to final assembly—and there was only one place to go. Even before the computer went on sale, Apple was urging partners from Singapore to Japan to set up operations in China, taking advantage of what seemed to be limitless pools of cheap labor in fast-forming bonded zones created for exports—areas within China featuring special trade terms and tax exemptions. Quanta, the assembler of the iMac G4, established Quanta Shanghai Manufacturing City, or QSMC, in 2001, with suppliers forming around it to establish a new industrial cluster. "It's not just that final assembly, test, and pack out needed to move into China, but the innovations in materials, fabrication, and inspection for Apple's designs needed to be nearby as well," Hillman says. These new local production sites

* In April 2002, Apple proposed a solution: a new all-in-one CRT with a G4 processor: the eMac. The CRT wasn't dead after all. The all-white, non-translucent computer started at $999 and had a seventeen-inch monitor, up from fifteen inches on the previous CRT. Apple marketed it as "a new desktop line designed specifically for education," but this was a half-truth. Really the eMac was just the "good" and "better" iMac that had been abandoned in Jobs's earlier excitement for the flat-panel design.

allowed Apple executives to travel from, say, an injection molding, sheet metal stamping, or machining facility to an assembly site in a matter of hours, even minutes, instead of summoning a person over from another country. Hillman describes the talent on the mainland as "woefully inexperienced," especially for the sophisticated designs Apple demanded. But that could change by investing in the people.

CHAPTER 15

"YOU'RE GOING TO GIVE US YOUR 'CHINA COST' FOR THIS"

David Tupman was in Scotland traveling to a wedding reception from the ceremony when an old friend said he'd just gotten a job at Apple. The chance encounter was in the summer of 2001, and it would alter the trajectory of his entire career. Both men had worked at Psion, a UK-based computing company that in the late 1990s made subnotebook PDAs, messaging devices with a full keyboard and packaged in a clever clamshell. Tupman was enamored with Apple designs and mentioned he'd love to work there. Well, good news: Apple was hiring engineers. Tupman sent over his CV, detailing his niche experience in Asia working with silicon and hardware to make handheld electronics. Within days he received a phone call from Tony Fadell.

Tupman, who gives off a sense of warmth in his soft-spoken English-accented speech, was living in London at the time. He agreed to fly over the Pacific for an interview in mid-September. A day before his flight, Al-Qaeda hijacked passenger jets and flew them into the World Trade Center. In the chaos that followed, international flights were delayed for a week. And when they resumed, Tupman waited another week, not wanting to take up a seat that might otherwise go to an American needing to get home. By the time he showed up in Cupertino, Apple's already rushed schedule was even more urgent, and Fadell had no time for a casual interview. Tupman was grilled by thirty people over two days, answering every conceivable question about electrical engineering without his even getting to ask what the job was. A week later his phone rang again. "So," Fadell said, "you want to get on this roller coaster?" Only upon accepting did Tupman learn he was the first electrical engineer hired for the iPod.

Tupman had another wedding to attend in two days and would need several weeks to get an H1B visa to work in the United States. No wedding and no time, Fadell explained. They didn't have a production-build prototype yet, but Steve Jobs would be unveiling it in just four weeks. Fadell had already taken the liberty of getting Tupman hired on a temporary basis with Inventec, the iPod's contract manufacturer, so he could begin work straightaway and work out his US visa issues—and his move to California—later. *Crikey,* Tupman thought. "Oh, and one more thing," said Fadell: "I bought you a ticket for tomorrow morning. It leaves at eleven a.m. You're flying to Taipei, so pack for two months and get going."

Tupman had no honeymoon period, no welcome, no introduction to Apple systems. But Fadell sent him schematics for the circuit board before he departed from Heathrow. During the twelve-hour flight, he made his mark spotting problems with the circuit diagrams—how the chips connect together and the resistors pass through the printed circuit layout. He knew this flight from his five years at Psion, which had also partnered with Inventec. The engineers did a double take when he walked in. They all knew him, and together, they got to work immediately on the problems he'd spotted. Then he got to hold a prototype iPod for the first time and immediately knew he'd made the right choice to join Apple. "It was like, 'This is so cool!'" he says.

Tony Fadell built a team of young engineers for the iPod; their reputations would rocket within the company over the next decade, reflecting the huge success of the music player. Among them were Tang Tan, Steve Zadesky, Andy Hodge, and DJ Novotney in Product Design;

James Wang was the key guy in Operations. Novotney, for one, began flying to Asia so often that even though he spent his weekends in the United States, he'd joined a basketball team in Taiwan and was reliably in town for Monday-night games.

This team worked on multiple hardware bugs that threatened to ruin the iPod launch. One they took to calling "Zombie Mode." About one in ten iPods would randomly shut down, and when plugged back in, would fail to recharge. Most would reset once the battery died, but that would usually take weeks. Apple set up a line with hundreds of units, then had operators from Inventec play a tedious game of iPod whack-a-mole, touching the scroll wheel every few seconds to keep the back-lit LCD light on and drain the battery. Then they could run tests to figure out which would wake up and which wouldn't, then circle back and solve the problem. When all the kinks were worked out, the first-ever consumer-ready iPod came off the line. The engineers loaded it with random music, used the scroll wheel to select "Artists," and played the first song in the alphabetical list. The catchy melodies of ABBA were heard through the white earbuds.

Teetering Edge

Steve Jobs held a comparatively low-key event for the launch. The live audience didn't seem to get it, and Apple got blasted for the $499 price point. More effective was a seven-minute marketing video set to pop music and featuring artists Seal, Moby, and Smash Mouth lusting after the device. "I might have to steal your prototype," says Moby. "I don't know who your product's designers are, but boy, you're not paying them enough."

In the holiday quarter Apple shipped 125,000 devices, a solid start. But a few months into 2002, sales petered out to just 20,000 a month. Cupertino worried the device was a bit of a dud. "The business was on the teetering edge," says an engineer who worked on several generations of the iPod. "We had a few months' sales where it was like, 'Oh my god, should we even continue this business?' And 'Will this survive?'"

Fadell, exhausted and frustrated, even tried to quit. Jobs persuaded him to stay, elevating his position to overseeing both hardware and software for the iPod. But there were conversations at a high level that if sales didn't improve, the device wouldn't be renewed. "We just kept our heads down and kept working on making the product better, better, better," an iPod engineer says. "We were pretty worried about [the low sales] from an overall business standpoint." The second-generation iPod came out in August 2002, just nine months after the original. But that unit didn't sell in impressive numbers either. The underwhelming figures contributed to that year's profit warning, its third in just four years.

Everyone at Apple agreed the iPod was awesome, yet it had done little to alter the company's finances. From March 2001 to March 2003, Apple revenues barely fluctuated, coming in around $1.4 billion every three months for nine quarters in a row. A major problem was that the iPod required a Mac to function. Giving the Mac features that weren't available on a PC, like iMovie and iTunes, was partly what had inspired the idea for the MP3 player. Jobs had hoped the iPod would generate more Mac sales, but few consumers were willing to splurge on a new computer just so they could buy a $500 music player. With Mac market share languishing around 5 percent, all that Apple's strategy was accomplishing was closing itself off to 95 percent of potential iPod customers. Ironically, this trivial share proved to be a major boon when Steve Jobs set out to launch the iTunes Store, where users could buy songs for $0.99. Jobs convinced all the major record labels to give it a try, explaining how the stakes were low because Apple was such a niche. It launched in April 2003 to rave reviews, but usage remained limited and frustrated Cupertino. Every high-ranking executive aligned against Jobs to convince him to let Apple write iTunes software for Windows—an idea he loathed. He backed down only after multiple experts demonstrated the revenue potential of expanding the iPod and iTunes markets. "Screw it," he told colleagues. "I'm sick of listening to you assholes. Go do whatever the hell you want."

When the iTunes Store for Windows emerged in late 2003, the third-generation iPod became a sensational hit. Record executives found they didn't have any leverage to oppose the expansion. Joe O'Sullivan, in Operations, calls the iTunes-for-PC move "the single biggest strategic decision that has enabled the company to be what it is today." Years later, Steve Jobs would offend by Bill Gates by comparing using iTunes on Windows to drinking ice water in hell. The results were spectacular. In the December 2003 quarter, iPod sales soared by 235 percent to 733,000, pushing total revenues up 36 percent to $2 billion. It was a four-year high, and the end of a rut. Apple revenues would never be that low again. Inventec, however, was struggling with the sudden burst in demand.

A Pivotal Shift

The third floor of Inventec's Taiwanese factory felt perfectly adequate when Apple was shipping iPods in the tens of thousands per month. When orders jumped to hundreds of thousands, it felt comically inadequate. "All of a sudden there were parts not only in the loading dock but up the stairwells in every cavern of that factory," recalls a product designer. "There were boxes of parts that just literally took over the entire factory building. It was overflowing into the stairwells and emergency exits. There were parts *everywhere*. It went from nothing to 'Oh my god, there's not enough space to build these things.'"

Inventec added production lines, then added more, but it faced difficulty hiring enough people and was running out of room. Apple, meanwhile, expected the price per unit to drop as more components were purchased in bulk. The problem had an obvious solution: Inventec proposed adding a second factory, in mainland China. "Inventec's like, 'We're going to China—China's offering all these incentives; we can build there,'" says Fadell. He remembers Inventec offering to move half the team from Taiwan to start building iPods immediately. "And we were like, 'Oh, well, how else are we gonna get the cost down?'"

Inventec had established its first Shanghai-based factory in 1992, and in the early 2000s the entire electronics supply chain was consolidating into China to take advantage of the lower costs and higher scale. China's entry into the World Trade Organization in December 2001 had a limited impact on direct US-China commerce, since preexisting tariff reductions already encouraged trade. But WTO membership spurred multinational investment and encouraged the trade of intermediate goods—like the hundreds of parts that go in an iPod—among dozens of countries. "All of a sudden, parts could start getting made in China," says a PD engineer on the product. In addition, there were no more labor shortages, and the people worked long and hard. More operations were slated for the mainland. Yet Inventec's initial expansion into China didn't impress quality-mad Apple. "It was rough," Fadell recalls. "They didn't even have internet connections to the factory yet. So we had to start from scratch there."

As much as Inventec wanted to drive the shift, a lot of production stayed in Taiwan for months, upsetting Apple and creating tension. Apple put the burdens of the delay on Inventec, squeezing it on margins. "We were pushing them, like, 'Look, you were supposed to move to China, and you haven't done it, so you're going to give us your "China cost" for this," says a person on the project. "It's not our fault you haven't moved yet.'"

Then someone at Inventec—it's unclear whether this was a rogue decision or an official directive—made a very bad move. The contract manufacturer was under financial pressure, likely owing to ruthless terms negotiated by Blevins and exacerbated by Apple pushing for lower prices with scale. Apple had Inventec running the iPod line on three shifts. But Inventec, according to Jon Rubinstein, was running four, creating its own supply of iPods and selling them out the back door. "They were selling on their own, and that really soured us," Ruby says.

An iPod engineer remembers some "shady business" but doesn't recall it being quite this blatant. "I don't remember it being this high-level conspiracy," this person says, explaining that Apple has exceptional quality standards and would reject certain units for cosmetic defects, but people within Inventec would refurbish them, and somehow nonofficial units would find their way to a Shenzhen market. "This stuff happens all the time in China," this person adds. The problem took weeks to discover. What happened is that customers would bring a broken iPod into an Apple Store for repair. The blue-shirted Apple employee would type in the serial number, receive an error message, then retype it, and get the same error message. "The serial number didn't exist," Ruby says.

As Apple worked on its next-generation iPod, a smaller version that would truly take the product into the mainstream, it needed a new strategy, and fast. Inventec helped to prove that if Apple was going to make products in mass quantities, China was the answer. What they hadn't proved was that Inventec should be the company to take them there.

CHAPTER 16

THE REPLICA—MAKING THE iPOD IN CHINA

The next time Foxconn really demonstrated its ambition and capabilities was for a product Apple hadn't even commissioned it to build. In the early summer of 2003, Terry Gou's company invited a group of people from Apple Product Design and Operations to Longhua for some show-and-tell. Gary Hsieh, a general manager at Foxconn whom one industry colleague describes as "a completely rogue entrepreneur," led the meeting. He unveiled a third-generation iPod—only, it wasn't made by Apple. It was a replica, made in-house. The Apple people passed it among themselves, marveling at Foxconn's ability to reverse-engineer the iconic music player. The replica had a different skin on the outside, but the same display, scroll wheel, and buttons. Even how it operated and played music was nearly identical to the real thing. "It was as if our own software-hardware team had built it," says an Apple engineer who was there. The point Foxconn was making was simple: *If we can build a replica of this quality without your training our staff or sending the official specs, imagine what we could build as real partners.*

Unbidden, Foxconn had orchestrated its own job interview and demonstrated a willingness to start that day. Hsieh and Gou took the Apple visitors on a tour, showing them a facility with capacity to build an immense quantity of iPods. "Terry's like, 'All this is at your disposal. We have all these great engineers. We've got all this stuff for you, and we're here to help,'" says a person present.

The Apple visitors included Tony Fadell, Steve Zadesky, and DJ Novotney, all from PD, plus Ops negotiator Tony Blevins. Foxconn's timing was impeccable. Apple was growing frustrated with Inventec, testing the assembler's limits as demand for the iPod finally picked up. Inventec was running short on good engineers, and its ambition to learn just wasn't in the same league as Foxconn, whose team absorbed information like PhD students. The difference mattered greatly, as Apple's Operations team was small in the early 2000s. They leaned heavily on the capabilities of their suppliers, not just to execute its orders but to develop new processes.

The Foxconn officials proposed to help in the development of the next iPod. They offered to do schematic layouts of the factory and perform much of the grunt work, like creating detailed digital models of the needed parts in CAD, or computer-aided design. Because it had such confidence in Apple's future, Foxconn said it would take on this work for pennies on the dollar. Tony Fadell credits Terry Gou with understanding the value of working with Apple better than anyone. "Terry was all about the relationship. He knew he needed to be with somebody whom he could grow with," Fadell says. "He just knew that if he had a really good relationship with us, he would be able to grow with it and get the capital he needed to be able to build the infrastructure ahead of everyone. And the other thing is, we trained all his engineers."

Gou even deployed a clever tactic to rotate his workers on Apple projects, to maximize the learning. "We trained all of them. Then one day we'd be like, 'Where'd those engineers go?'" says Fadell. He'd learn that they'd gone to work on other projects, using their new skills in areas that were more lucrative. Then Apple would be forced to teach a new cohort of people, as if a new semester had started.

Another person familiar with the replica show-and-tell says Foxconn "begged for the contract," but that's a bit unfair. The year before, in 2002, Foxconn had earned the title of China's number one exporter. The company wasn't desperate; it was savvy. Gou was a shrewd businessman and knew from experience that Apple was unlike any of his other clients. He didn't want to lose them.

And in 2003, that was a real risk. Foxconn had been supplying components to Apple since the early 1990s, making enclosures for them since 1999, and assembling the candy-colored iMac since 2000. But the work was dwindling. The major growth areas at Apple were laptops and the newer iMac, both assembled by Quanta, and the iPod, manufactured by Inventec.

Metals

Where Foxconn did have a strong hand was in serving as the go-to source for all things aluminum. Beginning in 2002, Apple made big investments in Foxconn, cooperating to build aluminum-clad cinema displays and the enclosure for the aluminum Power Mac G5 tower. Foxconn had won these orders after proving itself several months after the iMac G4 went on sale. Terry Gou had felt snubbed when Apple gave the final assembly order to Quanta, but from the prototype stage onward, it had played a role in the assembly and testing of the cable connectors. Seeking to earn Cupertino's respect, Foxconn built an expensive, complicated production line for the gooseneck, effectively taking a messy process involving three or four countries and placing it all in one factory. "This was one of Foxconn's real first forays into Apple cosmetic metal parts," says a PD engineer on the iMac project. Foxconn's investment was a major relief to Apple's Operations team, which had inherited a logistical nightmare of a project. "This happened right in the peak years of anti-Foxconn sentiment at Apple," this person says. "Foxconn's perseverance and over-the-top support of a quite outlandish Apple design proved that Foxconn's bad reputation as an undisciplined self-serving second source [contract manufacturer] was unjustified."

Meanwhile, Quanta duplicated its Taiwanese production line in mainland China, at Quanta Shanghai Manufacturing City, or QSMC.

"The sequence was: Everything was up and running in Taiwan. And then we tiptoed into China," Rubinstein says. "And basically, whoever was manufacturing in Taiwan set up a parallel factory in China. And we brought the product up on the factory in China. And then, over time, we started doing things initially in China." Foxconn's bet gave it experience just as the ID studio was making a strategic transition. Feeling like they'd mastered plastic on the design of the candy-colored iMacs and first iPods, Jony Ive wanted to push the boundaries on other materials, first with metals and later with glass.

"We wanted to machine aluminum," says Tony Fadell. "High polish, very accurate, detailed metals—and that's where Foxconn came in. Foxconn supplied all the metals for the Apple products, and Foxconn got tons and tons of money [from Apple] to go get all the equipment [needed] to make these high precision metals." Jony was enamored with the stainless steel back of the original iPod. Earlier reviewers of the device critiqued the choice of material because of the way fingerprints marred the chrome look. But this wasn't some oversight. It forced the user to polish the unit, and for Ive that created an unconscious, nurturing connection.

But now ID wanted to shift to anodized aluminum, a low-weight, easy-to-machine material that doesn't typically scratch or smudge. The process of anodization involves immersing the metal in a bath of sulfuric acid, which forms a protective oxide layer that prevents the aluminum from corroding. Introducing a dye can create a colored finish, allowing Apple to transition from the pure white iPod. "The shiny classic car fender iPod was meant to make a statement," says a former Product Design manager. "But if you wanted to ramp big, create a lot of these things that last for a longer period of time, anodized aluminum is such a good material."

Foxconn's replica paid off. It won the contract for the iPod Mini, an all-aluminum unit starting at $249 and available in five colors. Apple released it in February 2004, and it quickly became Apple's bestselling product ever.

Field of Dreams

The success of the iPod Mini all but assured Foxconn was getting the contract for the next iteration: the iPod Nano. But when Terry Gou invited Jon Rubinstein to Shenzhen to discuss the project, Apple's hardware chief nearly had a panic attack. "Terry points to an empty lot. And he goes, 'Here's your factory.'" Rubinstein looked into the distance, his bewilderment turning to anxiety. "I'm terrified," he recounts. "It's a typical Chinese field filled with garbage. I'm panicking. And he says, 'Don't worry, I got you covered.'"

Gou was putting on a strategic show for the American. He probably understood better than anyone just how quickly a greenfield site could be put up in China. He hadn't just overseen the construction of factories, but countless dorms, grocery stores, and entertainment venues over a period of nearly two decades. By the mid-2000s, the Longhua campus was known as Foxconn City. The workers living and laboring within its borders had reached more than 200,000—about the same as Salt Lake City. Rubinstein returned six months later to find a whole new building there, albeit not quite finished. "It was steel girders," he recalls, referring to the long metal beams that formed the skeleton of the building. "But the second floor was finished. Everything else was just girders. There was a stairway to heaven—right in the middle of the factory. I mean, literally. It was just a metal staircase that went upstairs. And you went up the stairs and through a door, and you were in a finished factory."

After another three months, the site had been transformed again. By then Foxconn had installed new machinery, hired tens of thousands of people, and had the production line up and running. The iPod Nano that Foxconn would begin building in the millions weighed just 1.5 ounces, about three-quarters less than the original. Jobs, wearing a black V-neck and a pair of dark blue jeans when he showed off the "impossibly small" device in September 2005, presented it by saying, "You ever wondered what this pocket is for?" A camera zoomed in on the small inner section of the pocket of his jeans as he pulled out the iPod Nano. "Well, now we know."

Rubinstein was floored by Terry Gou's ability to turn vision into reality at inexplicable speed. In America, he says now, nine months wouldn't be enough time for a greenfield site to have attained the permits to start building. "These aren't necessarily bad things, by the way," he says. "It's just not the way it is. And so we're not competitive." From a distance it appeared that Foxconn could go from zero products to 100,000 *per day* with ease. Other Chinese groups could best Foxconn in quality or match them in time to market—the period between taking a design and building the first batch. But nobody could match Foxconn in time to volume—how long it took to build a product in great quantities.

"Everyone could see Foxconn's operational superiority," says a PD engineer. Foxconn introduced an "all in one site" model for Apple projects, meaning FATP—final assembly, test, and pack out—would take place within a small area where it was also sourcing parts, making enclosures, and providing or facilitating services like stamping, molding, and forging. "Communication during development or when production issues arose was as easy as calling each other and meeting in five minutes in a meeting room to talk about issues, instead of summoning suppliers from a few hours away or another country," says the PD engineer.

Exposed

A lower price, a smaller form factor, and sleek styling, plus its availability on Windows and Foxconn's speed and scale, turned the iPod from a product that sold 937,000 units in 2003 to one that shipped 4.4 million units in 2004, then 22.5 million units in 2005. The success quickened Apple's consolidation into China. The low cost of manufacturing played a role, but it was the ubiquity of labor, workers' flexibility, the presence of "next door" suppliers, and tailor-made export policies that were groundbreaking. "Any time you had some problem or change, you could get a mountain of people to follow you down to the X-ray room or to the testing lab or to the sourcing lab to get materials or parts, or to try some machining or something. It was all right at your fingertips," says one PD engineer who also worked in Korea and Taiwan. "Anything we wanted, we could get it," this person adds. "If they didn't have it, they'd go buy it. We'd send 'em out to the store at two in the morning to get some measurement device or some material to remove something or to apply something so it would work better." Summing up what made the experience so distinctive, he said, "It was just the total control of those factories and the people there—whatever we needed, it would happen." A manufacturing engineer recalls trying to get somewhere during a shift change one day, when tens of thousands of people were exiting the factory and heading back to the dorms. "It would take you forty-five minutes or an hour just to go less than a kilometer," this person says.

The experience fundamentally reshaped Steve Jobs's perception of what was possible from a manufacturing perspective. In 2000, he'd clamored for Apple's own factories to take on more production. But by 2005, Jobs grasped that there was no going back. That year, a subordinate suggested that a certain project be done in the United States, and Jobs responded curtly. "I tried it. It didn't work." The results—in volume, efficiency, and price—were unmatched. But Fadell worried about vulnerabilities. Nobody at Apple had really architected the move to China; but in one opportunity after another, Apple operations were lured into the country. "We just got pulled in," he says. "I was always like, 'We're gonna get exposed. This is too much China exposure.'"

But the direction was set. Once a supplier shifted its operations to China, it forced rivals to follow. Within an organization building in multiple regions, everywhere else started to look expensive and constrained by labor shortages. Further and further down the supply chain, the electronics industry had found a new home. "It flipped so, so quickly," Fadell recalls. "Because China was subsidizing so, so, so much. Giving people free land, free everything . . . They made it so attractive to the outside world. It was, like, you'd be dumb [not to move to China]. And once one person moved, they all had to move, because of the cheaper labor."

The Divorce Avoidance Program

The eighty-hour workweeks and increasing need to be in Asia at inconsistent times, with little warning and often for unknown durations, caused massive stress on the engineers' mental health and their marriages. They were primarily men, and some of their wives took to calling themselves "Apple widows" because their husbands were around so infrequently.

So many marriages were broken up during the first years of Jobs's comeback that informal preventive measures were established to contain further damage. Engineers called it the DAP, or Divorce Avoidance Program. In the late 1990s, the acronym referred to when an engineer couldn't come in to work that day because his marriage was on the line. "It was like, 'Where's Glen this weekend? Why isn't he working?'" one engineer recounts. "And a colleague would reply, 'Oh, he's on the DAP.' The basic meaning was: Glen's about ready to get a divorce if he doesn't have a weekend with his wife. So Glen wasn't working that weekend. That kind of stuff happened on the team all the time."

Then the DAP evolved. The necessity of giving engineers respite to save their marriages was understood, but with Apple's ID studio continuing to push the boundaries of what was possible, workers were under constant pressure to perform. So instead of giving time off, Apple started to give out bonuses meant to assuage spouses. One engineer with more than two decades of Apple experience recalls calling his wife from the Apple office and telling her that he had to take another trip to Asia the following week. "And she just blew up. You could hear her on my phone speaker two offices away," he says. "The thing that made her calm down was that whenever I'd go to China on a project, if that project was completed and went to production, we got a $10,000 bonus." Engineers had a name for these bonuses: "Dan bucks" or "Danny bucks," in reference to Dan Riccio, the VP of Product Design. He'd played a role in negotiating for the bonuses. "We had these fake little vouchers that had Dan on them—he didn't look happy," an engineer says.

In those years, Apple conducted product launches in the first half of

January, for MacWorld, so the pressure in the final two months before that event could be particularly intense. "I'd miss Thanksgiving, Christmas, and New Year's," says one engineer. Apple started paying for the flights of spouses and children to join the engineers if a trip lasted more than thirty days. "It made a difference," this person says. They'd still be working seven days a week, but the hotels were nice.

Engineers said the pressure to put in the long hours was all but mandatory. Indeed, a decade later after Jobs created Apple University, a corporate institution meant to convey his values to a new generation of employees, Apple came close to codifying the principle that pushing employees to burnout was acceptable. In a slide deck called Leadership Palette, Apple states: "Fighting for excellence is about resisting the gravitational pull of mediocrity. It involves being dead tired and still pushing yourself, and others, to get it right, every time."

One engineer says the reason he left Apple after more than a decade is that during a routine medical appointment, his doctor noted his high blood pressure and said, "Okay, I need you to do two things for me: lose weight and quit Apple." The doctor explained that the stress would basically kill him. Some Apple engineers can even rattle off the names of people who died on the production line or upon their return from yet another trip to Asia. The engineers were often in their forties and fifties, and while it's not possible to conclude that overwork was their cause of death, many believe it was. One longtime veteran recalls that, during the funeral for one of these people, the number of Apple employees who left the Sunday service to join conference calls was unbelievable. According to Walter Isaacson, Jobs even attributed his own cancer to the volume of work he'd taken on in 1997. That's when he was running both Apple and Pixar, developing kidney stones, and coming home so exhausted that he had trouble speaking. "That's probably when this cancer started growing," Jobs told his biographer, "because my immune system was pretty weak at that time."

Jon Rubinstein, who worked for Steve Jobs on and off for sixteen years, called the long workweeks "shattering," and it's what led to his own departure later on. “A lot of people got sick at Apple,” he once said. “The list goes on and on of people who got terminally ill or really ill . . . and I worried that if I stayed, I’d end up damaging myself, and my health was, frankly, more important.” He added: “Steve used to always tell the groups, ‘This will be the high point of your life,’ and I was thinking, *God, I hope not,* right? Because that’s really a sad way to think.”

CHAPTER 17

PROJECT PURPLE IN ASIA

Tony Fadell could hear the footsteps behind him. Apple finally had its confidence restored after two decades of being beaten down, its near bankruptcy less than a decade earlier now looking like a distant memory. The iPod, after a slow start, had changed the face of the company. In the holiday period of 2004, Apple sold 4.6 million iPods—nearly as many MP3 players in a single quarter as the number of candy-colored iMacs sold in five years. Apple's share of the American MP3 player market had soared from 33 percent in 2002 to 82 percent in 2004.

This was a dominance and cultural relevance the company had never experienced before, and it only extended throughout 2005. That January, Apple launched the iPod Shuffle, a minimalist player without a display. In February, it unveiled the second-generation iPod Mini; in September, the Nano; and in October, the first iPod able to play videos. New iPods were emerging so quickly that on *Saturday Night Live,* Fred Armisen parodied Steve Jobs by announcing smaller and smaller versions until he held up nothing at all and proclaimed "the new iPod Invisa." In the holiday quarter of 2005, Apple sold 14 million iPods—triple that of a year earlier. The $2.9 billion of revenue generated by the music player exceeded the revenue achieved by the remainder of Apple's product line.

In a Silicon Valley culture captured by book titles such as *Only the Paranoid Survive,* Fadell began to worry about the sustainability of these sales. "You hear these heavy, stomping footsteps of the mobile phone industry. *Boom!*" he later told an interviewer. "And it's the feature phones at that time. They are adding cameras, they are adding color displays. And they are seeing the success of the iPod and going, 'That's just music. We have some storage. We can load music onto our phone, and we can do what the iPod does, plus more.' *Boom! . . . Boom!*"

Apple started to experiment. It partnered with Motorola to create a phone that played MP3s, but the result was embarrassing. Apple then worked on adding cellphone capabilities to an iPod, using the click wheel as a dialer, but that didn't really work. The company's engineers also made a full-screen iPod relying on a virtual click wheel, but that was inelegant. It wasn't clear what the future was. Whatever form the phone was going to take, Fadell's team was going to need to understand how to build not just one, but many. Apple had never made a product with cellular technology before, so Fadell sought more staffers competent in the field and sent them off to Asia to find quality suppliers.

Unknown to Fadell at the time, another set of heavy, stomping footsteps were behind him—those of rival executives clamoring for his influence and proximity to Steve Jobs. Nobody at Apple had ever ascended the ranks like Fadell. Joining as a thirty-two-year-old contractor in 2001, he was appointed vice president of iPod Engineering in 2004, and then senior vice president overseeing the whole iPod division in 2006. Executives who'd worked with Jobs since the late 1990s, or even earlier with him at NeXT, didn't wield nearly as much power. But Apple Computer was undergoing such a transformation that the word *Computer* would be dropped from its name in 2007. Fadell was the key executive in charge of Apple's most lucrative product line and, soon, its most promising future product, too. The resentment was palpable. *Boom! . . . Boom!*

The Trio

The three key deputies charged with bulking up Apple's cellphone expertise and touring Asia for the best suppliers were David Tupman and Steve Zadesky, who'd been working on iPods since 2001, and Rubén Caballero, an antenna specialist who joined Apple in 2005. Tupman and Zadesky knew the ins and outs of building handheld electronics at scale, while Caballero, who was born in Santiago, Chile, brought a more niche skill set. His family had fled Chile amid a civil war. Rubén's father, a businessman who refused to endorse the new dictator, was given twenty-four hours to depart the country. Some cousins who didn't leave were shot dead. Rubén was just seven years old when his family found asylum in Quebec. There he became fluent in French and studied electrical engineering. Then he spent thirteen years with the Canadian Air Force, learning English in his mid-twenties while serving as an aerospace engineer. In 2001, he joined a Silicon Valley chip start-up, Tropian, specializing in antennas and developing a system engineering team that worked on testing prototypes.

The trio was a small team with a big task, reflecting Steve Jobs's desire to build the phone the way a start-up would, disconnected from the rest of Apple. Jobs had become upset with the Mac team, feeling it was too bureaucratic. New product launches were driven by someone else's schedule—the release of new chip sets from Power PC and Intel—and a lot of the work was iterative. Compared to the dizzying releases of new iPod models, the Mac team's efforts seemed poky. He preferred controlled chaos and the ability to move on a dime, not rigid layers of order. "The Mac team, guys that had been there for thirty years, were like, 'Whoa, slow down there, whippersnapper!'" says a young iPod engineer. "They were gonna ship the next laptop in four years or something, and we're like, 'We ship products every six months, and we ramp the [production] lines to make orders of magnitude more units in a week than your product does in its lifetime.' So it was just a totally different culture."

Hyperbolic as that comparison is, it's close to how Jobs saw things. He made it clear that if Apple produced a phone, it would be more of an enhanced iPod than a Mac for the pocket. "You don't want your phone to be like a PC," he would later tell journalist John Markoff. Fadell's trio of deputies went into the deep minutiae of how phones functioned to avoid being subservient to the powerful telecoms like AT&T and Verizon, which largely dictated what features would be in every handset. Jobs had a particular disdain for them; he'd once explained Apple's reluctance to build a phone by saying, "We're not very good going through orifices to get to the end users." Fadell authorized his team to buy expensive machines that could analyze radio frequencies, or RF—cellular, Wi-Fi, and Bluetooth—so they could measure, tweak, and remeasure all the prototypes in development.

With Project Purple, as the secret assignment to build a phone was called, Apple was creating something from scratch, but also relying on the expertise it had developed in the prior half decade building the world's most popular handheld device. The iPod team had abandoned sampling—the testing of random devices in a batch, as a proxy for the whole batch—and instead validated every iPod through costly tests. Fadell wanted the phone to match that quality, costs be damned. The CMU 200, an RF frequency testing machine the size of a large stereo from specialty group Rohde & Schwarz, cost $146,000. These machines were made for test labs, but Apple, ever maniacal about reliability, began purchasing them in the hundreds to place directly on its production lines. Later, Apple purchased similar VCR-sized test equipment from LitePoint initially costing $50,000 per unit and similar machines from Agilent. In all three cases the orders overwhelmed the test-device makers, as Apple began to order more equipment than they could even supply. "They couldn't even comprehend what we were doing," says an engineer involved.

Apple treated them like any other component maker: It sent engineers over to bring up their quality, help them scale, and push down costs. The $50,000 machines got down to around $13,000. "That equipment is big, expensive, and slow," says another engineer involved. "And it's really general-purpose test equipment. Like, you would have it on your lab bench, and all RF engineers and testers knew how to run it. But if you're trying to build out your factory with five, ten, twenty, thirty, forty, fifty lines, and each of those lines has to have a tester or multiple testers along the line, then you start hitting the limit as to how many of these testers they can make."

The project was so secretive that they didn't dare ship any of the equipment to Apple's offices. Instead the machines were sent directly to several engineers' houses. To get them on production lines, engineers would put VCR-sized machines in their luggage and surreptitiously import them to China. "We were buying stuff and shipping it there by suitcases," a third engineer involved says. Once the orders were numerous enough, they went through more official, freight-forwarding channels, but in the earlier stages the team was working at a frenetic pace. Much later, when production was set up, two-thirds of the line was devoted to testing and validation—an unheard-of idea at the time, indicating just how seriously Apple was rethinking the rules of mass manufacturing. "Nobody would do that because of the cost," one of the engineers says. They were adamant that the thirty millionth unit be identical to the first. A Nokia engineer working within Foxconn in the late 2000s confirms this, recalling that Nokia had one test station for its phones. When he got a chance to see the Apple area—which was making fewer phones than Nokia—he was stunned to see fifty test stations. "It was incredible micromanagement of the whole process," he says.

Terry Gou's Yacht

In late 2005, at the same time Apple was secretly experimenting with a phone project based on an iPod-like design, two of Terry Gou's key deputies invited a handful of Apple engineers onto Gou's yacht for some sightseeing off the coast of Hong Kong. On the Foxconn side was Barry Chiang, director of the iPod division, and Louis Woo, a senior advisor and liaison to Apple. They were feeling upbeat, as Foxconn had just ramped iPod Nano production to more than 100,000 a day.

On the Apple side were at least five people, led by Rubén Caballero, the antenna engineer, and Chip Hills, an operations executive. Hills had joined Apple from GE Plastics and would soon become the de facto head of China for Apple and the point person for scaling the phone project. He was part of the crew scouring Asia, looking to find the best suppliers for the embryonic project. He was known as a finger-in-the-pie engineer, working directly on the shop floor to get things built. Although Apple was careful not to say precisely what they were working on, the Foxconn executives were keen to win the order. In considering which partners might make the phone, Apple's team had met with several Taiwanese contract manufacturers operating in China, including Quanta, its partner for the iPod Video; Pegatron, which assembled the iPod Shuffle; and Arima, a well-known manufacturer of Motorola and Sony Ericsson phones. Foxconn wasn't at all the most skilled vendor for the project, but what impressed the Apple crew out on the water was their hunger for the deal, their do-whatever-it-takes attitude. They were humble, with an eager willingness to learn and invest. It was perfect messaging. Apple wasn't interested in "best practices"; it wanted to upend how things were done. So Foxconn's ignorance was, in a way, a plus, coupled with its deep ambition to learn and proven ability to scale. Their attitude contrasted with the somewhat cocky approach favored by the more experienced cellphone manufacturers.

The yacht invite paid off. Hills chose Foxconn as the manufacturing partner for its nascent and still precarious phone project. Foxconn signed a vague Request for Proposal that told them virtually nothing about the gadget, but it called for Hills to develop a preproduction site within Foxconn, a sort of archetypal line that Foxconn would then duplicate every inch of to scale production.

Multi-touch

Around mid-2005, another project began to gain traction internally. The interfaces team had been toying with multi-touch technology for roughly two years, aided by a start-up Apple had purchased called FingerWorks. Senior engineers from Project Purple knew about it, but the original concept was about rethinking the Mac's interface. When Steve Jobs first showed Fadell the technology, asking if it might work for a phone, it was far from obvious that the enormous contraption Jobs pointed to was the future of something that would sit on your desk, let alone be shoved in your pocket. "It filled the room," Fadell recalled. "There was a projector mounted on the ceiling, and it would project the Mac screen onto this surface that was maybe three or four feet square. Then you could touch the Mac screen and move things around and draw on it."

As multi-touch developed, Apple believed they could use the technology to create a tablet. Hundreds of prototypes were built, including some models with electronics assembled by a small team in Foxconn, but the result was a tablet-like device that was fat, ugly, and slow. Semiconductors just weren't speedy enough to power the touchscreen interface of an eleven-inch screen. And because it took too much power, the battery was huge, so the device was huge. Meanwhile, the fear that the iPod business would be cannibalized by the phone giants continued to fuel anxiety and innovation. "It was an existential crisis," a senior engineer says. "[We were saying], 'You realize what's gonna happen here is this business we built on iPods is going to go away. We *need* to build a phone.'"

Jobs eventually canceled the other phone ideas and declared multi-touch the future. He was adamant there'd be no keyboard, so the phone would be as full screen as possible. Apple's engineers suddenly had to find suppliers that could build multi-touch displays at scale—something that didn't exist at the time. There was no way Apple could send the specs to some factory and wait for the parts to be built; instead, it sent teams of engineers to Japan, Korea, Taiwan, and China to find hungry vendors it could work with to co-create the processes. "There were a few truly groundbreaking mass production processes we were involved with, where we really had to go around to find the best people in the entire world—the peak of what humans have developed for some of these technologies," says a product manager. By early 2006, they had a full-screen prototype enclosed in brushed aluminum. Jobs and Ive "were exceedingly proud of it," journalist Fred Vogelstein would later recount. "But because neither of them was an expert in the physics of radio waves, they didn't realize they'd created a beautiful brick. Radio waves don't travel through metal well."

Negotiating for space within the phone was always fraught. If engineers had their way, it would've been twice as thick. But ID was unrelenting on the size, forcing the engineers to either compromise or innovate. The printed circuit board, usually flat, was folded like a sandwich to save on room, allowing the battery to be larger. So Caballero, the antenna expert, had to practically beg Jobs: "I need one inch of plastic." The ID studio didn't want to give a millimeter, but Jobs capitulated. "Rubén had to put the whole cell phone antenna there, the Wi-Fi antenna there, the Bluetooth antenna—all in that one inch of space," says an engineer. "In order to make it work, we had to drop the performance in the Bluetooth, to the point where you really had a hard time connecting Bluetooth devices to it."

The RF components giving the phone cellular, Wi-Fi, and Bluetooth capabilities were stuffed in the top of the device, covered by a black plastic housing on the outer metal shell. In that design the tests came back showing the antenna received a good signal. But around four months before the January 2007 unveiling, the engineers ran more tests measuring SAR—or specific absorption rate, which looks at the amount of radio frequency absorbed by the body—and the numbers were far too high. The RF team was concerned about how much energy was going to the user's head, especially after an academic study found an increased risk of brain cancer from using mobile phones. Caballero's team spent weeks tweaking the technology to get the SAR numbers down, to no avail. The only move that really helped was to play a Jenga-in-reverse game with the phone's inner parts: they took the RF components from the top and moved them to the bottom. That created distance between the radiation center of the phone and the user's ear. From the outside, the solution was elegant; from the inside, it was a fiasco. The modem couldn't be moved, so the team had to insert three special copper cables running the length of the phone to connect the components. "It took a good three to four months, working every night and day, every day of the week, to get it done," says the second engineer. Jobs was furious, placated only by the promise that it would be fixed for some future version. Besides, it was show time.

CHAPTER 18

THE ONE DEVICE

On January 9, 2007, Steve Jobs stood before a packed auditorium, once again in a black turtleneck and blue jeans. "Every once in a while," he said, "a revolutionary product comes along that changes everything." Then he introduced it—the iPhone—to an audience mesmerized by full-screen web navigation and the basics of multi-touch, like pinch to zoom and swipe to unlock, or the way the screen would bounce to indicate a page couldn't scroll any further. The prototype had experienced all kinds of software glitches in the days before, instilling feelings of anxiety and terror into a small group watching within the auditorium. "There we were in the fifth row or something—engineers, managers, all of us—doing shots of Scotch after every segment of the demo," a radio engineer named Andy Grignon once recounted. "After each piece of the demo, the person who was responsible for that portion did a shot. When the finale came—and it worked along with everything before it, we all just drained the flask. It was the best demo any of us had ever seen." The presentation was so good that some executives at BlackBerry maker Research in Motion thought it was faked somehow.

Two weeks after unveiling "the one device," Steve Jobs walked into a routine divisional meeting. He was in a bad mood and didn't look good. Then he pulled out his prototype iPhone, which looked worse. The keys in his pocket had cut a huge gouge across its plastic screen. He threw the unit onto the boardroom table toward Steve Zadesky and demanded: "Make it glass." It wasn't the first time the idea had come up. In September 2006, just four months earlier, Jobs had grown angry about smaller scratch marks and complained to a mid-level executive: "Look at this, look at this—what's with the screen?" The executive responded, "Well, Steve, we have a glass prototype, but it fails the one-meter drop test one hundred times out of one hundred times." Jobs cut the executive off. "I just want to know if you're going to make the fucking thing work." Now, in January, Jobs wasn't taking excuses. Apple had just announced the phone would be available in June; the date couldn't be pushed back. Six months would've been a rush job; but they had even less time than that. The display is a module that had to be ready months ahead of the assembly.

What followed is perhaps the best-known anecdote on the manufacturing of the original iPhone. Jobs reached out to Wendell Weeks, CEO of Corning, a glassmaker in upstate New York, saying he needed the hardest glass they could make. Weeks told Jobs about Gorilla Glass, something Corning had developed for fighter-jet cockpits back in the 1960s. They'd never found a market for it and abandoned the project. Jobs convinced him to begin production immediately.

The decision risked throwing Zadesky, who managed all the mechanical parts for the iPhone project, into a tailspin. He and Tang Tan, another iPod veteran, had to quickly put together a touchscreen supply chain, as glass and plastic function in totally different ways. Fadell likens this "crazy" phase to landing "a fleet of 200 jets on an aircraft carrier, all within minutes of each other. And all the jets were running out of fuel." Apple needed to find manufacturers that were highly competent, but with enough capacity to free up their top talent.

Among the suppliers it found was Lens Technology, a glass specialist Apple worked with to cut and place Gorilla Glass. It was founded by Zhou Qunfei, who dropped out of high school at age sixteen and left her impoverished village to work in the factories of Shenzhen. She found a job making watch lenses, earning about a dollar a day polishing glass. She hated the work but was eager to learn, and her boss offered her the chance to understand the science behind the manufacturing. Zhou—"Jane" to Apple engineers—eventually saved up $3,000, started her own company in 1993, and eleven years later was making small glass screens for Motorola with a team of 1,000 people. Apple engineers grew to have great respect for her operational skill and ability to leverage help through political channels. The company's main factory was in Changsha, the capital city of Hunan province where Mao was born. One engineer working in the factory recalls a time when power went out across the district. Lens couldn't operate. But Zhou was so well connected that, in a short period of time, multiple fire trucks showed up. Each carried generators, and soon Lens was back to tempering and precision shaping glass—the only factory up and running for multiple blocks.

Another important supplier was TPK, which placed a special coating on the Corning glass, enabling the user's fingers to transmit electrical signals. The Taiwanese start-up had been founded just a few years earlier by Michael Chiang, an entrepreneur who in the PC era had reportedly made $30 million sourcing monitors and then lost it all on one strategic mistake. In 1997 he began working with resistive touch panels used by point-of-sale registers. When Palm was shipping PDAs that worked with a stylus, Chiang worked on improving the technology to enable finger-based touchscreens, even showing the technology to Nokia. But nobody was interested until 2004, when a glass supplier introduced TPK to Apple. An iPhone engineer calls Chiang "a classic Taiwanese cowboy [who] committed to moving heaven and earth" by turning fields into factories that could build touchscreens. The factory was in Xiamen, a coastal city directly across from Taiwan. "The first iPhones 100 percent would not have shipped without that vendor," this person says. He recalls Chiang responding to Apple by saying, "'We can totally do that!'—even though [what we were asking was something] nobody in the world had ever done before."

Among the techniques Apple codeveloped with suppliers was a way to pattern, or etch, two sides of a piece of glass to do the touch sensor, at a time when film lithography processes were being done on only one side. Another pioneering technique is called rigid-to-rigid lamination, a process for bonding two materials using heat and pressure, which Apple applied to tape a stack of LCD displays to touch sensors and cover elements to create one material. The process was performed in a cleanroom environment with custom robotics.

Apple was secretive about each of these cutting-edge methods. One result of this is that outsiders failed to grasp the advancements taking place in China for the iPhone. In the Western press it was common to misrepresent China's role as being all about low-value assembly. These studies were based on opening an iPhone and breaking down where the display, chips, and other components came from. As most expensive parts were typically from Korea, Japan, and the United States, those doing the assessing would conclude that China's contributions were de minimis. "China [just] happens to be the last stop in a given product's long global supply chain," wrote the president of the Export-Import Bank of the United States. "The Chinese make products like the iPhone possible without reaping much of the benefits." Similarly, at one point, two scholars deduced that the work performed by Chinese workers contributed just 3.6 percent to the $179 wholesale cost of an iPhone. When *The Wall Street Journal* picked up on the study, it headlined the article: "Not Really 'Made in China.'"

The analyses were wrong. Apple was making spectacular investments in China; it's just that the contributions weren't found *within* the iPhone, but in the machinery and processes that made it. "Sure, the glass comes from Corning, but does it come in that shape?" says one manufacturing design engineer, referring to the US-made glass on the iPhone. "Corning glass is useless until Lens makes it useful." As for wages, observers were often counting only the steps in final assembly, oblivious to all the labor that went into building the components. Even so, it's true that Chinese wages per iPhone were a small percentage of the wholesale cost; however, this wasn't reflective of their insignificance but, counterintuitively, a sign of the China-based factories' importance. The low cost per unit reflected their efficiency.

Only after all this complexity making the touchscreen glass with cutting-edge processes did the tedious monotony of actually assembling the iPhone begin over at Foxconn. As *The New York Times* would famously recount later, once Apple worked out how to make the glass screens, a foreman roused 8,000 workers inside the Foxconn dormitories, gave each employee "a biscuit and a cup of tea, guided [them] to a workstation and within half an hour [they] started a 12-hour shift fitting glass screens into beveled frames. Within 96 hours, the plant was producing over 10,000 iPhones a day."

Lust

When the iPhone went on sale in July 2007, some higher-ranking executives were given theirs two days before launch. One made the mistake of using it in public at the Berkeley Greek Theatre. "When a few people recognized what I had in my hand, I nearly got mugged and raped," he says. His crude language is imprecise but meaningful—it connotes the animalistic *lust* people felt. Like many at Apple, this executive hadn't grasped the intensity of consumer excitement. When dozens of people camped out in front of the Apple Store for multiple days, employees didn't know if they should applaud their enthusiasm or kick them off the premises.

The hype was just enormous, as though people really did grasp what a cultural icon the iPhone was going to be. But even competitors that had a precise sense of the magnitude of Apple's achievement failed to understand the company's lesser-known advantages—its operational superiority and its newfound edge in eliminating defects. Quietly and without any fanfare, Apple had been building a yawning gap over the competition, improving hardware each year at a greater scale than the last. As Microsoft, Nokia, BlackBerry, and every other phone maker scrambled to respond, they found themselves fighting yesterday's war. They'd compete with the original iPhone, only to be outgunned by the following year's 3G model, which doubled the speed, halved the price, and was enhanced by an App Store fed by thousands of software developers worldwide.

The iPhone was such a watershed device that success in the decade following its launch was determined by how brazenly competitors copied it. All attempts to do something different failed. Within just six or seven years, Nokia was nearly bankrupt, BlackBerry was close to dead, and Microsoft's smartphone ambitions had been rendered irrelevant. But the cause of their demise wasn't solely Apple, whose global market share in the 2010s wouldn't exceed 18 percent. Rather, they were killed in two stages. First, by the likes of Taiwan's HTC and South Korea's Samsung, whose use of open-source Android software from Google enabled them to rival the best features of the iPhone. And then by new Chinese rivals, which were aided by the education in hardware excellence they'd all received from being part of Apple's China-based, world-leading supply chain.

As Apple grew its operations, more engineers were worrying about its dependence on China, which didn't appear to be opening to the world as they believed it would. Some shared stories of what they called "OIC events"—experiences that would occur only in China. One engineer recalls getting ready in the morning at a hotel in Shenzhen and glancing at the international news playing silently on his TV as he spoke with his wife back home in California. "The Dalai Lama came on," he recounts. "And I said to my wife, 'That's weird, the Dalai Lama is . . . '" Then the TV screen went blank. China's censors had cut the feed within seconds. Years later, he'd remember the incident as a foreboding sign.

"A Tony Blevins Special"

Terry Gou's perseverance had won Foxconn the exclusive contract to build the iPhone, but his strategy to make Apple dependent on his operations—so he could squeeze out more profit—failed spectacularly. Instead, Apple squeezed Foxconn, leveraging higher volumes to attain lower costs while obstructing Foxconn's efforts to choose which sub-suppliers to work with. In 2000, the first year Foxconn performed major operations for Apple, it had reported net margins of 10.6 percent. As it got more work with Apple, revenues soared while margins plummeted—to 4.6 percent in 2007 and then to 2.4 percent in 2011. So while Foxconn revenues more than doubled—from $53 billion in 2007 to $107 billion in 2011—profits merely inched up from $2.41 billion to $2.53 billion. "It was just brutal the way we'd work with suppliers," a former Apple VP says. "We wanted something, and we just got it. And they just wanted our business. It was incredible . . . The red carpet was rolled out everywhere we went."

For the original iPhone, Foxconn had even agreed to a no-quibble warranty, an onerous clause known internally as "a Tony Blevins special." It compelled Foxconn to take full responsibility for any iPhone failures within the first twelve months after purchase. "The no-quibble warranty meant that if we get a return, we're sending it back to you, and you fix it and deal with it," this person says. The clause was an incentive for Foxconn to maintain high quality standards—no funny business like saving on costs by using unauthorized suppliers, the sort of trick contract manufacturers were infamous for.

Blevins had already been a spectacular negotiator, and as Apple grew, he developed further ways to tilt the field. He'd organize suppliers into adjacent hotel rooms, then travel from one to the next, pushing prices lower and subtly indicating that some rival had just made a better offer. Blevins wouldn't let the suppliers order food or leave the rooms, and depending on the situation, he'd toy with the temperature. If it was the kind of hot and humid summer in Hong Kong when nobody would think to have brought a jacket, Blevins would crank up the air-conditioning in the hotel room, to the point where only the Apple team was appropriately dressed. "Then they would go all night till they made them cave," one colleague says. Apple's terms could be hard to say no to. In the 2010s, Apple would often ramp a product from hundreds of thousands of units to the tens of millions. Margins might be risibly low, but a supplier could become rich off the volumes.

Blevins couldn't be at every meeting, so he taught his subordinates the values he'd picked up working at a used-car lot as a teenager. When the procurement team would meet in Hong Kong or Shenzhen, each would be given the same amount of currency, then sent off to the local market for a set time. Whoever came back with the most silk ties was the winner. This game would be played over and over again, inculcating a sense of intense competition.

When members of Blevins's team negotiated contracts on his behalf and then gave them to their boss for a final sign-off, they found that he didn't have anything like a sophisticated review process. Rather, he worked on instinct, flipping through the pages and scanning for red ink—amendments asked for by Apple's counterparty. He didn't burrow into the details, but if there was too much red ink, he'd give it back. "He'd say, 'Do better, I'm not signing that,'" a subordinate says.

The no-quibble terms were a legacy of the iPod, a relatively simple product and one for which Foxconn was directly sourcing many of the parts. Apple had taken control of the more strategic and high-value-added items, but Foxconn had sourced commodity components on its own. Lacking any data on the iPhone before it was released, Foxconn treated it like an iPod and agreed to the same terms. But consenting to the same clause for such a different product proved to be a disaster. For the first iPhone, the percentage of units that came back within twelve months—what Apple calls TWR, standing for total warranty repair—was around one in seven. There were problems with the home button and the volume controls, and a spate of issues that didn't meet standards from a the perspective of field durability. Foxconn wasn't necessarily building it poorly; it was simply the first consumer electronics product of that complexity to be used multiple hours a day. Apple's quality standards were high, but they weren't built to meet smartphone addiction—a concept that hadn't really existed before. "You use an iPod occasionally, but you use the iPhone all the fucking time," says an executive involved in manufacturing the original unit. The no-quibble clause was maintained for least two to three generations of iPhone, until it got to a point where Foxconn was losing money and they had to plead with Cupertino to amend the contract. "It became untenable from a business standpoint," says a person familiar with the change.

That Foxconn would even sign such a contract demonstrated their willingness to do anything to work with Apple. Their hunger got to the point of being irrational—and Apple would fully exploit the situation. The ruthlessness of the contracts troubled members of Apple's team. One subordinate to Blevins recalls his boss handing him a thick stack of contracts and asking for an analysis by the morning. It was a kind of test. The subordinate came in the next day and said he'd often found the terms to be completely illogical.

"Why do you think that?" Blevins asked. The subordinate shuffled through the pages of one contract and explained that it imposed all kinds of risks on to the supplier—uncertainties they couldn't possibly control. Usually, the more uncertainties there are in a contract, the more these are priced in. A rational counterpart in Japan or Germany would go to the ends of the earth to ensure there was nothing in the contract they couldn't live up to, even if the risks were fancifully remote. But in this case, the risks were entirely lopsided to the supplier, and virtually none of it was priced in. "It's unlike anything I've ever seen," the subordinate told Blevins. "Anybody who signs that is insane."

Blevins looked at the colleague and revealed he was the author. "I'm very proud of that contract," he countered. "That's *my* creation."

CHAPTER 19

THE APPLE SHOCK

Years before Uber would become the largest taxi provider without owning a single vehicle or Airbnb would grow into the largest accommodation provider without owning any real estate, Apple was discovering how to be the world's largest manufacturer without owning any factories.

Apple was not unique in having its devices assembled in China by contract manufacturers. The country had been luring in countless companies, with local officials clearing all manner of hurdles to raise up factories faster than anybody else. Its currency was kept artificially low, boosting the value of exports while making imports expensive—an added incentive to make components in-country, further supported by strategic tariffs. It allowed manufacturers to work in bonded zones—areas designed to stimulate production by exempting them from paying certain trade taxes. And it encouraged tens of millions of migrant workers from the rural hinterlands to work on the coast, where they earned depressed wages and were treated as second-class citizens.

But Apple was taking advantage of the opportunities in unique ways. It was working so intimately with suppliers that it had come up with a new offshoring model altogether. It married the best of both worlds, imposing a zealous level of control over its manufacturing processes, but with the lower costs and added flexibility of not actually running a factory. Curiously, the nuances of Apple's strategy in China—what it was doing differently from everyone else—had been largely absent from media narratives, investor reports, and earnings calls. The few accounts of Apple in China to emerge were typically about the lives of workers.

The first major report was in the UK's *Daily Mail,* published in August 2006. It described workers at Foxconn's Longhua factory living in high-security dorms "100 to a room, arriving with a few possessions and a bucket to wash their clothes." Overtime, laborers told the journalists, was mandatory, and shifts could last fifteen hours a day. "We have to work too hard, and I am always tired," one worker said. "It's like being in the army. They make us stand still for hours. If we move we are punished by being made to stand still for longer."

The article went viral, and after conducting an audit, Apple acknowledged that more than a third of workers exceeded its maximum workweek of sixty hours. Within a month Cupertino established a Supplier Responsibility team, vowing to improve conditions and hold vendors to account. This cat-and-mouse pattern—of the media finding problems in the supply chain and Apple pledging to do better—would be replicated over and again in the decade plus to follow. The periodic exposés helped to shine a light on working conditions and likely caused some positive change. But the media's forays into what Apple was up to overlooked wider questions of company strategy, business development, and the management of product cycles. In histories of Apple, both in articles and books, China usually enters the conversation to explain the company's problems, not its successes. But an early exception emerged in a wonky report on supply chain efficiency that came out just before the iPhone went on sale.

Arms and Legs

Kevin O'Marah vividly remembers his confusion when Apple vaulted from out of nowhere into the number two spot on the Supply Chain Top 25, an annual ranking of the world's best-run corporate production and distribution systems. "Everyone was shocked," he says, recalling the moment in mid-2007. "It was like, 'What? This doesn't make sense. They have a terrible reputation.' "

O'Marah had created the list in 2004 when Apple wasn't exactly top of mind. Apple was entirely absent from the annual rankings for the first three years, so when it was abruptly ranked No. 2—just behind Nokia—he figured his researchers had erred and started to investigate Apple himself. What he found was that Apple was doing better than even its high score would suggest. In the 2007 data, P&G, Toyota, and Walmart all had a peer ranking at least double that of Apple. But when it came to a supply chain metric called inventory turns—a measure of goods sold versus inventories—Apple was in a league of its own. In other words, Apple was performing poorly on soft metrics, because none of its rivals knew what it was up to. But on hard metrics, it outclassed everyone. Tim Cook had once described inventory as "fundamentally evil," likening electronics to dairy products that might spoil. Another time he said, "I'd prefer to be able to talk inventories in terms of hours, not days." The results showed this was not a mere aspiration. Apple had 2.5 times better inventory turns than Nokia or Tesco, a grocer lauded for its efficiency, and it was 12 times better than Coca-Cola.

O'Marah might be the first person outside of Cupertino to really grasp that Apple was not outsourcing as the word was commonly understood. Instead, it was sending its top product designers and manufacturing design engineers from California and embedding them into suppliers' facilities for weeks or months at a time. There they'd whip local suppliers into shape, co-invent new production processes, and stay until the operations were up and running. "The thing that really stood out was not just that it's all in China, but that it's the most vertically integrated manufacturing system in the world and yet they don't theoretically own anything," he says. "They went far deeper and bigger than anybody had ever seen."

Instead of selecting components off the shelf, Apple was designing custom parts, crafting the manufacturing behind them, and orchestrating their assembly into enormously complex systems at such scale and flexibility that it could respond to fluctuating customer demand with precision. Just half a decade earlier, these sorts of feats were not possible in China. The main thing that had changed, remarkably, was Apple's presence itself. So many of its engineers were going into the factories to train workers that the suppliers were developing new forms of practical know-how. "All the tech competence China has now is not the product of Chinese tech leadership drawing in Apple," O'Marah says. "It's the product of Apple going in there and building the tech competence."

Apple was also investing heavily in the production process to build moats around its manufacturing innovations, while rivals were just giving suppliers spec sheets and saying, "Build this." Companies typically outsource because they don't want to deal with manufacturing; they want to focus on the higher-value parts of what's called the smile curve of product development. Think of how a product is made, sequentially. First is the higher-value functions of product conception and design; then the smile dips into the low-value function of logistics and manufacturing; then it curves back up to retail, branding, and services. By outsourcing the low-value functions, companies can avoid nitty-gritty details. But a great deal is missed in that thought process. "If your objectives are 100 percent aligned, then great—you'll get what you're hoping for," says an Apple procurement executive. "But that's rarely the case. The contract manufacturer is in it for them, and I'm in it for me, so if I just let them do their thing, it's going to come out best for them, not me."

So Apple did something totally novel. It purchased hundreds of millions of dollars of machinery, placed it in the factories of its supply partners, and "tagged" it for Apple use only. "They were doing more capital equipment buying than anybody I could see in the world, and yet they were not owning it themselves—they were putting it in other people's plants," O'Marah says. From when the iPod launched in 2001 to when the iPhone went on sale in 2007, the "machinery" that Apple owns—equipment used in supplier operations—quadrupled from $245 million to $1.1 billion. Such capital expenditures stunned O'Marah, yet in the next five years that number would soar to $16 billion. The investments allowed its suppliers to operate at a level they'd otherwise be incapable of. And it gave Apple considerable advantages. Not only did Apple disallow the supplier from using the equipment on rival products, but at any point Apple could drive a truck to the vendor and reclaim the machinery. If Apple wanted to reduce orders at one supplier and favor its rival, "Apple would have the machines shipped to another factory—no question, no discussion," says a manufacturing design engineer. In fact, around 2011 when Foxconn was attempting to exert leverage based on its dominant role assembling iPhones, Apple engineers showed up at a Foxconn assembly line and began unmounting expensive machinery from the floor, in broad daylight, before transferring it over to Pegatron. It wasn't necessary to shift a large percentage of orders to the Foxconn rival—just making the point was enough to instill order.

As iPhone volumes scaled up, Apple took the number one spot in the supply chain rankings for the following seven years, until Gartner—which purchased O'Marah's research company—took Apple out of the competition by creating a sort of "hall of fame" so someone else could win for once.

As a former Apple manufacturing design engineer puts it: "The model we had developed was: We're going to use your factory. We're going to use your people. But we're going to go in there and use them as our arms and legs. You know, 'You do this, and you go do this,' and 'You set the dials here.'" This person adds: "There is no supplier out there where we could just send a package of drawings and a pack of specs and get what we wanted without lots of work on our side. It just didn't exist."

The combination of big spending and a design-first culture enabled Apple to come up with production techniques that others couldn't afford or even imagine. In October 2008, Apple launched a "unibody" MacBook Pro made from a single block of aluminum rather than multiple parts, a feat of industrial engineering that offered "a level of precision that is completely unheard of in this industry," Jony Ive said at the time. This was accomplished using a CNC machine, which allows designers to conjure into reality a 3D image file of complex parts. These machines had been around for decades but, costing between $100,000 and $500,000 each, were used only to build prototypes. Apple dumbfounded the industry when it purchased more than 10,000 CNC machines in a single year, enabling a form of mass production that Steve Jobs called "a whole new way of building notebooks." Apple even made a deal with FANUC, an automation group, to purchase its entire pipeline of CNC machines for years to come—shutting out all its competitors from access—and then scoured the globe for more. "There were not enough CNC machines in the world to do the machining that we needed to do," one person says. "You have to understand that starting in 2009 we were growing exponentially. We'd go from building 10,000 parts a day one year, to 100,000 the next, and then 500,000, and then a million . . . Money was no object, basically."

When Jobs unveiled the unibody MacBook during a famous "one more thing . . ." moment, it marked the first time he spoke about Apple's operational edge at a major event, showing off a video of how it was made, featuring Jony Ive, Dan Riccio, and Mac hardware chief Bob Mansfield. "It put MD on the map," says one person involved in the effort, referring to Manufacturing Design, a part of Ops that intimately works with suppliers to figure out how to make Apple products. "We knew we had changed the world, from a design perception."

O'Marah, by tearing open devices to examine the parts and going through Apple's detailed job listings, was uncovering the least understood part of what makes Apple successful. It wasn't that its artists designed great products and then employed capable factories in China to produce them at scale. Apple's engineers were deep in the weeds building, and even inventing, those capabilities. Apple was doing this on such a scale that it created an entire organization within Ops dedicated to the procurement, planning, and deployment of this capital-intensive machinery. Apple understood manufacturing better than the manufacturers themselves. And when Apple cocreated processes with a supplier, it was often Apple that owned the intellectual property rights. True, how to enforce such rights in China could prove tricky, but the combination of ironclad contracts and large-scale orders was often enough to keep suppliers in line for a specified period, after which they might be allowed to use their newfound skills.

New recruits to Apple from top universities were just as surprised as O'Marah. It wasn't uncommon for a newly minted engineer at Apple to fly to

China within days of getting the job—often for the first time in their life—and come back shocked at the level of labor intensity and the tight control the company wielded over dozens of factories. "You'd have eight hundred people on a line, from start to finish in a process. And that's just one line, of many, in facilities the size of football fields," says a former procurement executive, describing their first trip to China with Apple just after completing a postgraduate degree. "After I started, I called my family and was like, 'Oh my god, this is ridiculous! Apple doesn't do anything the way I learned it.'"

O'Marah recognized that Apple's strategy was brilliant. It accounted for why the company was running circles around the competition, turning revered companies like Nokia and BlackBerry into case studies of strategic failure. But it had one major flaw. Whereas smartphone rivals like Samsung could bolt a bunch of off-the-shelf components together and make a handset, Apple's strategy required it to become ever more wedded to the industrial clusters forming around its production. As more of that work took place in China, with no other nation developing the same skills, Apple was growing dependent on the very capabilities it had created.

The upshot was startling. The open architecture of the IBM PC in 1981 was a major catalyst for the globalization of the electronics industry. Companies on any continent could compete in the supply chain, a phenomenon captured by Thomas Friedman with his phrase "The world is flat." Twenty-six years later, the closed architecture of the iPhone was driving a different trend: the Chinafication of the electronics industry. The more Apple scaled, the more economic sense it made for all the components inside its products to be made within the country. Some of the key parts would still be provided by American, German, Korean, Taiwanese, and Japanese companies, but as the years passed all were incentivized to build those parts within the borders of the Middle Kingdom.

As O'Marah says of Apple's supply chain: "It's not really a global supply chain. In principle, it is; but in practice it's this totally engineered stack of process and product, engineering and production, and it's all synced up in one place." After thinking about this for another moment, he adds, "They're going to have a helluva time getting out of there."

PART FOUR

INSATIABLE DEMAND—THE iPHONE IN CHINA

CHAPTER 20

THE MISSIONARY

The thirteen-hour flight to Beijing was uncomfortable. John Ford had three seats to himself, a small blessing for his 275-pound frame, but physical discomfort wasn't the issue. It was the nagging sense of total impostor syndrome. It was November 2007, and he was just beginning to process the magnitude of all he'd just signed up for. He'd been tasked with opening Apple's first store in the world's most populous country. It'd been only a few weeks since he learned that the company didn't have a game plan. Somehow, *he* was the game plan.

Steve Jobs had once said of hiring people: "It doesn't make sense to hire smart people and tell them what to do; we hire smart people so they can tell us what to do." Now it was dawning on Ford that he was the living embodiment of this idea, and that made him anxious. Apple had given virtually no thought to its retail ambitions in China. It didn't have a business license to operate a store, wasn't sure how to pay taxes, and didn't know if profits could be sent back to the United States. Even if these details were sorted out, the plan felt destined to fail. The iPhone had only just launched in the United States and was technically illegal in China. Cupertino hadn't started negotiations with any of the major telecom carriers, and expectations were so low that nobody really cared, either.

As the plane descended, Ford felt a sense of dread looking out the left-side window, unable to see the ground because of all the smog. In a few months, Ford's wife and their three school-age children would join him, but for now he was arriving alone in a city of 16 million people. There wasn't even a colleague to greet him at the airport.

The Brawn

When Ford was a six-three teenager he could bench-press 250 pounds and squat more than 600. With calves like tree trunks, he was a starting offensive lineman in all four years of high school. But lurking inside his beefy frame was an inquisitive mind more suited for hobnobbing with nerds. He'd grown up in a Mormon household with three older brothers. Their father served four tours in the US Air Force and then became a project lead for the B-1 bomber, an aircraft capable of delivering nuclear munitions at supersonic speed. Ford describes his dad as "a guy who excelled at everything," and he pushed his sons to travel and appreciate the world. John had grown up in nine cities across the country before attending high school in Lancaster, California. His best friend was a geeky girl with a pet rat, who became valedictorian. Her father was born in China but had embraced American culture so thoroughly that he named her Marlena, after a fictional scientist in a 1967 episode of *Star Trek*. Marlena and John hung out all the time, earning the nicknames "the Brain and the Brawn."

Upon graduating from high school, Ford played a year of junior college football but grew eager to dispel the notion that he was just some jock. His brothers all pursued missions abroad, in Uruguay, Chile, and England. Nineteen-year-old John chose to bring the Church of Jesus Christ of Latter-day Saints to Taiwan. He hoped that would give him the chance to learn Chinese and earn an intellectual edge over Marlena. Not speaking a word of the language upon his arrival, he pledged to advance his learning by avoiding English altogether. He took his classes seriously and socialized frequently, unashamed of his errors. He learned to read around 1,000 Chinese characters—not enough to master the written language, but missionaries persuade people in conversation, not in letters. He became charmed by foreign norms and developed a knack for understanding how other cultures thought about the world. He found himself intrigued by Taiwanese perceptions of wealth, which led, for example, to people owning nice watches and expensive cars but living in less-than-desirable homes. Outward appearances mattered greatly, he learned, but in Taiwan there wasn't a culture of having people over for dinner, so one's house decor didn't matter so much. As his father had hoped, language and travel were opening his son's mental world. "In roughly six months I was conversationally fluent," Ford recounts. "Within two years I could have discussions with Buddhist priests about the meaning of life." When the Brawn returned home to Lancaster, he could now visit the Brain and speak fluently to her father in Chinese—gleefully, since Marlena couldn't understand. "I always thought that was fun," he recalls with a laugh. "I tell people I learned Chinese out of spite."

After another year playing football at junior college, Ford earned a sports scholarship to Portland State. Then, in his sophomore year, an unexpected opportunity arose when Kathie Lee Gifford, the warm and sometimes wacky celebrity morning show host, burst into tears on live TV. It was May 1, 1996, and Gifford had been cast in the role of pariah. A labor activist had alleged that her clothing brand employed thirteen-year-olds in Honduras, often working in extreme heat and for up to twenty hours a day. The media storm frightened companies into better understanding their global supply chains, and Ford—thanks to his language skills— was offered a month-long trip to China. He jumped at the opportunity, then postponed his studies, stayed in China, and became a pioneer in social compliance auditing.

His role wasn't just translating language; he got to interpret culture for wealthy executives and travel well beyond the usual tourist meccas. All his previous conversations about culture were suddenly relevant. Repeatedly he'd find himself explaining different modes of thinking to frustrated Western clients. "We Americans have a phrase, 'Fool me once, shame on you; fool me twice, shame on me,'" he'd tell his clients. "The Chinese version of that is a little different. The general explanation of it is, 'If I cheat you and you don't catch me, it's your fault.'"

The concept of saving face was one he'd constantly clarify. Sometimes Americans would think of Chinese people as bad drivers because if they were cut off, the offending motorist could seem oblivious of the whole situation. "We're just misunderstanding the way that they think about driving," he says. "If I look at you and apologize for cutting you off, I lose face—I've acknowledged my error. The best way to avoid losing face is to not acknowledge the error. So if I cut you off in traffic, I just don't look at you."

After a year he came to recognize the unique value he offered. The consultancy he worked for was earning more than $2,000 a day from his services, but he was getting only $300. At just twenty-three and without a college degree, he launched his own firm. Pretty soon he'd hired ten employees, expanded beyond China, and was traveling the world. In 2000, the dotcom crash curtailed the business. But whatever, he was young, had learned a ton, and missed home. He sold his company and returned to studying in Portland.

Missionary Skills

After years of running his own business, Ford found earning a degree in marketing something of a bore. He got a side hustle at CompUSA, the electronics retailer that Steve Jobs had inked a deal with in 1997 to create a "store within a store." Ford took care of the Mac section for a manager who hated Apple, and as the iMac took off, the Apple section ended up supporting the whole store. Someone from Cupertino took notice of Ford's leadership, and the month he graduated from Portland State he was hired by Apple to help build the brand inside other retail stores.

Ford's father wasn't impressed. Two years earlier, John had been a CEO, leveraging his Mandarin and traveling the world. Now he was working at malls in Albuquerque—the only Apple employee in New Mexico—and his wage was $13 an hour. But he loved it. He was good at sales and could earn commission. Once again, someone in Cupertino took note. Soon he was hired as an assistant manager in Denver, where he quickly became a leader in teaching others how to engage with customers. "I use missionary skills," Ford says, "building relationships of trust with people just by being honest and trying to share with people something fun and factual. Open their minds up. Help them see value in what you're selling them."

Ford was promoted to store leader in Salt Lake City, where the culture was broken. He began by interviewing all the employees, then informing them that he was setting a new direction that would accept nothing but excellence. "About 70 percent quit within a week, and I was hated by everybody," Ford says. But a month later, employees were reporting that they liked the job a lot more. "Yeah," he told them, "because all the people who don't care aren't here anymore."

"Nihau!"

At an annual store leader conference in October 2007, John Ford's ears perked up. In one of the briefings someone had mentioned that a real estate developer had approached Cupertino, unbidden, with an offer: a prime two-story location at a new mall under construction in the Sanlitun subdistrict of Beijing. Apple had been told that if it secured the deal immediately, it could open the country's first Apple Store on the eve of the Summer Olympics. The Communist Party was spending lavishly to welcome nearly 11,000 athletes, turning the spectacle into a capstone of its opening to the world a quarter of a century earlier.

It was an intriguing opportunity to build brand awareness in a country where there was none. Just a few years earlier in 2004, the first full-time Operations employee in the country, Ying Liu, drove up to a factory entrance and told the security guard she worked for Apple. The guard asked her to open the trunk of her car. "After opening it, I asked him why," she says. "He said he wanted to see what kind of apples I brought into the factory." If brand recognition had changed much, it wasn't showing up in the numbers. So few people could afford Mac products that Apple's share of the China computer market in 2007 was less than

0.5 percent. “We weren’t even a rounding error on the computer front,” says a former Apple executive.

The few buyers who existed made their purchases at IT malls, vibrant tech hubs where customers could view the latest gadgets and haggle for discounts. Inquiring about the Mac was rare enough that it could get you escorted up the stairs and sat down for a drink. There, customers would be offered a deal packed with pirated software, including Adobe Creative Suite and Microsoft Office. “The Macs were literally on, but in shrink wrap so you couldn’t touch them,” the Apple exec says. Online banking was just beginning to take hold, but the services didn’t work on the Mac, so the IT malls would wipe the operating system and install Windows.

Apple hadn’t really been considering an expansion into China. The iPod had been a global sensation for several years, yet Apple hadn’t released a Chinese version of iTunes or launched an online store to sell its hardware to China. Total revenue in the country was less than $300 million, a blip. Besides, the Apple Store was largely an American phenomenon: By the time the first foreign store opened—in Tokyo, November 2003—there were more than seventy locations in America. Expansion was happening slowly. Apple Store hadn’t been launched in upscale Hong Kong, Paris, or Berlin, let alone a developing country with depressed wages.

But the offer was enticing. Chinese malls typically catered to the ultra-luxury class or to the bargain basement, whereas Sanlitun Village aimed at the middle and upper tier—the fastest-growing demographic, approaching 300 million people. The Apple Store team, led by Ron Johnson, didn’t believe high-priced Mac products would sell in big numbers, but the Olympics were a marketing opportunity for a global audience. The size of the proposed store was modest. But this, Apple’s team reckoned, was an advantage. A small footprint would contain costs for a project that was likely to lose money for years.

It was a few months after the deal was signed that Ford heard of the plans at the store leader conference. He raised his hand to get the attention of a recruiter in the room. “I speak Mandarin fluently,” Ford told him. “I’d love to help.” His thinking was humble. *I could be the big white guy who stands and speaks Chinese to people.* He was envisioning a role akin to a Walmart greeter in the United States, but he'd be able to start with a warm "Nihau!" His timing was opportune. The project's focus to date had been construction—importing glass from Germany, steel from Japan, granite stone from Italy, and hiring builders to bring Apple's iconic look to China.

Despite Apple's growing operational presence in the region, it barely had a team on the ground for selling goods. Its channel business—a marketing division in Beijing that did a bit of advertising and supported third-party sales and the education market—went back to 1993, but "every time they put somebody in China, they'd fire him within a couple of years for corruption," a former Apple executive says. In 2006 Apple had appointed the Singapore-based head of Asia-Pacific, Brian Lu, to run the China team. Colleagues liked Lu but also wondered, in the years ahead, how he'd attained such a high position. Lu was "an honest guy" but "hugely mediocre" and "terrified of being fired because everybody else before had been fired," this executive says. Lu was known as a curmudgeon who lacked the temperament to establish a distinct culture among his employees. He accepted the problems holding Apple back, instead of challenging them, and he was unduly deferential to the IT malls and government bureaucrats. "You needed the carrot and the stick," this executive says. "Lu didn't have enough of either to really drive things."

Apple's retail team knew it would take effort to find a skilled person to lead China sales. If they hired a local, they might need time to fly the person over to Cupertino and gain the trust of top executives. So, within an hour of raising his hand, Ford was introduced to Steve Cano, the senior director of Apple Retail Worldwide. Cano was an enthusiastic Californian with an athletic build and the demeanor of a Boy Scout. Like Ford, he got his start at CompUSA, before overseeing the October 2001 launch of Apple Store in Palo Alto—the outlet closest to Steve Jobs's home. Then he opened the New York flagship venue in July 2002, followed by Tokyo the next year.

Cano quizzed Ford and had a Chinese friend call him up to test his Mandarin. Over the coming weeks Ford fielded a bunch of calls, oblivious to what leadership was thinking. It was an awful lot of questions for the temporary greeting role that he imagined. Cano had come to see Ford as much more than a Chinese speaker with a grasp of Apple culture; he saw a crafty self-starter, someone who could overcome challenges on the fly with little infrastructure. Ford didn't know those skills were needed, but Cano did, and in November he dropped the bombshell: Apple needed a permanent head for the Apple Store in China, and they wanted him for the role. "How early can you go?"

This was the conversation when Ford realized just how much work awaited him. "We don't have anything," Cano told him. "You've got to figure everything out. You've got to figure out the whole operating process. We don't really have anyone on the ground. We have a small marketing group there that works for Apple, but they're a different entity than you. You'll have to go set the entity up. You'll have to figure all these things out."

Apple was accustomed to setting the bar high, on tight deadlines. But it accomplished these feats by hiring individuals it considered the best in the world. Around the same time, Steve Jobs needed a head of graphics, as Apple sought to design its own chips for next-generation iPhones. He'd narrowed his sights to Bob Drebin, a former Pixar engineer who'd done pioneering work for Nintendo and been the graphics technology chief at AMD, a chip designer. When Jobs heard he'd entered early retirement, he called him up with a job offer. Drebin demurred, saying he wanted a year to spend time with family and focus on hobbies like sports photography. "Okay," Jobs said, hanging up the phone. Three hundred and sixty-five days later, Drebin's phone rang. "So, you ready?" Jobs asked. Drebin accepted.

Apple's retail leaders were of the same ilk. The head of the Apple Store, Ron Johnson, was a fifteen-year veteran of Target credited with making the discount behemoth so distinctive that customers would jokingly pronounce it *tar-zhay*. Ford wasn't sure he fit the pattern of these high performers. "I really think that if Steve Cano had known the potential of China, I wouldn't have been the guy they sent over," he says. "It would have been an army of people going over, to figure out this opportunity. But they perceived it as a marketing opportunity with the Olympics. And that was it."

CHAPTER 21

THE SEWING MACHINE REPAIR SHOP

On one of his first big tasks in late 2007, John Ford proved Steve Cano's instincts right. Ford needed to obtain a license for the yet-to-be-built store in Beijing. But the laws, he found, contained a catch-22: You couldn't get a license without having a store, and you couldn't open a store without a license. Ford surmised the rule was created at the behest of bigger businesses to stymie competition. Or maybe it was supposed to be overcome by giving the right official a red envelope stuffed with cash. The truth of its origins didn't really matter; what mattered was addressing the rule without resorting to bribery.

Going through official channels, Apple would've been encouraged to form a partnership with a local business, or it could have received a license that limited its sales and distribution. Instead, Ford and a lawyer from Apple's channel business came up with a clever idea: Why not just acquire an electronics retailer, amend the name, and use that license? At first they were on the hunt for a large, respectable retailer, but one day Ford was out walking and randomly came across a cluttered store full of equipment. He looked closer. "There were just sewing machines everywhere: dusty, dirty, filthy; like a small mechanic shop," Ford says. "It was tiny. Ten square meters would be exaggerating—it was probably five." Sewing machines have chips in them, so technically they were electronics. And the store was in the same district as the mall, so the license could be transferred.

The store owner must have thought Ford was nutty. "I just walked in, started a conversation, and asked, 'If you wanted to sell your business, what would it take?'" He lightly interrogated the owner with niche questions about the license. Ford couldn't tell if the owner was brushing him off or just didn't understand. After a few minutes, he politely left. But he told Apple's channel business about the possibility, and within a few days they were back in the store to clinch the deal. They didn't reveal they were working for Apple, an admission that surely would have pushed the price higher. The owner agreed to sell for around $300,000, a life-altering sum. Within a few weeks the transaction was done: The license for a family-owned sewing machine repair shop became the legal basis Apple used to establish a multibillion-dollar retail presence that, by 2024, would include fifty-six physical stores and an enormous online outlet.

But first a dilemma emerged. How should the store be named? Cupertino didn't have a clear answer. Was the brand Apple or Pingguo, the name of the fruit in Mandarin? Ford presumed it should be Apple, but the answer wasn't obvious. Apple's local operations team, established around 2000, and the small corporate marketing group established in 1993, had both used Pingguo. Colleagues from these departments thought the English name might be insulting, whereas Ford assumed it was part of the appeal, especially when selling iPods to a new generation of go-their-own-way youth who venerated the American Dream. Looking to Japan wasn't much help; there the company was known as Appuru, a direct phonetic translation.

Ford sought guidance from Ian Duffy, head of Asia for IKEA. In China, Duffy had made the decision to brand the Swedish furniture retailer Yi Jia, which means "suitable home." Duffy told Ford this was his "biggest mistake," as it had deprived the company of its strong global image. Ford followed his advice. So amid the Chinese legalese on the store license, English characters were used to spell out Apple. And as Ford built a local team, he taught all the Mandarin-speaking employees to use the English words Apple, iMac, and iPod. In turn, they influenced Apple's marketing group and the wider masses. The decision didn't feel major at the time, but, nearly two decades later, the weight of it pleases Ford. "It's nice to have influence over the way a billion people think," he says.

Grand Opening

The license was a major win, but it was only the first of many challenges. Even "importing" products to China was a hurdle. Of course, virtually all of Apple products were manufactured in the country, but they were assembled in special made-for-export, tax-free economic areas. Rigid laws kept Apple from simply driving a few trucks over to Foxconn, loading them up with iPods, and distributing them neatly onto store shelves. To sell products on the mainland, Apple routed them 2,700 miles south to Singapore, where an Apple logistics team purchased the products, got them certified for sale in China, and shipped them right back. This all made little sense, but attempts to change the rigmarole went nowhere for more than five years.

In the months leading to the opening, Ford interviewed more than 500 people to fill 96 roles. Entire days went by where all he accomplished was grilling a few dozen recruits with questions. He was struck by the generational divide between candidates. Those born after 1980 were the first Chinese cohort after Mao's death. They grew up in the "reform and opening up" era, when the country experienced transformative growth as hundreds of millions of people moved from the hinterlands to the coastal cities. They embraced once-forbidden ideas and could earn more each month in factory jobs than their parents had made in a year toiling in the fields. Anyone aged thirty-five and above, Ford says, had "a blinders-on mentality" to everything: Don't question, don't ask, just do what you're told. "It was really hard to teach them, as leaders, how to think about experiential retail," Ford says. "But my younger people, they were just sponges. They were open to new ideas, open to change, open to different ways of doing things, open to making their own decisions."

By June, weeks before the Olympics started, construction of the

Sanlitun mall was done and the store was fully staffed. Worried that his employees wouldn't be able to afford to eat at the high-end mall, Ford arranged for lunch stipends. He'd been working sixteen-hour days for months, flying in and out of the country five times before finding a place for his family to live. They'd gambled on this thing working out, but Ford had no idea if it would. His biggest fear was that when he opened the glass doors each morning, nobody would walk in.

One night before the grand opening, he was sitting with Ron Johnson, Jerry McDougal, and Carl Smit, all from Cupertino's retail team, wondering what might happen when the doors opened. "What do you think you'll be selling—$12 million a year, $15 million a year?" one asked. Ford struggled to give an answer, murmuring something unintelligible. His gut told him things would be fine. But that feeling of dread was back. He had no idea that the store would double that prediction within twelve months. And he certainly had no inkling that, just three years later, the Sanlitun store would sometimes surpass those annual targets in a week.

The Gray Market

A lucrative gray market serving Chinese iPhone customers began to emerge as early as the summer of 2007, a year before the Sanlitun store opened and just weeks after the biggest fans in America slept outside the Apple Store overnight to be the first buyers. Reports that September suggested that China's IT malls were selling units obtained from abroad. Starting prices were 8,800 yuan, or $1,170—more than double the $499 cost in the United States. Savvy entrepreneurs had sensed an opportunity: they'd buy multiple phones in America, then smuggle them into China for a nice markup. As long as the phone came with a receipt from the Apple Store and remained sealed in the box, they had no problem finding buyers. The average hourly wage of an urban worker in China was around $2, so the resale of a single iPhone could earn someone a month's salary. "You could fly to the US, buy twenty iPhones, come back, and be an incredibly rich person," says a former Apple executive.

The three Apple Stores in Oregon, a West Coast state with zero sales tax, emerged as a popular location to buy as many phones as possible and then fly them to the country. When the iPhone 3G came out in July 2008, Apple broadened distribution and included Apple premium resellers in Hong Kong. It, too, lacked a sales tax, and so rivaled Portland as a go-to location for securing product for the China gray market.

Those sales, though, were barely on Cupertino's radar. In 2008, Apple had categorized China as a "third priority" market, one step below "priority two" countries such as Argentina and Uruguay. Cupertino thought the iPhone would be an object of desire, but not one to purchase. China's economy might've been booming, causing wages to double in the previous four years, but urban wages were around RMB 2,500 a month ($370)—not enough for a big market to take hold. Or so it seemed. Like numerous other Western companies, Apple was only interested in the high end of the market. The iPhone was so expensive even within the United States that Microsoft CEO Steve Ballmer infamously mocked its chances for success. In the much poorer country of China, Apple had sufficient reason to believe it would garner few purchases, and it made no effort whatsoever to broaden its appeal with lower prices.

Steve Jobs had been adamant that margins be maintained abroad, so for all international markets Apple would take the US price of its product, convert it one-to-one to another currency, and add other expenses such as value-added taxes and import fees. Sometimes the company would add in a few percentage points of "buffer" to account for currency fluctuations. Finally, Apple would round up to the nearest "nice price," like anything ending in 88, a lucky number in China. So an iPod retailing for $499 in the United States was priced at RMB 4,988, or $647—30 percent higher.

From 2007 through the summer of 2010, the gray market was disorganized and relatively small. It wasn't just that supplies were limited; demand was, too. Apple lacked any relationship with local telecom partners until late 2009, so the gray market phones weren't properly set up and often suffered from glitches. They couldn't always receive calls, and the voicemail feature didn't work. Even when Apple officially launched the iPhone 3GS with China Unicom on October 30, 2009, sales were okay but nothing spectacular. To comply with government standards, Apple had built custom iPhones lacking Wi-Fi so Beijing could push a short-lived alternative called WAPI. The day of the China launch—some four months after the 3GS hit shelves in the United States—*The Wall Street Journal* accurately suggested consumers were "anything but excited." A 32GB model went for 6,999 yuan, or $1,024, about three times the price of an average smartphone in China. The IT malls clamored to get Wi-Fi-enabled Apple products from abroad, but smuggling them en masse carried the risk of being arrested and, perhaps worse, having the expensive products confiscated. More common was that Chinese consumers traveling abroad for other reasons would pick up a few iPhones to carry back in their luggage. It was all pretty informal.

iPad Fervor

When massive crowds of people began to form outside of the Apple Store in Sanlitun on September 17, 2010, employees were confounded. They'd never seen so many people outside the glass walls before. Hundreds of people showed up in the wee hours for the chance to buy an iPad, a tablet that hit US shelves in early April and was only now coming to China. Steve Jobs had portrayed the device as a new product category—something between a smartphone and a laptop; the ultimate leisure device for browsing magazines, videos, and photos—and early sales indicated it might prove more popular than the iPhone. Before the store opened, Apple staff in their blue T-shirts counted down the final ten seconds, then high-fived the first entrants and applauded buyers as they left the store. To compare the crowd's enthusiasm to religious fervor might understate the scene. The first buyer had camped out for sixty hours and sported a custom-printed T-shirt that read "I BUY IPAD NO. 1." His friends hoisted him in the air as he exited the store, a tablet in each hand like Moses descending from Mount Sinai.

When new hardware launches, Apple tries to have two days' worth of demand at all its stores. The basis of the rule is essentially: *If you stand in line, you'll get the product.* But within five hours, inventory at Sanlitun was exhausted. The store had sold more than $3.7 million of iPads, all in cash, a worldwide record. When, a week later, the new iPhone 4 went on sale, the mismatch between supply and demand became even more stark. Despite the iPad bonanza, Cupertino felt it had little reason to expect so many people to show up for the new phone, so security was lax. Low sales of the prior model, the iPhone 3GS, coupled with the murkiness of the gray market, had clouded Apple's ability to forecast demand. In just a few days, Apple sold hundreds of thousands of the first Wi-Fi-equipped iPhones legally sold in China, clearing all inventory in the country.

The iPhone 4 had been unveiled three months earlier, in June, and it was a breakthrough design. Lead industrial designer Richard "Dickie" Howarth told colleagues he wanted it to feel smooth, like "it had been licked by thousands of kittens." Its deep black color, contrasted with a stainless steel frame, was made to look as if it'd been dropped from space. The first three iPhones had been copied mercilessly, all running Android and usually selling for lower prices. Collectively, Android devices would overtake iPhone by market share that year. Apple was under significant pressure to maintain its position as the lead innovator, justifying its higher prices. So the response by Cupertino was: "Let's make the next iPhone so damn difficult to copy that they'll go nuts or broke trying to copy it," says a manufacturing design engineer. The iPhone 4 was the first to use a custom chip designed by Apple, not Samsung; it was the first with a front-facing camera and to have a high-resolution retina display. And rather than cramming the antenna into the dense real estate inside, Rubén Caballero's RF team had found a way to house the antenna within the steel frame of the phone—an ingenious solution soon copied by the rest of the industry.

The first few days of iPhone sales in China had been great. But as news of massive demand for the new phone spread, a different sort of buyer began to fill up the lines: rural villagers and their shady scalper bosses. Unlike excited consumers, they were just there to make ends meet. The tension between them and genuine Apple fans escalated when scalpers started throwing their elbows around, bloodying the noses of others as crowds rushed the line. Ford had seen plenty of lines become unruly; so had the crowds. In a country of more than a billion people, it wasn't uncommon for a mass of people all trying to do the same thing to become rowdy. "In China, when there's a scarcity of product, you have to push to the front," Ford says. "If ever you try to buy a train ticket around Chinese New Year, you'll find that you have to shove your way to the ticket counter, throw your money up there, and hope that someone grabs your money and hands you a ticket."

Apple had some experience dealing with the gray market, but quite abruptly it became much larger and more organized. To restore order after fights broke out, the Sanlitun store shut down for a few hours. The fights and the closure made international headlines.

In hindsight, the unruly crowds in September 2010 hardly stand out. But at the time, it felt like a major failing. "We just lost control," Ford says. "We didn't have enough security. We didn't assume that people would be pushing to the front as much as they were. We didn't have crowd control outside, we didn't have good line maintenance. I think we had thirty to forty security people to manage the line outside." At future product launches, Apple would aim to have one guard per ten visitors, including plainclothed agents who kept an eye on poor behavior and prevented the otherwise inviting store from looking like a border crossing. As the lines swelled to thousands of people, hundreds of guards surreptitiously patrolled the lines to maintain a semblance of order. It sounded excessive, but it wasn't. Not at all.

CHAPTER 22

YELLOW COWS IN THE GRAY MARKET

John Ford wasn't certain the men he was speaking with were part of an organized crime syndicate, but it felt like a fair assumption. In part it was their bling, their uncharacteristic swagger, and the sovereignty they held over the thousands of people queuing up outside the Apple Store. These men wore gold chains around their necks, and some carried Louis Vuitton bags stuffed to their immaculately hemmed brims with 100-yuan notes—only around $15 each, but these were the highest denomination bills in China. The white-and-red notes featured the face of Chairman Mao looking into the distance, resolute and confident about China's socialist future. But thirty-four years after his death, in late 2010, these shady gangsters were orchestrating increasingly sophisticated schemes for the humble masses to purchase iPhones—pocket-size emblems of American capitalism—so they could sell them for marked-up prices around the country.

In Chinese these quasi-gangsters were known by the slang term *yellow cows,* referring to organized scalpers who find market inefficiencies and exploit them for profit. In the early 1990s, they established a lucrative trade in train tickets. As the economy boomed, authorities had been slow to expand rail car capacity. The yellow cows exacerbated the shortages by buying tickets in bulk at low fixed prices, then standing outside the stations hawking them for a small fortune. Some yellow cows went further, printing forgeries with special presses, paper-cutting machines, and reams of cardboard.

Within weeks of the iPhone 4 launch, the yellow cows had surmised that demand wasn't at all matched by supply. Apple was operating more than 300 stores globally by late 2010, but in Beijing, a city of nearly 20 million people, it ran just two stores. In Shanghai, whose population hovered near 23 million, it managed two more. In the absence of Apple Stores dotting the country, yellow cows took initiative and launched Apple's unofficial distribution arm to serve a billion customers.

Ford, at first unaware of how lucrative this trade was, experimented with a variety of tactics to get the resellers to go away. He tried requiring identification, or limiting sales to five per person, then two per person. In one instance he received approval to sell a scalper 2,000 iPhones, believing it would placate the man. The scalper readily complied—then showed up the next day for more. Ford was frustrated. The store sales were making him look good; the rowdiness of the lines wasn't. He started seeking answers, wondering what sort of deal might be possible so the scalpers would stop clogging the lines and allow ordinary consumers to experience the Apple Store and buy a product themselves.

The yellow cows' responses astonished him. "You could never run me out of cash," one told him. Ford wasn't convinced, but the reseller took him on a short walk, down a few blocks and around a corner, then past some informal security types. They entered a room, roughly 2,000 square feet in size, lacking furniture or anything else, save for one thing: renminbi. Piles of cash in neat stacks were at the ready to hand out to migrant workers so they could buy iPhones in the tens of thousands. No experience in the Mormon missionary's background had prepared him for this. Looking at the sea of renminbi before him, he estimated he was staring at a billion dollars. "I don't know what the number is for a room that size, but it was more money than I've ever seen in one space," Ford says. His estimate is, of course, imprecise. It could be wildly off. But as Apple's popularity grew, it wouldn't be uncommon for Ford and his team to spend hours counting a few million dollars' worth of renminbi from a single day of sales, in preparation for an armored truck to haul it off. (Soon, these trucks were showing up several times per day, as the back room of the Apple Store wouldn't suffice for the amount of cash coming in.)

The yellow cow told him: "You keep selling, and I'm going to be here buying until people don't want to buy it anymore." He then explained a bit about how his business worked. By hiring ordinary people in the hundreds to buy multiple iPhones each, his gang could amass the world's most iconic product by the thousands, then have the devices shipped to another major city where the gang would be the exclusive vendor. The opportunity was vast. America had only four cities with a population over two million; China had at least forty. Few Westerners at this time had heard of Chongqing in southwestern China, but in 2010, when *Wired* magazine called it "the fastest-growing urban center on Earth," the sprawling city's population had doubled to 32 million in under fifteen years. What that example pointed to was that a single reseller and his ragtag army of "bag ladies" could become the sole distributor in a metropolis the size of South Carolina with a population greater than Texas. Until Apple had its own stores in such cities, the Beijing resellers and their cash rooms weren't going anywhere.

The yellow cows filled the lines by advertising jobs in regional newspapers and busing in migrant workers. What emerged was a gig economy. The yellow cows paid hundreds of people to line up at China's four Apple Stores hours before they opened, offering each person around 100 yuan for every iPhone or iPad they could secure. Apple had stipulated that buyers must have a valid ID, but beyond that it couldn't pick and choose who it would allow in the store. Brady MacKay, a US special agent for the Drug Enforcement Administration living in China, recalls the "feverish pitch of the Chinese people" as thousands of consumers fought with each other in line. Apple staff, he says, used ropes and banisters to section off people and keep things orderly. "It was almost riotous, and John's trying to keep a lid on this, trying to keep control of the masses, the crowds, the cheating, the dishonesty, and yet still selling the product," MacKay says. "People would walk out with two new phones—they'd get mobbed. There'd be buses and people being dropped off to wait in line to buy their two phones. It was just an unbelievable circus."

Speaking to Cupertino, Ford struggled to convey just how powerful the demand was. One time, when he told an Apple executive visiting Beijing that he needed such and such number of iPhones, the executive looked incredulous. "You're asking for a quarter of the entire planet's supply of iPhones!" Ford looked back at the executive. "Yes! Welcome to China!"

Massive Growing Pains

In theory, there were plenty of places in China to buy an iPhone. In addition to Apple's four official stores, Cupertino had expanded the number of authorized third-party dealers by 800 in the first three months of 2010, bringing the total to 2,000. China Unicom, Apple's only telecom partner at the time, alone had more than 100 outlets scattered around the country. In practice, though, this wasn't much help. Some stores were allocated no more than a few dozen iPhones, and given the demand, it was easy for anyone with iPhone inventory to make good money selling them on the side. Apple executives weren't sure any of the phones meant for China Unicom were being sold at the prices they'd set.

China Unicom had demanded more iPhones, but they must have overlooked an important clause buried more than ninety pages into its contract. What the legalese made clear is that Apple's four official stores had priority in terms of price, volumes, and timely allocation. Plus, iPhones purchased from Apple were contract-free, whereas Unicom required a two-year sign-up. Also disadvantaging the telecom was that, in a market rife with counterfeit products, people wanted to buy iPhones directly from Apple.

Throughout October 2010, sales at the four Apple Stores were overwhelming. At times, the Sanlitun store was processing fifteen iPad sales per minute—a pace not even physically possible in a normal Apple Store. But this wasn't normal. The yellow cows were so attuned to the rules that the people they paid to stand in line would each carry the same wad of cash in hand. Apple employees responded by having iPads at the ready—in whatever quantity they deemed the limit—plus the exact change precounted. "We had money counters on the top to double-check. We'd hand customers their change, hand them their units, and they're out the door," Ford says.

The Sanlitun store employees were selling Apple products with the same conveyor-belt logic, efficiency, and monotony of their comrades 1,300 miles south in Shenzhen, who'd assembled and packaged the same units just days earlier at Foxconn. Demand was so great that Apple closed the Genius Bar just to make room for cash registers, and at peak hours there were thirty registers running at once, each processing a transaction every two minutes. "Nobody had seen that kind of volume in retail before," says another Apple executive. "It just happened. There were massive growing pains."

In the days and weeks that followed, the four Apple Stores would receive more inventory, but again and again they were outflanked by the yellow cows. The resellers were becoming more organized and sophisticated. Some of the yellow cows in command of the groups had the capital to buy hundreds of phones each day. They'd be "waiting outside our stores with suitcases to put all of the phones in, to take to IT malls," an Apple executive says.

Apple had hoped to quell demand with the October 2010 launch of the online store, but that channel broke down, too. The resellers viewed the online store as either a threat to their business or an opportunity to get more product, so they found ways to capture all the inventory and book up all the reservations. Apple responded by limiting advance reservations to just one day and strengthening its ID verification processes. "But within twenty-four hours they'd hack into our system, and they'd either deny service—so that nobody could get an appointment—or they'd take all the appointments," a former Apple executive says.

Apple's coding team struggled to understand how the resellers were operating so quickly. They assumed bots were booking the appointments, so they installed CAPTCHA systems to weed them out. That didn't work. They sought the help of Ticketmaster to review Apple's systems and see if there were better ways of keeping the resellers out, but Ticketmaster determined the systems in place were fine. They were just being outnumbered. Even years later, Apple executives recounting the episode would repeatedly say that their systems were "hacked"—but they were using the term imprecisely. There was no actual security breach; the resellers had just paid throngs of people to flood the website. Just as Apple, in the factories of China, had determined that masses of low-wage labor could often perform more efficiently than expensive machines, the resellers had learned that hordes of people were more effective than bots.

Back in Cupertino, the teams tasked with allocating global supply would meet with others forecasting demand in China. Together, they could do little more than guess. It wasn't appropriate to present to top executives estimates based on hunches, but if they relied on the usual evidence-based reasoning—per capita income and the like—the projections would be wildly off. "It was pulling numbers out of your ass—no matter what you did," says one person involved. Another says they'd look at sales in the prior year, then assume a double-digit growth number that sounded impressive. "But it was never high enough. We were always wrong," they added. The next year they'd double the estimate, cross their fingers that they weren't over-projecting by half, then discover that they'd been far too cautious. "My friends were always asking, 'Is it a marketing strategy to keep demand low?'" says one executive. "But it wasn't a strategy. We just got it wrong all the time."

Apple commissioned a series of customer interviews to better understand the Chinese consumer. The results contained some insight into the power of the Apple brand: a fifth of respondents had been to the Apple Store more than ten times; two-fifths were "very likely" to buy an iPhone, and even more indicated a desire to buy a Mac. But overall the study just underscored how elusive the whole forecasting project was. For starters, Cupertino learned that metrics such as median income were useless, even misleading, in a country of more than a billion people. Statistics were sometimes based on average incomes nationally, giving undue weight to the hundreds of millions of people living in the hinterlands. But even when Apple looked at Beijing-specific incomes, the projection math didn't add up.

To be more precise, Apple ran in-store interviews to ask customers directly about their wages, but to no avail. The average reported incomes were lower than Apple anticipated, but somehow this had no significance in terms of sales. In one instance a post office worker had used 30 percent of his entire annual salary to buy an iPhone. "When people see me with the iPhone," he told Apple researchers, "I'm not just a mailman."

Status Symbol

Demand for the iPhone in China stunned executives in Cupertino. After revenues in Greater China shot up by four times to $2.6 billion in the holiday quarter of 2010, Tim Cook called the growth "absolutely staggering." It's hard to fault Apple for not predicting the demand, since throughout much of the 2000s the opposite error was far more common. In the absence of solid market research, multinational executives would spend time only in top-tier cities like Shanghai and Beijing, then wrongly apply their impressions to more than a billion consumers who had much lower incomes, different tastes, and more basic needs. Stories abound of Western companies forced to rein in lofty expectations after it emerged there was little demand for their product outside of the top markets. But for Apple, *status symbol* hardly begins to describe what the iPhone meant to a generation of people abruptly able to participate in a market economy.

China's urban population had grown from less than 20 percent in 1980 to more than 50 percent by 2012. As hundreds of millions of people were lifted from poverty, many wanted to show it. The ultra-rich purchased $12,000 Louis Vuitton purses or drove around town in BMWs, but for the burgeoning middle class, the iPhone was both accessible and conspicuous. Brady MacKay, the US special agent who was working on the US ambassador's team as attaché, stresses that in just a single generation China had gone from a time "when chairman Mao and the Communist Party would purge you for being a private entrepreneur, and you could end up in a gulag, [to a time when] everybody's making money, including the senior party leadership, living a lifestyle that they couldn't even imagine two decades earlier."

MacKay had first visited China as a nineteen-year-old in 1979 and attended university there in the 1980s. When he was a student, he says, everyone dressed in proletariat blue or People's Liberation Army green. "There were no private cars, very few private restaurants. If they had ten items on the menu, they may have actually had two in the restaurant." So when people in China started to make money, he says, "they really didn't know how to display it, how to control it. And Apple," he goes on, "was in the middle of that. Not only were they manufacturing there, but they were selling this product on a retail level that was in such high demand. And it was every time Apple launched something. It was what the Chinese with money wanted. Because it was a symbol. It wasn't even the phone—it was the *symbol* of the phone." MacKay tries to think of a Western analogy that might convey the feeling but can't. "You'd have to go back to the 1880s, when the first cars came out," he says. "It'd be like being one of the first people with a car instead of a riding a horse on a muddy stream."

Thousands of people who couldn't afford iPhones found ways to buy them anyway. *China Daily* reported that a study of college students in Wuhan found that 20,000 had taken out loans with twelve-month interest rates as high as 47 percent to buy "fancy electronic products," 90 percent of which were Apple. Perhaps the most widely publicized incident was that of a seventeen-year-old who underwent black market surgery to sell his kidney in exchange for enough cash to buy a new iPhone and an iPad.

The gray market became lucrative enough that some smugglers

carried out ambitious plans ranging from the loony to the ingenious. In one case, six men used a crane to lift tote bags stuffed with iPhones and iPads, then sent the bags down a zip line from an apartment complex in Hong Kong and across the border into Shenzhen. In countless other instances, smugglers were caught "wearing" tens of thousands of dollars' worth of iPhones. Sometimes the units were strapped to their bodies; other times the smugglers placed dozens of them into custom pockets knit into their shirts. A Chinese housewife was once caught with sixty-five iPhones strapped around her waist. She'd stuffed at least twenty more in a handbag.

Demand for iPhones became so normalized that, at the official stores, Ford established relationships with the resellers, replete with unwritten rules and a system of wordless dialogue. It was too difficult to discipline the individuals paid to be in line. They were generally poor, only standing for hours because their commission could outweigh a week's worth of factory work. MacKay recalls watching Ford stand at the entrance, a solitary figure of authority before 3,000 people, maintaining order with his gaze and a flicker of the hand. If he gently raised one finger, it signaled "one mistake"—a warning that the crowds had become unruly. Someone might have butted ahead in line, yelled too much, or thrown an elbow. In the event of two mistakes, he raised two fingers, then closed the entrance and stopped selling for fifteen minutes. If Ford had to raise three fingers, the store would close for an hour. But that was rare. "Because every time I stopped selling, they stopped making money," Ford explains. "They were just buying the product to flip it. All they wanted was the volume throughput."

The simple system worked well—until it didn't. The next major incident was so bad it ended with photographs of a bloodied man on the ground, unverified reports of an Apple employee beating a customer with a metal rod, and Ford's being led away in handcuffs. Worse, it was caught on videotape, and the video was sent to Steve Jobs.

CHAPTER 23

"FIRE THAT MOTHERFUCKER!"

Steve Jobs was rarely happy when he called, but seldom was he *this* angry. When the phone rang, Ron Johnson, the senior vice president in charge of Apple Retail, had already been reading the negative headlines emerging from China. A day earlier, on Friday, May 6, 2011, Apple's China outlets had started selling the iPad 2, and the effect was like pouring fuel on a fire. Lines outside the Apple Stores were already more chaotic than usual, owing to the prior week's release of an all-white iPhone 4. Now reports from China suggested that an altercation had broken out involving an Apple employee at the Sanlitun store. Apple had locked the store doors in response, heightening the tension and causing the likes of CNN to pick up the story. The incident, captured by Apple's security cameras, was sent to Jobs. In the grainy video, without sound, a young Chinese consumer got in the face of a tall American employee—a beefy guy wearing a blue Apple T-shirt—and the employee responded by shoving him to the ground. The young Chinese man writhed in pain, remaining on his backside and twitching. Chaos ensued as security forces defended the Apple employee and got him to safety, out of frame. Jobs seethed as he watched the video. He called up Johnson and delivered three choice words: "Fire that motherfucker!"

Three months earlier, the Apple CEO had introduced the new iPad, a presentation that left many commenting on how emaciated Jobs looked.

He'd been diagnosed with cancer in 2003 and underwent major surgery the next year. It was believed to have been successful, but the cancer returned in 2008 and Jobs took a second medical leave to undergo a liver transplant. He took a *third* medical leave in early 2011, during which time he lost considerable weight from a reduced appetite. His presence at the iPad 2 "special event" was unexpected and garnered much applause.

Frailty aside, Jobs delivered a compelling presentation, explaining how the original iPad had sold 15 million units in its first nine months—a faster start than the iPhone and more units than the entire tablet PC market had ever sold, he said. Executives had eagerly looked forward to the iPad 2 launch in China. Now that weekend had come and it was complete turmoil.

Johnson did his best to calm down Jobs. Not an easy task in any situation, and this one was especially fraught. He explained that the employee wasn't some random hire, it was Beijing store leader John Ford—the de facto general manager for all of China retail. Ford had brought his family over to China and had been working his ass off for Apple. But it was difficult to placate Jobs given the current situation: Ford had been arrested after the confrontation. Johnson didn't have all the details. He'd spoken only with his deputy, Steve Cano, who'd received an unwelcome call from Ford in jail. Although Ford had said not to worry, Cano was stressed. How could he not worry? A story from the Associated Press was being republished around the world, describing how "a fight broke out between an employee and a customer at an Apple store in China's capital city." A photograph accompanying the story was the stuff of PR nightmares: an injured young man lay on the ground; beside him, a sullen woman looked up toward the camera, her hands clasping tissue paper soaked in blood. A Chinese witness related that "a foreign" Apple employee had gotten into a scuffle with a local customer. Netizens took to Sina Weibo, a microblogging platform akin to Twitter, with wild allegations that the foreign employee had "beat one Chinese man with an iron rod."

The situation was fast-moving and complex. Ford, Cano learned, had been in touch with the office of the US ambassador to China, Jon

Huntsman Jr. The Apple Store in Beijing was closed for hours. Carolyn Wu, Apple's PR representative in China, was fielding calls and emails from international media. "The store team acted to protect themselves and our customers by closing the doors and preventing the group from entering," Wu told the AP. The closure only exacerbated the chaos. The hundreds of people standing in line were not Apple fanboys; they were resellers, and the store's closure robbed their ability to earn a week's worth of wages.

Mobs of angry migrants protested the closure by shaking the transparent doors so violently that they shattered. That, too, was photographed and distributed around the world. In the telephone game that followed, panic ensued. Some executives in Cupertino had begun to fear the worst. There were murmurings that the Communist Party had sent Apple's Beijing store leader to a gulag.

"China's Bloody Apple Brawl"

Had the security footage leaked, it almost certainly would've been John Ford's last day at Apple and his family's last week in China. But the video didn't leak. Reports that a foreign employee had beaten up a Chinese consumer circulated widely, but nobody worked out the details. Ford's name or position didn't make the newspapers even when, two days later, the *People's Daily* reported—wrongly, as it turns out—that the "beaten man" had been given 20,000 renminbi (about $3,000) to cover medical costs.

What really happened that day was less dramatic than what the grainy security video appeared to show. Ford had been walking among the crowds outside the Apple Store, speaking to people in Mandarin and trying to create a more relaxed atmosphere. At the back side of the glass building—far from the main entrance where the press was set up—a woman became aggressive, grabbing Ford's arm and digging in her fingernails as she begged to jump the queue. Ford maneuvered away from her, only to be confronted by a young man, who came inches from his face. To create some distance, Ford pushed him back. "The guy just collapsed," says an Apple retail manager who watched the video. The young man flailed to the ground dramatically, like a professional athlete knowing the referee was watching. "It was complete setup," says another witness to the video. The young man's performance became more emphatic on the ground as he bellowed in pain and quivered. A crowd of angry consumers descended on Ford, compelling his security guards to cut through the crowd, grab him, and usher him to safety. "The video didn't look good; the video looked awful," Ford acknowledges. "I barely touched the kid, but I'm a big guy, I'm not small. So I don't doubt that he got a shove, but he overplayed it."

With no media witnessing the exchange, it's unlikely the confrontation would have garnered much attention. But the shattered glass doors were proof that the rowdy crowds had become more raucous than ever before. Reports on some Chinese news websites said three or four customers were injured. One person told reporters he'd tried to avoid the drama, but that someone had thrown a bottle, creating a gash on his head. Newspapers clamored to cover the event. *The Week* headlined its story: "China's Bloody Apple Brawl." Others said the crowd had rioted, though the reality wasn't so intense: when the crowds shattered the door, they didn't yell with delight and try to break the next thing; they fell silent. They hadn't meant to break anything, and now they were worried they might be arrested by the district's police chief, Mr. Du, who was right there. Ford knew the incident would be deeply embarrassing to Mr. Du, whom he'd known for more than three years. "His only job is to keep the peace," Ford says. "I mean that literally: 'Don't cause waves in my community and my bosses won't fire me.' That's what the Chinese police system is built for."

How the police functioned was something Ford had taught his school-age children living in China at the time. "My kids learned at a young age: When a cop comes up and asks you to do something, check if he has a gun. If he doesn't, ignore him. If a cop comes up and he does have a gun, do whatever he says because that's an army policeman. But the non-army policemen have no power whatsoever."

When Ford's brother came to visit him in China, John would teach this same lesson in a more fun, slightly dangerous way. "My brother loved driving with me and my car in China, 'cause I could pull up next to a cop at a red light, then run the red light in front of him," he says. "My brother would laugh and say, 'How do you get away with that?' It was because the cop assumed that if I was doing it, I must be *able* to do it. If he pulled me over, he'd be risking getting fired by this powerful person who clearly knew he was powerful enough to pull around the red light right in front of him."

Ford recounts how, in one instance, a man came in with twenty-five government-issued IDs. Each featured the same headshot, but there were twenty-five different names. Apple had a limit of two iPhones per person, and the man asked to buy fifty iPhones. Ford was amused, but he wasn't going to sell the phones. The man surprised him by calling the police. His surprise deepened when Mr. Du came over, listened closely, and concluded: "Well, sell him fifteen phones." The response was ridiculous but not surprising—compromise was part of the culture. Ford protested: "Mr. Du, don't you care that he's got twenty-five fake IDs right here?" The policeman responded: "Well, how do I know they're fake?" Incredulous, Ford said because there are twenty-five different names for the same headshot. "Yes," Mr. Du said, "but one-on-one, I can't tell individually if each one is fake."

Ford realized he'd inadvertently placed Mr. Du in an awkward position. More than anything, the policeman's role was to keep a semblance of order. His actual authority was limited. If this scalper had twenty-five legit-looking fake IDs, he might be an important person with government or triad connections. If Mr. Du arrested him, he might wind up dead the next day. "I don't know if that's what he was thinking, but there was something, culturally, that was causing him to want to deflect," Ford says. "Keeping the peace to him meant, 'Let's just find a way to give him something so he goes away.'"

Understanding which officials had authority and which didn't had been very important in Ford's years running the Apple Store. In China, it was all too common for Ford to find himself in hot water for not placating authorities who expected special treatment. Government officials, for instance, would threaten the Apple Store with fines if Ford wouldn't give special discounts on iPhones. But Apple had an express policy not to offer bribes, nor would Ford personally allow it. At times the store was issued bogus penalty fees, but Ford refused to pay them. "I would just flat out say no," Ford recounts. "You have to play positional power as if you have it, even if you don't."

Dealing with the higher echelons of police required a much more gingerly approach. They didn't mess around. Their job was less to keep the peace than to instill fear and maintain order at any cost. One time, in 2010 at Apple's Pudong location in Shanghai—where consumers pass through a cylindrical glass entrance before heading down a spiral staircase—an enormous crowd of more than 7,000 scalpers got angry when Apple ran out of inventory. "Look, we have no more stock. There's nothing we can do," employees told the crowd of villagers bused in to purchase iPhones. Apple tried to close the store, but the villagers wouldn't let the security guards physically shut the doors. Some grew violent: one threw a stool at an employee; others made death threats. For hours, hundreds of security guards hired by Apple to maintain order couldn't get the enraged customers to leave; they were staging a sit-in and the local police were equally ineffectual in breaking it up. An armed division of police arrived on the scene, to no avail. Even the mayor of Pudong showed up and told them to vacate. But the villagers had a reason for being stubborn—some of the yellow cows paying them were linked to violent criminal organizations. The villagers were far more worried about retaliation from these bosses than about the police. The situation escalated until, after eleven p.m., central authorities in Beijing called in an elite special unit of police—100 guys wearing all black with expressionless faces that, according to a person present, handled security for senior members of the Chinese Communist Party. Another person present called them "the SWAT team."

This elite unit directed Apple store managers to cut the security cameras, cordon off the staff, and isolate the whole area. The black-clad cops told the villagers: "You're either going to leave voluntarily or leave in body bags." As the size of the crowd dwindled to under 1,500, a young female villager pulled out her smartphone to snap a photo. A member of the elite unit of enforcers knocked her on the floor, grabbed her by the scalp, and dragged her behind the Genius Bar. "They beat her pretty badly," says a person present. Fourteen years after the episode, he still has nightmares about it. "She was screaming in pain."

For the next forty-five minutes the other villagers were beaten one by one. Part of the tiled floor was left so bloodstained that Apple had to replace the stones. Employees present had their phones wiped. No record of the event exists. "It shows you how quickly the Chinese can brush everything under the carpet," says a person present. "It was like a mini–Tiananmen Square."

Few people understood China's police better than MacKay, the US special agent. "They are ruthless," he says. "They had surveillance teams on me 24/7 for the three years I was working there as the attaché. They would break into our homes and place bugs, get into our computers, play all the espionage games on us. They wouldn't even hide it. We'd go to church on Sunday, come back, and there's cigarette smoke throughout the house. And our computers have been accessed and, you know, all kinds of stuff—bugs in the house, cameras in the house. They were essentially saying, 'We can do what we want.'"

Ford had all this background knowledge on the day the glass doors shattered in Beijing and the media started reporting on his altercation with the young man. He realized what a major problem it could be as the story went viral. A foreign Apple Store employee pushing a Chinese man to the ground was the sort of event that could spark an international incident. None of this looked good for Mr. Du, with whom Ford had developed a trusted relationship. So Ford made two concessions. First, though the young man who'd been shoved to the ground had no medical bills to speak of, contrary to what *The People's Daily* reported, Ford agreed to give him several iPhones. Second, Ford offered to be arrested. "In case the story got bigger, Mr. Du needed protection from his people, because he needed to show that he did something," Ford says. "And the easiest thing he could show was that he'd put the big powerful American executive into his jail cell."

Uncertain how long it would take for the story to go through its media cycle, Ford stayed in jail for four days. The stunt, he says, "scared the crap out of my wife and a few other people." Conversations with Apple weren't exactly smooth. In Ford's mind, he'd preemptively de-escalated a chaotic situation and got the local authorities on his side. Here he was, just sitting in a room, hanging out, and making calls from his iPhone to inform his network of political connections not to worry if they read that he'd been arrested. But back in Cupertino, executives were losing trust.

China had abruptly emerged as the biggest market outside of the United States, and it seemed that Apple's de facto head of retail couldn't keep order. It didn't help matters that prior to the incident Ford hadn't spent a lot of time currying favor among the company's top executives. He just liked doing a good job and solving problems; he wasn't maneuvering to climb the corporate ladder and saw little reason to defend himself. When executives from Apple would visit China and see the challenges with the iPhone, they'd throw up their hands in anger and blame Ford. "They'd say, 'Well, John's just not organizing the store well enough,'" he recounts. "And I'm like, 'No, we have a supply chain problem. We don't have enough distribution points.'" Repeatedly, Ford would relay to his superiors of all the problems in China, only to receive basic advice such as "Why not just call the police?" The people he reported to just didn't understand China. As his frustration grew, the gap between how Ford experienced things on the ground and how Cupertino viewed them from abroad was widening.

This gap had been noticeable even in the first weeks of the Sanlitun store opening. In the final days of the Olympics, the home page for the iTunes app in the United States had prominently displayed an album called *Songs for Tibet,* a compilation of music and a fifteen-minute talk from the Dalai Lama. Apple didn't have a Chinese iTunes store, but the US version was frequently accessed by users in China. A day after the album went live and some American athletes in Beijing had downloaded it, the entire store of 8 million songs was blocked.

The disruptions went beyond ordinary consumers. The internet went down in Apple's corporate office and other services were shut down. Apple was caught off guard. It was an early instance of Cupertino's not really understanding local culture and sensitivities. It'd be one thing for Apple to choose free speech over sales in China, but that wasn't what happened. They were just oblivious, as in 1997 when the Think Different campaign included the Dalai Lama. "People in Cupertino weren't really thinking about China in '07, '08," Ford says. "They weren't even thinking of the implications of it until we started opening stores." He'd sent a message back to Cupertino: "This stuff will kill our business here if we're not careful."

CHAPTER 24

TWIN BETS—FOXCONN AND TSMC

The global financial crisis had a profound impact on Beijing's world view. Washington had for years been incentivizing China to be a member of the US-led global order rather than work outside of it or seek its overthrow. But the wars in Afghanistan and Iraq were twin quagmires, and by the autumn of 2008, it appeared Western capitalism itself was on the brink of collapse. When Vice Premier Wang Qishan had the chance to meet US Treasury Secretary Henry Paulson amid the economic downturn, Wang told him: "Hank, you were our teacher. But now our teacher does not seem so smart."

With the rest of the world in recession and China's exports plummeting, Beijing's leadership understood it could no longer rely on global demand to keep its factories humming; instead, it would build its way out of the slump. In 2009, it orchestrated a staggeringly large fiscal stimulus, directing state-controlled banks to issue $1.4 trillion of loans, with at least half devoted to infrastructure spending.

Never one to miss a chance to expand his empire, Terry Gou pounced. Apple was inexperienced with Chinese politics, but Gou was keyed in. Not only did he know what it took to build up entire factory towns, he also understood how to pit government officials against each other to extract major incentives. He knew that when a directive went out from Beijing, mayors and governors of different regions were eager to demonstrate their commitment. So Gou went looking to strike a deal. The biggest projects received the biggest incentives, and there was no bigger client than Apple.

"Terry has an intuition about how to get government incentives that is hard to rival," says a former Foxconn executive. "Nobody in the West can ever understand how China [attracts] so many factories. It's literally—you're given land. They'll build the infrastructure for you. If you expect the buildings, they'll build them for you. They'll help you with your interprovince migration. If there's not enough labor in the zone they want you to go on, they'll get you the people and they'll bear that cost." This person adds: "The caveat is: you better deliver on your export commitments."

Around early 2010, Apple chief operating officer Tim Cook arrived in Shenzhen to meet with Gou and discuss two major products: the iPhone 4, which featured a breakthrough design, and the first iPad. Both would hit markets that year. The two executives discussed numbers in detail, including the price of components, labor costs, and how many they should build. Gou listened to Cook intently, felt perplexed by his conservative outlook, and opted to make the biggest bet of his career.

"Terry basically said, 'This is sandbagging—your numbers are way off,'" says Alan Yeung, a former Foxconn official. "I think your numbers are going to be multiples of what you're presenting."

Cook, risk-averse by temperament, wasn't so sure. But prior to the meeting, Gou had already met with Apple engineers in China, who were feeding him details and forecasts that were more optimistic than the views in Cupertino. So Gou made a handshake deal on the spot. He offered to personally facilitate the necessary actions to establish mass production, in exchange for taking all the orders when—he believed—they inevitably emerged. "Foxconn is going to underwrite the investment," he told Cook. "I'll build two campuses with Chinese government partners, along with the provincial and central government. And when your volume is there, I'm going to build the products for you."

Harmonious Society

When *The Atlantic* journalist James Fallows reported from China in the late 2000s, it wasn't skylines or high-speed trains that startled him, but the sheer size of China's manufacturing hubs in Shenzhen and the broader Guangdong province. "From the major ports serving the area, Hong Kong and Shenzhen harbors, cargo ships left last year carrying the equivalent of more than 40 million of the standard 20-foot-long metal containers that end up on trucks or railroad cars," he wrote in the summer of 2007. "That's one per second, round the clock and year-round—and it's less than half of China's export total."

By 2010, the fishing villages in Shenzhen had transformed into a city more populous than New York City, replete with dazzling skyscrapers. The problem was that this building craze was not representative of the country. Wealth was concentrated in the coastal cities, but as Premier Wen Jiabao told a press conference in 2011, China remains "a developing country" with "a weak economic foundation," "uneven development," and 150 million people living below the poverty line. Beijing was worried about exacerbating inequality trends. The Chinese migrants moving to the coast were required to have a permit to work in the city. The Chinese Communist Party (CCP) encouraged this migration—it was critical to keep GDP growing by 10 percent a year—but officials were also anxious about the political ramifications. They were trying to be more methodical about the building of factories, wanting to slow down growth in overcooked top-tier cities and instead create higher-income jobs away from the coast.

In the CCP's five-year plan running through 2010, a central theme had been *building a "harmonious society"*—a phrase that, Fallows quipped, passed the lips of Chinese officials as often as "global war on terror" had been uttered by their American counterparts. The subtext was that as Beijing embarked on a spending spree to get through the global financial crisis, it wanted to invest in ways that were sustainable.

Beijing was worried that an economic downturn could have the greatest impact in the poorer areas, and who knows what the implications of that might be. "The Chinese government's greatest fear was revolution," says an Apple executive who traveled to China after the financial crisis. "It's still their greatest fear."

China was only entering its third decade of a transformative change. As economist Yi Wen puts it: "China compressed the roughly 150 to 200 (or even more) years of revolutionary economic changes experienced by England in 1700–1900 and the United States in 1760–1920 and Japan in 1850–1960 into one single generation." The industrial advances in the West had of course been remarkable, but for the Communist Party they were also ominous. England was in a near-constant state of war for the two centuries following the Industrial Revolution. America was involved in the slave trade and descended into a civil war that killed 2 percent of its population. Japanese society underwent great upheaval as it became an imperial power. The challenge for China was to replicate the successful growth of its industrial predecessors but avoid the social instability and misadventures. And it sought to achieve this balance within a novel political system characterized by one observer as having "no ancient wisdom [and] no followers."

Income growth in China's top-tier cities was exponential, and so were real estate prices. "Everything was just growing off the hook," observes the former Apple executive. "People were sending their daughters away to work in these factories, because in one year of work they could bring home a dowry that could sustain them for five or ten years in the small villages."

Churn

Terry Gou's bet exemplified his tenacity, ambition, and daring disposition. What made him such a good competitor was his ability to predict his clients' needs before his clients did. By the time Apple realized it needed to double production of some hit product, Foxconn would've already increased capacity by expanding its factory and moving the precision machinery into place. But more than that, the bet demonstrated Gou's political savvy. When the global financial crisis hit, big investors and entrepreneurs based in Taiwan and Hong Kong retreated from China, a natural response, as demand for goods from North America and Europe sputtered. Gou, by contrast, was willing to invest, and he did so in ways that aligned his political interests with Beijing's.

Indeed, what Gou was promising Cook was not simply factory capacity, but new campuses far from the coast. He pledged to build a compound for making iPhones in Zhengzhou, and another for building iPads in Chengdu, two emerging cities hundreds of miles from Shenzhen or Shanghai. There were, of course, selfish reasons for the move. Six Foxconn workers had attempted suicide in the first quarter of 2010; four died. One of the survivors, a seventeen-year-old, was a migrant worker responsible for spot inspections on the iPhone 4 production line, a job she took to help look after a brother who was born deaf. After a month of work, she hadn't received pay owing to a clerical error. Lonely and overwhelmed, she'd jumped from the fourth floor of a Foxconn factory. The impact caused her to become paralyzed from the waist down.

By the end of 2010, the number of attempted suicides rose to eighteen. Foxconn became a household name for all the wrong reasons, and Apple was accused of "iSlavery." Whatever his other skills, Terry Gou didn't exactly come out of this crisis looking like a media-savvy CEO. He installed nets all around the factories, to prevent workers from jumping to their deaths, and compelled workers to sign a pledge not to commit suicide. Describing his hopes for the new factories in Zhengzhou and Chengdu, Gou said that workers living inland and closer to their families would feel less anxiety. "There will be hospitals, there will be other facilities, there will be sources of entertainment," Gou said in September 2010. "And if people still decide to kill themselves, then no one can blame me."

There was also less competition in the interior. Shenzhen was a hotbed of innovation and rivalry in a way that Zhengzhou wasn't. Foxconn was looking for ways to lock in the Apple partnership while achieving lower costs and fewer responsibilities with migrant labor. Specifically, Gou was trying to focus on managing factories, not the dormitories, cafeterias, and hospitals he'd felt compelled to set up in the 1990s when China was vastly underdeveloped. Rather, he would enlist "local governments to build towns to house Hon Hai's staff and take over the social functions that the company has long kept in-house," according to *The Wall Street Journal,* which interviewed Gou for three hours in September 2010. "I told the Chengdu government: I'm investing $3.5 billion and we want you to invest $7 billion" to create a place for Hon Hai workers to live, he told the newspaper. Gou emphasized that the new factories would have a larger mix of older workers who could mentor and comfort the young.

At times Gou was apt to frame the shift as being less about his own motivations and more about alleviating pain points suffered by Apple. In early 2010, America was still in the wake of the subprime mortgage crisis, with near double-digit unemployment. But China was experiencing the opposite problem: labor shortages. Unskilled workers were being offered signing bonuses as factory wages shot up 20 percent in just a matter of months. Some manufacturers were weeks behind schedule and short of hands. Production lines were closing and factories were looking at hiking prices, which would have heightened inflation in the United States just as the country emerged from recession.

"Rising wages suggest the re-emergence of a worker shortage that was becoming evident before the financial crisis," reported *The New York Times.* "A government survey three years ago of 2,749 villages in seventeen provinces found that in 74 percent of them, there was no one left behind who was fit to go work in city factories—the labor pool was dry." Throughout the 2000s, manufacturing labor costs rose by 15.6 percent a year. The starting point was less than $0.50 an hour, but the trend nevertheless spooked Western executives involved in making long-term commitments. An Apple manufacturing design engineer from this time says shifting production to the hinterlands might not be a long-term solution, but "you could basically reset the clock to five years prior."

Another factor was churn. Although there was no shortage of migrants applying to Foxconn, retaining them was a challenge given the monotony of the work. Turnover at major electronics contract manufacturers in China can reach 300 to 400 percent yearly, according to Ken Moon, who teaches operations at Wharton. "This amounts to replacing an entire factory workforce several times over, inside a year," he says. Indeed, the Pegatron factory in Shanghai, near the Pudong airport, was, by 2014, employing 100,000 laborers in a standing state—that is, before production ramp-up—and at times experienced attrition of 25 percent *per month,* according to a China-based Apple executive at the time. "They were losing 25,000 people a month, which means they needed to hire 25,000 just to stay in a steady state." An internal "attrition memo" corroborates this, saying: "Worker exit rates at Pegatron Shanghai averaged 6% per week, and average tenure was only 68 days."

Finding that amount of labor was becoming increasingly difficult as smartphone production consolidated into China in general, and into the Pearl River Delta area in particular. Apple, through its suppliers, was in competition for labor with emerging Chinese brands Xiaomi, Vivo, and Oppo, as well as Korea's Samsung. All these suppliers depend on an ecosystem of labor brokers who take empty buses out to villages in the interior of China, where they recruit workers. "So there's a whole ecosystem even around obtaining the workers to keep the system going," Moon says. "Those are government-licensed brokers, and the government has stayed involved and has a very heavy stake in keeping these systems stable."

Churn was especially high around Chinese New Year, when factories shut down for two weeks and migrants return to their families. A 2009 documentary, *Last Train Home,* captures what it calls "the largest human migration in the world," as more than 130 million migrants return home in a single week. The grueling journey can take multiple days, in trains so packed that restroom breaks aren't possible and passengers have to resort to wearing diapers.

Back then, millions of workers each year would opt to remain in their village, finding it too difficult to head back to their monotonous jobs after being home with family for just a few days. Internal reports suggest that some Apple suppliers experienced attrition rates north of 50 percent at Chinese New Year. Unhappy with the disruption, Apple spent years trying to reduce the churn, even working with researchers at five major universities, but with little effect.

"Everybody got their extra month bonus right before Chinese New Year, and then people wouldn't come back," says an Apple manager. "And then [Apple's suppliers] started saying, 'Well, we're only going to give you half [of the bonus now], and you get half when you come back.'" Even then, a large portion didn't return. So instead of a bonus split 50–50, the suppliers experimented with 25–75, 20–80, and so on, but none of the strategies really worked. "The only thing it changes is [that] you had a bigger exodus after Chinese New Year [rather than before]," the Apple engineer says.

Uncle Terry's inland investment was a risky gambit. In late 2010, Gou was expecting half of all Foxconn workers to work and live inland within two years, versus 20 percent at the time. The bet paid off handsomely. Annual iPhone shipments nearly quadrupled to 93 million between 2009 and 2011, while the first iPad was so successful some pundits wondered if it would eventually outsell the iPhone. The business logic of the deal was unimpeachable. It really only had one downside: The production of Apple's two most important products was now even more firmly fastened in China.

TSMC

Another company made a fateful gamble on Apple around the same time: Taiwan Semiconductor Manufacturing Company, or TSMC. Like other companies dealt a blow by the financial crisis, TSMC initially reacted by cutting staff. When workers protested, the famed founder and chairman of the company, Morris Chang, retook the reins. The seventy-seven-year-old had retired in 2005, but after the initial success of the iPhone, he leapt on an historic chance to win Apple's business.

The opportunity had presented itself after Apple got upset with Samsung for copying the iPhone, which led to years of courtroom battles on three continents. Any company mimicking the look and feel of the iPhone would draw the ire of Steve Jobs, but with Samsung, such actions felt like betrayal. The Korean giant had been a close partner, providing chips for multiple iPods, as well as supplying flash memory, displays, batteries, and processors. Nobody in Cupertino was pleased with Samsung's first chip for the iPhone, known as the H1, so Apple's custom silicon team—led by Alan Gilchrist—got deeply involved in the process. Apple bulked up its understanding of chips with the purchase of P.A. Semi in late 2008, a hugely consequential deal allowing Apple to take greater control of the chips inside its phone—and, eventually, across its entire lineup of products.

The Apple-Samsung partnership was more intimate than is widely known. The Korean company even had separately badged engineers working full time at Apple's Infinite Loop campus, on the bottom floor of De Anza 3. The top two floors housed Apple's semiconductor team, led by Johny Srouji, a chips savant who'd worked at IBM and Intel before Apple hired him in 2008. The two companies jointly worked on the design of the subsequent iPhone chips, so when Samsung then copied the iPhone with an Android-enabled device, Apple wanted to distance itself.

In 2010, Apple operations chief Jeff Williams reached out to Morris Chang through his wife, Sophie Chang, a relative of Terry Gou. Dinner between them launched months of "intense" negotiations, according to Chang, as Williams pressed TSMC on prices and convinced the Taiwanese group to make a major investment. "The risk was very substantial," Williams recalled at a gathering for TSMC's thirtieth anniversary in 2017. "If we were to bet heavily on TSMC, there would be no backup plan. You cannot double-plan the kind of volumes that we do. We want leading-edge technology, but we want it at established technology . . . volumes."

Williams's narrative leaves out some of the most interesting facts about the early partnership. One is that Chang wouldn't commit to Apple's demands. In a 2025 interview with the podcast *Acquired,* Chang said that TSMC would've had to raise substantial amounts of money, either by selling bonds or issuing more stock. Williams had another idea: "You can eliminate your dividend." Morris balked at the aggressive suggestion. "If we do what Jeff Williams says, our stock to going to drop like hell," he recounted. Chang agreed to take only half of Apple's order. Even this partial commitment forced TSMC to borrow $7 billion, so it could invest $9 billion and devote 6,000 full-time employees working round the clock to bring up a new chips fab in eleven months, according to Williams. "In the end, the execution was flawless," he said. The partial commitment forced Apple to toggle between Samsung and TSMC, which some in Cupertino saw as a plus—it meant that Apple wasn't beholden to just one supplier for what serves as the brain within the iPhone. But Srouji's team found it nightmarish to manage both suppliers. So Apple turned to TSMC on an exclusive basis, establishing over-the-top contract terms to protect itself. A person familiar with the contract characterized it as saying: "We need to make sure that you're gonna go out of business—if you're gonna put us at risk of going out of business." It was a "mutually assured destruction" type of situation, this person says, because if TSMC didn't perform in any given year, there'd be no iPhone. So the Apple decision was made: "We are going to put all of our eggs in one basket, and then we're gonna guard the basket."

TSMC's bet would prove critical for making it the world leader in semiconductor fabrication, with Apple as its biggest client. From Cupertino's perspective, it was a shrewd move that aided Samsung's biggest competitor and helped to ensure the iPhone had a computing edge over its biggest rivals. But since Taiwan is considered a rogue region that could eventually be reincorporated into China, possibly by force, the shift doubled Apple's exposure to the geopolitical risk of a more belligerent Beijing.

iSad

Steven Paul Jobs died on October 5, 2011, aged fifty-six, leaving behind a company worth $350 billion and a trusted lieutenant, Tim Cook, to manage it. Millions of people mourned, often leaving bitten apples at the company's stores or holding up digital flickering candles on their iPads. In China, social media sites recorded 35 million tributes. The *New York Post* captured the sentiment of many with its one-word lead: "iSad." Despite the loss, Apple's stock continued to climb, peaking eleven months later, in September 2012, when its market capitalization surpassed $620 billion.

But then investors started to worry about Apple's prospects. Over the next twelve months the stock fell around 40 percent. Investors and journalists focused on a perceived lack of creativity. Analysts were clamoring for "the next big thing," another hit product to succeed the iPhone and iPad. They obsessed over the iPhone market share, which stagnated between 15 percent and 20 percent worldwide, while Android's share of the smartphone market shot up from 10 percent in late 2010 to 40 percent within three years. It was far from clear that Apple could battle so many competitors collaborating on software and hardware then undermining the iPhone on price. It looked like the PC battle all over again.

But the ensuing years would prove this wasn't a repeat of the 1990s. Apple had captured the richest consumers around the world, and developers knew that iPhone owners spent more money not just on the phone, but on their apps. Horace Dediu, a former Nokia executive turned market analyst, calculated that iOS users were spending, on average, four times as much as Android buyers. "Half the users, paying four times as much, means double the income," he wrote. If anything, developers prioritized iOS.

Apple's ecosystem was being wildly underestimated. Whether it was the way its products synced content across devices or locked the consumer in, the company's dual control of hardware and software acted as a protective moat from the onslaught of new competitors. Investors worried that cheap Chinese handsets would emerge as a massive threat—but they were more of a threat to Samsung's dominance, not Apple's. While Samsung, relying on Android, struggled to differentiate its phones and would see its sales in China plummet, Apple's narrow focus on the high end paid off. In hindsight, Apple's share price and media image were suffering for all the wrong reasons in 2013. The company *was* facing an existential threat—but it wasn't from Android; it was from Beijing.

CHAPTER 25

"THE NAVY SEALS"

John Ford was arriving in Beijing from abroad in the spring of 2011 when his phone started pinging with notifications. Four American contractors working the security line at the Apple Store in Sanlitun had been arrested; their passports had been confiscated while they sat behind bars. Unlike his own arrest a few months earlier, this wasn't a voluntary gesture. Once again, Ford would have to work his connections. What ensued was a headache but also something of a personal victory.

Cupertino's concern with the resellers had been escalating. Around-the-block lineups for iPhones in China were a gravy train for Apple. But managing the crowds proved so difficult that they had to stop selling iPhones every afternoon. "We did phones in the morning until about one o'clock. Then we stopped selling phones so you could come in to buy a computer, etcetera, later in the day," Ford says. "You could view the phones, you could play with them. You just couldn't buy them." Ford, with the backing of Ron Johnson, had tried to inform Cupertino that the problem wasn't cultural. "This is a distribution issue," the two declared. "The resellers are taking advantage of a distribution challenge that we've created."

Unsure if Ford was part of the problem, Apple flew in "hot teams" from the United States to help manage the issue. Tactically, these security teams were top-notch; it seemed obvious they had military backgrounds. Ford half jokingly calls them "the Navy SEALs." But it soon became clear they hadn't spent much time in China. They tried to impose order in a Western way: *Set the rules and be firm. Don't let people break the rules.* They implemented a hard approach, restricting who could enter the store, in direct opposition to the soft, relationship-building approach that Ford favored.

But Chinese law didn't allow that. If a store was open to the public, it was open to everyone. Efforts to exclude people proved disastrous. Trying to impose order, the Navy SEALs turned physically aggressive, a tactical no-no, culturally. "We're in *their* country," says MacKay. "And they're very sensitive to Westerners telling them what to do and taking advantage of them." The resellers responded by having their minions flood the store, clogging the sales channels to such a degree that sales would freeze. "They'd all come to the front, where the cash register is, screaming and yelling and holding out money: 'I want my phones! You're selling phones! I want my phones!'" Ford recounts. The resellers were sending a message: *Work with us, or we're going to shut you down so nothing happens.*

Once again, Mr. Du was on the scene. But with Ford on an airplane, out of reach and unable to placate him, he got angry at the disorder. He told the Navy SEALs to follow him to the police station and hand over their passports. Lacking cultural savvy, they did as they were told. Ford, reading updates as he arrived in Beijing from a business trip, called the US embassy looking for MacKay, who'd often dealt with Chinese police and could help sort out the situation. They were able to negotiate for the contractors' immediate release, on the condition they left the country right away. Ford scolded them for heavy-handed tactics as he put them in a car to the airport.

His handling of the situation earned him some credibility in Cupertino. It was now easier to accept that a soft approach to the reseller issue wasn't the problem. But as Apple's business boomed in China, the yellow cows were just one challenge. More broadly, Ford worried that Apple was losing leverage with the Chinese government and failing to exert its own power. As early as 2010 he'd told Bob Mansfield, Apple's head of hardware: "All you gotta do is open up a factory in Vietnam and you're gonna get some nervous Chinese government officials."

But as Apple grew exponentially, it doubled down on manufacturing in China. A few peripheral devices such as keyboards and cables were shifted to Vietnam, where labor was cheaper. But these were tactical moves to save on costs, not strategic shifts to de-risk China exposure. Executives had presumed that doubling down on China helped their cause—"look at how many jobs we're creating!"—but Ford's understanding of Chinese culture was more nuanced. "They call it big potato, small potato," he says. "It's an analogy for social status." Sure, Apple was creating a lot of jobs, but it was also making a lot of money, so these things balanced out—China didn't "owe" Apple anything. The job creation didn't give Apple leverage; it just deepened its vulnerabilities and reinforced that it was the small potato. "I didn't think Apple understood China very well," he says. "I don't think the American government does, either. They don't get the culture of how the Chinese operate or how the [Chinese] government works. We approach everything from this Western mindset of fairness. The Chinese approach it from positional power—who's got more strength?"

Ford reckoned that Apple had more pull than it understood, but it was unwilling to make the necessary moves. As a result, the company still faced major problems "importing" products made in China, opening new stores, and getting help from local police to manage the networks of yellow cows.

American Dream Kids

The huge success of the Apple Store in Beijing and Shanghai convinced the company it needed to build more locations. Real estate developers were happy to help. Each store was pulling in more than $200 million in revenue, so there was a sense that putting one in your mall would be a cash cow for the entire project, says a former Apple executive. Ron Johnson had predicted in 2010 that Apple would have twenty-five stores in China by the end of the following year. But actual growth happened far more slowly. By the start of 2015, the store count in China was just fifteen. The company found that it lacked the right political connections. The IT malls had felt threatened by Apple, and since they were often controlled by wealthy entrepreneurs with political clout, they'd successfully put up roadblocks. Without a keen understanding of regional politics and institutions, Apple wasn't able to grow where and how it wanted to. Its second store in Beijing, for instance, was a two-story location descending into the basement of an older mall called Xidan Joy City, right next to an old septic tank. Every few days the tank's seal would break, releasing an awful odor into the basement and then up the spiral staircase.

Apple's diminishing leverage became more apparent in 2012 when a lawsuit emerged over its use of the term iPad. The trademark had been filed in 2001 by a Taiwanese company called Proview Technology. Before unveiling the iPad, Apple had set out to purchase naming rights around the world. It cleverly obfuscated who the "real" buyer was in these transactions, aware that sellers would inflate the price if they knew Apple was involved. It set up a British company called IP Application Development—abbreviated to IPAD. The entity paid £35,000 to Proview, securing the rights. But once the iPad became a massive hit, Proview felt tricked. Its China subsidiary argued the trademark sold to Apple was valid only in Taiwan and that it still had rights to the name in mainland China.

Ford found the argument dubious. And when, during the dispute, a Chinese government authority attempted to confiscate iPads from the Apple Store, Ford walked to the inventory room where his staff was bundling them up for the official and told him to "fuck off"—in English—declining to hand over a single iPad. He had his team translate his frustration on his behalf, a face-enhancing move that gave him leverage. "You want to create an impression that you're an executive who is at a level where it's not required to speak their language," he says.

Ford's next move with the visiting government official was to argue that the trademark covered only the original iPad, not iPad 2. He offered to quarantine the original model, and he then proceeded to negotiate for the sale of the newer one. Compromise, as ever, was a winning tactic.

Years of living in Taiwan trying to convert people to the Mormon faith, coupled with his time in China, had taught Ford unwritten rules. He possessed street smarts that let him work the system in Apple's favor. But he struggled to convey these concepts back to Cupertino and grew dismayed by some of their decisions. In 2012 higher executives chose to deal with the iPad trademark problem by paying Proview $60 million. It was a decision they could easily rationalize—global iPad sales that year would soar 61 percent to $31 billion. But to Ford, this rationalization missed what the fine signified.

By late that year, he was done with the long hours and frequent debates. The work had been exhausting for everyone. Apple's global revenues had climbed from $42.9 billion in 2009 to $156.5 billion in 2012—but the pace of growth in Greater China was in a different league altogether, rising 2,830 percent, to $22.5 billion. In the summer of 2012 Ford and his family left China, and a few months later he departed Apple, too. He felt confident in the company's future. Apple didn't have a great understanding of China, he thought, but the problem was likely to go away as Apple built more stores and the country liberalized. China's economic success, it seemed, was really fueling change, and the growth was just phenomenal. "China [is] building the square-foot equivalent of Rome every two weeks," observed *New Yorker* writer Evan Osnos around that time.

The generational divide Ford had been observing for years gave him hope. He'd nicknamed the younger staff on his team the American Dream Kids. "They were going through this 1950s Americana growth phase, [believing they could] do whatever they wanted and the opportunities were limitless," he says. "They thought everything was possible.

And the mindset I had was that by the time these kids become fifty, that'll be the mindset of all the Chinese."

It wouldn't be long before he realized just how wrong he was.

Burned-Out iPhones

Just as the yellow cows in the 1990s train-ticket scheme progressed from cornering the market on tickets to acquiring expensive machinery to print forgeries, so, too, did the yellow cows running the gray market for iPhones grow more sophisticated. What happened with the SWAT team in Shanghai's Pudong store got back to the villages, frightening would-be participants in the scheme. At the same time, the resellers orchestrating the long lines to acquire Apple products were increasingly mixed up with organized crime, and they sought ways to inflate their margins.

They began buying Apple products in large quantities in the United States, where iPhones could be acquired more readily, at a lower price, and without sales tax. Some of the yellow cows found yet another advantage: if they purchased iPhones through a carrier such as T-Mobile or Verizon, they could use fake IDs and acquire new iPhones with just a down payment on a twenty-four-month contract—with zero intention, of course, of ever paying the next twenty-three installments. So instead of purchasing an iPhone for, say, $500, then finding a Chinese city where Apple products were scarce and a willing buyer existed to pay a price marked up by hundreds of dollars, they found an ingenious but illegal way to acquire iPhones at less than $100, dramatically increasing their profits.

The problem with these iPhones is that they were carrier-locked—that is, they were restricted to a specific US network and wouldn't function in China. But as the yellow cows elevated their tactics and grew more cunning, they developed technical know-how through factory connections. There were, after all, huge sums of money involved as the number of iPhones sold in China expanded from hundreds of thousands in 2009 to more than 20 million in 2012. At these factories the yellow cows found ways to "burn out" the main computer chip within the iPhone. They were deliberately breaking the unit, but in the process, masking its retail market country of origin. Then they started paying Chinese migrants to show up at the Apple Store and complain that their new iPhone didn't work. Store employees at the Genius Bar were at first oblivious of the scheme and couldn't make heads or tails of these units. Using special tools, the Genius Bar employees would open the iPhone and confirm it to be brand new, but with the processor zapped. In some instances they reported to their bosses that the returned phones had existing customers' details attached to them—US names and addresses—which flummoxed them because that wasn't possible for a new phone. Uncertain what was going on but wanting to provide Apple's famously courteous customer service, the staff gave some customers brand-new iPhones—a delight to the reseller bosses who'd devised the scheme. "This was like cocaine to the yellow cows," says a former Apple executive familiar with the episode. "They were making a fortune."

In other instances, and especially as the scheme went on, customers had to wait as Apple sent the burned-out units to a logistics hub in Singapore, where a special team could replace the chip and send the phone back to China. For an ordinary customer, this would've been a perfectly fine outcome; but the migrants and their yellow cow overlords were anything but ordinary. They needed mint condition iPhones with full warranties to attain the highest possible price in the gray market. A "refurbished" unit wasn't good enough.

Upset, they began to complain about Apple, saying the arrogant Western company was treating Chinese customers unfairly by repairing, rather than replacing, broken units. The complaints made their way up the various political channels, and eventually they were conveyed to China Central Television, a mouthpiece for the party. And this is the secret origin, unreported until now, of *Consumer Day* in March 2013—the story featured in this book's Prologue—when Apple was viciously attacked in a state-sponsored media blitzkrieg until it apologized. The scheme to deceive Apple was left out of the narrative.

Complicating the situation, the complaints of the yellow cows had been amplified throughout 2012 by ordinary customers who struggled to purchase iPhones at the prices set by Apple. And when customers had problems with their phones, booking an appointment could often prove tough as the resellers began using mainframe computers in warehouses that either reserved all the spots or crashed the system. Then they'd stand outside the stores selling the appointments. "It was much more sophisticated than you could possibly imagine," a former Apple executive says of their tactics.

The challenge was exacerbated even further by legitimate customers taking their broken iPhones for repair to fake Apple Stores that had no interest helping them. There were so many of these stores, from corner shops claiming to be official resellers to large, quality-engineered locations that mimicked the look and feel of the real thing, that some retail employees jokingly competed in private chat groups over who could find more of them. When Apple hired an investigative third party to gauge how large the problem was, the estimate of fake stores to come back was above 10,000—a difficult to verify number, especially as Apple executives balked at the approximation as outlandish. Whatever the real number, the point is that by late 2012 it was becoming clear that Cupertino was in over its head in China. Behind its unprecedented financial success in the country was a dizzying array of problems, and the tech giant had far too few people on the ground with the cultural and political acumen to address them. Then, amid the confusion, Beijing selected a new general secretary to lead the Chinese Communist Party.

PART FIVE

POLITICAL AWAKENING

CHAPTER 26

THE DESPOT

It was as if the maxim "bide your time" had been personified and come to life as a world leader. Appointed general secretary of the Communist Party on November 15, 2012, Xi Jinping was something of a cipher—few outside the country knew who he was or what he stood for. As Xi stood in the Great Hall of the People in Beijing, accepting his new role, his calm demeanor and warm smile gave little away. Wearing a dark suit, a crisp white shirt, and a wine-red tie, Xi apologized for keeping the press waiting. Then he delivered anodyne remarks on China's 5,000-year history, including how the CCP helped to make New China more prosperous. "We have every reason to be proud—proud, but not complacent," he said. The only real policy initiative he mentioned in this first speech was fighting corruption. That was something anyone could applaud. It took years to fully grasp that the anti-corruption drive was air cover for toppling political rivals, so Xi could nominate loyalists into key positions and consolidate power.

That Xi had managed to remain an unknown quantity was striking given that he'd been a public figure for three decades. He'd governed two of China's most successful provinces and, in 2007, was elevated to the Politburo Standing Committee—the nation's highest decision-making body. He was already appointed the heir of Hu Jintao, president and general secretary. But for many Chinese he was better known as the husband of Peng

Liyuan, a celebrity singer nine years his junior who once serenaded China's troops in Tiananmen Square following the bloody crackdown in 1989.

Xi was also a "princeling," born to what might be thought of as Communist royalty. His father, Xi Zhongxun, was a close ally of Mao in the Red Army and head of the Propaganda Department in the 1950s. After being imprisoned and purged during the Cultural Revolution, the elder Xi was rehabilitated. He was chosen to be a top official in Guangdong, where he evolved into a fervent supporter of opening the economy through capitalist experimentation. When confronted in a conservative Politburo meeting in 1987, he fumed: "What are you guys doing here? Don't repeat what Mao did to us!" He lost the battle, was again stripped of his titles, and died in 2002. Now, a decade later, there was hope that the younger Xi, too, might be a closet reformer and revive his late father's legacy.

The world's inability to understand China's impenetrable leader was largely due to his enigmatic, unassuming character, coupled with the general opacity of the CCP's operations. But it was also due to the distracting scandal of Bo Xilai, the populist party secretary of Chongqing widely expected to be elevated to the Standing Committee. Bo was a handsome, charismatic hard-liner nicknamed "little Mao Zedong." He'd built a reputation fighting corruption at a time of secret deals and lavish spending among cadres. His father was one of the "Eight Immortals" of the Communist Party, an exclusive circle of elders that included Deng Xiaoping. Some observers believed he was positioning himself to push Xi aside, seize power, and implement one-man rule. But his entire career collapsed in spectacular fashion when, in February 2012, Chongqing's chief of police took refuge in the US consulate, providing officials with a lurid story that gripped the nation: A British consultant found dead three months earlier hadn't died of alcohol poisoning, as believed; he'd been murdered with cyanide by Bo's wife. Newspapers called it "the biggest Chinese political scandal in at least two decades." Bo was implicated in the murder, stripped of all titles, and sentenced to life in prison that September. His downfall helped clear the path for Xi to assume unprecedented power.

The party Xi inherited was losing its vision and credibility, and observers inside and outside the country could see it. In 2012 democracy scholar Larry Diamond predicted that Communist Party rule will end "much sooner than I used to suppose." There was a pervasive sense that a strongman was needed, following two terms of weak leadership under Hu Jintao and Wen Jiabao, a time when multinationals could do as they pleased, rules weren't enforced, and reforms had stagnated. Critics called it a "lost decade," bereft of vision or real leadership. Power was so dispersed across the Standing Committee that it became known as the "collective presidency." Hu Jintao, mocked for his inability to take action, was nicknamed the Woman with Bound Feet. China was still growing quickly, but that growth was directionless and likely unsustainable as the cost of labor climbed. "For all its impressive economic gains in low-cost manufacturing, China had little to show in the way of innovation or the development of the service sector, the markers of the world's advanced economies," wrote the scholar Elizabeth Economy.

Just a few weeks into his new role, Xi showed his face in Guangdong. He railed against "nihilism," exhorted his colleagues to be firm in their commitment to Leninist values, and portrayed the fall of the Soviet Union as a historic failure—not of an economic system, but of particular individuals who didn't have the courage to deploy "the tools of dictatorship" and fight for the party. "Nobody was man enough to stand up and resist," he exclaimed. In early January 2013, Xi made it abundantly clear to listeners that China's new leader was more Mao than Deng. "Facts have repeatedly told us that Marx and Engels's analysis of the basic contradiction of capitalist society is not outdated, nor is the historical materialist view that capitalism will inevitably perish and socialism will inevitably triumph outdated," he told the CCP's Central Committee. "This is the irreversible overall trend of social and historical development, but the road is winding. The ultimate demise of capitalism, and ultimate triumph of socialism, will inevitably be a long historical process."

Both these speeches were behind closed doors. A summary of the first was leaked in January 2013; the other was kept secret for six years. Publicly, Xi honed a far more conciliatory image, one based on achieving the "Chinese

Dream" through hard work and national pride. For Cupertino, this friendlier image of Xi made it all the more jarring when CCTV, the party mouthpiece, attacked Apple on *Consumer Day* in March 2013—just one day after Xi completed his transition to power by becoming president—followed by *The People's Daily* scolding Apple for its "incomparable" arrogance.

Exploit and Plunder

Xi Jinping had plenty of reason to be upset with Apple. Global revenues at the tech giant had soared from $6 billion in 2003 to $157 billion in 2012, and though Apple's success had much to do with product conception and design, its ability to build and distribute its hardware couldn't be accomplished without operations in China. In addition, Chinese consumers had been Apple's biggest source of growth during the prior three years. As Xi took power, he emphasized a policy of "in China, for China," and it didn't look like Apple was sharing the wealth.

Apple's net margins had jumped from 1.1 percent in 2003 to 26.7 percent in 2012; profits, in the same period, expanded at a meteoric rate from $69 million to $41.7 billion. Yet the company's chief assembler, Foxconn, appeared to be getting a raw deal. Foxconn had been a more profitable company than Apple in the early 2000s. But as iPod and then iPhone volumes took flight, Apple's margins soared while Foxconn's collapsed by two-thirds. And far from being some outlier, Foxconn was among the chief beneficiaries—indeed, one of the chief enablers—of Apple's growth. Plenty of other suppliers would work for Apple on several generations of a product and become overly dependent on the tech giant for revenue, only to find that its technology wasn't needed in the next generation of hardware, lose Apple as a client, and go bankrupt. "If it's even slightly convenient for them, they'll knife you," says the top executive of an American supplier that suffered such a fate.

Worse, Apple had become so successful that negative stories involving the company attracted global attention portraying China in a poor light.

Beginning in 2010, the wave of suicides at Foxconn had put Chinese working conditions in the international headlines for months. When, in September 2012, some 2,000 Foxconn staff in the city of Taiyuan rioted, the assembler responded by sending in 5,000 police. Mayhem like this wasn't at all atypical in China; what was rare was the international media coverage. Journalists devoted outsized attention to the uprising because the factory played a role in supplying iPhones. From Beijing's perspective, Apple's attempts to evaluate its supply chain challenges and set the problem straight didn't necessarily help. After Apple commissioned an independent evaluation, it acknowledged that 60 percent of the 229 suppliers audited had failed to comply with 60-hour maximum workweeks; about half worked improperly with hazardous chemicals; and more than 100 facilities failed to pay proper overtime. When Cupertino published the report, the context was an American company playing the role of white knight, cleaning up the supply chain. The unspoken subtext suggested that, if left unsupervised, Chinese factories would exploit workers and endanger their lives—an embarrassing message for an ostensibly socialist country.

Then there was Apple's signature line: "Designed by Apple in California. Assembled in China." For some, the statement diminished the importance of China's contributions. The country had developed extensive world-class industrial clusters on a previously unknown scale. Thousands of skilled engineers using sophisticated machinery had played a critical role in making Apple products functional and beautiful. Assembly wasn't at all the crux of the partnership. The signature line looked outdated, seemingly structured to keep China in its place.

For any hard-liners, these suspicions were brazenly confirmed by Apple's organizational structure. The ideal template for a Western company, from Beijing's perspective, was a joint venture—a partnership with a local company in which the multinational gets access to a billion customers but the local partner learns the ins and outs of operating the business so it can eventually flourish on its own. In the 1990s, such "technology transfer" was critical for China to avoid forever being a haven for low-skilled cheap labor. They could play that junior-partner role for a while, to lure in capital and provide jobs, but the goal was for Chinese firms to eventually compete on their own. For Western companies, such arrangements could be very lucrative. Volkswagen was the first major carmaker to sign such a deal in 1984, and within a few years the JV was the largest carmaker in the country. As China's new-car market outpaced America's, VW's leading position helped it overtake GM as the world's largest carmaker.

But the arrangements could also be dangerous. Numerous companies avoided entering China in the 1990s due to the risks and uncertainties of IP protection. Once China entered the WTO in 2001, however, explicitly conditioning market access on tech transfer was illegal in most sectors. As President Clinton had put it: "We don't have to transfer technology or do joint manufacturing in China anymore." But the practice didn't really end; instead, the pressure turned informal. The Chinese market was so large that foreign companies would sometimes "voluntarily" enter such agreements. A textbook example occurred in the early 2000s when China planned the largest high-speed rail network in the world. The potential orders to foreign companies were enormous, creating a Prisoner's Dilemma among Siemens, Bombardier, and Kawasaki. In the end, all three agreed to transfer technology to state-backed companies in exchange for market access. By 2010, policy had shifted to favor local industry; the foreign companies struggled to compete in China, and the local companies began exporting their technology abroad. As one Japanese executive involved put it: "[The Japanese and Europeans] were afraid this situation would happen in the future, but they thought it would take more time. The Chinese catch-up speed was so fast; they could not have imagined they would be competing [with the Chinese] for contracts in the US."

For many foreign companies the go-to structure became the wholly owned foreign enterprise, which ostensibly allowed companies to protect their intellectual property and license their tech to Chinese factories. But Apple's oldest business in the country—the third-party channel sales unit, which distributes Apple products to authorized partners—was neither a joint venture nor a wholly owned foreign enterprise. Instead, Apple had classified the business unit as a trading company, a designation that was practically offensive. The term was associated with the Dutch and English East India Companies, colonial-era businesses involved in China's "century of humiliation." Back then, Western powers annexed Hong Kong and Macau and forced China to import opium, a premodern equivalent of fentanyl that had a disastrous effect on the population. Trading companies were linked with exploitation, plunder, and unequal treaties. It didn't help that Apple had created zero R&D centers in the country, while the likes of HP, Microsoft, and Motorola had established theirs a decade earlier. Nor did Apple have formal partnerships with local companies, while Samsung alone had more than thirty-five.

The Party Leads Everything

On the morning of the original CCTV episode on March 15, 2013, some ten hours before the first attack on Apple aired, Apple Store employees in Shanghai were confronted by a cohort of media, including CNN and local outlets seeking comment from the tech giant. The journalists had been prebriefed about the coming *Consumer Day* episode by Mofcom, China's Ministry of Commerce, which manages media relations in the country by preapproving government messaging and coordinating missives across departments. Store managers felt blindsided by allegations that Apple had mistreated Chinese customers, yet they couldn't respond without first informing Cupertino. It was late in California and senior executives couldn't be reached, resulting in awkward silence for hours as news crews waited impatiently. When an emergency conference call with half a dozen senior leaders came together, Tim Cook coolly rejected the allegations that Apple treated Chinese customers poorly. He took the bold stance that he ran the world's largest company and didn't need to apologize for anything. Over the following three weeks, as the media attacks widened, Cupertino learned that treating Chinese government officials like vendors in their supply chain wasn't going to fly. Only then did Cook pen an apology letter, in Mandarin, for Apple's China website. (According to one person, the

Apple CEO also flew to Beijing for a secret meeting with China's top officials. "The Chinese would never accept a written apology," this person says. "You have to lose face in front of them, and bow.")

To secure Apple's China business, Cook amended its warranty policy in the country, pledging that eligible customers with broken phones would be given new units. The enhanced policy was like a godsend to the yellow cows. It turbocharged their illicit scheme to such an extent that Apple Stores in China soon had a separate line just for iPhone returns. When their turn came, some migrant workers would unpack entire backpacks filled with iPhones, returning each for a brand-new unit. The updated warranty policy had given the yellow cows a new source of iPhone supply: existing models. They began stealing them from consumers, in China and abroad, and then deployed special tools to amend the fifteen digit IMEI number—which in those days was printed on the back of the iPhone and again on the SIM tray inside. In some cases, the yellow cows would obtain a top-tier iPhone, take it apart and separately sell pricey components like the memory chip, replace them with inexpensive lookalike parts, and then return the tampered unit for a brand-new model. The yellow cows became so adept at this that even a well-trained Genius Bar worker couldn't detect which phones had been tampered with.

Successfully clamping down on these practices would take several years and involve a series of stunning discoveries. Apple began holding onto returned units for thirty days, using that time to figure out which had been compromised. Their systems allowed them to type in the IMEI number, and if the number was legit, then the system would indicate they were holding the correct unit; but sometimes the data would indicate the IMEI was an activated phone still in use on the other side of the world. That confirmed they were holding a manipulated unit, allowing them to deem it ineligible for return. As the scam went on, Apple learned to place the units under a special X-ray-like microscope, providing a near-atomic view that outclassed the resellers' ability to fool them. It would take Apple more than five years to deter the bad actors, by serializing every major component within the iPhone, pairing the display, battery, and camera to the logic board. The move caused blowback from right-to-repair activists, as it inadvertently made it more difficult and costly for legitimate third parties across the world to help customers with broken iPhones. But the blowback was considered a small price to pay for ending the devious trade-in scheme Apple was facing in China.

Back in 2013, the magnitude of the problem facing Apple wasn't at all understood—not by Apple, and certainly not by Western media. Indeed, the consensus narrative to emerge was that Apple had gained the upper hand against the Chinese government. Beijing's attack on the company had "largely backfired," *The Atlantic* wrote, as "hundreds of thousands of Weibo users—students, intellectuals, white-collar workers and celebrities—voiced their support for the American technological behemoth." In *Forbes,* Gordon G. Chang mocked Beijing for an obvious goof when a celebrity actor with millions of followers took a hard stance against Apple using his Weibo account, but ended his screed with the words ". . . Post around 8:20." Whoops! The actor had included part of the instructions. Who wrote the instructions wasn't entirely clear, but in a country where a motto is "the party leads everything," Chinese netizens had an educated guess. "Users began posting acerbic comments with the #PostAround8:20 hashtag," Chang wrote. "Weibo censors later deleted tens of thousands of postings with that hashtag."

But whatever the failures of the digital blitzkrieg were, Cupertino was made to understand that it was China that had the leverage, not Apple. While Beijing was unlikely to take hard action against Apple's manufacturing operations, given that its economy depended on attracting Western companies to build things in the country, it seemed completely willing to attack Apple's retail presence and digital offerings. For hard-liners, the iPhone was often a symbol of the younger generation's materialism, individualism, and fascination with the West—all trends they were happy to crush. As one editorial in the *Global Times* opined: it was "shameful" for the Chinese to go gaga for the newest iPhones at inflated prices. "For now," the editorial said, "if you see someone with an iPhone 6, cast your eyes on them contemptuously."

CHAPTER 27

THE GANG OF EIGHT

The coordinated attack of Chinese media exposed that Apple's supply chain—the envy of the tech world—contained something close to an existential risk as the country turned inward and belligerent. Apple's response to this vulnerability wasn't the subject of media articles or earnings calls, and certainly Cupertino wasn't issuing press releases about it. But in 2013 the company began to carefully and deliberately shift how it operated in its most important market.

Apple had built strong, unrivaled connections across the supply chain. But partners led by Foxconn had largely taken care of dealings with provincial officials. When *The New York Times* detailed the billions of dollars' worth of incentive packages, subsidies, and other preferential policies that government officials in China offered to build "iPhone City" in Zhengzhou, it quoted Apple as saying "it was not a party" to the negotiations. This sounded implausible for the detail-oriented company, but it was true. Operational moves occurred purely at the business level.

Within two years Apple had assembled a team. They called themselves the Gang of Eight. The group was composed of three new hires and five executives already working for Apple, spanning all major aspects of its business in China: operations and procurement, retail and marketing, government affairs, and Apple University. They would be Cupertino's eyes and ears in the country. The first major task for the

Gang of Eight was to work out what Apple's story was. *Why was Apple in China? How was it contributing? What did Apple have to do to demonstrate its commitment?* Very little thought had been put into these questions. More broadly, their role was to find ways for Apple to contain its China risk and placate authorities so the company could continue to grow. It was an enormous mission. But even though Apple was under intense scrutiny and selling pressure on Wall Street, its biggest challenge was ill understood and all but ignored.

Rory Sexton, Steve Marcher, and Jun Ge

The leader of the Gang of Eight—and the de facto head of Greater China—was Rory Sexton, an Irish-born engineer who'd joined Apple in 2001 and risen to the rank of vice president. Sexton, who moved to Shanghai around late 2013, was known for his keen grasp of details. This was a skill honed from more than a decade working closely with Deirdre O'Brien, a member of Tim Cook's innermost circle. Sexton had developed a deep understanding of how Apple functioned, from the temperaments and preferences of its top executives to the niche inner workings of how ideas could become reality. His role was to localize Operations—the team of engineers responsible for scaling Apple hardware into the tens of millions of units. He was tasked with growing the 1,000-strong team in China and creating a more rigorous organization while serving as its liaison to Cupertino.

Sexton was Apple's first vice president to live in China. Before him, the key decisions had been made by people flying in from Cupertino on a regular but fleeting basis. These Apple envoys would spend sixteen-hour days in the factories, living a Groundhog Day existence, with the same routine, the same conference-call times, the same meals. They weren't pondering affairs of state. Politically, the company had accumulated shockingly little savvy, especially at the regional and institutional levels outside of Beijing. But now Apple would have someone with clout to represent the division in-country and streamline production. Within a few years that team would grow to 4,000 engineers, reflecting a profound shift in how Apple operated in the country.

This shift had the potential to create tension. Cupertino has always been the center of power, and typically the engineers working in China wanted to report back to the mother ship directly. It was how you gained recognition and moved up the ranks. But Sexton was in a strong position to command respect. Subordinates describe him as a likable colleague who at times could be full of jokes, but his default mode was to be tough as nails. Sexton wasn't the sort of engineer who walked a production line, spotted problems, and started fixing a machine; but if he was informed of some niche issue affecting iPhone ramp-up, he'd be the first person to hop on a four a.m. flight to Zhengzhou and coordinate whatever was needed to solve it. His specialty was understanding what remedial actions needed to be taken, working with the vendors to avoid delays, and then communicating what was going on back to Cupertino.

This reputation earned him respect and a little fear. One subordinate describes how Sexton would walk into a meeting, take a look at whatever numbers were being presented on a spreadsheet, and with a manager's eye, zero in on some problem. "A number would jump out at him and he'd say, 'That number doesn't make sense to me . . . tell me about this number,'" the person recounts, imitating Sexton's gruff voice tinged with his Irish accent. Then some junior person would stand up, voice shaking, body quivering, to explain. "Invariably, Rory was correct," this person says. Then he'd leave the room and move on to the next problem.

Sexton was joined, in late 2013, by Steven Marcher (pronounced Marker), a Brit with a degree in applied physics who'd lived in Beijing since 2002. Marcher had slick short blond hair, the build of a rugby player, and tattoos around his shoulders. He looked tough and had trained as a Muay Thai fighter, but he was a calm, soft-spoken Buddhist with a penchant for saving dogs. Marcher had spent a decade at Nokia from 1997 to 2006, when the company was easily the most dominant phone maker in China. He'd played an instrumental role helping the Scandinavian company relocate more of its design and R&D centers from Europe to China, as part of a wider effort to source more local components and better compete with fast-moving regional competitors. Nokia had built a strong partnership with Foxconn during his tenure, and that led him to join Terry Gou's company as a vice president for the antenna unit. It was rare if not unprecedented for a foreigner to head a division at Foxconn, and he stayed for four years.

Marcher had wide experience and the knowledge of what it took to operate in China in ways that appeased local officials. Several colleagues describe Marcher as a nice guy, but remember him as elusive and hard to read. For years he'd struggle to fit in with Apple, and colleagues would debate whether the problem was his level of competence or merely that he'd never worked in Cupertino.

Marcher had a broad skill set and was fluent in Mandarin, but it wasn't actually clear what his role would be. As it had done with John Ford, Apple expected *him* to tell the company what he should do—not the other way around. He soon made it his task to open Apple's first research and development hubs in China, just as he'd done for Nokia.

A second key hire was Jun Ge. He joined Apple in mid-2014 to lead government affairs. Jun, a native speaker of Chinese with a law degree from Northwestern and an MBA from the Chinese University of Hong Kong, had nearly two decades of experience at Intel. There he rose to the level of vice president, building the company's presence and strategy in China, negotiating with officials to establish multibillion-dollar projects in multiple cities. He was a known quantity within regulatory circles and could help Apple navigate them. Before Jun, in their overtures to China, Apple's top brass routinely met only with high-level ministers in Beijing. The executives were often oblivious to the country's regional political differences or to the dispersal of power across competing bureaus and departments. Apple's operational division had a headquarters in the Pudong district of Shanghai, a provincial city of 23 million, but seemingly nobody before Jun could name the mayor or understand that Pudong, as a special economic zone, had its own administrative structure distinct from that of Shanghai's. He reported to Cupertino-based Lisa Jackson, who'd run the US Environmental Protection Agency before joining Apple's executive team in May 2013 as head of environment, policy, and social initiatives.

At Apple, Jun would be based in Beijing but spend much of his time in other cities, chiefly Shanghai. His responsibilities included regulatory policy, social responsibility matters, and strategic initiatives across Greater China. Before Jun, Tim Cook relied on Cathy Novelli, Apple's vice president of worldwide government affairs from 2007 to 2014. When Cook needed to get things done in China, like open a new store, it was often Novelli who'd fly over and figure out who to talk with. Novelli was supposed to be a pro at this—she was a former US trade representative during the Clinton administration and a future under secretary of state—but China wasn't her specialty. Jun was the first senior person living in China directly tasked with elevating Apple's navigation of the political system.

The Others

Three other members in the Gang of Eight are less important to this narrative but deserve a mention: Brendan Lawry had joined Apple in 2005 in its strategic silicon division, then moved to Shanghai in 2011 as the in-region director of procurement. Denny Tuza, who'd joined Apple as a senior director of retail in 2009, was appointed the head of China retail sales a year after John Ford left. Brian Lu, a longtime executive from Singapore who'd moved to China in 2006, was Apple's head of third-party sales for the region.

Then there was Chip Hills, the de facto head of China before Sexton. More than anyone else, Hills had been responsible for scaling iPhone operations in the country, racking up air miles from his home in Charlotte, where he and his wife were raising three daughters, to various production sites in Asia. He'd been the key Ops guy who signed Foxconn to the iPhone contract on Terry Gou's yacht. Colleagues remember him fondly as someone who trusted his staff and gave them latitude to get their projects done. One specialist recalls working side by side with Hills late into the night on a project for which Hills didn't have the requisite expertise. He was so committed that he would do whatever was needed, like moving boxes or making coffee, until the task was done. The colleague compared it to a heart surgeon helping out a brain surgeon, demoting himself to handing over a scalpel. Unfortunately, Hills's tenure with Apple was cut short when, in 2014, he was diagnosed with pancreatic cancer. Albert F. Chip Hills III passed away on October 27, 2015. When Jeff Williams gave the eulogy, he told of finding notes he'd written when he first interviewed Chip. Williams had written, in big letters, "WARMTH."

A Timely Firing

The final member of the Gang of Eight was Doug Guthrie, the most instrumental character in Apple's political awakening. Guthrie, a China expert, had become the youngest dean in the country when, aged thirty-nine, he was asked to lead the George Washington University School of Business in 2010. He was a fluent Mandarin speaker and a specialist in economic sociology, a niche field emphasizing the importance of state and local governments and regional institutions in economic development. Guthrie's appointment as dean had received widespread media coverage; but just three years later *The Washington Post* and the *Financial Times* were all covering his firing over a budget dispute. The articles showed pictures of his boyish, contemplative face, his big round eyes, his combed-back salt-and-pepper hair and his dark, structured eyebrows. Joel Podolny, head of Apple University, sensed opportunity. The two had struck up a relationship years earlier when they were both teaching at Harvard. Podolny had tried but failed to lure him into a permanent position in Cambridge. But here was a second chance.

Podolny teased an intriguing possibility—move to sunny California and teach Apple executives about China. At first Guthrie didn't care much for the idea. But he'd keenly observed the CCTV-led assault on Apple earlier in the year and thought the company had handled it badly. China *wanted* something from Apple, he surmised, and Cook's apology hadn't delivered. Plus, his work over the past decade had increasingly shifted to grasping the nuances of China's economic model. The idea of putting these abstract ideas into practice at the world's largest company felt like a lucky break. His public firing had been a humiliating affair, and he was already planning to leave Washington.

Still, he had zero interest in teaching executives in California. Over the past decade he'd developed a well-deserved scorn for pundits who possessed lofty thoughts about China's economy but little experience on the ground. And China was changing so rapidly that a common joke was that if you hadn't visited in the previous six months, you might as well never have visited. Over the course of a few calls, the idea gained traction. Guthrie accepted but with one condition: "I'll take the role," he said. "But send me to Shanghai."

CHAPTER 28

THE CHINA WHISPERER

Doug Guthrie had struggled from an early age in Pittsburgh. He found words on the page to be incoherent: *d-o-g* would read *o-d-g* and leave him confused. He didn't know it, but he suffered from dyslexia, a learning disability that went undiagnosed and was misunderstood by the adults around him. For some children, such disabilities force them to adapt in extraordinary ways, and in Doug's case he developed a compensatory technique called audiographic memory. When his mother read him a story aloud, he'd encode the text into his mind and, on subsequent nights, pretend to read it back to her. By the fourth grade, his recall was so developed he felt he'd tricked the whole school when he won the spelling bee.

Another challenge complicated his childhood. He suffered from Bipolar II, a disorder causing mood swings. Sometimes he'd stew over his inability to read properly or live up to his mother's lofty expectations. He'd experience a sense of anxiety that would last for weeks. More often, however, he'd feel unusually energetic, focused, even obsessed. His experience in these periods was so distinct that he'd thought of himself as inhabiting a whole new character: Super Doug. As a kid, he'd call on Super Doug to stave off Depressed Doug and overcome his dyslexia. Super Doug could study well past midnight and exist on just a few hours of sleep.

Guthrie's ability to focus helped him become a top student, though he struggled to reconcile his high IQ with the recognition that he'd never read a real book the whole way through. In high school he met a Taiwanese classmate, Leo Hsu, who by chance would profoundly influence his life. Usually, when a Chinese speaker teaches a white guy the four tones of Mandarin, it comes out sounding horrible. The non-native struggles to distinguish a high-level tone from a rising-falling pitch and can amusingly say "horse" instead of "mother." But when Leo asked his friend to sound out the tones *bī, bí, bǐ,* and *bì,* Doug recited them back with the fidelity of a recording. Leo turned this into a juvenile game, commanding his human parrot of a friend to walk up to some random lady and say, in perfect Mandarin: "There's a caterpillar behind you."

Guthrie and Hsu became college roommates at the University of Chicago, where Guthrie opted to study economics. To fulfill his language requirement, Doug accepted Leo's dare and signed up for an intensive course in Mandarin. Guthrie had no formal exposure but quickly excelled. Much of the learning took place in language labs, where students listened to dialogues and tried to memorize them. As Guthrie's peers plodded through the same 45-minute dialogue on repeat, every day, pausing to imitate the words, Guthrie could listen just once and then go for a run or train with the university's cycling club.

More significant is that he quickly discovered his learning disability had vanished. The way Guthrie's form of dyslexia works in the brain is that the letters on the page get transposed. English is alphabetic, with each letter representing a sound; when the letters are all jumbled, sounding out the words or decoding their meaning becomes difficult. But Chinese is logographic: each character is a morpheme, or unit of language. There is no equivalent of letter-to-sound conversion, and sequence matters less. For the first time in his life, reading was a pleasure. Finally, he was highly skilled at something. Super Doug's ability to focus accelerated his learning of thousands of Chinese characters, while his audiographic memory turbocharged his ability to speak and comprehend a tonal language.

Soon Guthrie was supplementing his Mandarin with courses on Chinese literature and history. It felt like destiny was calling when, in the spring of 1989, pro-democracy students assembled across Tiananmen

Square clamoring for democracy with their makeshift Statue of Liberty. His form of bipolarity, Guthrie says, can lead to rash decisions, and he abruptly made plans to take a year off and visit Beijing. He borrowed $1,500 from his grandparents and sorted out the admin to ensure he wouldn't lose his student aid. Then came the crackdown. On June 4, the Communist Party ordered its troops to end the protests. The army killed hundreds of students, possibly thousands, before dawn.

His dreams of visiting Beijing abruptly died, too; he was sickened by what happened, but also wanted to understand *why* it had happened. He opted to spend a year abroad in Taiwan, hoping to become fluent in the language. Taipei is a basin surrounded by mountains, and soon after arriving, Guthrie went cycling in his best tight shorts and most colorful racing shirt. He was laboring up the Yangming mountain range when one cyclist, then another, and soon a whole group flew by him. When he arrived at the peak, face sweaty and ego bruised, the entire squad was waiting for him, impressed. Guthrie surprised them by speaking in pitch-perfect Chinese. He took a closer look at their jerseys and realized they were Taiwan's national cycling team. The coach invited Guthrie to train with them.

Soon he was waking up early to meet his cycling pals at four a.m., then spending four hours with them conversing in Chinese. "It was the best immersion ever, because these people didn't speak a word of English," he says. The experience led him to dream of becoming a Chinese scholar. Returning to Chicago after a year, he switched majors and engrossed himself in the history of Chinese civilization. Then he enrolled in a program to earn a sociology PhD at Berkeley, home to some of his favorite China-focused scholars.

A Friend of China

The average sociology PhD takes seven years; Super Doug took just five. The degree culminated with Guthrie living in Shanghai for a year, where he interviewed eighty-one factory managers to study how capitalism was taking root. Shanghai was in the early stages of an incredible transformation. Men were wearing suits with the price tag still on the cuffs, signaling that wealth was becoming a badge of honor. Guthrie rode around the city on a one-speed Flying Pigeon, a Chinese bicycle that in the Mao era served as a symbol of an egalitarian society. Now it was being used to study how people got rich.

When Nixon and Kissinger had visited China two decades earlier, they were given Potemkin village–style tours—visits to beautiful factories that didn't represent the country. Guthrie sought to strenuously avoid that. He'd set out to interview each manager in a structured way, asking the same questions to all. The idea was to capture qualitative, on-the-ground research, but with a big enough sample that it would achieve statistical significance. Berkeley had a relationship with the Shanghai Academy of Social Science, which oversaw his research. In name, this sounded fine, but the think tank was a propaganda machine. It had no interest in allowing Guthrie to do the research he wanted. Doug didn't know it at the time, but Li Yihai, his handler, was a hard-core, ambitious member of the Communist Party. Li told him: "You're not seeing just any factory; we will decide what factories you're going to visit." Guthrie felt his whole project might be in peril. But he discovered an annual archive listing every local industrial enterprise. He made copies and started making phone calls. He had a big plan to visit the factories on his own.

One visit was different from the rest, and the episode would haunt Guthrie for years. During the interview with a manager, a young man was present. He was educated and spoke English, although he'd been silent throughout the interview. When Guthrie was saying goodbye, the young man followed him outside and whispered, "Do you know East China Normal Park?" The man spoke so quietly, so carefully, that Guthrie could hardly make out the words. He told Guthrie not to look around. "Meet me there tomorrow morning at eight-thirty."

The next morning the young man was waiting. "You should know that everything you're doing is being tracked by the Security Bureau," he said. The man explained that as soon as Guthrie had departed from the factory, the Security Bureau called for a readout of all that was said. "If I were you, I'd be a little nervous."

Guthrie, just twenty-five, was disoriented and fearful. It felt unlikely he'd be put in prison, but he worried his thesis work would be in jeopardy. Amid his confusion he made a naïve error: He went to Li Yihai and told him about the encounter. As soon as the words left his mouth, he realized what a stupid decision this was. Li didn't deny that Guthrie was being watched; he just wanted to know who the young man was. Guthrie wouldn't say but feared Li would figure it out; he begged Li not to do anything. This got the Communist official's attention. He asked Guthrie, in an ominous tone, "Well, are you a friend of China?" Guthrie worried his laptop might be confiscated. Li said he could get in trouble from Guthrie's unauthorized factory visits and started asking about his conclusions, about what positive things he might say about the country.

The encounter shook Guthrie, but he didn't fully grasp the implications until much later. Only in retrospect would he recall the episode with a fuller understanding: China might be reforming and opening up, but this wasn't some adoption of laissez-faire capitalism; the Communist Party was firmly in control. Guthrie had been a believer that economic reforms would lead to political change, and in the late nineties he would testify in Congress, advocating for China's entry into the WTO. Only later, living in Shanghai and working for Apple, would Guthrie come to fully realize how closely the party was tracking and monitoring what foreigners in China were doing. The party's whole reform program was meant to lure in capital and Western businesses as a way of learning, so China could reverse-engineer the technology, replicate it, and then replace it.

Dragon in a Three-Piece Suit

Upon becoming a lecturer, Guthrie taught students that China, unlike the caricature of the Communist country so often disseminated in

Western media, was actually a more decentralized nation than America. China featured federalism on steroids, contrasting wildly with Soviet Communism. Beijing sets the goals in substance and pace, but it's up to the provinces, municipalities, and counties to figure out how they meet them. The system—what the scholar Chenggang Xu calls "a regionally decentralized authoritarian regime," or RDA—is an enormous meritocracy for officials from provincial governors down to the local cadres. They're given wide latitude to incentivize businesses and work with them hand in glove to achieve fast growth and high employment. As Xu puts it: "The central government has control over personnel, whereas subnational governments run the bulk of the economy; and they initiate, negotiate, implement, divert, and resist reforms, policies, rules, and laws." Such decentralization allowed for experimentation on a grand scale: what worked in Guangdong could be replicated in Shanghai. But Beijing was often patient: It waited for the results of these experiments rather than rushing ahead with them. This combination of decentralized decision-making, experimentation, and gradual adoption of new policies played a critical role in how China became a manufacturing powerhouse.

Guthrie knew his students were familiar with the basic story of China's emergence on the modern stage under Deng Xiaoping, when it started to experience double-digit GDP growth after decades of tumult and chaos under Chairman Mao. But he thought most people didn't understand much about the drivers of those changes. Economists liked to portray the growth story as one of markets. A Communist society had loosened state controls, enabling human ingenuity to flourish; pockets of capitalism ushered in a wave of changes, rewarding people for hard work and creating a virtuous circle that gave rise to both supply and demand. Guthrie didn't find this view wrong per se, but the absence of local context was painful for his sociologist brain. The narrative didn't pay enough heed to facts on the ground. The "ruins" of China's previous system had, he argued, shaped the new systems as they emerged. So Guthrie put special focus on Chinese culture and local institutions. What emerged was a nuanced view of a China in transformation.

Western academics had a tendency to view China through their own lens. They saw entrepreneurs as motivated by profit maximization and would interpret certain actions, such as the mid-1990s adoption of codified labor standards, as driven by the desire to be more efficient. Guthrie in contrast viewed these moves by China's business sector as mimicking Western practices, a fake-it-till-you-make-it approach. A factory owner would adopt labor standards because the optics were good, and it would attract more foreign investment. These differences in motivation might sound subtle, but the ramifications were deep. China might be mimicking the West, but it wasn't actually *becoming* Western, as so many assumed; it merely looked that way. China, to quote the title of Guthrie's PhD-thesis-turned-book, was a *Dragon in a Three-Piece Suit.*

This insight led Guthrie to take a different view of the administrative state. It was common to predict that the party's role would simply wither away, but Guthrie observed that it was evolving. Government officials were no longer a heavy bureaucratic hand weighing on development; in their relationship with local and foreign companies, officials were acting more like venture capitalists—the kind that take a cut of equity, sit on the board, and aim to promote growth.

An economist who mistakenly believed China was growing in double digits solely because it had loosened the shackles of Communism was prone to believing that this growth would inculcate Western values, creating a self-reinforcing momentum that would lead to the collapse of the Chinese Communist Party. Such a view has a certain intellectual laziness to it, akin to nineteenth-century anthropologists whose social Darwinist perspective viewed other cultures as being in an earlier phase of a linear human development. Such views were, by the mid-twentieth century, recast as racist. But mainstream economics hadn't undergone the same change.

The fact was, China wasn't just catching up to the West; its system was maturing into something novel. "One of the great ironies of our time," Guthrie told students in 2013, "is that the largest Communist society in the world is also the most dynamic capitalist economy in the world. There's a tremendous amount that we can actually be learning from China." To drive home the point, Guthrie gestured with his hands and drew a continuum. On one side—his hands gesticulated to the right—were those who believe China is a corrupt "house of cards." On the other side—his hands pointing left—were those who are "very bullish on China." Describing his own view, Guthrie walked left until he was out of frame. "I'm, like, somewhere over here," he said to laughter. Guthrie could sound so laudatory regarding the Communist Party's ingenuity that the FBI had once shown up in his office asking questions, worried the professor might be a Chinese asset.

CHAPTER 29

VOLUNTARY IS THE NEW MANDATORY

As Guthrie was preparing to move to Shanghai for Apple and in the months after arriving, he began to observe that Xi Jinping was deviating from the script Washington had written two decades earlier when China was going to be the next great democracy. In the autumn of 2013, Xi announced the Belt and Road Initiative, a grandiose project to link China by land and sea to some 140 countries across the developing world. Among the BRI's goals was lessening China's reliance on exporting to the West and establishing a new model in which China could lead, not just fit within an existing consensus. Another Chinese government document spoke of the "seven unmentionables"—a list of ideas to be vigilant about, including freedom of the press, the party's historical errors, and judicial independence. Xi also began laying the groundwork for Made in China 2025, a blueprint for the country to achieve self-sufficiency in advanced electronics, biomedicine, and aerospace.

Washington immediately saw the plan as a rebuke of open markets and economic interdependence. "The program," wrote the US Council on Foreign Relations, "aims to use government subsidies, mobilize state-owned enterprises, and pursue intellectual property acquisition to catch up with—and then surpass—Western technological prowess in advanced industries." The Information Technology and Innovation Foundation, which counts Apple as a member, would later characterize the plan to Congress as "an aggressive by-hook-or-by-crook strategy that involves serially manipulating the marketplace and wantonly stealing and coercing transfer of American know-how."

Guthrie felt that China was at a pivotal juncture, but he was surprised how difficult it was to get the message across. He'd once told students: "Doing business in China means you have to have a deep understanding of local institutional conditions." But living in Shanghai and wanting to learn from the best—from Apple, the Western company that had cracked China—he was finding that the company didn't have a deep understanding at all. Certainly, not a nuanced sense of the "local institutional conditions" he deemed so important.

In light of Xi's other actions, the *Consumer Day* attack on Apple the year before didn't look, to Guthrie, like some one-off misunderstanding that Cook had neatly solved with an apology. It was a signal that Apple was in trouble. Guthrie began to see that Beijing was pivoting in ways that were bound to catch Apple off guard. It was becoming clear Xi would welcome foreign corporations only if they were "in China, for China"—and if they didn't like it, they could leave. Guthrie began to fret that Apple's enormous operations and retail presence in China were at great risk.

He tried to sound the alarm in Cupertino, but he had little influence or clout. The company was racking up record sales. Whatever problems Xi had expressed when he first entered office had—apparently—been solved. So when Guthrie would show up in Cupertino trying to deliver the message that Xi Jinping was taking China back to the 1990s—an era of "technology transfer" when accessing the Chinese market also meant handing over secrets to a local joint venture partner—he was easy to ignore.

Until, that is, his predictions started coming true.

The Floating Population

Lawyers in Cupertino were frantic and confused about China's newest ordinance—the labor dispatch law of mid-2014, which limited the share of temporary workers a company could employ to just 10 percent. The new rules wouldn't be enforceable until March 2016, but as soon as they were Apple's most important suppliers would be in violation. The lawyers looked at each other in dismay. "There's no way we can comply with this!" When they called up Doug Guthrie in China, the professor's response only confused them further. "That's the point," he told them. "You're *supposed* to be out of compliance." They'd protest: "How does that make any sense?" And Guthrie would explain: "Because you're supposed to go figure out what the mayor of Zhengzhou wants from you."

Cupertino's alarm was appropriate. The flexibility of Chinese labor was a key ingredient in the secret sauce that allowed Apple to function so efficiently. China didn't have plentiful labor just because it was a large country; the state orchestrated second-class migrants into a "floating population" of more than 220 million adult workers—a larger workforce than that of the entire United States. State-backed organizations commissioned companies to drive buses into rural areas to hire unskilled workers—so-called dispatch labor—and move them to Apple's vast network of suppliers for seasonal production. Internal documents obtained for this book detail how Apple's need for Chinese labor would fall below below 900,000 in the slow months of spring, but then ramp up to more than 1.7 million in the peak season before iPhone launch. Under the new law, which set a company's maximum temporary worker level at 10 percent of the total workforce, this could no longer happen. Apple's operations in China looked to be in serious peril.

Assessing how damaging the impact would be, Apple surveyed 362 factories in its supply chain and found that nearly half went beyond the 10 percent threshold, including 80 factories that relied on dispatch labor for more than 50 percent of their workforce. During product "ramp," when Apple often ships more than a million units per day of certain hardware, some factories' share of temporary labor exceeded 80 percent. "Our 'surprise and delight' business model requires a huge volume of labor for only a short period of time as we ramp products," an internal Apple presentation in 2015 said. "We are making it difficult for our suppliers to comply with this law as 10% dispatch is simply not enough to cope with the spikes in labor demand we require during our ramps."

No Western lawyer would have been trained to understand what was going on, though in principle it was fairly simple, akin to how a nuisance lawsuit is filed not to win but to extract a settlement. The Communist Party had little intention of enforcing the labor dispatch law by issuing fines, let alone ending the practice of deploying migrant labor to factories around China. The whole notion of a floating population was government-driven and had been for decades. In Mao's China, who lived where was so tightly controlled that it was illegal for individuals to reside outside of their registered area—their *hukou*—without official permission. When the Chinese economy began to open up in the early 1980s and experimental zones were flooded with foreign investment, rural villagers were allowed to find work in the city. But they were systematically discouraged from putting down proper roots. They faced obstacles accessing social services and had few labor rights, and their children couldn't attend urban schools, which meant they typically stayed back in the village. Even so, factory life was vastly preferable to toiling in the fields under the hot sun, so hundreds of millions of villagers flocked to cities like Dongguan and Shenzhen.

The flexibility of this exploited population was instrumental in China's rise. There was no way Beijing was doing away with it; instead, the regime was designing legislation to compel companies like Apple to respond with favors. The labor dispatch law was federal, but enforcement was local. So if Apple realized its operations ran afoul of the new rules, it had three choices: overhaul the way it did business; leave China; or find out what the local officials wanted. In this circuitous fashion, Beijing was telling Western corporations that if they wanted access to China's 1.4 billion people, they'd have to give up something.

Behind the basic principle was a wider legal history in China. Unlike the Rule *of* Law developed in the West, Xi was returning China to a Rule *by* Law tradition, a system of governance dating back more than 2,000 years. Rule *of* Law is about creating an impartial framework; Rule *by*

Law is about controlling the population—or in this case, nudging corporate behavior. Beijing was not *explicitly* demanding anything for market access—that was illegal under WTO rules. But it was redesigning the system to make wink-wink arrangements more likely. As one Western businessman living in China at the time characterized the changes, "voluntary is the new mandatory."

A Top-Down Project

Guthrie's opinions were again in demand in 2015 after—as he predicted—Apple received a terrible result in China's study of corporate social responsibility (CSR). The scores were published by SASAC—the State-owned Assets Supervision and Administration Commission of the State Council—an institution that has no equivalent in the United States. SASAC was among the most important organizations in the country. It was the largest shareholder of China Mobile, a dominant carrier with some 800 million subscribers, as well as China Telecom, its biggest rival. When SASAC published its first CSR report in 2015, Apple received a rating of 22.5 out of 100, the lowest of any large multinational.

The low grade baffled executives in Cupertino. Lawyers called up Guthrie with naïve hopes of getting an explanation of the situation. *Didn't China know Apple had spent years improving its environmental impact? Weren't they aware that in 2007 Steve Jobs had outlined plans to rid products of toxic chemicals? Had Beijing not seen Apple's annual reports on cutting carbon emissions and using more recycled materials?*

Guthrie explained Cupertino was missing the point. The rankings had little to do with Apple's environmental practices. The report made this clear in a subtle way: In the list of some forty companies, Apple was the only foreign corporation missing a label to indicate "joint venture." *That* was the point—Apple wasn't engaged in technology transfer with a local partner. As a study nearly a decade later would conclude: "In the West, CSR is a bottom-up form of private business self-regulation by which companies volunteer to support societal goals of a philanthropic, environmental, or human rights nature, [whereas] CSR in the Chinese context has been a top-down project in which companies support the political agenda of the ruling Chinese Communist Party (CCP) and government, including poverty reduction (which strengthens party legitimacy), environmental protection (which seemingly has become a personal preference of China's paramount leader Xi Jinping), and the CCP's goal of 'national rejuvenation.'"

Through this lens, it wasn't difficult to see why Samsung had attained best-in-class marks. The Korean giant had dozens of formal partners, its own multibillion-dollar manufacturing sites, and formal joint ventures going back decades that allowed Chinese partners to "capture" technical know-how. Samsung had prominently recognized the importance of China early on and had expanded from low-skilled production to cutting-edge chip fabrication. Apple had no formal joint ventures, did not engage in tech transfer, and operated in the shadows. Before 2012, when Apple came under pressure to publish a document listing its main suppliers, few people had any idea which factories supplied it with components.

The challenges kept coming. Apple engineers found that rules limiting their stay in the country were suddenly being enforced. Some even had to pay fines on the spot. Supplies going from one factory to another hit inexplicable road blocks. A US State Department official living in China at the time recalls that such unexplained inconveniences—known as *bu fang bian* in Mandarin—went from relatively rare, before Xi took over, to pervasive. Individuals they'd been working with would be "invited to tea" by the authorities, who'd make it clear they shouldn't work with the Americans.

Then in September 2015, China accused Apple of underreporting sales. The Ministry of Finance asked Apple to pay the equivalent of more than $80 million in unpaid taxes and fines. Cupertino grasped that the lights were flashing red. "We're watching you" is how Guthrie characterized the challenges. "And just like on *Consumer Day,* we can hit you if we want."

Self-Criticism

Guthrie was asked to put together a presentation on modern China. He began regularly flying into Cupertino to brief senior executives, including members of Tim Cook's innermost circle such as Services head Eddy Cue, explaining how Xi Jinping was charting a new course and brainstorming what might be required of the company. "It became increasingly clear that China could do serious things if it wanted to," he recounts. "And that was, I think, what got the executive team's attention. And that's where I started to get more attention as I was predicting this."

Wanting to help Apple's relations with government officials, Guthrie set out to study its supply chain. He conducted hundreds of interviews with vendors, just as he had in 1994 when he was a PhD candidate studying China's industrial transformation. At the start, he'd believed he would end up recommending that Apple build joint ventures with local partners—a prominent display of support for China that, he knew, would be anathema to Cupertino. But if Apple didn't act, the consequences could be dire. Anyone could see that. In 2013, Reuters reported on a meeting in which a senior Chinese official had threatened thirty foreign companies with antitrust fines and recommended they write "self-criticisms" about their behavior. "The message was: if you put up a fight, I could double or triple your fines," one participant told Reuters. In the first three years of Xi's reign Beijing launched antitrust investigations of Microsoft and Qualcomm, while IBM and Cisco suffered as their Chinese clients were incentivized to buy Chinese-branded machines. Each of these Western brands responded to Beijing's authoritarian tendencies by establishing new joint ventures, or in the case of IBM, agreeing to provide a Chinese partner with what *The New York Times* described as "a partial blueprint of its higher-end servers and the software that runs on them."

Qualcomm's case was the most public. China possessed great leverage over the California-based chip designer, an instrumental force in creating the 4G and 5G tech used in smartphones. The case has broadly been seen as a shakedown. Qualcomm revenues rest on being paid a licensing fee for every smartphone using its technology. As China became the world's largest market for smartphones, Beijing demanded the fees be cut. Qualcomm put up a fight, but there was little it could actually do. In 2015 it agreed to launch a joint venture and pay a $975 million fine, the largest in China's corporate history, to end the state's three-year antitrust investigation. "They held us hostage for a billion dollars and stole our intellectual property. And there was no negotiating. We were just grateful that we got to keep our business model," says one Qualcomm executive. During one ten-day period, two Qualcomm executives say the company grew so concerned about arrests that it stopped sending its people to the country. "We were afraid they would get kidnapped," says one. The single negotiator Qualcomm did send opted to sleep on the company's private jet during his stay. "He'd go to the meetings, but then he'd go back to the plane and would spend the night [there]."

CHAPTER 30

THE APPLE SQUEEZE

The most insane statistic about Apple's business is this: The iPhone accounts for fewer than 20 percent of smartphones sold around the world, yet it routinely boasts more than 80 percent of industry profits. In no other market does a minority player command this kind of dominance, and yet Doug Guthrie felt the media had failed to really investigate how it could be true. Insofar as the statistic was discussed at all, it was chalked up to Apple's brand appeal and its ability to sell more expensive phones than its rivals. But Samsung and others sold expensive phones, too. How was Apple so thoroughly dominating the most iconic consumer product category of the twenty-first century to the point that more than a dozen competitors were left fighting for four-fifths of the global market share, then divvying up less than 20 percent of the profits?

The statistic is quietly published each year by Counterpoint Research. When Guthrie first encountered it in 2015, he was determined to understand how it was possible. He knew Apple had long taken a majority of smartphone profits, but as prices of Android-based devices collapsed in the prior few years, Apple's profit stranglehold had only strengthened. iPhone prices weren't just stable; they were going *up*, contradicting some of the most basic premises of technology and economics. Compare the situation to what was happening with the PC, whose average price in 1990 was $4,000. As a result of competition and economies of scale, the average PC price fell below $1,500 by 2005. But the iPhone, starting at $499 in 2007, was, by 2015, fetching $649. How did Apple do it?

Wanting to help Apple understand its predicament in China, Guthrie started traveling and interviewing suppliers. In his talks with dozens of them, a common theme emerged. "Working with Apple is really fucking hard," suppliers would tell him. He'd respond: "So don't." And they would demur: "We can't. We learn so much." He soon grasped this dynamic wasn't at all the industry norm. Suppliers to Apple's rivals typically worked on a limited number of units, as Android phones and Windows-based computers catered across the price and geography spectrums. That meant each brand would sell dozens of different models per year, with varying components. For these companies, their higher volume products were in the lower end, where they could make use of standardized parts and wider tolerances. And they'd play suppliers off one another based on price. But Apple was different: under the design direction of Jony Ive, Apple's product portfolio remained radically simplified. Even by 2015, Apple was only releasing two new iPhones a year. They were hand crafting luxury phones but doing it in mass-market quantities. In their search for suppliers, Apple gravitated toward quality, not price. To reach that quality, Apple had to come up with new processes to make the phones; but until Apple chose a new design these processes wouldn't exist. So it had to work far more intimately with suppliers. "Apple influenced the entire manufacturing process because what they were doing was so unique. Nobody else was doing this, so Apple had to fund that equipment," says Brian Blair, a tech analyst who repeatedly toured Apple's suppliers back then. He uses an analogy from the automotive world: it's one thing for Volkswagen or GM to make 10 million cars a year; what Apple was doing was akin to making 10 million Ferraris a year.

The risk of this approach is that it that gives too much power to the supplier. So under Tim Cook's leadership, Apple had built redundancy into the supply chain, teaching multiple vendors how to do the same thing to mitigate risks of overdependence. "Every year there'd be discussion about our huge reliance on a small number of companies. What would happen if one of these companies were to stumble?" says one manufacturing design engineer. "Certainly at the component level," this person adds, "even Foxconn didn't have the space for the machines to make the components we needed, so we were kind of forced to find second sources, third sources."

Given Apple's scale and manufacturing concentration, the result of this strategy is that Apple spawned the formation of major industrial clusters in which engineers from Cupertino would teach multiple factories how to, say, shape glass for the iPhone. So instead of being beholden to Lens Technology—the company that cut and tempered Corning glass for the first iPhone—Apple would constantly send engineers from Cupertino to train its rivals. That kept Lens on its toes, lest Apple choose a different supplier for the next-generation iPhone—a potential catastrophe as Apple, by 2015, was producing a quarter billion iPhones per year. Moreover, it kept Lens from raising its prices. So any company supplying Apple with some component was preemptively thwarted from believing it had any power to exert, because Apple made it known that it had options.

These tactics, coupled with Apple's always wanting its next product to be a breakthrough, enabled the company to operate at incredible efficiency and earn way fatter margins than the rest of the industry. "Those factories are willing to forgo profit so that Apple ops engineers would come and teach them how to be efficient," Guthrie says. The explicit deal—let's call it the Apple Squeeze—was that Apple's engineering and operations teams would rigorously train local partners, in the process giving away manufacturing knowledge, in particular how to efficiently scale while maintaining the highest quality standards. In exchange, the local supplier would work for soul-crushingly low margins with the understanding that it could profit from the incredible volumes Apple demanded. It could also use these new skills to win orders from other clients, charging them more for similar work. So in 2016, when iPhone margins were 33 percent, Chinese rivals Oppo, Vivo, and Xiaomi were earning 7 percent, 6 percent, and 2 percent margins, respectively. In other words, the Apple Squeeze was instrumental to how Apple attained industry-leading margins. The message was: *We won't pay you much, but the experience will be invaluable.*

Apple took extraordinary control over its suppliers to ensure it was getting the appropriate prices. It demanded access to every detail about the supplier's operating costs, from the wages of its workers and the cost of its dormitories to the bill of materials and expense of the machinery. In fact, Apple often had a better sense of the suppliers' operational costs than the supplier itself. Because rather than have the supplier purchase the raw materials needed for whatever component it was manufacturing, Apple procured these components on their behalf—a power move that obfuscated from the supplier what the prices were. The tactic had emerged around 2010, when Foxconn was trying to earn extra money by purchasing components at one set of prices, then billing Apple a higher cost. Apple responded by "disintermediating" Foxconn. Another motivation was simply that, when annual iPhone shipments ran into the tens of millions per year, and then into the hundreds of millions, Apple realized it wasn't good enough to assume its suppliers would secure enough raw materials—the only way to ensure this was to be involved in negotiations directly. The power this team wielded was enormous: up to 1,300 people all reporting to Tony Blevins.

Suppliers would put up with this seemingly inequitable deal because they got something less tangible but more valuable than profits. They got engineering help from Apple's best—tuition-free, on-the-ground training—for multiple hours a day, day after day, for weeks and months leading up to a product launch. "So the reason Apple gets Chinese suppliers to work for them, for zero profits, is because the Apple ops engineer, following Tim Cook's orders, is sleeping on a mat in their factory and helping them make that line efficient," Guthrie says.

In numerous cases Apple wasn't just training employees, it was purchasing equipment and placing it on the factory line of its suppliers. Recall that in the late 2000s, supply chain researcher Kevin O'Marah had been blown away when he observed Apple spending hundreds of millions of dollars on machinery to put in its suppliers' factories. By 2018, the value of that machinery specifically for China—known as China "long-lived assets" in the company's annual reports—had grown to $13.3 billion. These staggering expenditures allowed the factories to operate at a scale they otherwise couldn't afford to.

Birthing China's Smartphone Market

In the early years of the iPhone, Apple was adamant that the processes it cocreated with suppliers were its intellectual property. When Apple believed Samsung had copied the iPhone, Steve Jobs was furious, and Apple sued. Tim Cook, speaking about the lawsuit in 2012, called it "the worst thing in the world" to be ripped off like that. "From our point of view, it's important that Apple not be the developer for the world," he said. "We can't take all of our energy and all of our care and finish the painting, then have someone else put their name on it."

But over time, Cook's team grew to understand that the innovations it came up with would be mimicked in China, usually within a year. This was simply the cost of doing business there. Ideally, Apple could keep secret particular processes, or demand exclusivity, but the duration of such agreements rarely went beyond twelve months. Efforts were made to prevent suppliers from brazenly offering the exact same thing to Apple's rivals, but suppliers could at least approximate what they'd accomplished and offer it to others. The suppliers weren't necessarily copying Apple in ways that violate patent laws or were illegal. Apple had been training them for more than a decade, and they'd become world class in both quality and scale.

Still, particular engineers at Apple would become irritated, even furious, that something they'd worked on for countless hours over months was copied and commoditized for the rest of the market. When Jony Ive, in 2014, was asked about the likeness of the latest Xiaomi phones, he fumed: "It really is theft and it's lazy and I don't think it's okay at all."

But such outbursts became rarer with time. As an organization, Apple understood that the overall effect of mimicry was that competitors were always one step behind. "They were trying to copy what Apple's shipping versus what Apple's going to ship," says one senior executive.

Besides, Apple realized where their bread was buttered. Suing Chinese companies for patent infringement ran the risk of being seen in China as a bully. Even if Apple had a patent upheld, enforcing it was understood to be impossible. And Apple had learned that its multicountry, multiyear battle with Samsung had done it no favors. Cook, asked in an interview about the patent wars, responded that they were "a pain in the ass."

The shift in thinking was also driven by the practical realities of how the iPhone's exponential growth impacted its top suppliers. Apple had instituted a rule so that its vendors wouldn't be more than 50 percent reliant on Apple for their revenues. Overdependence on Apple could create trouble, because Cupertino had a propensity to shift directions. So if, say, a company providing a key component was 80 percent dependent on iPhone revenue, and Apple made a design change obviating the need for that component, that company might collapse. In fact, many did; this happened repeatedly, and it caused Apple problems, including negative headlines in the media and bad will from suppliers. So Apple learned to find a sweet spot: to be the most important client for its suppliers, so it had leverage, but not so much that the supplier was overly reliant.

The upshot of this policy, as a senior executive put it, was that "whatever rate we're growing at, they have to grow that fast with someone else." So as iPhone shipments soared, Apple encouraged its China-based suppliers to feed the Android market. As a result, Apple gave birth to the Chinese smartphone industry. In 2009, the majority of smartphones sold in China were produced by Nokia, Samsung, HTC, and BlackBerry. But as Apple taught the supply chain how to perfect multi-touch glass and make the thousand components within the iPhone, Apple's suppliers took what they knew and offered it to homegrown companies led by Huawei, Xiaomi, Vivo, and Oppo. Result: the local market share of such

Chinese brands grew by leaps and bounds, from 10 percent in 2009 to 35 percent by 2011, and then to 74 percent by 2014. It's no exaggeration to say the iPhone didn't kill Nokia; Chinese imitators of the iPhone did. And the imitations were so good because Apple trained all their suppliers. Cook didn't want Apple to be the developer of the world, and it wasn't. It did, however, become the developer for China.

Indeed, the industrial clusters supported by Apple's gargantuan investments were so significant that other phone makers came under tremendous pressure to keep up. But lacking a playbook or the detailed knowledge of how Apple operations worked, they turned to Chinese suppliers for help, giving over intellectual property in exchange for a speedy response. "They all completely abdicated," says Horace Dediu, the former Nokia executive who now runs the market intelligence group Asymco. Apple, in other words, set in motion a series of events that helped Chinese suppliers win more orders and advance their understanding of cutting-edge manufacturing. At the same time, Western manufacturing of electronics atrophied.

Any number of Apple engineers, and certainly its top executives, already knew all of this. But what Guthrie drew from it was novel: If Beijing and provincial officials were told about the Apple Squeeze, he argued, they'd understand it to be a superior form of technology transfer than the joint venture model. In a typical JV, the foreign corporation doesn't actually want to give away its technology, so it would keep a certain distance whenever possible. Apple, by contrast, created intimate connections to make the supplier work well beyond their own perceived capabilities, and then actively encouraged them to thrive independently so they wouldn't be overly exposed. As Apple's engineers spent thousands of hours codeveloping processes with local suppliers, they were modeling a domineering attention to detail and teaching problem-solving techniques with specialized machinery and different materials.

"I don't remember, ever, a strategic withholding of information," says a former Apple industrial designer. "All we cared about was making the most immaculate thing . . . We were inventing every day. Every day you'd invent your way through a problem. It was absolutely wonderful as an experience. But I guess we were unwittingly tooling them up with incredible knowledge—incredible know-how and experience."

Or as a former Apple VP said to this author over coffee: "Are you sure you're not overthinking your thesis? You keep talking about geopolitics, but I was there in the 2000s when we were setting up production in China, and I can tell you, we weren't thinking about geopolitics at all."

Precisely.

Registered Capital

Hard-liners in Beijing had viewed Apple as an exploitative power because through their conventional lens, it looked that way. Samsung had several dozen formal partnerships in the country; Apple had none. Samsung had its own manufacturing plants; Apple had none. But Guthrie's argument turned this logic on its head. He emphasized that Apple was embedding its top engineers into more than 1,600 factories, making a few dozen partnerships look paltry. The difference was that the likes of Intel and Samsung were trumpeting their joint ventures and investments in the country, while Apple was silent. Worse, Apple was allowing Foxconn to take credit for all manner of investments that ultimately traced back to iPhone and iPad demand.

Guthrie argued this was a mistake. And he was purporting to solve a major riddle: why Apple was perceived as a negative force in Beijing. Apple contributed greatly, creating millions of jobs and supporting a sophisticated supply chain that ricocheted well beyond its own needs. But its contributions were unknown because of Apple's secretive, insular culture. He advocated something radical: Get the message out to everyone, sing it from the hilltops if necessary, until every government official understands just how much the country is gaining from Apple's presence. "China wants the constant learning," he says. "The fact that Apple helps bring up 1,600 suppliers for China—it's an incredible benefit."

Guthrie's thesis immediately met resistance. Cupertino viewed its operations strategy as its secret sauce, not something to be broadcast. Executives were also acutely aware that the scale of its investments in China could be politically charged in Washington. As one American executive involved in Apple strategy around this time put it: "Nobody likes to portray it that way, because that gets you into deep trouble with the regulators here."

Michael Hillman, who spent years in Asia bringing up the competencies of entire supply networks, says Apple's reticence to articulate the impact of its actions goes all the way back to its first days in China in the early 2000s. "There was this allergic reaction from Apple executives, but that's exactly what was fucking happening," Hillman says. He recalls speaking to Jon Rubinstein, senior vice president of hardware, about teaching the Chinese how to do their job, only to be "corrected" by his boss. "You can't say that; that's not what you're there doing," Ruby said. "Okay, well what am I doing? What am I missing?" Hillman asked. "I was trying to be respectful. But it was this open, nasty secret that the competencies weren't there. And the only way we were going to ship a product was by embedding Apple engineers and Apple operations staff into vendors to get the quality, the yield, that we wanted."

In Hillman's view, Apple hadn't entered China with a clear strategy to build industrial clusters; it was just something that evolved with time as the company solved one problem after another. "That whole process started early on and kept growing and growing," he says. "So it wasn't some genius move; it was just a gradual accretion of capability, and Apple taking advantage of it, and then you combine that with our contracting getting ever more sophisticated, and the amount of control authority that Apple had. We could basically call the rules."

Guthrie declined to share the specific findings of his supply chain study, but other sources provided internal documents that expand upon his research and demonstrated Apple's impact on the country's development. These documents show that in 2015, Apple's investments in China had totaled $55 billion per year, an astronomical sum that, through political channels, could easily demonstrate the company's commitment to the country. This estimate wasn't overinflated for impact, but it contained some creative logic that's worth unpacking. The figure looked at investments that remained in China, not overall spend—a much higher figure that would include the cost of components in its devices, known as the BOM, or bill of materials. Apple does not release these figures, but third-party BOM estimates for the iPhones selling in 2015 are above $200 per device. Multiplied by the 231 million devices Apple made in China that year, the iPhone BOM would alone be around $50 billion—and that's before adding the component and material costs for the iPad, the MacBook, and all the other Apple hardware.

On this wider measure of spend, Apple was in the top-tier of corporate spending, but it wasn't unique. Several companies spend tens or even hundreds of billions of dollars in China. Walmart sales in 2015 were $485 billion, and by some estimates more than 60 percent of its products come from China. But almost none of that spending is investment. If Walmart calculated its investment in China, it wouldn't make sense for it to include, say, the wages of the Chinese workers making toilet paper, pet supplies, or kitchenware. Such wages are spend, not investment.

But this is where Guthrie's argument got clever, relying on his niche expertise. China, he knew, had a concept called registered capital, referring to investments made by foreign companies in the initial buildup phase. An automaker operating a joint venture, like GM or Volkswagen, can initially count wages as registered capital because they are investing in worker training. After a year or two, when a car's production line is up and running, wages cease to be investment and become a part of spend.

Guthrie argued that much of Apple's spending in China was more like GM's than Walmart's—it wasn't classified that way, but it should be. Because a sizable part of the wages Apple paid to workers across its supply chain was akin to training costs. And whereas an auto company trained workers in the setup phase for a new car, Apple was constantly innovating, teaching new skills and processes to refresh its multifaceted product portfolio. And it wasn't doing so in a joint venture or two, but with hundreds of suppliers.

That's how Apple's estimate got to $55 billion. The figure included wages for the 3 million people it pays down multiple tiers in the supply chain, plus the billions of dollars Apple spends each year on machinery that it places in its suppliers' factories, as well as the construction of its retail stores. "What we have to convince the Chinese government of is there's a big play here," he told colleagues. "Apple isn't just sitting in a trading company office in Pudong and buying touchscreen glass from Lens. We're actually helping all of these suppliers build these things."

In total contrast to his earlier assumption that Apple might need to overhaul aspects of its China operations by establishing joint ventures, Guthrie realized that more than anything, *Apple just needed to market what it was already doing.* The hard-liners in Beijing had seen Apple as an exploitative trading company that offered nothing in return, but in fact Apple was the world's biggest corporate investor in China, a mass enabler of "indigenous innovation."

Apple's own balance sheet tells the story: The value of its "machinery, equipment and internal-use software"—namely the instruments placed in third-party factories for production—totaled less than $2 billion in 2009, but then soared beyond $44.5 billion by 2016—more than four times the value of all "land and buildings" owned by Apple—as the company took unprecedented control of its supplier network.

Cupertino's resistance to Guthrie's ideas began to gave way. Soon the question turned to: *How do we tell Beijing?*

CHAPTER 31

A MARSHALL PLAN FOR CHINA

Tim Cook and operations chief Jeff Williams each wore dark formal suits and white dress shirts with matching blue ties. A photograph snapped by Chinese media shows both men standing with one hand clasped over the other, a formal stance befitting a high-stakes event. Behind them is Lisa Jackson, the head of Environment, Policy, and Social Initiatives, in a black blazer. Williams, with a furrowed brow, appears focused but apprehensive about their meeting. Jackson has a serious expression, looking composed. Cook is more relaxed, practiced, and calm—more confident. The three executives were on the grounds of Zhongnanhai, the headquarters of the Chinese Communist Party. Cook had been there at least once before, in March 2012, when he met with vice premier Li Keqiang, who the following year would be appointed the number two to Xi Jinping.

The closely guarded compound, in central Beijing near the Forbidden City, was quite the location to meet executives from an American company. Zhongnanhai, strictly off-limits to the public, is where Mao told a Soviet ambassador in 1958 that he was prepared to mobilize the entire population of China for a new world war he expected to break out within a decade. It had long been a place to host foreign dignitaries, including Che Guevara and Richard Nixon. And now, in May 2016, it was where Beijing had summoned three top executives from Apple.

Just a few months earlier, Apple's China business was the star of its holiday 2015 earnings. Global revenues had inched forward only 2 percent, but China sales had climbed 14 percent—carrying the whole company into growth. Apple was sitting on an enormous cash pile of $216 billion. "We have the mother of all balance sheets," Cook boasted. And the future looked bright: for the first time, Apple's installed base—the number of active devices out in the wild—had crossed 1 billion. So even if the smartphone market was saturated, Apple had a new opportunity to sell consumers higher-margin services, like music, movies, and other entertainment.

But the first four months of 2016 were troubling: the March quarter experienced an abrupt U-turn, driven by China sales collapsing by 26 percent. Instead of carrying Apple, the China disappointment forced the tech giant to report its first year-over-year decline in *global* revenue in thirteen years. Its shares plummeted 7.9 percent, and Apple issued a gloomy outlook. The March quarter would turn out to be the start of a six-quarter streak of earnings decline in China, when iPhone market share in the country would fall from 15 percent to 9 percent. An internal study at the company would later say of the period: "Apple had not seen a downturn like this in China in over a decade."

That same month, April 2016, China's State Administration of Press, Publication, Radio, Film, and Television suddenly shut down the iTunes and iBooks stores, which had only been launched half a year earlier. The regulator now said Apple would need a joint-venture partner to run the services. *The New York Times* called it a startling move with major significance. "The company may finally be vulnerable to the heightened scrutiny that other American tech companies have faced in recent years," it reported. The pressure may have stemmed from China's homegrown competitors, who were upset that the iPhone offered proprietary content and services inaccessible to the Android universe. The regulatory move thwarted Apple as it expanded into entertainment and services, which made it more like a Google or a Facebook. Bloomberg noted that Apple had been "allowed to grow almost unimpeded in China" in the previous decade, but now it looked like Beijing wanted to tilt the field in favor of domestic companies.

When the trio of Apple executives traveled to Beijing a few weeks later, they were in damage control mode. Cook and his team were there to meet with China's economic planning agency, the National Development and Reform Commission. They were more than just prepared. They were ready to sign an extraordinary agreement—a pledge to invest $275 billion in China over the next five years. The meeting was part of a wider campaign to forgo its usual secrecy and begin trumpeting to Beijing just how seminal Apple's influence was on the country's tech sector. The meeting reflected how successful the Gang of Eight and the government affairs team had been in getting Cupertino to fit Apple's business narrative into language Beijing would appreciate. But whereas Guthrie advocated broadcasting this message loud and clear, Cook had opted for a different route: to deliver the message quietly to a select audience of top officials. No doubt this was politically necessary. At the time, Donald Trump was campaigning for president on his "America First" platform, threatening 45 percent tariffs on Chinese imports and promising, "We're going to get Apple to build their damn computers and things in this country!" One of his top advisors, Peter Navarro, had cowritten a book called *Death by China*. If Cook had held a press conference from Zhongnanhai, it would have been suicide.

The Local Language

The optics were extraordinary. The waiting Apple executives stood near the red-coated gate to the main entrance, called Xinhuamen, the Gate of New China. It was flanked by two banners: "Long Live the Great Communist Party of China" and "Long Live the Invincible Mao Zedong Thought." The scene underscored just how much had changed since 2000, when the first China-made iMacs rolled off the assembly line. Back then, Washington was encouraging China to join the World Trade

Organization. Many officials believed that trade would empower China's middle class and perhaps topple the Communist leadership; instead, foreign investment strengthened the Communist Party. No corporation was a bigger investor than Apple, and that was the message the executives were here to convey.

The $275 billion pledge from Apple was so large that other corporate investments pale in comparison. Apple was promising that it alone would invest more in China, for the coming five years, than all Canadian and American private investment into Mexico from the signing of NAFTA in 1993 through 2020. Indeed, it was large enough to eclipse some of the largest government-backed nation-building programs ever. Between 1979 and 2007, for instance, the Japanese Overseas Economic Cooperation Fund granted ¥2.54 trillion worth of loans to China—around $30 billion in 2016 dollars—to help the country's development. Ezra Vogel, a biographer of Deng Xiaoping, said of the financial aid: "During Deng's years at the helm, no country played a greater role in assisting China build its industry and infrastructure than Japan."

Or consider the 1948 Marshall Plan. That involved America's spending $13.3 billion over four years to spur post–World War II development in sixteen European countries—or $131 billion in 2016 dollars. The chief administrator of the Marshall Plan once called it "the most generous act of any people, anytime, anywhere, to another people." Yet Apple, in China alone rather than in sixteen countries, was telling Beijing it would invest more than double that amount by 2021. It's been estimated that every dollar of Marshall spending stimulated $4 to $6 worth of additional European production. And as historian Niall Ferguson has noted, the gift to the continent "played an important part in moving Europe from a dysfunctional system of labor relations based on strike action and class conflict to one based on wage restraint and productivity growth."

Cook's goal was to convey a similar message, to demonstrate to Chinese officials that Apple's success in China had ripple effects across the advanced electronics industry. By investing in and teaching local suppliers, Apple was inculcating a corpus of hands-on knowledge, both in tangible skills and abstract concepts, which applied well beyond serving its own needs. True, this was fairly unintentional; Apple hadn't designed its supply chain to spur innovation at its suppliers. Yet that's exactly what it had accomplished. And Apple's investments weren't just large, they were ruthlessly efficient and narrowly targeted in the advanced electronics sector—"by far the most important" thing desired by Xi, according to China scholar Barry Naughton. Conveyed in the right language, this impact was wildly supportive of Beijing's goals to learn from the West and move up the value chain.

Thinking of Apple's investment like a government program is instructive. Year in, year out, China didn't have the talent or expertise to build the products that Jony Ive's studio conceived, but the engineers Apple hired out of MIT, Caltech, and Stanford, or poached from Tesla, Dell, and Motorola, routinely got them up to speed. Apple could send a caliber of talent to China—what one Apple veteran calls "an influx of the smartest of the smart people"—that no government program ever could. And the culture was such that the Apple engineers would work up to eighteen hours a day. Moreover, whereas a government program could at best train a workforce to engineer products, it wouldn't have the ability to actually purchase the goods. But Apple could and did.

In economic terms, Apple was creating the whole market—supplying inputs in the form of worker training and machinery, then purchasing the outputs. The suppliers who won Apple contracts were given a massive order book and were taught to ramp up at a pace none had ever experienced. Better still, Apple had put so much design, brand image, and superb marketing into its products that even without commanding a dominant market *share,* it nevertheless attained a dominant market *style.* A new Apple product would set into motion the look, feel, and substance of what a laptop or smartphone should be. So the processes it often co-invented with China-based suppliers were in great demand.

And it wasn't just a transfer of knowledge from America to China.

Apple had a specific team of Subject Matter Experts, whose job was to research new processes, new materials, new tools, and new machines. "If the current machines, the current technologies in Asia, were not enough for what we were looking for, the SME team would go to Europe or Japan to search for new technologies," says a former manufacturing design engineer. "They'd try to find new technologies, new labs, new research facilities, whatever—and if they could find it, they'd try to transfer that to China and make in China what we couldn't do with the current technology." This person adds: "This happened every year when we had to launch a new product. Because every year we were pushing the envelope and we'd need something new . . . Apple identified a lot of technology, for example, in the watch industry and jewelry industry in Switzerland, Germany, and Austria, and they'd go to those places, find these special machines—these special technologies for very refined high-end products—and try to adapt those machines into making an iPhone or iPad or Mac."

What Apple had realized was that, unwittingly, its presence in China was enabling technology transfer on an extraordinary scale. As mind-bogglingly large as its $275 billion investment was, it was not really a quid pro quo. The number didn't represent any concession on Apple's part. It was just the $55 billion the company estimated it'd invested for 2015, multiplied by five years. That earlier estimate had little to do with politics; the figure was enormous because Apple was wildly successful and had heavily concentrated its operations in a single country. Indeed, the five-year pledge would rightly be seen as a low-ball projection, given that it assumed no growth. What was new, in other words, wasn't Apple's investment, but its *marketing* of the investment. China was accumulating reams of specialized knowledge from Apple, but Beijing didn't know this because Apple had been so secretive. From this meeting forward, the days in which Apple failed to score any political points from its investments in the country were over. It was learning to speak the local language.

"Music to the Ears of China"

The investment took the form of a nonbinding Memorandum of Understanding, a 1,250-word document that had many authors. Former Apple executives familiar with the memo say it was built upon the research of at least three members in the Gang of Eight—Guthrie's supply chain study, Steven Marcher's work on how local R&D hubs would help China, and input from the local government affairs team headed by Jun Ge. But it had largely been drawn up by a Cupertino-based subordinate to Jackson, David McIntosh—a Pittsburgh-born policy wonk in his early forties.

McIntosh, who has an understated, scholarly demeanor behind his dark-framed glasses, had joined Apple only the year before, but he already had the trust of Jackson from serving as a top political advisor when she was heading the Environmental Protection Agency. McIntosh has described his position with Apple as a "troubleshooter of Chinese regulatory problems." In his six-year stint, he took forty-five trips to China, often accompanying Tim Cook. His LinkedIn profile includes a photograph of himself aboard Apple's private jet, looking both relaxed and focused in a spacious cream-colored leather seat next to tables set with white linen cloths. He has captioned the photo: "Shuttle diplomacy."

The fact that McIntosh was so involved in crafting the document had irked members of the Apple government affairs team in China. The Harvard Law graduate was no China expert, hadn't lived in the country, and didn't speak Mandarin. "There was a lot of friction between David and other people in terms of how this was being put together and how this was going to be worded," says a person familiar with the tension. "The importance of this was huge . . . to be seen engaging at that level with the Chinese government, so you have to be treading carefully."

Exactly what Apple's trio of top executives told Beijing leadership that day isn't known. But what they were directly signaling to Beijing was that Apple wasn't just creating millions of jobs in the country; it supported entire industries by facilitating an epic transfer of "tacit knowledge"—hard-to-define but practical know-how "in the art of making things, in organizing practical matters, and in the way people produce, distribute, travel, communicate, and consume," as the China-born Federal Reserve economist Yi Wen defines it. For Yi, it was the acquisition of this tacit knowledge, rather than democracy or property rights, that acted as "the secret recipe" behind England's Industrial Revolution in the eighteenth century, as well as China's over the past four decades. Or, to put it more simply, quoting the late Harvard economist David Landes: "If the gains from trade in commodities are substantial, they are small compared to trade in ideas."

Whatever difficulty Apple executives had in drawing up the document, it served its intended purpose. "That was music to the ears of China," says one Apple executive familiar with the talks. Beijing had spent decades trying to catch up to the West's lead in advanced industry, scientific research, and economic might. It often resorted to spying, outright theft, or coercive tactics. Or it would orchestrate complicated schemes, like pitting multiple high-speed rail groups against each other to win major contracts, all the while learning from each and synthesizing the different technologies into something "new." Or it would lure expertise from abroad, such as the Thousand Talents program—a government-sponsored effort to bring outside experts to China. But here was America's most famous tech giant *volunteering* to play the role of Prometheus, handing the Chinese the gift of fire.

Apple's messaging wasn't public, but if it had been, it would've turned received wisdom on its head. In 2017, a *Wall Street Journal* article had opined: "Longer term, though, Apple's business is out of step with the Chinese government's goal to reduce its dependence on expensive foreign technology, and facilitate the development of homegrown competitors like Huawei." In fact, the opposite was true. The technology transfer that Apple facilitated made it the biggest corporate supporter of Made in China 2025, Beijing's ambitious, anti-Western plan to sever its reliance on foreign technology.

Ludicrous Mode

The paradigm shift Apple initiated was so consequential that it left Chinese officials convinced that its JV model was broken. In 2018, officials in Shanghai allowed Tesla to become the first foreign automaker to establish a manufacturing plant in the country without a local partner. It was characterized in the press as a sweetheart deal, as if government officials had succumbed to the charm of Elon Musk. But China was acting in its own interest. When Musk proposed to open the factory within two years, the mayor of Shanghai convinced him to fast-track the effort to just twelve months, offering big incentives, including affordable land and tax benefits. "It was probably the fastest and most CapEx-efficient factory ever built in the car industry, let alone EVs, in the world," says Harsh Parikh, then the head of global supply management for CapEx at Tesla.

Why the rush? China had first opened its doors to foreign carmakers in 1984, when bicycles dominated the landscape. Within a few short years Volkswagen's first joint venture became the country's largest automaker, and Mercedes and BMW mimicked the strategy. The Germans proceeded to dominate China's premium car market for three decades, with a collective market share north of 70 percent in 2016. The whole point of the JV model, as the CCP-run *Guangming Daily* put it in 1985, was for China to replace "the formula of 'the first machine imported, the second machine imported, and third machine imported,'" and replace it with: "the first machine imported, the second made in China, and third machine exported." Yet in more than three decades of the JV model, no Chinese car brand ever became competitive enough to vie with the Germans. In 2016, each of the ten premium brand leaders were foreign. Plenty of local brands served the lower-end local market, but none were so evolved that they penetrated foreign markets in large numbers. As *The Economist* later put it: "For all its manufacturing might, China never mastered internal-combustion engines, which have hundreds of moving parts and are tricky to assemble."

Electric vehicles changed the game. But more specifically, Tesla did. China's ambition in electric vehicles goes back to around 2001, and with hefty government incentives, EVs became embedded in the public transportation system about a decade later. The sector had been so awash in incentives and subsidies that Shenzhen alone had 17,000 electric buses at a time when all of Europe and North America had practically none. Consumers who purchased EVs were often able to get a free license plate, which are otherwise tightly controlled and sold at auction. Despite all this support, EVs and plug-in hybrids together accounted for just 4.8 percent of the new car market in 2019.

Tesla broke ground on the Shanghai Gigafactory in December 2018; by late 2019 China-made Model 3 vehicles were coming off the production line. Immediately they were a massive hit, and the Tesla Model 3 was China's bestselling EV in 2020. Chinese consumers "didn't want to buy anything being manufactured by Chinese brands; they all wanted Tesla," says Parikh. "As soon as Tesla came, there was a paradigm shift from consumers, and that's something the Chinese government saw. This was an opportunity to have the entire EV industry in China compete with, and learn from, Tesla."

In China, this phenomenon has been called the catfish effect. The idea is based on the fact that when sardines are caught at sea and placed in a tank for their journey back to shore, they become sedentary and die. But sardines kept alive tend to have better flavor and texture, and thus fetch more money. The story goes that a Norwegian fisherman figured out that if he threw a catfish into the tank, the sardines would keep swimming and fight for survival. The presence of a single predator causes the whole tank of sardines to better themselves. Beijing, it's often said, wanted Tesla to play the role of the catfish for the EV industry.

The theory is partly misleading. It implies that Tesla just *inspires* competitors to do better, but Tesla works intimately with and improves its third-party vendors, who then supply the local EV brands such as BYD. This, of course, is the Apple model, and Parikh—who played a key role in establishing the Shanghai Gigafactory—specifically hired engineers with Apple experience to set the plan into motion. "Working with

Tesla is not easy," Parikh says. "But the mindset of suppliers is 'We're going to become very strong if we can adapt.' It's just like working with Apple. If they can unlock the scalability, then they can grow with Apple, or grow with Tesla, and become world-class suppliers."

Tesla's investment in China has worked out brilliantly for China's EV sector, with quality improving across the board. The share of EVs and plug-ins soared from under 5 percent in 2019 to 38 percent in 2023. And the investment has certainly worked out well for Tesla: Shanghai now accounts for half of the company's global production. But there are longer-term uncertainties and unanswered questions. "In this game, one American company—Tesla in cars and Apple in phones—gets to win," says another former Tesla executive. "They don't care if all their US competitors lose. It's actually better for them. But on the other side, all the Chinese companies win. They all get to step up and create a massive market where none previously existed."

CHAPTER 32

BUREAUCRATIC PROTECTION

Jean Liu's meeting in Cupertino was already shaping up to be the most important of her career when, just days before in April 2016, China's regulators shut down Apple's iTunes and iBooks stores. For Liu, the thirty-seven-year-old president of Didi Chuxing, a ride-hailing start-up, the abrupt move made for impeccable timing. Didi was spending truckloads of money in a battle for supremacy with Uber, and the cash burn was only going to get worse if Didi opted to invest in autonomous driving technology. Liu needed some financial help. But more than that; she wanted Apple's endorsement. The request was audacious, but she happened to be catching Apple at just the moment Cupertino was eager to alter its narrative in China. Beijing's attack on Apple's digital stores meant that future growth in services and content would be constrained. Worse, the regulatory move likely signaled more trouble to come.

Cook had cautiously chosen to broadcast Apple's $275 billion deal with Beijing quietly, so Cupertino needed to take other action as well. In effect it deployed a two-track approach. The private investment demonstrated its positive impact across multiple industrial clusters, while a second track would more publicly showcase new partnerships, more job creation, and the local R&D hubs. Liu might not have known all the details of Apple's predicament, but she was no amateur in getting deals done with strategic rivals and potential partners.

The COO-turned-president of Didi had joined the company in July 2014 when it was already two years old, yet her work was so important that she'd earned the title of cofounder. Born in China—her given name is Liu Qing—and educated in computer science, Liu had spent more than a decade at Goldman Sachs, climbing from junior analyst to managing director in Hong Kong. When she first became interested in Didi, it was just one of thirty ride-hailing companies in China. Not having a driver's license in Beijing, Liu found it difficult to navigate the city with her three children and was thankful for Didi's service. She tried to invest on behalf of Goldman, but Didi had little problem raising money in its early years and rebuffed her. Eventually she told them, "Well, at least let me join you." She'd almost immediately made her mark by orchestrating a dramatic merger with its chief rival, Kuaidi, leveraging relationships she'd built as an investment banker.

In just two years Liu, who has expressive eyes and dark, wavy hair that falls to one side of her face, had become something of an ambassador for Chinese tech. Her rival at Uber, Travis Kalanick, was known for dropping out of college, breaking rules, and throwing frat-boy parties. By contrast, Liu had graduated from Peking University, then Harvard; she came across as poised and methodical, listening intently before speaking and then conveying both warmth and ambition. Whereas Kalanick spoke of disrupting taxi networks, she spoke of collaborating with them. Liu dealt with difficult questions in an unapologetic, matter-of-fact style. Once, defending Didi's cash-burning tendencies in its battle with Uber, she told investors: "We wouldn't be here today if it wasn't for burning cash."

Meeting with Cook, she broke the ice with a joke: "Our company's legal name is called 'little orange,'" she said. "We figured a company named after a fruit could always achieve something big." Cook was charmed. He'd later say he was impressed by Liu's environmental ambitions and messaging on social responsibility. "Jean has . . . built a company that is dedicated to serving the community around it," he wrote in 2017. "By analyzing commuter patterns the way oceanographers track the tides, Didi may help traffic jams go the way of the flip phone."

Here to Stay

Just twenty-two days after their meeting, Apple announced a $1 billion investment in the ride-hailing start-up. Liu said it happened "like lightning." The investment stunned tech observers. Sure, Apple had acquired plenty of companies outright in the past, and it certainly had the cash, but the Cupertino behemoth almost never took a stake in a start-up—especially not an app developer that competed against rivals within its own ecosystem. It was the largest single investment Didi had ever received. Cook's explanation didn't exactly hold water: "We are extremely impressed by the business they've built and their excellent leadership team, and we look forward to supporting them as they grow." His comments weren't wrong so much as beside the point. Hundreds, even thousands of app companies would have been good investments since the App Store debuted in 2008, but Apple hadn't bought a stake in any. Most observers had an inkling of what was really going on. "The deal seems like a calculated move by Apple to curry favor in China," wrote *The Information*.

Even Apple executives were surprised. "That was a signpost event," said one person who'd helped Apple build out its Asian supply chain in the early 2000s. "Like, this is how organized the graft is. It used to be a roll of hundreds out of your pocket, under a table in a restaurant. Now it's in public: 'You're going to write us a billion-dollar check to invest in our autonomous driving and machine-learning start-up.'" Apple executives in the immediate aftermath told this person that Beijing had specified the investment and that Apple followed through to "show we're committed to the CCP." This, however, is unlikely. Chinese politics rarely work that way. Rather, officials set the conditions where such demonstrations of commitment are warmly welcomed, but the commitments are not well defined. That way, nothing untoward is put into writing, China avoids breaking WTO rules, and the corporation is left wondering if its actions are enough.

There's a parallel here to Apple's own negotiating tactics. People familiar with Tony Blevins say he was averse to drawing red lines or asking for specific prices; rather, his feedback, until a contract was signed, would consistently involve uncertainty. He created the conditions where suppliers would pitch selling components well below the price he'd hoped for. But now the tables had turned, and these tactics were used by a nation-state against Apple.

Both parties downplayed this narrative. When Liu was asked if the deal could help Apple's political standing in China, she demurred, saying there was a "good foundation where we can help each other in many ways." But it surely hadn't escaped Cook's notice that his new partner was the daughter of Liu Chuanzhi, among the most politically connected tech entrepreneurs in China. Jean's father founded Lenovo in 1984, building it into China's largest PC maker by the late 1990s, then expanding internationally by purchasing the IBM ThinkPad PC business in 2005 and Motorola's handset business a decade later. Lenovo was born out of the Chinese Academy of Sciences, a government research institute that had remained its biggest shareholder. A variety of US government bodies have reportedly warned about the risks of using Lenovo equipment, citing cybersecurity concerns. For Apple, Lenovo's proximity to the state wasn't a liability, but its attraction.

The nature of the Didi investment would set an Apple precedent. Nothing it did was pure political window dressing. The team was getting savvy in how to work the political system in China, and if it had to make political overtures, it would do so in ways that achieved other aims, too. The Didi investment served at least two functions. At the time, the Next Big Thing in Silicon Valley was self-driving cars—a technology that, according to Google cofounder Larry Page, might be "bigger than Google." Apple wasn't immune to the hype, and in 2014 it had launched Project Titan, a secretive car project envisioning a driverless ride-hailing service in both the United States and China. Didi could offer Apple a "fast track into the world of autonomous vehicle and mapping," says a former Apple engineer on Project Titan, explaining that autonomy requires mapping out the roads and that foreign companies aren't allowed to collect such data. If Apple was serious about autonomy, it had to establish the right connections. And Didi had them, including a relationship with a Beijing-based mapping company called Auto Navi, the best and most widely used such service in the country.

The second function the Didi investment served related to Apple's surprise at how slowly its digital payments platform, Apple Pay, was taking hold. It saw Didi as a solid platform for expansion. At the time, WeChat Pay and Alipay were vying for dominance, spending as much as RMB 40 million ($7 million) per day to acquire new customers. Apple was looking for a way to compete. An investment in Didi and a relationship with Liu helped Apple establish *guanxi*—political relationships—in two budding industries, aided by Apple taking a seat on the board. Meanwhile, the Apple investment gave Didi international name recognition, further fueled by Cook. The week Apple's investment was announced—five days before his secret meeting at the CCP headquarters—Cook met with Liu in Beijing, where they hailed a ride together and visited an Apple Store. The next year Liu was named one of *Time* magazine's 100 most influential people in the world. Her profile was penned by Cook.

Each of these moves was part of a wider effort to give Apple what one scholar of China calls bureaucratic protection. The moves were carefully calibrated and had the fingerprints of the Gang of Eight all over them. The investment in Didi was the first concrete action demonstrating that their key argument—Apple needed to demonstrate how it was creating partnerships and "giving back"—was taking effect. Cook amplified this narrative by pandering to his audience, declaring China not just an important market but a bedrock of technological ingenuity. "The thing I like to do most in China is to spend time with entrepreneurs," he told *Xinhua*. "There are so many entrepreneurs that are driving the next wave of innovations."

If Cupertino was looking for signs that this new plan was working, all they had to do was tune in to China Central Television—the state broadcaster that had laid into Apple for its warranty deficiencies. "Apple had no investment strategy in China before. Its strategy used to be 'sell products only and invest nothing,'" an analyst said on CCTV. "Its investment now may not necessarily reverse its downtrend for good, but it may contribute to formulating a layout for the next growth engine."

R&D

Cook's visit to Beijing that week was the first of three trips he would take to China in 2016, reflecting just how loud and clear he'd received the message that Apple needed to launch a charm offensive. By August he'd returned to China, touting to officials including Vice Premier Zhang Gaoli that Apple was launching its first R&D lab in the country. In October, Cook told the mayor of Shenzhen that Apple would open a second R&D hub in the vibrant city. Chinese media trumpeted the centers as a sign that Apple recognized the need to compete with homegrown competitors. In March 2017, Apple announced two more R&D centers, in Shanghai and Suzhou. Documents from Apple explained to the officials what sort of innovation the centers would work on, but they were carefully crafted so as not to give away anything confidential or to provide competitors with clear direction as to what Apple was up to.

Although none of the four centers were joint ventures, they employed hundreds of local staff and demonstrated to a variety of officials that Apple was committed to China. "It was about making sure that Apple, as a company, doesn't just use people but actually allows them to grow in terms of competence and respect for what people do," says one person familiar with the company's interactions.

The extent of the actual importance of the R&D hubs, beyond politics, was hotly debated in Cupertino. "It was all a facade," says one former senior executive. "And we knew it, internally. But we were stuck in China." An American engineer based in China says tension with the local employees was often palpable. This person was involved in hiring and says the caliber of the R&D hubs was "much lower" than what Cupertino would accept. During a web-based interview, "You'd be asking them a question and you'd hear the keyboard clattering—and it's like, 'Hey, can you come back on camera?' And they're, like, doing a Bing search of 'metal springback' or something." The experience solidified the manager's view that the hubs were primarily for political optics.

The R&D hubs were overseen by Steven Marcher, the former Nokia executive in the Gang of Eight. Those who dismissed the R&D centers as window dressing saw his ambitions as doomed to fail from the start. Apple needed to win political points by charming local politicians with new investments and jobs, but Marcher failed to recognize the reality of his role and took himself too seriously. "Steve was a complete outsider with a mega ego," adds one former Apple executive.

Others, though, say real work was performed by the China hubs; it was just "noncore" work that didn't conflict with Cupertino. Much of the work was software-based, such as building a Mandarin-speaking Siri and ensuring that iOS worked well for Chinese users. The Beijing lab was the most software focused, working on wireless payment technology and issues with telecom carriers. Shanghai focused on hardware, including a battery testing lab. The Shenzhen hub did so much manufacturing and supply chain work that visiting Apple engineers from California would be perplexed at finding the lab mostly empty. It wasn't thinly staffed, though—the local engineers were just working intensely in suppliers' factories.

Supporters of the R&D hubs say the negative view of them reflects the insecurities of engineers in Cupertino, who were losing their power as more decision-making got done in China. Before the hubs were built, Apple had been sending so many engineers to China on temporary trips that Cupertino convinced United Airlines to begin direct flights from San Francisco to Chengdu, three times a week, arguing that Apple would regularly buy enough of the thirty-six first-class seats to make it profitable. The 6,857-mile flight became United's longest nonstop flight. Two years later, Apple again convinced United to begin flying nonstop—to Hangzhou, a tech hub on the outskirts of Shanghai. "Hangzhou is a bit of a schlepp from Shanghai," says a former Apple executive. "Yes, you can take a bullet train, but for all the American guys getting off the plane from Cupertino, navigating the train station is kind of complicated. So Apple basically said to United, 'Look, you put up a flight to Hangzhou and we'll fill it for you.'" Apple's signature line had long been that its products were "designed in California," but the hubs began to indicate otherwise. China's influence was growing, and as the hubs performed more work, the engineers there would openly question the need for so many of their counterparts to constantly fly in from America.

Whatever the quality of work in the R&D hubs, Cook used their opening to hammer home Apple's new narrative to local media. "We're not just someone who's here to access the market," he told the Chinese magazine *Caixin*. "We've created almost five million jobs in China. I'm not sure there are too many companies, domestic or foreign, who can say that . . . There's deep roots here. I think very highly of the country and the people in it. We're here to stay."

App Bans

But if the Gang of Eight could pat themselves on the back for a job well done, the next eighteen months would demonstrate the limits of their approach. However effective Apple's friendly tactics in China were, the country was still led by an increasingly powerful ruler intent on remaking China in his image. In the process, Apple risked having its image remade, too.

In late December 2016, Apple pulled *The New York Times* from its China App Store, following a demand from local authorities. Apple told the paper its app was in "violation of local regulations," though it didn't disclose which. Tim Cook acknowledged: "We would obviously rather not remove the apps, but like we do in other countries, we follow the law wherever we do business." But this "other countries" defense lacked substance. Phillip Shoemaker, head of the App Store from 2009 to 2016, says the entire app review team during his tenure was in Cupertino, with one exception—a single employee in Beijing. "If any ministers in China had an issue with apps on the store, they had a hotline to my employee, who could call me," Shoemaker says. "I didn't do this for any other country."

Beijing even employed app developers to test the vulnerabilities of the App Store. "The Chinese government would put things in our store, to see if they'd get by the review process," Shoemaker says. "And then during the negotiation process they'd bring it up: 'Hey, by the way, we have an app in the store that, when you play the game, each time you kill an enemy, a contact is deleted from your list of contacts, just randomly.'" The claim was alarming. The App Store was designed to be both safe and open, a hybrid that maximized the closed system of Apple's OS with the openness of a PC-style platform. Cupertino's original idea was that the store would be "curated," each app rigorously reviewed one by one by a dedicated team. But the App Store had proved so popular that the team was almost immediately overwhelmed. In internal documents, one of Apple's top fraud detection engineers compared the App Store review process to being more like "the pretty lady who greets you with a lei at the Hawaiian airport than the drug-sniffing dog."

In this instance, the Chinese government had exposed a security gap that the review team simply hadn't conceived of as a potential problem. "Nobody checks to see if contacts are being deleted," Shoemaker says. "Why would a contact be deleted?" But sure enough, Shoemaker's team found a Breakout-style game that deleted random contacts from the user's address book as they played. Apps were supposed to be "sandboxed," meaning a malicious app couldn't access data from other apps. But if a game got user permission to, say, access the user's contact list to invite friends, all bets were off. The game developer—in this case a state-sponsored one—might even be able to upload the user's contacts to the cloud, compromising user privacy. "There were no other checks and balances in place," Shoemaker says. "Because once you grant access, they can do whatever the hell they want." It's not clear any users had their contacts stolen this way, but that wasn't the point. Beijing was looking for vulnerabilities and telling Apple what it'd found. It was a show of power.

When Beijing asked for *The New York Times* to be removed, it requested that the app be removed from the *global* App Store, not just China's, Shoemaker says, adding: "Because they know their citizens can get on VPNs and go to a different [geographical] store and still download it and learn all about the Dalai Lama." Apple didn't accede to the demand. But a few months later, when Beijing called for virtual private networks to be removed from the China App Store, Apple complied, and 674 VPN apps were deleted. This was a massive concession, placing all iPhone users in the country in a splintered-off version of the internet. ExpressVPN called it "the most drastic measure the Chinese government has taken to block the use of VPNs to date, and we are troubled to see Apple aiding China's censorship efforts." The compromise reflected just how different reality was from expectations. In 2000, before China joined the WTO, President Clinton sarcastically wished Beijing "good luck" in their efforts to crack down on the internet. "That's sort of like trying to nail Jell-O to the wall," he said. But seventeen years later, China found it didn't need to pin anything to the wall—the world's largest corporation was happy to just hold it for them.

Hubris

In 2017, Beijing passed a cybersecurity law requiring local user data to be stored in the country. Such data residency rules were not unique to China, but unlike in other countries, Apple couldn't simply build a facility to house all the data. Or rather, it could—but to comply with local laws, the data center would be jointly owned by a Chinese government partner. Apple met with officials numerous times throughout 2016 to argue that its consumer-oriented cloud service shouldn't be subject to the same laws as corporate-oriented cloud services such as Amazon and Microsoft. When regulators disagreed, their lack of a countermove demonstrated Apple's diminished leverage in the country. The result was Apple's first joint venture.

As with the Didi investment, Apple sought to take a long-term strategic view. Some on the government affairs team recommended that if Apple was going to be forced to invest in infrastructure, it should at least do so in an area where it could score political points. They recommended Apple build the data center in Guizhou, an impoverished province in southwestern China where they believed Apple could have more influence with local officials. Those officials, in turn, could influence Beijing and allow the company to maintain control of customer encryption keys. That way, Apple could continue to tout its narrative on user privacy, something Cook would later call "one of the top issues of the century."

Whether Apple managed to win this concession is disputed. In May 2021, *The New York Times* reported that "Chinese government workers physically control and operate the data center" and that "Apple abandoned the encryption technology it uses in other data centers after China wouldn't allow it." However, the report didn't find evidence that the government had accessed the user data of Chinese iPhone owners; rather, it said Apple "has made compromises that make it easier for the government to do so." Apple posted a vigorous response: "In China, the law stipulates that iCloud data belonging to its nationals must remain in the country. We comply with the law, but we make no compromises on user security. We retain control of the encryption keys for our users' data, and every new data center we build affords us the opportunity to use Apple's most cutting-edge hardware and security technologies to protect those keys."

Another reason Apple was angling to build the data center in Guizhou was hubris. The company's government affairs team understood that when Beijing launches its five-year plans, it sets into motion a growth competition between the Chinese municipalities and provinces. The Guizhou governor, Chen Min'er, was an up-and-coming Communist Party official and a potential successor to Xi Jinping. The government affairs team wanted to place a bet on Chen, hoping that Apple's investment might give him additional clout and increase his chances of being the next paramount leader. "We were making a prediction," says a former Apple executive. "Usually at the beginning of a president's second term, the president will name a Standing Committee, and one of those people would be named successor. We were all sure that Chen Min'er would be there." But in October 2017 the seven-member Standing Committee was revealed, and fifty-seven-year-old Chen wasn't on it. In fact, no heir apparent was named, breaking from recent tradition, and "Xi Jinping Thought" was enshrined in the Constitution. China observers immediately understood the implications: Xi had no intention of serving just two terms. The prediction Apple's China team had made was wrong. "It was like, 'Fuck,'" the former Apple executive says, "'we just built these data centers in Guizhou for nothing.'"

PART SIX

RED APPLE

CHAPTER 33

COGNITIVE DISSONANCE—SUPPLIER RESPONSIBILITY

Early in her tenure as Apple's head of Supplier Responsibility, in 2013, Jacky Haynes was auditing a Chengdu-based Foxconn factory when New York–based China Labor Watch published a damning report on a Pegatron factory in Shanghai making iPhones. The activist group had sent in an undercover team posing as workers where, for several weeks, they witnessed thousands of "underage and student workers" routinely working overtime, violating Chinese law and Apple's code of conduct. Workers slept twelve to a room, took cold showers, and rarely got a day off. The report was biting in its analysis. "Apple has zero tolerance for lapses in the quality of its products," China Labor Watch wrote. "If a quality issue arises, Apple will do everything it can to have it corrected immediately. But a lower level of urgency apparently applies in responding to labor rights abuses." Receiving the report, Haynes immediately dropped what she was doing and hopped on a flight to Shanghai, some 1,180 miles away.

The urgent flight signaled just how seriously she took the role, but in retrospect her dutiful conviction in the meaning of her work also appears innocent and idealistic. It was a time when Haynes was eager to create change—before her hopes got crushed by the twin realities of Apple's demanding operational culture and Beijing's crackdown on labor rights advocates.

Passion Project

Haynes exuded an aura of warmth and confidence. Her smile was natural and offered a hint of mischief, while her ocean-colored eyes conveyed curiosity. She was good with numbers and in an alternate life might have been a sports analyst. Instead, she'd taken up industrial engineering, graduating from the Georgia Institute of Technology in 1981. Haynes then began a thirteen-year stint at IBM, overlapping for more than a decade with Cook and Williams. IBM selected all three as promising future leaders and sent them off to complete an executive MBA from Duke. In the mid-nineties, Haynes spent three years as a vice president for Intelligent Electronics, where Cook was a top executive of the reseller division. After he was lured to Apple in 1998, Haynes was invited to follow. She spent eight years in senior director roles, managing business initiatives in the supply chain and customer service, before entering early retirement at age fifty-one. But after Cook's ascension to CEO and media reports that dozens of Foxconn workers had jumped off the roof to their deaths, Apple was battling "iSlavery" accusations. Haynes returned in 2012 to lead Supplier Responsibility as a passion project, reporting directly to operations chief Jeff Williams. "I would not have come back from retirement to take this job if we did not have a management team, up through and including our CEO, Tim Cook, who was totally committed to the work we are doing," she said in a 2015 interview.

Haynes set out to make a difference. She called factory workers her "clients" and wielded her influence to expand the supplier responsibility team from just a handful of people to around a hundred in four years. She initiated conversations with civil society organizations, formed an eight-person advisory council of independent scholars to enhance the accountability of her efforts, and asked groups like China Labor Watch if they'd periodically meet to discuss how to promote real change. "It was a real go-go time," says Desta Raines, who led Apple's labor and human rights team. "Lots of momentum and resources," she adds. "It was really a heart and soul effort. Apple really cared. The feeling was, 'We need to understand this.'"

The challenge Haynes had been assigned was immense, and she relished it. "Jacky had a memory like no other person I've reported to and a work ethic so diligent that she was reachable at virtually any time," says Raines. "She advocated stakeholder engagement, wanting the team to be more proactive in speaking with investors and non-governmental organizations, to share all the good things Apple was doing. Jacky would say: 'We're not leading unless other people are following.'" A regular at the Top 100, Apple's annual retreat for top executives, Haynes had deep connections to Cupertino's top brass, and she represented Apple at the Electronic Industry Citizenship Coalition, a nonprofit seeking to improve factory conditions.

Supply chain executives describe her in glowing terms. "She was highly authentic—could not be bought," says one. "No shortcuts. No greenwashing. She wanted to do the right thing. And she worked for Apple because she believed they wanted to do the right thing." Another says, "Jacky brought in a mature business acumen. She had a very balanced approach . . . It felt like we could get somewhere with Jacky."

By all accounts Haynes was a force to be reckoned with and a positive advocate for laborers in the Apple supply chain. She'd written a tome on compliance, detailing how to improve conditions for workers and radically increase the scope and quantity of factory audits. In 2013, her organization "conducted 451 core audits at all levels of our supply chain—an average of more than one each day, and a 51 per cent increase" from 2012, she wrote. "Our goal is not simply to identify problems, but to actively fix them."

"Disappeared"

Haynes championed what Apple called the working hours report—a monthly assessment aggregating data from each of its suppliers. The report detailed the number of people working in its supply chain, including the hours they worked, in an attempt to track and improve compliance with Apple's standards. A former Apple executive characterized this as a huge effort to really improve outcomes. "For a company the size of Apple, with the supply chain it had, it doesn't matter what you're trying to do—just giving everyone a Biscoff cracker with their lunch every day would be a sizable feat," this person says. So for Haynes to engineer a working hours report that was actually adhered to, at over 400 companies with a standing state of 1.7 million workers—and ramping to much higher during [new production introduction] launches—that's remarkable."

Cook, for one, was emphatic in his support. "We've put a ton of effort into taking overtime down," the Apple CEO had told the All Things Digital conference in 2012, alluding to how Apple was working to assess suppliers so it could make necessary changes. This was one of Cook's first major interviews since the death of Steve Jobs. Sitting in a red chair and peering through thin-framed glasses, Cook even compared the reports to the US government's monthly payrolls release, calling the work hard and complex. He spoke as if taking greater control of how Apple conducted business would shape his legacy. "I hope people rip us off blindly," he quipped, meaning that he wanted other companies to follow Apple's lead.

But time and again, according to Apple colleagues and contract manufacturing executives, the realities of responding to Cupertino's high demands made compliance nearly impossible. Under Haynes's leadership, Apple pressured suppliers to cut worker overtime, remove underage workers, improve work conditions, and invest in safety. But its need for quality, speed, and price was no less unrelenting. A supplier investing to become a leader in compliance needed extra margin to make good on those commitments, but Apple's global supply managers—the team assigned to purchase components—were judged on achieving scale at low prices. "Jacky wanted to do the right thing, she felt it was possible," says one contract manufacturing executive. "But she didn't have the authority to talk about money. So we'd work with her, and then we'd work with Tony Blevins. And it's not that they weren't talking; it's that he just didn't give a fuck."

Every supplier knows that if it can't meet its commitments to deliver a defined number of units, it faces a legal fight with Apple or risks not being chosen for the next product. So when push came to shove, suppliers knew what to prioritize. "They were always willing to do the right thing until it wasn't economically feasible to continue to do the right thing," says an Apple engineer who managed product launches. "If you make an organization choose, they will choose profits."

Another Apple executive referred to the statistic that iPhone accounts for less than a fifth of global smartphone shipments but garners 80 percent of industry profits. "To do that, you need to be creating competition at every level in the supply chain. You need to be ruthless," this person says. "But you can't do that and also be compliant." A manufacturing design engineer at Apple recalled a day when Cook sent a note about the importance of corporate social responsibility. Such notes were meant to convey something important: *We care about this at the highest level of Apple.* But that same day his more direct bosses were demanding improvements to output. "The two messages were opposed to each other," he says. But there was no genuine recognition of that. Apple as an organization was a living, breathing manifestation of cognitive dissonance.

A senior executive at Foxconn, Louis Woo, once told reporter Rob Schmitz that if a client abruptly needed to ramp up production by 20 percent, Foxconn could either hire more workers immediately or compel its current workers to put in more hours. "When demand is very high, it's very difficult to suddenly hire 20 percent more people," Woo said. Schmitz added: "Especially when you have a million workers—that would mean hiring 200,000 people at once."

In 2016, Haynes's advocacy abruptly halted. It's not entirely clear what happened internally, but contract manufacturers who'd worked closely with Haynes say she was moved from her role, either sent off on a paid leave or assigned to special projects that no longer involved supplier responsibility. "She was disappeared," says one close partner. "She grew a monster that Tim couldn't manage." Li Qiang, founder of China Labor Watch, says she got sidelined. "Jacky entered her position aiming to promote real changes," he adds. But she'd learned that her goals were "fundamentally at odds with Apple's corporate goals."

Apple quietly stopped publishing the monthly working hours report. The removal was abrupt and unexplained, reversing the pledge Cook had made for transparency just a few years earlier. Executives familiar with the shift say the point of the reports was for Apple to tout its improvements to compliance. But then the numbers started to go in the opposite direction, undermining the company's messaging. "It was impossible to meet the compliance targets," says one Apple executive familiar with what happened. "Why set a target if we couldn't meet them? So instead of showing that we missed it, we just dropped it."

Li Qiang says it wouldn't be fair to conclude that Apple doesn't advocate for better working conditions across its supply chain. It does. And when Apple makes the case that it's a leader in this area, it's not necessarily wrong. But the general conditions of manufacturing electronics in China are poor, and he says Apple's demanding culture promotes a "do whatever it takes" approach among suppliers. That routinely leads to subpar conditions and invariably leads to some instances of illegal practices. Apple, he believes, is capable of doing far more, but chooses not to because it would compromise its other goals. He is reminded of a biblical passage from Luke 21:1–4:

> As Jesus looked up, he saw a rich man placing his gifts into the temple treasury. He also saw a poor widow put in two very small copper coins. "Truly I tell you," he said, "this poor widow has put in more

than all the others. All these people gave their gifts out of their wealth; but she out of her poverty put in all she had to live on."

"Apple," says Li, "is the rich man."

Crackdown

The wider context of what was going on in China explains much about why Haynes's goal of working with civil society groups became increasingly difficult. Near the end of Xi Jinping's first term, Beijing was brutally crushing the nascent labor movement. Police were arresting peaceful protesters, raiding NGOs, and striking fear into the movement. Labor advocates had experienced "regular rounds of repression" for twenty years, "but this most recent repression is more serious," Eli Friedman, a professor of labor at Cornell and a founding member of Haynes's advisory council, wrote in early 2016: "It seems that the Communist Party is intent on stamping out labor activism in civil society once and for all."

A few months later, Beijing passed a new law "restricting the work of foreign organizations and their local partners, mainly through police supervision," as *The New York Times* reported. The rules impacted more than 7,000 NGOs, requiring them to get an official Chinese sponsor or to cease operations. By August, after some stories that were considered embarrassing for Xi, Beijing's grip over local media tightened as journalists were told they would be personally liable for negative reporting. "The new rules placed responsibility squarely on head editors, saying news sites must monitor their content 24 hours a day to ensure 'correct orientation, factual accuracy, and appropriate sourcing,'" reported the Associated Press.

Heather White, founder of Verité, a nonprofit consultancy advocating for responsible supply chain practices—the consultancy Apple commissioned in the wake of the 2006 *Daily Mail* article alleging that Foxconn was an abusive sweatshop—had spent the mid-2010s filming a documentary on worker conditions in the electronics supply chain. She says conducting interviews went from dangerous in Xi's first term to impossible in his second. "We could never have even tried to make that film there if we'd begun in 2017, because of Xi Jinping's attacks on worker organizations," she says. "All the worker organizations I worked with . . . they were effectively gone by 2017."

White says people tend to think that China's authoritarian turn has been bad for Apple, and they presume that Cook and others would prefer that China adopt Western values. But she reckons the opposite is true: "Apple has benefited tremendously from the crackdown that Xi Jinping has been waging. Normally Apple would be under pressure over working conditions, but basically there's no voice calling out Apple for working in a digital surveillance totalitarian environment."

Cook, often asked how he feels about all this, has suggested Apple is some kind of change agent. "Your choice is, do you participate? Or do you stand on the sideline and yell at how things should be?" Cook said in 2017. "My own view—very strongly—is you show up and you participate. You get in the arena. Because nothing ever changes from the sideline." But White says Cook isn't participating so much as being used—like when he accepted, in October 2019, a role as chairman of the advisory board at the Beijing-based Tsinghua University School of Economics and Management. "The role that they want Tim Cook to play is Useful Puppet, one that they can use for propaganda purposes," she says. In her view, Samsung operates at a considerable business disadvantage because South Korea is a democracy with NGOs, trade unions, and a vibrant press that, for instance, has interviewed grieving parents after some workers developed leukemia from working in factories. "Apple doesn't have any of that possible pressure," White says. "Apple actually has a government that prevents all of those key stakeholders in society from writing an article or appearing on television. They can't even protest."

The stark difference between how exposed to the light supply chain problems were twenty years ago compared to deep into Xi Jinping's reign can be observed in the X archives—formerly Twitter—of Students and

Scholars Against Corporate Misbehaviour, a Hong Kong–based group founded in 2005 to advocate for workers' rights. In the summer of 2018, SACOM's account repeatedly posted about illegal student labor and protests, demanding compensation for workers sickened by silicosis—a lung disease that countless Chinese laborers have developed from working without adequate protection. Some of the rallies the posters highlighted were especially vexing to Beijing because protesters carried portraits of Mao, sang socialist anthems, and were espousing "the very ideals that the government fed them for years in mandatory ideological classes," *The New York Times* reported. As one protester put it: "We are Marxists. We praise socialism. We stand with workers. The authorities can't target us."

That summer SACOM had exposed the illegal use of student interns in Apple's supply chain. The group had interviewed twenty-eight students forced to work at a Quanta factory assembling the latest Apple Watch. They reported that "significant numbers" of students were compelled to work overtime under threat that they wouldn't graduate without this "work experience." On November 7, 2018, nine students stood near the front of an Apple Store, each displaying a sign indicating their support for workers' rights. The students were smiling, hopeful. And then the police showed up, arrested a protester, and sent a message to the others. SACOM tweeted a video of the scuffle, and over the coming week it bravely posted about other detentions and house arrests. Then the posts stopped. After thirteen years of advocacy, the group disbanded. Some of its leaders went into hiding.

Potemkin Factories

In the years following Haynes's departure in 2016 and Apple's discontinuance of its monthly working hours report, the company has nevertheless continued to publish an annual supplier responsibility report. But whereas New York–based China Labor Watch sponsors undercover investigations, with people posing as workers for weeks at a time, Apple's reports are self-assessments. Individual factory audits aren't made available, nor is there anything like off-campus interviews of employees. Reading the reports is, in Heather White's expert opinion, "a waste of time." Even if the reports were written with the best of intentions, they'd be of dubious value. Suppliers know their business rides on passing inspections.

One former Apple executive points out that the auditing teams typically arrived on a schedule, which gave suppliers time to prepare in advance. Often, he recalls, the sequence of events was like watching bad actors in an amateur theater production. In one audit, a group of laborers were busily stacking a bunch of pallets, ostensibly demonstrating how they were recycling the trays as part of some new environmental initiative. "The trays were stacked on a pallet, and [one of the workers said], 'These are going to the recycling center!'" At that point, the executive asked, "How are they getting to the recycling center?" And the worker replied, "They'll get picked up by a forklift!" The executive looked around the room, noticing there was no exit wider than a standard door. So he asked, "How's the forklift going to get in here and collect the pallet?"

"That's when you saw the penny drop," the executive recalls, "when you realized that they got a couple of guys to bring the empty pallet in sideways, put the pallet on the ground, and stack a whole bunch of empty trays on there. They hadn't thought about the fact that they were going to tell people that a forklift needed to come into the room to collect the pallet."

Unannounced visits from Apple could get around these problems. But suppliers have clever work-arounds. They might play a particular song throughout the factory, which serves as an urgent signal: ALL UNDERAGE WORKERS LEAVE THROUGH THE BACK DOOR. Apple could get wise to that sort of tactic if it really wanted to, but "you've got the fox guarding the henhouse," says Friedman. He quit Apple's advisory council after concluding that few of the things he wanted to accomplish were possible. "Why would Apple want to rigorously enforce things that would hurt their bottom line?"

Besides, after Haynes left, Apple's ambitions were diminished. Beijing's wider crackdown on civil society groups had destroyed her attempts at radical accountability. The groups were facing arrest, office raids, and harassment, rendering attempts to meet with them moot. Cook had wanted other companies to see Apple's supplier responsibility efforts and "rip us off blindly." Instead, Apple's own supply chain reporting became more opaque. Haynes moved on to other projects. Several years later she fell ill. Jacquelynn Haynes peacefully passed away on April 12, 2022, in Colorado. She was sixty-four.

CHAPTER 34

THE FIGUREHEAD—ISABEL MAHE

Apple's operations team in Shanghai had a surprise for its annual town hall meeting on Friday, May 26, 2017. The last such meeting had gathered only dozens of people, but this time Apple told many staff attendance was required. The entire China Ops team was invited, with engineers journeying to the location from around the country. Several VPs from California flew in, including Manufacturing Design head Nick Forlenza and Product Design lead Dan Riccio. Invitations were sent by Rory Sexton, the head of in-region operations.

When Apple staff arrived at Caffè Macs, they found it was packed with hundreds of people drinking beer, eating pizza, taking their seats at the round tables, or gathering in the mezzanine upstairs. Phones weren't allowed, since Apple would be giving employees a confidential overview of how the business was doing, revealing the latest numbers. Amid the hoopla came the evening's big announcement that Isabel Ge Mahe was permanently moving from Cupertino, taking on a newly created role: Managing Director of Greater China.

The attendees exchanged glances and politely applauded. Many had never heard of Mahe, Apple's vice president of wireless technologies for more than nine years. The Apple she'd joined in July 2008 was mostly known for iPods and Macs, products that didn't have cellular chips. She'd grown a 25-member software team into a group of 1,200 as the growth of the iPhone and the birth of the iPad, AirPods, and the Apple Watch put her in charge of a team whose responsibilities spanned all Apple products containing cellular, Bluetooth, near-field communication (NFC), and Wi-Fi chips.

Mahe, who exuded a sense of elegance in her carefully chosen designer clothes, agreed to take questions from staff. A Chinese employee in her thirties was among the first to take the mic. Looking for inspiration, she asked Mahe about the secret of her success as both a mother and a powerful executive. Mahe's answer got many side-eyes. "I have many helpers," she responded, referring to nannies and house cleaners. "That's what you need. You need to get many people to help you." A person present quips that you could hear crickets. As another person present tells it: "The way the woman phrased the question was: 'I have a family. I travel a lot for work. How do I make it in the corporate world—as a woman who also wants to be a mom?' And Mahe answered almost like she was aristocracy or something. Like, 'Well, you have to make sure you have a good housekeeper.'"

It was a softball question, and Mahe had stumbled badly. A few moments later a young Chinese man asked a far more sensitive question: "How can we have more control over decisions here in China? Are you going to help us with that?" She responded matter-of-factly that decisions for China would be made in Shanghai and Beijing. But this answer was so unsatisfying that the man stood back up, grabbed the mic from the person passing it around, and tried again: "No, I mean why do we have to wait for people in Cupertino to wake up in the morning to answer an email so we can make a decision? Why can't we own that decision here?"

Mahe hadn't spent enough time in China to understand the context. The local Operations team had been skirmishing with the Product Design team, which was mostly in California but had been building a more permanent presence in China. Ops often resented the power of PD, believing their own skill set had provided Apple with enormous value as Apple scaled. When Ops met with vendors, the local teams wanted to be empowered to make the decisions rather than defer to the Cupertino-centric PD team. This tension was core to the company. There was a strong sense in parts of Cupertino that Operations—particularly outsourced Manufacturing Operations—was expendable. What differentiated Apple, in this view, was breakthrough industrial and product designs. But people within Ops tended to view their work as the whole reason Apple hardware was so ubiquitous and profitable. "You can talk about touchscreen glass and the end of the BlackBerry keyboards all you want, but what really matters is having the genius to figure out how to produce a million of them each day," says one person present. So what the questioner was asking Mahe was, in effect, *Whose side are you on? Are you aligned with Product Design, or will you respect Ops?*

Mahe was being tested, but she hadn't been briefed well enough to understand. Flummoxed, she darted her eyes around and looked at Rory Sexton for help. "I remember that moment," says another person present. "It was either, like, 'Rory, please save me!' or 'Rory, why did you let this happen?'" She managed to murmur an answer about why it was important that local teams seek advice from Cupertino rather than act independently, and then her words trailed off. Articulated more clearly, this might have been the right answer in Cupertino, but Mahe was in the belly of the beast of Shanghai-based operations. In this very building were the offices of Sexton, Brendan Lawry, and Steven Marcher—the three Gang of Eight members representing Ops, Procurement, and R&D.

Engineers in the audience went away unimpressed. "It gave her the appearance of being unqualified for the position," says one. "She's a nice person and everything. She's not an idiot. But they should have coached her for a month or two . . . Apple's notorious for that. They just throw you into the fire and expect you to put it out."

Bad Mess

Isabel Ge Mahe was born in Shenyang, the largest city in China's northeastern province of Liaoning. Her father was a college professor in China, and when Isabel was a teenager, he was offered a mining consultant job in Vancouver, British Columbia. He intended to bring Isabel's older sister, but she had a boyfriend in China and wouldn't go. Isabel jumped at the chance, keen to learn English and get an international education. Later, when her father's company no longer needed him in Canada, she convinced him to stay so she could continue her studies. The former professor sacrificed for his daughter, taking odd jobs like delivering pizza and working at gas pumps while she contributed by busing tables and selling shoes by day and studying at night.

The hard work paid off: In 1992 Mahe received a scholarship to Simon Fraser University, where she completed undergraduate and graduate degrees in engineering. She joined PDA maker Palm in 2002, staying for nearly six years as it struggled to reinvent itself for a smartphone future. Mahe had built a wireless team for Palm almost from the ground up, catching the attention of Cupertino, and a few months after the iPhone was unveiled, Apple recruiters started a year-long campaign to draft her. She rebuffed them, believing that leaving her team would be a betrayal. But the recruiting intensified, culminating in Steve Jobs inviting Mahe over for dinner. He impressed her, although he lied about the dinner. "Just water for the whole two hours," Mahe once told *Fortune*. "So that was a little bit of bait and switch!" Jobs, listening to her concerns, allowed her to bring over key members of her Palm team. According to Mahe's account, he clinched the deal with this line: "You can stay with Palm and drive a bus full of people off a cliff, or you can come to Apple and give them a better place to land."

In the next nine years Mahe demonstrated her technical competence, but she also developed a reputation of being difficult to work with. "She fought with everyone," one colleague recounts. When a product includes both hardware and software, it's not uncommon when problems arise for people in one group to blame the other. If there's an issue with calls being dropped, for instance, it could be the antenna, but it might be the baseband software. The ideal Apple engineer would take a self-incriminating approach, addressing the problem with the feeling that, as one engineer put it, "I'm guilty until proven innocent." But insiders say Mahe was the finger-pointing type, and the attitude cascaded down across her whole team. She'd grown "very protective and very isolated in Cupertino," says someone who worked closely with her. "Nobody wanted to work with Isabel."

In the *Harvard Business Review,* Joel Podolny, the former dean of Apple University, once pointed out that creating products at Apple can be "messy" because multiple divisions are involved. So Apple encourages its leaders to feel accountable for the whole product, "even though you don't control all the other teams." He explained: "'Good mess' happens when various teams work with a shared purpose . . . 'Bad mess' occurs when teams push their own agendas ahead of common goals." As Podolny put it, those who become associated with bad mess "are removed from their leadership positions, if not from Apple altogether." In Mahe's case, she was sent to China.

The Gang of Eight had been working behind the scenes in China since 2014, successfully helping Apple to shape its image, and collectively they started to clamor for something more public—a more organized China team, headed by a strong lead. According to some colleagues, Rory Sexton wanted the role. In fact, he was already the head of Greater China in all but name. He had the clout, was a VP, and was the closest thing Apple had to a power broker in the country. Sexton led a team of engineers, worked closely with suppliers, and frequently spoke with government officials. "He was a master of analyzing the political game and figuring out how to build the team while not being worried about who gets credit," says a colleague. One time he defused a government threat to shut down Pegatron's iPhone assembly operations after an Apple employee was caught leaving the bonded zone with uncertified prototype iPhones slated for testing on local networks. But Sexton wasn't Chinese and didn't speak the language.

Steve Marcher was another possibility. He did speak Mandarin, had been in China for fifteen years, and he, too, had relationships with local officials. But he was relatively new to Apple and simply wasn't a known quantity throughout Cupertino. One colleague says Marcher often had good ideas, but when he tried to get senior executives on board he would be met with a condescending "Who are you, again?" Besides, Apple cares a lot about optics, and a white guy officially leading the company's efforts in China wasn't going to fly—especially given that one of its core goals was ingratiating Apple with Chinese officials.

Doug Guthrie recalls the first time he met Mahe. He was one of the people advocating for an official head of China, but he didn't play a role in the selection process or know who she was. So he was surprised when, on one of his trips to Cupertino, she asked him to come by her office. It was after Chinese New Year, in early 2017, a time when Guthrie had developed real influence with senior executives. He walked to her office in Infinite Loop and exchanged pleasantries. Mahe gazed at him and said, "So I guess I have you to blame?" Guthrie's eyes widened; the question felt aggressive. "We've never met," he responded. "Have I done something?" And Mahe said, "Well, I'm getting on a plane and going to China, and it's because Tim [Cook] said, 'You better listen to Doug Guthrie.'" Within a few minutes it became clear Mahe wasn't just referring to a typical jaunt over to China; she'd been asked to take on a major career challenge, one that would involve moving to Shanghai with her non-Chinese-speaking husband and their children.

Apple formally announced Mahe's new role on July 18, 2017, some six weeks after the town hall Q&A. Internal murmurings that she wasn't the right person for the role plagued her from that first meeting. From the outside, it looked like a superb choice: Mahe was a vice president and had led a large team on critical technologies. But though she'd been born in China, she'd moved to Canada at age sixteen and hadn't lived in the country since. Though someone like Jun Ge or Steve Marcher might have possessed the local knowledge and savvy to navigate the political landscape, it was far from clear that Mahe did.

The Only Managing Director in the World

The mismatch was more the fault of Apple. The role called for someone who knew a lot about US-China relations and how local institutions worked, or someone who was multiple levels deep in Apple operations. Mahe was neither. She was a technical expert, no doubt, but she didn't have the right skill set. The fact that she was Chinese was supposed to be a plus, but really it just demonstrated how superficial, even cynical, Apple was being. Cupertino wanted "the face of China" to be Chinese; the fact that her career experience didn't align with the role was a distant consideration.

What frustrated employees disappointed by her appointment was that Apple had several Chinese-speaking women who were more qualified. Iris Cui was one. She was a tough, powerful, bombastic Taiwanese woman who'd studied at Peking University in the 1990s and became a director of Apple operations. Another was Villa Wu, the deputy head of government affairs. She'd studied in Shanghai and worked for Intel before joining Apple's government affairs unit, building Apple's credibility and facilitating connections with local government authorities. One challenge, however, was that if someone is doing well in their job, Apple doesn't want to take them away from it.

The bigger problem was the role itself. "Managing Director of Greater China" was a titular position that mostly existed for political reasons and simply didn't align with how the company operates. Unlike a conventional company where the business is divided into units, each with their profit and loss statements overseen by a general manager, Jobs had put the whole company under one P&L. Then he divided it into functions like marketing, engineering, and finance, each overseen by a technical expert. The company has no general managers—and yet here was Isabel Mahe, general manager of China. The odd position cast her in a state of ceremonial limbo. On paper, she'd be overseeing 14,000 employees in Apple's most important region. But Apple is a deeply hierarchical company, and the retail workers at Apple Store, the operations engineers, the R&D specialists, and the government affairs team all have independent reporting lines within China or back to Cupertino. None of these functions would report up to Mahe in any meaningful way.

Colleagues say Mahe tried to make a mark in R&D, taking on

greater responsibility. But her expertise was confined to baseband software, and the teams back in Cupertino had no respect for her hardware chops. Instead, she started writing a monthly report on the China market, summarizing local conditions and noting her observations about the marketing campaigns launched by Apple's rivals. Some on the China team enjoyed the note, seeing Mahe as a champion of their desire to be empowered. Another colleague says Mahe tried to find time in her calendar to meet with people, but there was little clarity on what her role was. She couldn't garner respect and didn't develop a keen sense of what was going on beneath her. "She was wheeled out as the China face, meeting officials," another colleague says. "She only showed up when there was an event she needed to show up for, and then read the script. I had no respect for leaders like that."

Multiple engineers who spent years flying into China say that they didn't know who Mahe was. Those who lived in the country say they still have little idea what her role is seven years into the job. "She's kind of the leader of R&D in China, but that's more figurative," says one director. "What's important for Apple is product—and she doesn't really own a product." Mahe, too, has alluded to her role being unique within Apple, entailing a grab bag of tasks that overlap with the portfolios of more well-suited specialists. "I've had to write my own playbook," she said in 2019, "since there's never been a managing director role anywhere in the world at Apple. I've had to learn new skills, like influencing, leading cross-functional teams like sales and marketing, who have way more expertise in those areas than me. I'm meeting with government officials, business partners, and giving speeches like this."

But speeches, it turns out, aren't really her specialty. In the few talks or interviews available on YouTube, Mahe comes across as poised and gracious, but also prone to giving trite answers, recycling Apple clichés, and speaking in buzzwords lacking substance. Asked to give advice to MBA students, her remarks included: "When times are tough, believe in yourself. And also know that it is these challenges that make you stronger." Those banal tips are a part of a rehearsed four-point answer that includes "Keep an open mind" and "You can never spend too much time with your loved ones."

Rock Star

Internally, it was clear to Cupertino by early 2019 that the position hadn't worked out. Mahe had become a figurehead with no major responsibilities. She was a general manager in a company that didn't have general managers. But Apple needed the role for political optics, and moving Mahe would've been fraught. Apple had recently lost retail head Angela Ahrendts, the former CEO of Burberry and one of Tim Cook's signature hires, as well as Denise Young Smith, the head of inclusion and diversity. Both women had been on the company's male-heavy leadership page. The prospect of losing another woman, and the only Chinese person on the executive team, was a nonstarter.

Besides, Mahe wasn't a threat to anybody. Cupertino concluded it was best just to leave her in a cushy role. When she tried to establish a media presence for herself, she wasn't allowed to, so she sought out other work to create her image in other ways. She joined the board of Starbucks in 2019 and Lululemon in 2022, and now serves as a governor of the China division of the American Chamber of Commerce.

To outsiders, these positions have made her look like a rock star. *Fortune* has repeatedly named Mahe to its "Most Powerful Women" lists. And in the rare instances she's mentioned in the media, reporters make the natural assumption that Apple's success in China is somehow reflective of her leadership. The company's secretive, insular culture has masked the reality that she's been playing a largely ceremonial role.

CHAPTER 35

THE RED SUPPLY CHAIN

Tim Cook was all smiles as he walked the production line, passing by young Chinese workers in their white protective coats and matching hats. Photos from the day, December 4, 2017, show Cook in blue factory smocks, stopping at several of its hundred-plus manufacturing stations—and, if the pictures are anything to go by, making all those around him guffaw. Beside him was Grace Wang, founder of Luxshare Precision, a Chinese contract manufacturer that had outmaneuvered its Taiwanese rivals earlier that year and won a major order to assemble AirPods.

How Wang won that order has become part of Apple lore. The story is that procurement head Tony Blevins struck a deal for Luxshare to assemble the earbuds at cost—no margin at all. But unlike so many similar stories, this was less about Blevins's ruthlessness and more about Grace Wang's craftiness. She agreed to do the work for free on one condition: that Tim Cook visit her factory and be photographed on the assembly line. It's difficult to confirm the margins really were zero, but on that day in December when Cook visited Luxshare's factory northwest of Shanghai, he offered toothy grins and praised all that he saw. "This is an extraordinary example of a Chinese dream being realized," Cook said. He even took to Weibo, China's answer to Twitter, to proclaim that Luxshare was making AirPods with "phenomenal precision and care," and that "Chairman Grace Wang has built a culture of excellence that starts with people. We are thrilled to work with them!"

A "news report" trumpeted on the Luxshare website milked the visit, saying that after Apple had dispatched its engineers to train Luxshare staff and smooth the production, they came away dazzled. "Mr. Cook said he had been extremely impressed with Luxshare's staff," the text says. "Mr. Cook said that, personally, he very much approved of Luxshare Chairwoman Grace Wang's idea on employee welfare."

The Apple CEO's visit was a stroke of brilliance on the part of Wang, described in the puff piece as someone who knows "the various Apple products like the back of her hand." What she understood is that profits from the deal hardly mattered relative to the public prestige of working with Apple. Cupertino has long been famously secretive about its supply chain operations; companies can face penalties for even mentioning that they make goods for the tech giant. But Cupertino's desire to enhance its narrative in China presented an opportunity. Wang orchestrated an event that elevated the perception of Luxshare from "one of many suppliers" to a real partner. As the website article proclaimed: "Birds of a feather flock together."

Wang (pronounced "Wong") had two major audiences in mind. One was the capital markets. Wang and her older brother founded the company in 2004 and hold at least 39 percent of its shares. Over the prior ten years, Luxshare had earned $782 million of net profit. Its owners stood to make far more in the stock market than from low margins on final assembly. By turning Cook's visit into a media event, Wang delivered a message to investors: Luxshare was on the up-and-up, and its rise would come at the expense of Foxconn. On the day Cook visited, Luxshare was worth $12 billion—validating how successful it had become from supplying components to Apple for nearly a decade. Still, that was only one-fifth of Foxconn's $57 billion valuation. Within two and a half years, Luxshare's market value would soar to $38 billion, overtaking Foxconn's own dented market value at a time when the Taiwanese group was bringing in thirteen times more revenue. Any financial analysis would struggle to reconcile how that could be. The two companies were in the same low-margin business, using the same techniques, and servicing similar clients. But Chinese investors know their own country's politics well, and they saw the writing on the wall. Foxconn, too, understood the challenge, and in 2019 it set up a task force to study its Chinese rival to understand its technology, expansion plans, hiring strategy, and whether the company was supported by any Chinese government entity.

The second audience for the photographs of a smiling Cook was Chinese government officials. Wang, who earned her assembly chops as one of the first migrant workers on the Foxconn production line in 1988, came to understand the Terry Gou–led company's political savvy. She realized that Apple orders, if they could be secured, could be parlayed into getting factory land and other incentives. One industry colleague calls her an "active member of the Party" who pitched Luxshare as a Chinese alternative to Foxconn, made good on some early promises, and was lavishly rewarded for doing even more. "She's got massive government support," this person says. "She cracked the whole government thing—she can get anything she wants." Wang is known to be tough-minded, smart, and strategic, though not charming. "It's definitely not her elegance," this person adds.

The ascent of Luxshare has been remarkable. In 2009, the first year it began making connector cables for Apple, it earned just $81 million in revenue. The company's strategy was to mimic Foxconn's culture, work ethic and hunger, even its uniforms. Terry Gou–like sayings were plastered to the walls: "Don't put off until tomorrow what you should do today." Or: "Successful people look for ways; failures look for excuses." Keen to meet Apple's demanding standards, Luxshare engineers and managers once slept at the factory for an entire month.

By 2016, its revenues had shot up to $1.9 billion. Then the real business started. After winning the AirPods order in 2017, Luxshare began assembling Apple Watches in 2019 and, in 2021, became the first mainland Chinese business to manufacture the iPhone. Between 2016 and 2023, its revenues soared 1,455 percent to more than $32 billion, with

Apple accounting for three-quarters of sales. Remarkable as Luxshare's ascent has been, though, its early success was a harbinger of a much larger trend driven by two intersecting forces.

Designed by Apple in California, Made in China 2025

After Tim Cook, Jeff Williams, and Lisa Jackson journeyed to the Communist headquarters and pledged a $275 billion investment, something unexpected happened: It spurred competition. For years, many suppliers had been frustrated by Apple's high demands, overbearing control, and low margins. They viewed Apple as the "prom queen"—beautiful to look at but unwise to date because of all the drama, says one former Apple vice president. "At the end of the day, she'll leave you hanging, your heart will be in your hand, and then you'll be out—that's Apple's business," this person says. But part of this frustration was a misunderstanding. Chinese suppliers often didn't grasp what Terry Gou had figured out in the late 1990s: that the value of working with Apple was the learning. But once Apple marketed its impact on the country to government officials, Chinese suppliers perked up.

Xi Jinping's Made in China 2025 plan, published in 2015, had asked Chinese companies to "master core technologies, perfect the industrial supply chain, and form our own development capabilities." What became clearer to Chinese companies in 2017 was that the best way to support these goals was, ironically, to work intimately with the mother of all capitalist companies. Apple, for its part, wasn't necessarily aiming to have more Chinese companies in its supply chain, but the Apple Squeeze tilted the field in favor of local rivals. They were the ones who could work for the experience, because they could most readily access cheap capital, government subsidies, land approvals, and access to pools of labor. As a former Foxconn executive puts it: "The faucet was being turned off" for the Taiwanese—who had largely built China's manufacturing sector over the past four decades—but it was free-flowing to an emerging class of mainland suppliers known as the Red Supply Chain.

Apple's own annual lists of its top suppliers demonstrate the effect. The number of Chinese companies in Apple's list of around two hundred top suppliers each year climbed from sixteen in 2012—the first year it was published—to forty-one in 2019, when they surpassed the number of American suppliers for the first time. By 2021, the number of Chinese suppliers had hit fifty-one, overtaking Taiwan for the top spot. As *Nikkei Asia* observed at the time, "the number of mainland Chinese companies had tripled since 2012 while the number of US counterparts has fallen [by a third]." Moreover, the size of Chinese factories can often dwarf those in other countries, rendering any quantitative analysis misleading. For instance, in 2018 the total "labor demand" at Apple's fourteen suppliers in Vietnam totaled 45,000, far less than the 72,000 people needed at a single Chinese glass supplier, Biel Crystal, according to two internal presentations.

Significant as those numbers are, it actually undersells the story of China's dominance in Apple's supply chain, since the vast bulk of international companies contributing to Apple products do so from *within* the country. As *China Daily* observed in 2023: "Currently, 151 of Apple's 200 major suppliers, including foreign and Chinese ones, have a manufacturing presence in China."

Besides Luxshare, the other three major indigenous contract manufactures making Apple products are BYD Electronic, a major supplier of hardware enclosures and assembler of iPads; Goertek, a maker of AirPods and AirPods Pro; and Wingtech, which manufacturers Mac Mini desktops and MacBooks. These groups collectively reported $6 billion of total revenue in 2015; by 2020 their revenues had quadrupled to $25 billion, and in 2025 their sales are expected to exceed $52 billion. Apple has been instrumental to their success, shifting orders from Taiwanese leaders Foxconn, Wistron, Pegatron, and Quanta. As David Collins, an Asia-based manufacturing consultant, said of the Red Supply Chain in late 2020: "Foxconn's share price is down roughly 50% from two years ago. They see blood in the water."

The rise of the "big four" in the Red Supply Chain underscores how Apple has sleepwalked into a new reality: China has become the only place in the world where it could possibly build hundreds of millions of iPhones each year, and an ever-increasing number of the companies involved are Chinese rather than Taiwanese, American, or global multinationals. This Chinafication of the electronics industry stands in direct opposition to the "Made Everywhere" slogan that Apple has been touting to credulous investors. Despite the many assumptions and articles to the contrary, Apple has only gotten closer to China in the past decade.

Cupertino understands that openly supporting Xi's plan for tech supremacy is politically taboo. But Apple's message in Chinese media is, if not wildly supportive of the effort, then at least in sync with it. When *China Daily* reporters met Isabel Mahe in 2023, they quoted her saying: "Apple is happy and willing to help the country's transition to smart manufacturing." It paraphrased her, saying: "Previously, smart manufacturing equipment in Apple's supply chains came mainly from non-Chinese companies, but now such equipment of local origin has become more common." Mahe, like Cook, has portrayed these partnerships as "win-win," seemingly oblivious to a quip that goes back at least a decade: "In China, 'win-win' means China wins twice."

Red Flags

The increasing presence of the Red Supply Chain raises troubling questions about Apple's future. The Taiwanese suppliers Apple worked with in the last twenty-five years were profit-first organizations that primarily existed to serve the client. Apple, in other words, was the power they aimed to please. But Chinese companies exist in a different framework, one in which bringing glory to the Chinese state and upholding the party's principles is paramount. These goals aren't necessarily in conflict with Apple's priorities, but they introduce risks that are difficult to understand or predict. For instance, the Chinese companies' prime directives were why Jacky Haynes's monthly hours report was abandoned. What happened, one executive says, is that Apple found itself working with companies that didn't care about overtime maximums. "She was about doing the right thing, and the Chinese suppliers were never about doing the right thing," they add. The challenge was not that the Chinese were less ethical; they just had different incentives and more readily responded to political goals. Pleasing Apple or making short-term profit might still be important, but there was more of a political dimension to learning all that they could, so they could ascend the ranks of suppliers, achieve long-term control by pricing out international rivals, and be rewarded as leaders in "indigenous innovation."

Just how well Cupertino understands the dynamics at play in China is hard to know, as none of these issues are publicly addressed in any meaningful way. Privately, some former executives describe the increasing presence of Chinese companies in Apple's supply chain in "strictly business" terms: Apple would open bids for an order, and the companies most capable of offering low prices and quality processes just happened to become more localized with time. There is some merit to this argument. With Apple's help, the Red Supply Chain has indeed become more sophisticated, and Apple, ever keen to obtain better pricing and slash its capital expenditures, has taken advantage of their eagerness. The value of Apple's "long-lived assets" in China peaked in 2018, at $13.3 billion, and in the years since has declined by almost two-thirds to $4.8 billion, the lowest since 2011. This sizable drop reflects how Apple stepped back and let the Red Supply Chain pick up the tab on expensive equipment. The move was highly supportive of Apple's margins, which have been increasingly important since iPhone sales peaked in 2015. In the past decade, Apple hasn't experienced any growth in iPhone shipments, but it has managed to please investors with higher-priced units—the average selling price of an iPhone has climbed from $756 in 2018 to $908 in 2024—and lower costs in procurement and assembly. Meanwhile, operating margins for the iPhone jumped from 26 percent in 2018 to 34 percent in the first half of 2024, according to Counterpoint Research.

But the "strictly business" narrative fails to grasp the nexus between supply chains and local politics. As Taiwanese scholar Wu Jieh-min argues, the role of the Chinese state "is exceedingly understated" in most research. The "underpoliticized" narrative, he writes, overlooks how "the Chinese government invested capital and selectively nurtured" certain industries, including telecommunications and cellphones. Such help allowed local suppliers to purchase their way into Apple's supply chain. Luxshare, for instance, got into iPhone assembly after buying two China-based subsidiaries of Wistron, a Taiwanese rival, for $472 million, in July 2020. The following year, BYD Electronic spent $2.2 billion to purchase the Chengdu- and Wuxi-based electronics manufacturing facilities of Jabil, a US contract manufacturer that had been supplying Apple for fifteen years. And with cheap access to capital, they could acquire workers from Foxconn and other suppliers who already had Apple experience. These tactics have been so successful that they've helped to drive a shift of geopolitical proportions. According to Apple insiders, 100 percent of final assembly, test, and pack out of Apple hardware was performed by Taiwanese companies in 2012; in the years since, that percentage has fallen below 50 percent—reflecting a staggering shift toward Chinese suppliers that has made Apple hugely popular in government circles.

Apple engineers recall that talented workers at its closest partners in the late 2010s were being heavily recruited by the Red Supply Chain companies, as well as the smartphone brands such as Xiaomi, Vivo, and Huawei. "People were leaving in droves," says a former manufacturing design engineer. Another says Chinese smartphone recruiters would wait in the parking lot to poach particular individuals, like the guy who ran CNC programming and had fifty technicians under him. "They'd hand him a check that is double his pay," this person says. A third Apple engineer said the recruiters couldn't be more explicit in how they approached potential new hires, saying, "What do you know? Tell us *everything* you know!" Then the companies would use this experience in their marketing materials. "It was like, 'We have this many people with

Apple experience on our team, so you should pick us over some other [contract manufacturer],'" one of the engineers recalls. According to *The Information,* Luxshare "hired away more than half of Quanta's Apple Watch team in 2019."

The practice became so brazen that in 2022 Taiwanese prosecutors accused Luxshare of stealing commercial secrets from Catcher, a local contract manufacturer, and poaching its workers to win Apple orders. In May 2024, Taiwanese law enforcement accused eight Chinese companies, again including Luxshare, of surreptitiously setting up operations on the island with the goal of stealing know-how and talent.

Such tactics accelerated after 2017 but had been going on for years. One former Apple executive recalls, around 2012, being with one of Terry Gou's top executives when they saw indigenous Chinese companies holding signs outside the Foxconn factory, recruiting talent. "Holy shit, I'm gonna lose my best guys here!'" the Foxconn executive exclaimed. Recognizing the two, a top engineer walked over and offered his hand: "It was a pleasure working with you. I'm working for Huawei now." As the engineer walked away, the two executives were silent for a few seconds. Then the Apple executive turned and said, "Who the fuck is Huawei?"

CHAPTER 36

"5 ALARM FIRE"

Tim Cook was in Europe when he received the latest, gutting development relating to iPhone sales. The day before, October 26, 2018, had been the official sales launch of the iPhone XR—a budget-friendly handset aimed at the Chinese consumer with features like a dual SIM card slot. Saori Casey, a VP of financial planning, had written to Cook with updated projections indicating that iPhone sales in the holiday quarter would be up to 7.1 million units short of the prior estimate. The finance team had characterized the new guidance as "an extreme problem," mainly reflecting weak demand for the XR. Cook sent back a curt reply: "This is obviously a disaster," he wrote. "We need all hands on deck now."

The new ranges indicated "a huge drop of $3.5 billion" for the quarter—"in, literally, a 24-, 48-hour kind of window," Cook would later say in a deposition, cited here for the first time. This and all other email exchanges in this chapter come from a trove of internal documents, emails, and depositions of senior Apple executives made public in court discovery but hitherto unreported on. They offer unprecedented insight into the granular sophistication of how Cupertino tracks sales and then uses that data to chart the future. When Kevan Parekh, a VP of sales, marketing, and retail finance, forwarded Cook's message, he added dryly: "It's going to be a fun few weeks leading up to Thanksgiving . . . "

What Cook *Knew*

Early warning signs for the XR had emerged two and a half weeks earlier, during prelaunch on October 8. By October 19, the Worldwide Reseller Operations team was reporting internally that preorders were a whopping 79 percent less than for the iPhone 8 and 8+ a year earlier and "softer than expectations across all reporting partners."

The tepid sales on launch day reinforced the narrative and were immediately understood by Cupertino to be a major problem. "We definitely had some concerns based on preorders . . . but the wheels fell off on Friday 26th," Donal Conroy, another finance VP, later wrote to colleagues. In his email to Cook and finance chief Luca Maestri, Conroy had written that sell-in—the total number of all iPhone models that Apple, globally, would ship for sale in the holiday quarter—was likely to fall to 73.2 million units, or possibly to as low as 67.5 million—declines of 5 percent to 13 percent from the prior year.

Just why the numbers were coming in so low wasn't immediately understood, but it soon became clear that local consumers were comparing the features of the latest iPhones to what was on offer from Huawei, China's "national champion." Huawei was beginning to penetrate the premium market with slick phones featuring multiple cameras codeveloped with Leica, the prestigious German camera group. Positive reviews around the world made it a symbol of national pride, and Chinese customers were flocking to Huawei's stores.

For Cupertino, understanding the disappointing trajectory of the latest iPhone was especially urgent because Apple would report quarterly earnings in just a few days, on November 1, when it would give investors a projection for the all-important holiday quarter. Investors were anticipating that Apple would forecast sales of $93 billion, and they were keen to know how the company was doing in China, whose economy had been decelerating for months. "China is the greatest unknown given macro uncertainties," UBS analysts wrote.

In the days ahead, things weren't looking good. By late October,

Apple cut its internal revenue outlook in China from +4 percent to −1 percent. Revenues weren't just growing slowly in its most important overseas market; they were *shrinking*. The new forecasts set off something close to panic in Cupertino. The holiday quarter was shaping up to be the biggest financial disappointment in the twelve years of the iPhone. Chief financial officer Luca Maestri immediately met with the sales team to run through different scenarios on how to boost revenue. "Their original view was a low of $87 billion," Maestri wrote to Cook on October 27, referring to the low end of a new revenue forecast. That was a massive $6 billion less than what Wall Street was expecting. "The whole issue is of course XR," he acknowledged. But during the discussion, the group agreed to revise the low end of the estimate to $89 billion. The hard data wasn't pointing that way, but could get there "with a few assumptions," Maestri wrote.

That same day, worldwide sales head Mike Fenger emailed his staff "Urgent Q1 Action plans," asking what they could do "given the current performance indications of the iPhone XR." Fenger acknowledged the task would be difficult, like pulling "a rabbit out of our hat." This action plan, he noted, "is of the upmost [*sic*] urgency given the fact we need to lock earnings guidance in a few days." He concluded the email with an exhortation: "Go, go, go."

But the situation continued to deteriorate. China Mobile, the world's largest carrier, sent Apple two requests to stop shipments. Apple had delivered 254,000 XR units to the carrier, over and above the 241,000 requested—which counted as additional revenue—but customer demand was low, and the carrier didn't want to be stuck with inventory. "Partner explicitly said if Apple cannot keep our practice to maintain healthy channel inventory, [China Mobile] will consider hold payment to future shipment," internal emails said. China Unicom also had too many units and told Apple it "will consider not accepting shipment and hold future payment."

On Sunday the twenty-eighth, Mark Anderson, a senior manager of iPhone sales finance, characterized the challenge as "a 5 alarm fire"—the highest level of urgency at fire departments, when as many as a hundred firefighters are called to the scene. He asked his team to consider "chessboard moves," such as cutting prices to boost revenue. "We need to shift gears into actions mode and come up with some things we can do," he wrote. The plans they came up with felt implausible to Larry McDevitt, senior director of finance. "Luca asked me to find $800 million to $1 billion!!" he wrote on October 31. Mike Fenger cited the "performance indications of the iPhone XR" and asked a colleague to "urgently marshal your best thinkers" to drive additional revenue. With Cook as their CEO, this team of executives was deeply experienced in the art and science of reading spreadsheets and plotting out sales trajectories, and McDevitt characterized the idea that sales of the iPhone XR might recover as fanciful. "Let's just hope N84"—the code name for iPhone XR— "is on a curve we've never seen before and it surprises us all with week on week strength through end of quarter!"

Two days before the earnings call, on October 30, staffer Rachel Yong sent an "N84 China update" to more than a dozen colleagues, informing them that "key partners" accounting for 85 percent of sell-through channels have requested that Apple stop shipments of the XR. She cited a new demand prediction that was bafflingly low, later characterized by a VP of sales as "massively muted" and "nothing like an iPhone NPI"—or new product introduction.

A big question weighed on Tim Cook and Luca Maestri: What should they tell Wall Street?

What Cook *Said*

Hours before Apple's earnings report, Tim Cook wrote an email to the board of directors. He summarized that revenue was solid but warned there'd likely be pressure on the share price once Apple revealed low guidance for the holiday quarter: "Sales of iPhone XR began last Friday and were muted despite the most positive product reviews we've had in years." He went on to explain: "We have no historical experience to project the demand curve for this type of product and therefore have a higher range of potential sales outcomes."

It was an awfully sanguine message that failed to capture any of the drama taking place over the prior three weeks—"extreme problem," "5 alarm fire," or "obviously a disaster." The "higher range" of sales outcomes idea rested on the data being murky. Apple had staggered the launch of three iPhones that year, beginning with two higher-end models followed by the XR. A year before, two entry-level models were released first, followed by the higher-end iPhone X. This reversal in order, Apple lawyers would later argue, clouded Apple's ability to make forecasts.

But this was only partially true. Looking at the same set of data, Apple's Operations team held its weekly meeting that day and discussed slashing production of the iPhone XR. The next day, they followed through and cut production plans for the iPhone XR "further than discussed" by 11 million units in the quarter and a cumulative 17 million through the next quarter. In other words, Apple's operations team wasn't allowing time for different "potential sales outcomes" to unfold; the data was convincing enough for them to slash production of the XR for the next five months.

But Cook's email to the board was a model of transparency relative to what he and Maestri would tell analysts on the earnings call just a few hours later. They informed Wall Street that Apple was expecting $89 billion to $93 billion of revenue in the holiday quarter, underwhelming investors. But they didn't say a word about the muted sales of the XR, or the difficulties of forecasting, or that Cupertino now expected China revenues to shrink. Instead, they soothed investors with cheery sentiment. The obfuscation was brazen. Asked specifically about the XR, Cook replied that it'd been on sale for just five days so "we have very, very little data there." Asked about "deceleration" in emerging markets including China, Cook said it was a "great question" and mentioned "we're seeing pressure in . . . markets like Turkey, India, Brazil, Russia." Then he switched to China, subtly moving from present tense—the nature of the question—and looked back a quarter: "In relation to China specifically, I would not put China in that category. Our business in China was very strong last quarter. We grew 16 percent, which we're very happy with. iPhone in particular was very strong, very strong double-digit growth there."

Not saying anything was part of the plan. In prep notes for the call, Apple staffers had prepared Maestri for the question: "Why are you guiding revenue growth of 1 percent to 5 percent ($89 to $93 billion)?" His rehearsed answer is one of enthusiasm: Apple has the "strongest product lineup we've ever had heading into the holiday season." The notes go into some detail on the launch schedule of different iPhone models, but they don't mention the troubled XR or the idea that forecasting might be particularly difficult that year. Instead, the notes mention "the impact of macroeconomic uncertainty in some emerging markets," but China—its biggest overseas market—isn't named. Instead, the notes say to mention currency headwinds, and "if pressed," Maestri should cite Turkey.

Four days later, on November 5, Apple's head of PR, Steve Dowling, forwarded a story from *Nikkei Asia* to top executives. The news Cook and Maestri concealed from investors was leaked: The *Nikkei* reported that Foxconn and Pegatron had halted plans to boost XR production. Foxconn would devote forty-five production lines to the XR, rather than sixty as originally envisioned, according to a source that estimated it was cutting production by 100,000 units per day "to reflect the new demand outlook—down 20 percent to 25 percent from the original optimistic outlook." The situation was similar at Pegatron, while Wistron—on deck to start production in case the XR was a hit—had been told to stand down.

Priya Balasubramaniam, Apple's VP of iPhone operations, confirmed to Operations chief Jeff Williams that the *Nikkei* report was accurate. "Given how close some of the numbers are to facts," she wrote, there was "no doubt to us that a lot of the information on production line and daily production volume has to be directly from Foxconn." The sixty-two production lines making the iPhone XR at Foxconn, she said, were "big lines" capable of making 590 units per hour, and Apple had cut the number to forty-five. She also confirmed Pegatron was not running at capacity, and that Wistron had indeed been told to stand down. "The leak is infuriating," Williams wrote to a colleague. Tim Cook weighed in, suggesting Apple hold its manufacturing partners to account. "The leaks will continue until there is a substantial financial penalty," he advised.

What Cook *Wrote*

The revenue warning hit Wall Street like a shock wave. On January 2, 2019, Tim Cook issued an ad hoc statement saying revenue for the holiday quarter would be "approximately $84 billion"—$7.5 billion lower than what he'd forecast just eight weeks earlier, and further still from the $100 billion that Apple executives had hoped for back in mid-October, before the official launch of the XR. It was Apple's first revenue warning in nearly sixteen years. Tim Cook cast the net of blame widely, but acknowledged the main culprit was China.

What exactly was the problem in China? Cook was mighty vague. He assigned responsibility to "economic deceleration," noting that growth had slowed in the second half of 2018, a trend exacerbated "by rising trade tensions with the United States." He cited third-party market data to suggest "the contraction in Greater China's smartphone market has been particularly sharp." And he pointed to how "uncertainty weighed on financial markets," leading to fewer customers visiting the Apple Stores "and our channel partners in China."

The statement had implications well beyond Apple. The *Financial Times* reported that Apple "has stoked fears over the health of the global economy, rattling financial markets." Apple's stock dropped nearly 10 percent, its sharpest one-day fall in six years.

Close readers of Cook's letter pointed out that the reasons he cited didn't really add up. "Cook said two months ago that Apple's China business was 'very strong,' even amid signs of an economic slowdown and months of headlines about trade tensions with the US," wrote Bloomberg columnist Shira Ovide. She said the trends Cook pointed to were obvious to anyone outside the Cupertino bubble. "Apple failed in the No. 1 mission of being a public company: being honest with investors about its business," she concluded. "The company simply denied the reality that was staring it in the face, until denial was no longer an option." At Yahoo Finance, Brian Sozzi said Cook now had "a major credibility problem" with investors. Daniel Ives, a Wedbush Securities analyst known for his bullish takes on Apple, titled his note to investors: "Apple's Darkest Day in the iPhone Era."

What Cook *Omitted*

What Apple didn't tell investors in November 2018, or say in its January 2019 revenue warning, was that sales of the XR weren't simply attributable to a cooling Chinese economy. Instead, Chinese consumers were choosing to buy phones from Huawei. Apple had dealt with copycats since the earliest days of the iPhone, but most Chinese rivals could be ignored—they catered to the low end of the market. Huawei was different. It competed with Apple in the top tier, and in 2018, Apple executives began observing that Huawei's latest Mate phone was awfully good, outshining Apple in features rather than just price.

Four days before the November 1 earnings call, Cook had held a Sunday meeting with other executives. "In China, we're worried about the new Mate devices," he told the team. He was right to be concerned. Just a few years earlier, the gap in quality between iPhones and Chinese handsets was stark. But Apple had brought up quality across the region, and the gaps were closing. Within a year, Huawei would be outselling Apple not just in China but globally.

CHAPTER 37

THE HUAWEI THREAT

Tim Cook's obfuscations and omissions on the November 1 earnings call infuriated investors. The revenue warning he issued two months later caused Apple's market value to fall $75 billion, and investors, led by the UK's Norfolk county council, sued. When the case moved forward and lawyers for Norfolk asked that documents from "relevant" individuals be made available in discovery, Apple surprised the opposing lawyers by not including emails from Isabel Mahe. The plaintiffs thought they were onto something. They accused Apple of "attempting to unjustifiably circumscribe discovery" by excluding such an important individual. They demanded her inclusion, perplexed that Apple "somehow concluded" that the managing director of Greater China wasn't relevant in a lawsuit concerning the economic conditions, sales, forecasts, and production of iPhones—*in China.*

But Apple *had* handed over the relevant material concerning the "flow of relevant information." It's just that Mahe wasn't in that flow. The omission wasn't indicative that Apple was hiding something; it was an unwitting, glaring acknowledgment that its managing director of Greater China was a figurehead. This was made even clearer in a deposition of Tim Cook. Upon asking the Apple CEO to name his direct reports, Cook didn't name Mahe—despite the "Apple Leadership" website explicitly saying she reports directly to him. Nor did Cook include her in a list of the top ten to twelve people who attend the Monday-morning meeting of the executive team, a group described by Luca Maestri as "the most senior people in the company—all of them report to Tim." The discovery made it abundantly clear that Mahe wasn't involved in any of the key decisions. She wasn't even copied on the emails when sales forecasts and production were slashed. And yet Mahe did produce her monthly sales report on November 1, the morning of the earnings call, and it's more revealing regarding why Apple was struggling in China that quarter than anything Cook or Maestri has said or written.

Bitten Apple

As early as April 2018, Cupertino was getting concerned that China's phone brands were penetrating the top tier of design and quality. It had become clear that these brands had managed to rival the iPhone X—the $999 flagship that Apple had started selling the prior November. The "tenth anniversary iPhone" had been a breakthrough, enabling the user to unlock the phone with Face ID rather than their thumbprint. That allowed Apple to create an Infinity Pool–like design, arguably the biggest change since the 2007 launch. In a sea of similar-looking smartphones, the iPhone X really stood out, demonstrating Apple's innovative edge—but only for five months. Kevan Parekh—who in late 2024 would be appointed Apple's CFO, succeeding Maestri—wrote to a colleague stunned that the newest Huawei, Oppo, and Vivo flagship devices had managed to mimic Apple's latest innovation so quickly. "Incredibly," he wrote, "they all look similar (to varying degrees) to iPhone X, right down to the wallpaper, portrait lighting UI [user interface], and even the marketing how-to-videos. I expect Q3 to be challenging for us."

When the iPhone XR began to disappoint, Mahe determined that the underwhelming trajectory was less about a decelerating economy and more about the rise of homegrown competition. In late October she emailed colleagues in the United States to say the iPhone XR wasn't really on the Chinese consumer radar, relative to Huawei. "Everywhere I look I see Huawei Mate 20's advertisement (airports, billboards) and all sorts of news article [*sic*] on social network [*sic*] about how great Mate 20 is," she wrote. "News and information on Mate 20 dominate the internet. Frankly I don't see a lot of buzz on the new iPhones anymore, especially not much on XR."

The China sales team put together a six-page note titled "Huawei: Competitive Analysis," comparing Apple's newest iPhone models with Huawei's. The flagship Mate 20 Pro's features easily rivaled those of the higher-end iPhone XS, but Huawei had surprised Apple by positioning its pro model against the lower-end XR, even undercutting it on price by 17 percent. The Mate 20 Pro featured a larger screen with better resolution, three back cameras instead of one, double the memory, a bigger battery, and a faster recharging time.

In her monthly report on November 1, Mahe told sixteen of Apple's top executives that Huawei's "aggressive pricing in China" had diluted launch momentum for Apple "and prompted confusion on the positioning of the iPhone XR." She said the iPhone XR launch "has been somewhat overshadowed" and called the Mate 20 Pro a "Worthy iPhone Competitor" priced "nearly USD 360 cheaper than our entry iPhone XR." Further, she noted: "Huawei also recently opened its flagship retail store in Shanghai, which looks shockingly familiar to our new Apple Store designs."

Over the coming year, the onslaught from Huawei would be intense. China's national champion increased its share of the local market from 20 percent in the first half of 2019 to 27 percent in the second half, and then to 29 percent in early 2020. It began outselling the iPhone three to one in China, particularly threatening because it was taking a bite out of Apple's luxury dominance. In China's "premium market"—phones priced between $600 and $800—Huawei share soared from 10 percent in early 2018 to 48 percent a year later, causing Apple's share to fall from 82 percent to 37 percent. Apple's hold in the "super premium" market—phones priced above $800—was still impressive, at 74 percent, but it had fallen from 90 percent a year earlier.

If Huawei's success had been confined to China, the damage would've been limited. But in 2019 the Chinese brand overtook Apple sales globally. It shipped 238.5 million phones—more phones than Apple had shipped even in its peak year of 2015. The student, as they say, had become the master.

Trump

How Apple got out of this mess was a surprising twist, the stuff of novels. Donald Trump had ascended to the US presidency threatening Apple; instead, he saved it. In May 2019 the Trump administration alleged Huawei was a security threat, citing alleged ties with the Chinese government and the potential for its communications equipment to be used for espionage or cyberattacks. It soon imposed unprecedented sanctions, depriving Huawei of Google services, including the Play Store, Gmail, YouTube, and other Android tools—a crippling blow for Huawei phones distributed outside of China. Washington also disallowed American companies from shipping fifth-generation cellular chips to the group. Phones equipped with 5G had only just started taking off. Huawei, which makes cellular infrastructure in addition to smartphones, was an early leader. Its first 5G phones hit the market in August 2019, fourteen months before Apple, and by June 2020 it was selling 7 million such devices per month. But when the sanctions hit, Huawei's smartphone business collapsed. It lost $30 billion of revenue in a single year. It was also forced to spin off Honor, its sub-brand, avoiding job cuts and enabling the budget-oriented division to survive because it would no longer be subject to the same sanctions.

Apple was suddenly the only game in town for premium 5G phones. Huawei's share of the Chinese market plummeted from a peak of 29 percent to just 7 percent; Apple filled the void, its China share near doubling from 9 percent to 17 percent. In a matter of months, the Washington-Beijing trade war had unexpectedly morphed from threat to boon.

None of this was foreshadowed in 2016 when Trump was running for election on the most anti-trade, anti-China platform in modern American politics, with tariffs promised as a flagship policy. Trump's rhetoric was imprecise and erratic but often centered on China and went after Apple directly—far more so than the CCTV or *People's Daily* had in 2013. When, in a complex episode, Cook refused to assist the FBI by developing "backdoor software" to open a dead terrorist's iPhone, candidate Trump told his supporters: "What I think you ought to do is boycott Apple until such time as they give that security number. How do you like that? I just thought of it. Boycott Apple!" Trump said. "Tim Cook is looking to do a big number, probably to show how liberal he is. But Apple should give up—they should get the security or find other people."

When Trump entered office in early 2017, Cupertino was on high alert. Executives were far more concerned about Trump than they ever were about Xi Jinping. Beijing's ruler was a despot, sure, but he was a rational actor whose interests, broadly speaking, neatly aligned with Apple's. Neither Beijing nor Cupertino wanted iPhone product to be shifted out of China. But that's precisely what Trump wanted. "Tim, unless you start building your plants in this country, I won't consider my administration an economic success," Trump said he told the Apple CEO, in July 2017. Cook, according to Trump, had promised Apple would build "three big plants, beautiful plants." Clearly understanding the risks of the insurgent presidency, Cook made a point of calling Trump, even visiting the president every four to six weeks. "Cook, this big southerner, was calling Trump all the time—he was nice to him," says Margaret O'Mara, tech historian and author of *The Code*. "He was so savvy navigating the broader currents of global trade."

His diplomatic overtures climaxed in November 2019 when Cook personally gave President Trump a tour of a Texas factory churning out Apple's Pro lineup of Macs. After the event, Trump tweeted: "Today I opened a major Apple Manufacturing plant in Texas that will bring high paying jobs back to America." The tweet was patently false. The owner of the plant was contract manufacturer Flex, not Apple; it had been assembling Macs for six years; and rather than representing some milestone, the factory had been demonstrating just how difficult it was to make computers in America.

The origins of the project were political. Apple had been hammered in the Obama versus Romney presidential election for outsourcing jobs, and Apple felt it needed to demonstrate a commitment to America. Working with Flextronics—later renamed Flex—it planned for Mac Pros to be made in Texas. The sleek all-black cylindrical product was chosen for its high margins and low volumes, so it was seen as low risk. But in fact "the Trash Can Mac," as it was nicknamed, was highly complicated. Apple had it made in Texas and China, and both production sites struggled, reflecting its complexity. But the Texas experience was considered "an unmitigated fiasco," as one Apple engineer called it. "The worst project I ever worked on at Apple was bringing up Flextronics for the Mac Pro in Texas," says a second engineer. A third calls the experience painful and embarrassing:

> There was a bunch of stuff that we at Apple were very used to doing, that just didn't work anymore. Like, we're very fond of making custom fastening hardware, custom screws—you know, little nuts and stuff like that. Well, in China, if you're building and it's like, "Oh, shit, the screw is too short," and like, "I need a longer one," you call someone on a cellphone and 1,000 are at the factory tomorrow. That was not a thing in Texas. It would take two months. It was absurd.

A fourth person recalls speaking to one of the Flextronics workers, described as an overweight fifty-year-old white guy, who told him: "All the engineers are so frustrated with us because we don't move at 'China speed.'"

Even working with local supplier Texas Instruments was difficult, because the semiconductor maker was producing parts overseas, testing the parts overseas, and then reimporting them. "That caused a bunch of tax realities that they didn't like," one of the engineers said.

"So it was a six-month negotiation to honor the same prices they would give us in Asia to deliver the same parts in Texas." A fifth engineer says that ramp—the time when production scales up—officially began in July, but really started the following October, because it took the next six months to get the required finish on the aluminum housing. "You could tell Tim just hated it," a sixth engineer says, referring to Cook. "It felt so forced."

In the end, Mac Pros were indeed shipped from Texas, and Apple made a snazzy video demonstrating the processes—scoring whatever political points it could. But the project made it only because Apple leveraged relationships with suppliers in the one country where it knew the talent existed. "We flew people from China to get it fixed," one of the engineers says. "People working for Foxconn." The irony is hard to overstate. After more than a decade of sending its top engineers to China, to train staff on how to build things at Apple quality, Cupertino needed to fly Chinese engineers into America's heartland to complete the project. Apple had closed its American factories only a decade earlier, but as one of the engineers put it, "It was a very formative decade."

Just a few years earlier, Intel cofounder Andy Grove had warned that without manufacturing, America might lose the ability to innovate. Certainly that was the case for any number of hardware companies that sent blueprints off to Asia for someone else to turn into gleaming products. In Apple's case, Grove's worry was only partially true, but in revealing ways. Apple still knew *how* to manufacture; the problem was that it couldn't *execute* these plans without China. As Michael Hillman, a fifteen-year veteran of Apple and the Product Design head for the iMac G4, astutely puts it:

> If you're shipping a million of anything a day, there are only a handful of companies on the planet that can do it, and Apple found itself in that place with many technologies. You look at all the innovations, all the bespoke things Apple was doing—electronic components, surface mount technology processes, test processes—everything, even

> the data management for manufacturing one million units a day, all of that was proprietary to Apple. All protected in-house. Apple engineers were the general managers for this manufacturing supply base. But there wasn't any way to do it, anywhere, but in China.

So, in 2019, standing beside Trump in the Flex factory as the president proclaimed untruths about Apple's newest Mac Pro, Cook didn't see the need to correct the record. How could he? Apple had become utterly reliant on China, and the unexpected election of Trump had threatened the goodwill Cook had built up in China for nearly two decades. Trump was slapping tariffs on Chinese imports of up to 25 percent. If that applied to iPhones, it would've hammered Apple's margins or forced the company to inflate prices in its biggest market.

Politically, Cook's move was a masterstroke. Apple survived a trade war between the United States and China by gaining exemptions on tariffs from the Trump administration. And even though Washington kneecapped Huawei, Beijing didn't retaliate, because Cook had already made it clear just how much Apple was investing in the country, raising quality standards across its electronics supply chain. As the decade concluded, Apple was doing great. For its holiday 2019 quarter it posted a record-high $91.8 billion of revenue, a return to form made possible by Trump's sanctions taking Apple's biggest rival off the game board.

Guthrie's Departure

Late 2019 is also when Doug Guthrie left Apple. He'd been battling depression for years, increasingly relying on Super Doug, who'd obsess over work and be ultra-productive, to stave off Depressed Doug. He'd thrived in his twenties and thirties, living off three to four hours of sleep each night. But in his late forties, he found the lack of rest was catching up to him. He was falling into deeper bouts of depression, to the point of ideating suicide. "I came very close to not being here," he says. What saved him was a visit from a childhood friend whose father had died of suicide when he was just twelve years old. Guthrie, a dad himself, asked his friend how long it took to get over his father's death. At the time, Doug was in a deep depression and looking for absolution, someone to tell him it was okay to say goodbye to the world. His friend responded with both care and anger. "I don't know what you're thinking of, but that was thirty-six years ago, and not a day has gone by that I haven't thought about it—and been hurt by it. You don't get over something like that." The interaction shook Guthrie out of his state and compelled him to seek medical help. Only then was he diagnosed with Bipolar II, giving him a new lens to understand his entire life.

Guthrie felt it was best to leave China and to depart Apple. For more than two decades leading up to Xi's ascent, Guthrie had been a China bull—an advocate for the theory that more trade and commerce would inevitably create the rule of law and a liberal society. But Xi changed the country so, so radically, a political hardening made clearer to a wider audience as Beijing forced minority Muslim groups into indoctrination camps and cracked down on pro-democracy protesters in Hong Kong. "When you stake your life, your identity, on and around certain ideas, you sort of fight for them," Guthrie says. "Xi Jinping kind of broke my heart . . . I was sitting there, in China, in my dream job, and I'm watching Xinjiang's internment camps. I'm watching China tearing up a fifty-year agreement over Hong Kong."

Apple, meanwhile, had become too intertwined with China. Guthrie had been hired to help understand the country and to navigate it. And Apple had followed through—very successfully. But it had burned so many boats, as the saying goes, that Guthrie felt its fate was married to China's and there was no way out. "The cost of doing business in China today is a high one, and it is paid by any and every company that comes looking to tap into its markets or leverage its workforce," he later wrote in a blog. "Quite simply, you don't get to do business in China today without doing exactly what the Chinese government wants you to do. Period. No one is immune. No one."

CHAPTER 38

GLOBAL PANDEMIC

An Apple engineer was in Wuhan with his wife when the city entered lockdown on January 23, 2020, an extreme measure designed to isolate a threat the authorities had ignored, downplayed, and covered up for weeks. A novel coronavirus called COVID-19 was rapidly spreading, leaving behind a trail of dead bodies and unanswered questions. The couple wanted to return to the United States but domestic flights from Wuhan to the East Coast of China were abruptly canceled. The authorities barricaded the streets, blocking cars from moving from one area to the next. The couple's desire to get home turned into a desperate need. They sought local help and arranged a complex escape plan by traveling from one checkpoint to another in a series of taxis. They'd pull up to a barrier in one car; another would be waiting on the other side; they'd transfer their baggage from one trunk to another, pay the driver, and go. The 520-mile drive from Wuhan to Shanghai usually takes under nine hours; this journey took three days. Arriving in Shanghai, the couple still weren't sure they'd be able to get on a flight. Travel restrictions were tight, but there were flexible policies for people taking their pets out of the country. "It was, like, a mercy mission type thing," says a person familiar with the episode. The couple prepared to adopt a cat to aid their escape, but after seven nights in a Shanghai hotel they were able to fly back to San Francisco without such a charade.

Two weeks after their arrival, on February 17, Apple issued a revenue warning for the March quarter—just thirteen months after it had cut guidance before. China was again the problem, but this time, of course, the issue wasn't poor iPhone sales; quite the opposite, *making* iPhones was now the problem. Chinese New Year fell on January 25 that year. Factories often empty out for a solid two weeks for the celebrations, as migrant workers head back to their villages. This year, many employees didn't come back. "We are experiencing a slower return to normal conditions than we had anticipated," Apple told investors.

Cupertino had been expecting revenues that quarter to rise 9 percent to 15 percent, an unusually wide estimate that already reflected COVID-19 uncertainties from late January. But the situation was fast evolving, and now Apple wasn't certain it would grow revenues at all. The main problem was that suppliers were ramping up more slowly than anticipated. But in addition, all forty-two Apple Stores in the country had been closed. Given its deep operations and near real-time understanding of consumer trends, Apple unsurprisingly was the first major corporation to issue such a warning.

Within three weeks, COVID-19 swept across much of the world. Offices were closed, workers sheltered at home, and the stock market crashed. By early March, Apple shares had collapsed by nearly one-third—losing $440 billion in market value and returning to the $1 trillion valuation first reached in August 2018. But in the coming months, Apple—at first—defied dire predictions by demonstrating the resiliency of its China-centric supply chain.

For years, Cupertino had flown engineers into China by the planeload to oversee the ramping up of new products. Prior to COVID, Apple was booking "50 business class seats daily" from San Francisco to Shanghai, according to an accidental leak from United Airlines revealing Apple as its largest corporate customer. Suddenly that wasn't possible. But every product Apple made had an in-region support team, and they were forced to step up their game. Apple's partners, too—from Foxconn, Luxshare, and BYD to deeper layers in the supply chain—knew what they were doing. Apple had trained their engineers and, at times, orchestrated mini-crises to let the schedule slip and see how the suppliers would react. "I intentionally let one whole build just basically crater," says a former engineering manager, describing an event before the pandemic. "It was an example for them to learn what it takes." It was like the old parable about teaching a man to fish. "All of these suppliers, or a lot of them, have gotten to the point where they understand what it takes to develop an Apple product," this person says. "And so when we stepped away, there's a machine that's already enabled, that knows what it takes to build a product."

Apple staff, too, had broad experience working over Webex—Cupertino's preferred video-conferencing tool—from just a few years earlier. The building and opening of the company's new "spaceship" headquarters, Apple Park, had caused all kinds of disruption ahead of its 2017 opening, forcing teams to work remotely and, though it was unappreciated at the time, giving them a preview of what it would be like to work during a pandemic. The 2,000 or so staff at Apple's Chinese R&D centers, too, became critical. Even executives who believe those hubs were just political window dressing now acknowledge they were a massive help when Apple was suddenly short of hands.

Still, Cupertino wanted to send engineers to China and offered bonuses between $500 and $1,000 a day for people to go. But flights had been dramatically reduced. United halted nonstop flights from San Francisco to Shanghai from March to October 2020. So Apple scrambled the jets. In the spring, Cupertino began sending engineers to Shanghai on private planes departing from San Jose, with a pit stop in Alaska. "Each jet could hold thirteen people, but we only sat six," says a person familiar with the flights. "We wanted room and, you know, we're Apple."

Upon arrival the team of engineers had to go undergo health tests and perform nearly three hours of paperwork using a digital app in Chinese. Then they checked into a dingy, state-run hotel for fourteen days of quarantine. "It was dicey as hell," says one person. To help out, Apple sent a few people from the local Asia Procurement Office (APO), which had prearranged for the new arrivals to be put in bare-floor hotel rooms. They had learned that state workers never really cleaned the carpeted floors—they just sprayed them down with chemicals. Bare floors were the way to go.

Once they were checked in, the team took the escalator up and got a full view of their surroundings. It looked like a zombie movie, a desolate area with ad hoc test stations, staffed with Chinese officials in their all-white full-body protective suits. These officials earned the nickname "White Guards," a play on Red Guards, the all-too-zealous enforcers of Mao doctrine in the Cultural Revolution. The White Guards gained a reputation for "surrounding people, beating and dragging them away, or knocking on their door to put pressure on them to submit to a PCR test [with the possible result that they might] leave home for an isolation camp," according to Radio Free Asia.

In the engineers' hotel rooms, APO staffers had left "goodie bags" with a yoga mat, a collapsible camping bucket for washing clothes, and what appeared to be a long-stemmed lint roller. Folded sheets were on the bed. The guests soon figured out what the lint roller was for: If you rolled it across the bed, it came back disgusting. Somehow the APO colleagues had arranged for China Eastern Airline to provide first-class food. That sounded better than it was. It's a decent meal on a single flight, but three times a day, for two weeks, was a bit much. Trapped in their rooms at all hours of the day, the engineers had only one other option for finding nutrition: They could order a cup of noodles on Taobao, a shopping platform. And every night, the White Guards plunged long Q-tips deep into the team members' nasal passages, leaving the probes in for ten seconds as the COVID testing rules required.

After the fourteen-day quarantine, it was a totally different reality. While much of the Western world was sheltering at home, China's strict lockdowns, mandatory quarantines, and other "zero-COVID" measures had allowed for relative normalcy by the summer of 2020. Early fears that a global pandemic originating from China would wreak havoc on Apple's supply chain never really materialized. COVID-19, of course, swept the world, killing people by the millions and disrupting businesses. And supply chain woes that once might have seemed mundane were now front-page stories: carmakers short of semiconductors; grocery stores emptied of food; hospitals lacking protective gear. Westerners fretted about the supply of everything from toilet paper to Peloton bikes. Billions of dollars' worth of goods were stuck at port. But Apple had few problems making their products en masse, and even fewer challenges convincing people to buy them. Its suppliers had difficulties, no doubt; but Apple is nearly always their most important client, so if the maker of some component had their capacity cut in half, by and large Apple was still getting its share. One bank estimates that in the four years from the onset of COVID, component shortages reduced Apple revenue by $30 billion—a massive amount in absolute dollars, but just 2 percent of company revenue owing to the fact that Apple had experienced a surge in orders from consumers upgrading their home offices.

In the holiday quarter of 2020, Apple revenue jumped 21 percent to $111.4 billion. Buoyed by the sanction-induced collapse of Huawei, sales in Greater China played a starring role, soaring 57 percent. The following year was even better. In fiscal 2021, global revenue shot up 33.3 percent. COVID-19 hadn't harmed Apple; ironically, it helped the company enjoy its strongest growth in a decade. On the first trading day of 2022, just twenty-one months after the depths of the COVID market crash when Apple's value sank to $1 trillion, its market value surpassed $3 trillion—a first for any company.

Crackdowns and Lockdowns

Amid stunning success, the unpredictable risks of Apple wedding its fortunes to China continued to spill into view as Xi Jinping made it abundantly clear just how seriously he expected corporations to heed his authority. In the early months of battling COVID-19, Beijing enacted a major crackdown on its own tech giants by launching "investigations" into dozens of companies that had, in varying ways, challenged its power or ignored its requests. The crackdown's poster child was Jack Ma, the billionaire founder of e-commerce giant Alibaba. In late October 2020, after Ma critiqued Beijing governance and compared state-owned banks to pawnshops, regulators called him in for "supervisory interviews." They soon canceled what would have been a world-record $37 billion fundraising effort for the initial public offering of Alibaba's sister company, Ant Financial, a lender disrupting state-owned banks. Investors had valued Ant at $316 billion—exceeding even JPMorgan Chase. But Ma disappeared from public life and Alibaba's stock price fell nearly 50 percent.

The crackdown included more than thirty-five antitrust investigations and other security probes into data collection. State-backed entities purchased corporate stakes and installed themselves on the board of major tech firms, including TikTok owner ByteDance and Sina Weibo, China's Twitter-like service. Other companies were wholly acquired by the state. "Today, many entrepreneurs are now concerned that they will be persecuted or their property will be confiscated," wrote two China scholars in their book *Mao and Markets*. By February 2022, the sell-off had wiped out $1.5 trillion of market value. Among the victims was Didi, the ride-hailing group Apple had so publicly invested in, and to whose board it had appointed its VP of corporate development. Didi had opted to list its shares in New York despite warnings not to do so by Chinese regulators. Ten days after going public, Beijing launched an investigation, and the following month it ordered app stores to remove the Didi app from their platforms, in effect depriving the business of user growth. Didi shares fell by more than 80 percent.

Apple was spared. Its lobbying efforts had successfully demonstrated to Beijing that Apple was providing tremendous benefit to the country, and the company was careful to refrain from commenting on China's authoritarian turn. But then, as the Omicron variant of COVID-19 began to spread in Shanghai, a city of 25 million and the headquarters of Apple's

China operations, Apple found itself challenged by the pandemic in a way that it hadn't previously. Officials reacted with draconian "zero-COVID" measures, confining most residents to their homes for two months beginning on April 1. In the previous ten years authorities had never issued a decree so directly opposed to Apple's business interests.

The strict response to COVID's initial outbreak had been understandable given mass uncertainty over the deadly nature of the virus. It was a time when medical experts couldn't agree on even the basics: *How important are face masks? Is it dangerous to meet outside? Are children as vulnerable as the elderly?* Factories in China had closed in 2020, but that was far from unique; in the United States, California's demand that Tesla close its Fremont factory spurred an incensed Elon Musk to move the company's headquarters to Texas.

The Shanghai lockdown was different. By April 2022, much of the world had normalized, and vaccines had been distributed for more than a year. So it made sense that Apple would find the latest measures to be unwarranted and highly disruptive. One logistics manager described commercial transportation across the entire Yangtze River Delta region—a megalopolis around Shanghai with a GDP similar to all of Japan—as "basically stagnant." Even a senior Huawei executive warned that a prolonged lockdown "will pose severe consequences and massive losses for the whole industry." In the case of Apple, more than half of its 200 primary suppliers were impacted, disrupting production of iPhones, MacBooks, and iPads. Tim Cook estimated damage to revenue in the range of $4 billion to $8 billion, the starkest warning of the COVID period.

The twin threats of a tech crackdown and zero-COVID rules disrupting Apple's operations underscored the company's vulnerabilities. But as 2022 wound down, Apple stepped up its efforts to aid Beijing's Made in China 2025 plan, agreeing to work with state-backed Yangtze Memory Technologies Corp or YMTC—a semiconductor producer making memory chips. The new partnership was a glaring illustration of just how much the foreign policy interests of Washington and Cupertino had diverged.

In Washington, under President Joe Biden, a hard-line stance countering China had become the most bipartisan issue in Congress. The United States saw China's efforts to build chips on its own as one of the twenty-first century's biggest threats. Beijing was intent on advancing its chip fabrication capabilities, which can support both consumer electronics and military weaponry. It had established the Big Fund—officially known as the China Integrated Circuit Industry Investment Fund—a multiyear effort costing tens of billions of dollars with the goal of making China self-sufficient in semiconductors. Washington diplomats were pressing Japan and the Netherlands to choke off China's homegrown semiconductor market and were sanctioning Chinese companies that posed a threat. Meanwhile, Beijing was responding by accelerating efforts to de-Americanize the chips supply chain, and America's biggest corporation was only too happy to help.

"Apple is playing with fire," Marco Rubio, Republican vice chair of the Senate Intelligence Committee, told the *Financial Times* in September 2022. "It knows the security risks posed by YMTC. If it moves forward, it will be subject to scrutiny like it has never seen from the federal government. We cannot allow Chinese companies beholden to the Communist Party into our telecommunications networks and millions of Americans' iPhones." In Congress, a bipartisan group of senators including Democrats Chuck Schumer and Mark Warner had urged the Biden administration to put YMTC on a Commerce Department blacklist that would effectively bar US companies from providing technology to the Chinese group. Apple acknowledged it was "evaluating sourcing from YMTC . . . to be used in some iPhones sold in China," but it was adamant these chips wouldn't be used in iPhones in America. Yet that's almost beside the point. As Michael McCaul, the top Republican on the House Foreign Affairs Committee, put it: "Apple will effectively be transferring knowledge and knowhow to YMTC that will supercharge its capabilities and help the CCP achieve its national goals." Apple, under pressure from US lawmakers, said it had suspended the partnership.

CHAPTER 39

"AN UNPRECEDENTED NIGHTMARE FOR APPLE"

Beijing's crackdown on its own tech sector and the unrelenting zero-COVID measures were a massive show of force accentuating just how much power Xi Jinping had accrued as he neared the end of a second term in office. Xi's actions made Washington's hopes from two decades earlier—that it could export democracy through capitalism—look almost willfully naïve.

One episode demonstrating Xi's hold over the party was captured on film. As Xi was poised to accept a third term as China's ruler, his predecessor, Hu Jintao, was sitting right next to him at the 20th Congress of the Chinese Communist Party, on October 22, 2022. When seventy-nine-year-old Hu reached for a red folder in front of him, another Chinese official removed it from his grasp. When Hu again attempted to grab it, Xi signaled to an aide, issued a command, and within seconds two aides lifted Hu by the armpit and escorted him out. As China journalist James Kynge writes: "As Hu was hustled out, none of a seated row of top officials even so much as turned to wish him well. They stared straight ahead, studiously ignoring his humiliation." Inside the envelope, some experts believe, was a dossier that would have demonstrated that Hu's key protégé wasn't being elevated to the seven-member Politburo—the highest organ of the Central Committee. Xi had stacked the Politburo with allies, consolidated more power than any Chinese leader since Mao, and was set to rule for life.

If China's authoritarian turn was problematic for Apple, we might expect to see its revenue suffer, its margins fall, its operations deteriorate. But just a few days later, on October 27, 2022, Tim Cook appeared triumphant. Apple was reporting to the world that it had earned nearly $400 billion of revenue in its fiscal year, a new record following fourteen consecutive quarters of rapid growth. The results, which would surprise Wall Street amid a macroeconomic storm hurting every Big Tech rival, were all the more remarkable given that Cupertino had recently weathered two Black Swan events: four years of the Trump administration and three years of COVID-19. Both threatened to strain Apple's relationship with China, where virtually all of Apple's products were manufactured; yet Apple didn't merely struggle through these two episodes, it thrived because of them.

Luca Maestri, Apple's cheerful Italian-born CFO, was especially ebullient when he spoke to the *Financial Times* half an hour before Apple's earnings went public. The number of iGadgets in the wild "set a new record in every geography and in every product category," Maestri said. But what he was most happy about was the outlook for Apple's lucrative holiday quarter, because for the first time since the onset of the pandemic, Apple's supply chain was under control. "We didn't have any meaningful significant supply constraints either from COVID or from silicon shortages," he said.

Within days of Apple's report, the iPhone maker's market capitalization shot up to exceed the combined value of Google parent Alphabet, Facebook parent Meta, and Amazon—three of the four other Big Tech companies. Apple's lead over number two Microsoft was $720 billion, a gap large enough to encompass Tesla. Apple was in a league of its own.

But one week later, a crisis emerged at Foxconn's most important factory, where the supplier builds Apple's most important product, at the most important time of the year. The sprawling campus of 200,000 workers in Zhengzhou, known as "iPhone City," experienced a COVID outbreak. Foxconn, desperately wanting to keep the factory churning out products for the holiday season, introduced a "closed-loop" system that barred employees from leaving the factory's environs. As false rumors spread that 20,000 people in iPhone City had tested positive for COVID, hundreds of workers, fearing China's prisonlike levels of detention during a pandemic lockdown, fled the scene by tearing down security walls and scaling fences topped with barbed wire. Some opted to walk more than sixty miles back to their rural villages. Those who stayed experienced food and medical shortages and found their movements restricted to crowded living quarters. When workers protested, riot police beat them with batons.

This single event, three years into a global pandemic, dramatically exposed a risk to Apple that had been latent for nearly two decades: its deep concentration of manufacturing operations in a single country. "The Zhengzhou debacle is being talked about as a result of China's zero-COVID policy, but what it really shows you is systemic weaknesses in the way manufacturing is organized," a well-placed person involved in supply chain audits in China for more than a decade told the *Financial Times*. One analyst called the scene "an unprecedented nightmare for Apple."

For years, Cook had resisted calls to really diversify Apple's operations. Speaking to investors in April 2020, he said: "If you look at the shock to the supply chain that took place this quarter—for it to come back up so quickly really demonstrates that it's durable and resilient. And so I feel good about where we are." Some investors, journalists, and other executives at Apple believed Cook was being complacent. But it was only in November 2022 that clear proof came crashing down. The protests in Zhengzhou became a media spectacle, catalyzing similar demonstrations against COVID lockdowns in at least a dozen cities across the country. Together these protests formed the biggest challenge to Communist Party rule since students took over Tiananmen Square in 1989. Activists became famous for holding blank white sheets of paper, a poignant symbol of "everything we want to say but cannot say," as one participant put it.

Apple was forced to issue yet another revenue warning—its third in four years, each due to problems in China—saying that supply chain disruptions would derail production of the highly sought after iPhone Pro, its most lucrative model. Later, it posted its first revenue decline in nearly four years. Trying to soothe, Apple offered some comments about sorting out its factories, but it was careful not to support the protesters. In fact, the company restricted use of its file-sharing tool AirDrop after it emerged that Chinese citizens were using it to organize. The move was similar to how, in October 2019, Apple removed from its App Store a mapping application used by pro-democracy protesters in Hong Kong, just days after being criticized by Chinese state media for allowing it to be downloaded. In the words of Democrat Mark Warner, chair of the Senate Intelligence Committee, removing AirDrop was tantamount to "doing the bidding" of the Chinese Communist Party.

Getting China Wrong

Both Hu's unceremonious removal from China's Congress and Beijing's crackdown on its own tech giants for stepping out of line might have been on Tim Cook's mind in early December 2022 when he was confronted by a reporter on Capitol Hill, en route to meeting privately with senior lawmakers. "Do you support the Chinese people's right to protest? Do you have any reaction to the factory workers that were beaten and detained for protesting COVID lockdowns?" asked Hillary Vaughn of Fox News as Cook walked through the building. "Do you think it's problematic to do business with the Communist Chinese Party when they suppress human rights?" Cook ignored Vaughn, eyes cast downward as he changed direction to avoid her.

One supply chain executive characterized the confrontation as "the worst forty-five seconds of Cook's career." But his biggest, most astute critic might have been . . . himself. In 2017, explaining why corporate executives should be more up-front about their values and "lead accordingly," Cook had told journalist Megan Murphy that "silence is the ultimate consent." He went on:

> If you see something going on that's not right, the most powerful form of consent is to say nothing. And I think that's not acceptable to your company, to the team that works so hard for your company, for your customers, or for your country. Or for each country that you happen to be operating in.

The forty-five-second clip of Cook ignoring questions about China played repeatedly on US cable news. Cook's silence—his ultimate consent—was highly indicative of just how beholden America's most valuable company had become to an authoritarian state.

The point, however, isn't to condemn Cook or Apple. It's to convey the predicament they're in. At the turn of the millennium, Washington made a bet on China—a bet that free trade would liberalize the country and perhaps catalyze the creation of the world's biggest democracy. Instead, trade enriched China and empowered its rulers. Cook shouldn't be blamed by politicians for enmeshing Apple's operations in China two decades ago, but he has erred by doubling down over the past decade despite mounting evidence that Xi has been ramping up repression at home and taking a more combative stance in international affairs. "You can say that we read them wrong, that we misunderstood China. But Jack Ma read China wrong, too. Every entrepreneur read China wrong," says a supply chain expert who has lived in the country. "You look at what Deng Xiaoping and Hu Jintao were promoting—the [business class] didn't see this coming. Xi changed the game completely. He's another Putin in the making." This person adds, "Look, I'm not a Cook fan. But you have to be sympathetic. He didn't know what he was dealing with. Nobody did."

CHAPTER 40

PLAN B—ASSEMBLED IN INDIA?

The Shanghai lockdown and COVID-related protests in Zhengzhou were a major moment for Apple—like the CCTV-led attacks a decade earlier—to pause and really digest the vulnerabilities of being so dependent on a single authoritarian regime. The assessment was sobering: Chinese brands had accounted for just 23 percent of global smartphone shipments in 2013, the year of Apple's political awakening. But their share surpassed 50 percent in 2020. Brands led by Huawei, Xiaomi, and Vivo gave Chinese companies, in 2022, a cumulative market share in both China and Russia of 79 percent; in Indonesia, 73 percent; in India, 66 percent, per Counterpoint Research. In fact, Samsung and Apple were the only two sizable non-Chinese companies still making smartphones. Taiwan's HTC, Korea's LG, Canada's BlackBerry, and Finland's Nokia were all basically gone; Motorola was now owned by China's Lenovo; and global sales of Google Pixel were so low as to be subsumed into the "other" category. Moreover, Samsung didn't share Apple's vulnerability. After peaking in 2013 with 20 percent of China's smartphone market, Samsung's share collapsed to just 1 percent. It closed its Chinese plants in 2019, diversifying its supply chain to such an extent that more than three-quarters of its handsets were assembled in six countries from Argentina to Vietnam; less than one-quarter of its units were outsourced to contract manufacturers in China. The ascent of China's smartphone sector spoke volumes about Apple's dependence on the very capabilities it had orchestrated, underscoring how China had gone from a land of cheap labor to one of sophisticated automation. Now, the important players in the country were no longer just manufacturers but design-driven brands taking significant market share around the globe.

Until the Shanghai lockdown, there'd been no major plans to shift iPhone production out of China. To avoid the threat of tariffs on China-made goods during the Trump administration and to take advantage of lower labor costs, Apple had made notable shifts in where it manufactured some of its other products, diverting them to Vietnam and Thailand. According to Apple insiders, by 2022 more than 70 percent of AirPods production, nearly a third of Apple Watch assembly, and about a quarter of iPad manufacturing had moved out of China. That's a far faster shift than recognized by independent market intelligence groups, but it hasn't been in Apple's interest to tout these moves given political sensitivities in China. An analysis of 1,000 financial filings from Apple's four biggest Taiwanese manufacturer partners supports the conclusion that diversification efforts have been substantial. According to TD Cowen, the research arm of investment bank TD Securities, from 2018 through 2023, these four groups spent $16 billion—on land, construction, and machinery—diversifying production away from China to India, Mexico, the United States, and Vietnam. By contrast, iPhone production had barely diversified before the Shanghai lockdown, owing to its complexity and a lack of will at the highest echelons of Cupertino.

Apple, with partner Foxconn, had tried manufacturing iPhones in Brazil since the early 2010s, but volumes had been negligible—estimated to be 1 percent or less of all production. The expansion was a matter of avoiding heavy tariffs in the region, not creating a manufacturing hub for exports. But engineers who worked on the Brazilian project called it a disaster. There were still lots of taxes to pay; none of the factories rivaled the scale of China; the political environment was unstable; and the labor force was unreliable. One Foxconn worker sent from the Czech site says there were even problems with armed gangs attacking the factories.

Apple had also been making iPhones in India since 2017. As with Brazil, volumes were limited and the shift had largely been driven by the desire to avoid tariffs. But unlike with respect to Brazil, there were forces within Cupertino lobbying for a much bigger push. The effort hadn't received much traction, but the Shanghai lockdown of 2022 proved a major catalyst for change. "Overnight," a former executive says, "China went from being a reliable supplier to a completely unreliable supplier." Plan B for iPhone manufacturing got approved.

Made in India

The push to India has been led by Priya Balasubramaniam, VP of iPhone operations. Former colleagues describe her as great at negotiating with vendors, running the supply chain, and rolling up her sleeves to figure things out. One manufacturing design engineer says she is "very, very sharp—can cut right to the chase." But they say she's not necessarily all that technical or inventive. "She's a person who will work harder, work harder—not smarter," says one. Several people say the jury is still out on whether she can lead a major shift from China to India. The implication: If the skill set needed is brute force and sixteen-hour days, then Priya—as everyone at Apple calls her—is great for the role; if it requires fundamentally rethinking things, she might not be.

India, a democracy with English as a second official language, offers fewer geopolitical risks than China and, with its rising middle class, could become a huge market in the coming decades. As an internal memo prepared for Tim Cook in October 2018 put it: India is poised for a "China-like trajectory." The memo compared India's economy to China's in 2008, cited projections that GDP would grow 7 percent a year for the next five years, and referenced an estimate from McKinsey, the consultancy, saying "India's 'consuming class' is expected to almost triple to ~90M households by 2025." India, in 2018, was already the third-largest smartphone market in the world, with 124 million users, and it was projected to soon surpass the US market of 176 million users. The memo called India's smartphone market "a vast pool to be exploited."

But Apple's push to India was tepid in the five years following that memo, until the Shanghai lockdown. The slowness had reflected Cupertino's caution and New Delhi's unwillingness to be as welcoming as Beijing had been two decades earlier. When Cook had personally met with Prime Minister Narendra Modi in 2015, he lobbied to open an Apple Store in the country. But protectionist rules required that foreign companies selling goods directly to consumers must source 30 percent of components locally, and Modi wouldn't offer an exception. When the rules were relaxed in 2017, Apple suppliers began assembling some iPhones in India—with Taiwanese partner Wistron—a move that allowed Apple to avoid hefty tariffs. That made the iPhone more affordable to a rising middle class. But in India an online Apple Store didn't launch until 2020, and the first physical Apple Stores didn't open until three years later—fifteen years after the first store in China.

Priya's team has made tangible progress since 2017. They've moved from making the entry-level iPhone SE models to, in 2020, producing the flagship models. In addition, they've sped up the mass launch in India, trimming the lag between iPhone distribution from China and iPhone distribution from India from many months to just a few weeks. By 2023, there was actually no lag at all—made-in-India iPhones were available on the same day. Another milestone was reached in September 2024 when Pro models were made in India, too. And Apple wasn't just supplying the local market; consumers in Europe, among other places, took to social media with their surprise that their newest iPhone was "made in India."

Despite this progress, Apple is only in the earliest phases of diversifying iPhone production. As Morgan Stanley analysts estimated in mid-2023: "90–95% of Apple's production is still in China; we believe a full decoupling would likely require *hundreds of billions of dollars* of investment at least, which would prove an outsize burden for the supply chain." Indeed, the pace of growth in Apple's operations in India is nothing like that of China a decade earlier. From 2016 to 2023, iPhone production in India grew from zero to around 15 million units, accounting for 7 percent of global shipments. China, between 2006 and 2013, ramped production from zero to 153 million units. So, at best, India is taking on iPhone orders at one-tenth the rate China did a decade earlier.

And yet, even that vastly overstates things. Most operations that suppliers have set up for Apple in India are FATP—final assembly, test, and pack out—a labor-intensive process performed with components largely flown in from China and then assembled mostly by Taiwanese companies Wistron and Foxconn. One manufacturing design engineer says, only slightly joking, that the phones "made in India" are assembled in China, disassembled there, and then sent to India for reassembly. As of late 2024, Apple's India operations are only in the early stages of building up capacity for "new product introduction," a much wider effort involving a greater depth and breadth of operations to source components, build prototypes and test them, and ramp to mass production. Apple does intend for India to become fully capable in every respect—but that's likely to take a minimum of five to ten years, if it can be accomplished at all.

A former senior Apple engineer agrees Cupertino now has major ambitions to orchestrate "next-door" suppliers in India—industrial clusters comprising operations from a diverse set of vendors close to final assembly. But, this person says, the pace of development hasn't been quick. If those clusters can be established, it would be a big deal, but in the interim, having iPhone assembly in both China and India dependent on the same supply chain adds more complications than resilience. "You have to add in that time cycle—from that part coming from China and into India," this person says, pointing out that the lower labor costs of India get offset by the added logistics of sending freight from China. Historically, this engineer points out that when Japan, then Taiwan, and then China made their mark in global electronics manufacturing, they all started by supplying components, creating a foundation of technical expertise. Only afterward would a supplier of, say, motherboards, begin to vertically integrate and expand into taking on final assembly, test, and pack out; by contrast, Apple in India has been doing FATP for seven years and is only now trying to build up the competency of suppliers making parts. "My sense of it is, [Apple is] doing it ass-backwards," this person adds.

Rivaling China

Engineers and executives with years and decades of experience at Apple are deeply divided on whether India has what it takes to rival China—and to what extent Apple's investments can be a game changer. There are some who are extremely bullish. One current Apple operations engineer, having just returned from both countries, estimates that India will account for a stunning 60 percent of Apple's manufacturing by 2030—meaning that *more Apple products will be made in India than in China*. Several former engineers believe that's feasible, but many others find it wildly overconfident, exuding hubris in Apple's abilities and ignorance regarding just what a unique, crafty, determined, and powerful role China has played in the prior twenty-five years. If anything even resembling this operations engineer's prediction is accomplished, it would be an extraordinary achievement that would significantly de-risk Apple's operations and, in the process, accelerate India into a manufacturing powerhouse.

The two major arguments supporting India's potential are its enormous workforce and its cheap labor. In 2023, its population of 1.43 billion overtook that of China; that number of willing hands could be a major asset versus, say, the resources that exist in Vietnam, which has a skilled population but is only one-fifteenth the size. Average monthly manufacturing wages in India, as of 2024, were just $195, versus $1,139 in China (and $5,912 in the United States). It's common to hear that India today is similar to the China of two decades earlier. Certainly, the potential is enormous. Bain, the global consultancy, estimates that manufacturing exports from India could more than double from $418 billion in 2022 to more than $1 trillion in 2028, driven by policy support and low costs. Bain further estimates that electronics exports alone will grow at an annual rate of up to 40 percent. And Apple is playing an active role making changes on the ground. In 2023, Apple and Foxconn successfully lobbied for a landmark bill in the Indian state of Karnataka to liberalize labor laws. The new legislation allowed factories to run twelve-hour shifts, up from nine hours previously. Karnataka also eased rules on nighttime work for women, who dominate electronics production lines in Southeast Asia.

But these "India is the new China" arguments can feel superficial. China's strength has been less about the abundance of labor and more about their allocation and flexibility. Jenny Chan, coauthor of *Dying for an iPhone*, which details the lives of Foxconn workers who assemble Apple products, argues that state support in filling factories with migrant labor has been critical. "This is really important, because you will not get [much interest from workers] in assembling an iPad or iPhone," she says. "It's repetitive work and you are just rendered as a robot—a tiny cog in a huge machine." But India doesn't have a culture of internal migration. In one study, India had "the lowest rate of internal migration" among eighty countries.

Moreover, wages in China have soared, but they've soared for a reason—reflecting the skill sets of experienced workers, the competitive edge of its industrial clusters, and world-leading investments in automation. Or to put it simply, the Chinese worker comes *with* a robot. According to the Information Technology and Innovation Foundation, robot adoption in China is in "a class of its own, with its national and provincial governments committing massive amounts of money to subsidize adoption of robots and other automation technology." As of 2022, the number of industrial robots deployed in China was above 290,000, more than half the global total; in India, it was 5,400, according to the International Federation of Robotics.

Indeed, China sports a level of technical sophistication that multiple experts struggle to even comprehend. The layperson often believes Foxconn could just open a factory in a different country; but the Foxconn hubs in China are surrounded by hundreds of sub-suppliers all ready to compete for the next major order. "For Apple to give that system up is tricky," says Jay Goldberg, founder of D2D Advisory, a tech consultancy. If Foxconn, for example, needs to install sonic welders—a process to merge different metals or plastics with ultrasonic energy—it can call up any number of firms to run the line and hire the labor. "There's all these subcontracted, specialty niche firms, and nowhere else does that exist," Goldberg says. What China offers, in other words, is not simply labor, but an entire ecosystem of processes developed over more than two decades.

Then there is the cultural dimension. In China, suppliers and government officials took a "whatever it takes" approach to win iPhone orders. Operations in India are not run at that sort of pace, says a former Apple engineer, adding: "There just isn't a sense of urgency." China's top-down ambitions were aided by docile, hardworking laborers systematically exploited by the state; by contrast, India's government is fragmented and less powerful, its officials aren't incentivized to boost growth the way Chinese cadres are, and Indian workers have more of a voice. In September 2024, some 1,500 Samsung workers in India formed a union and went on strike, demanding higher wages. Their story was broadcast worldwide by the BBC, in effect shaming the Korean company into prioritizing compliance. In China, such dissent would receive no media support and be crushed.

As far as intentions go, it's evident that Cupertino is now making serious efforts to de-risk from China by asking its supplier partners to replicate their China-based capacities in India. One supplier executive said Apple is pushing them "like hell" to move. But even if suppliers prove capable and New Delhi invests in infrastructure, the pace of Apple's moves is likely to be constrained due to China's interest in retaining control of Apple operations. "It's clear Apple is slowly inching away, but they have to walk a fine line. They don't want to run away—but they can't crawl," says Goldberg. "They have to walk at just the right pace. If they move too quickly, China will get mad at them. And if they move too slowly, they'll get stuck."

Sensitive to its vulnerabilities, Apple has portrayed its move in private conversations as an expansion to India, not a retreat from China, former Apple executives say. In addition, Cupertino has been telling Beijing: *Yes, some production is moving to India, but our Chinese supply chain is becoming more Chinese.* This strategy has put Foxconn in a tight spot. The push to India has so far been led by the Taiwanese assembly giant, but to a large extent this change in geography has been happening against its will. Multiple people familiar with the relationship say Foxconn has limited interest in establishing iPhone operations in India, given the vast scale of its investments in China, its understanding of the politics and culture, and the credibility it's built from operating there for nearly four decades. But Apple needs to make the shift, and it has basically told Foxconn: *if you want to hold on to your iPhone work, you need to expand in India.*

How Beijing has responded to Apple's diversification efforts isn't entirely clear. But the Chinese government definitely wants the country's firms to retain their competitive edge in manufacturing, so as Apple has made moves to diversify production to India and Southeast Asia, members of the Red Supply Chain have helped with the efforts. In Vietnam, more than a third of Apple's top suppliers are from China, including Luxshare, Goertek, and BYD. In early 2023, Bloomberg reported that around fourteen suppliers—led by Luxshare—received a green light from New Delhi to establish operations in India, "after Apple named them as companies whose services it needs to increase its presence." As one former product manager says, "I think if [Apple is] successful in India, it will be with the Chinese government's support." Just look, this person adds, at the major contributions China is making in Africa, where it has development arrangements with virtually every country and a vast hold over the continent's mining capabilities. "They are actively participating in helping to build out portions of Africa," this person says. "If you think that they're not willing to do that in India to benefit themselves, you're crazy." But the situation is delicate. In early 2025, it emerged that Beijing had suspended Chinese equipment exports and Chinese worker visas to India, creating a stumbling block for Foxconn's expansion. Foxconn instead sent workers from its Taiwan-based operations. The episode suggests China wants technology transfer to be a "one-way gate"—the information flows in; it doesn't move out.

Meanwhile, conglomerate Tata Group has emerged as the most ambitious Indian company wanting to serve as a local "anchor" to bring in more suppliers for iPhone production and, using incentives from New Delhi, attract other Indian companies. The group launched Tata Electronics in 2020 and entered the iPhone supply chain by making casings and cables. Then, applying the "buy your way into it" lesson from the Red Supply Chain, Tata purchased Wistron's India iPhone assembly plant in 2023, for $125 million. In September 2024, Tata said it would hire more than 20,000 people at its iPhone assembly plant in Hosur, doubling its workforce there. Then, two months later, Tata acquired a majority stake in Pegatron's only India-based iPhone factory. Long term, India wants to bring the entire value chain inside its borders, says Prabhu Ram, head of industry research at CyberMedia Research—and the government will do all it can to help. "This isn't just about Tim Cook's legacy," he says. "This is about Prime Minister Narendra Modi's legacy."

CHAPTER 41

A STAGGERING VULNERABILITY—TSMC

Even as Apple has made some moves to diversify away from China, other aspects of the company's strategy have intensified its vulnerabilities. In particular, a 2020 decision to move away from Intel chips for Mac desktops and laptops had the consequence of doubling down on its China risk. For the prior fifteen years, the CPU chips across its desktop lineup were made by US-based Intel, which designed and fabricated them in the United States and Israel. But Cupertino abandoned the American chipmaker in favor of "Apple Silicon"—chips designed in-house and exclusively manufactured in Taiwan by TSMC. Apple had already pursued this strategy for portable products, namely iPhone and iPad, following its shift away from Samsung chips. At a pure business level, the 2020 decision had merit: It gave Apple even greater control over its hardware, replicating the sort of lead it has long held in handsets across its portfolio. But it also had a clear downside. Today the main "system on a chip" in every iPhone, iPad, MacBook, desktop Mac, AirPod, and Apple Watch is being made on one small island. That concentration of risk would be extraordinary in any environment, but it's especially troubling given China's authoritarian turn.

To be clear, Taiwan is not itself a geopolitical risk; it's a thriving democracy and strong ally of the United States. But Xi Jinping has repeatedly threatened the country with war, calling for "reunification" and pledging to "resolve" the Taiwan question "in this generation." The message has felt more ominous since 2019, as Beijing crushed Hong Kong's autonomy and then jailed pro-democracy activists. In January 2024, when the Taiwanese people elected Lai Ching-te as president, Beijing denounced him as a "stubborn worker for Taiwan independence" and responded with a show of force. It staged mock attacks in the Taiwan Strait that the People's Liberation Army described as tests of its ability to "seize power" over the island. Such actions have become increasingly frequent, highlighting advances in the Chinese military's technological prowess. In September 2024, China fired an intercontinental ballistic missile into the Pacific Ocean, the first such test in more than four decades. When on October 1, 2024, the Communist Party celebrated seventy-five years of ruling China, Xi reiterated his desire to "reunify" with the island democracy, saying "Taiwan is China's sacred territory" and that the two are connected by blood. "It's an irreversible trend, a cause of righteousness and the common aspiration of the people," he told thousands of supporters. "No one can stop the march of history."

Any military action would immediately threaten TSMC, which is responsible for making at least 80 percent of the world's most advanced chips. In war games involving an invasion of Taiwan by China, Taiwan's semiconductor industry doesn't survive. "It would go out of business on day one of the war," according to Chris Miller, author of *Chip War*. "The moment fighting starts, TSMC facilities would stop producing. It would never be reopened." Such a cessation in production would have disastrous effects on the world economy. Avril Haines, US director of national intelligence, estimates that if Taiwan were prevented from exporting chips, the global loss would be "somewhere between $600 billion to more than $1 trillion, *on an annual basis*, for the first several years." Indeed, the *New York Times* columnist Nicholas Kristof has credibly called TSMC "the only corporation . . . in history that could cause a global depression if it were forced to halt production." For Apple alone, the impact would be the equivalent of a meteor strike. Even a naval blockade or "quarantine" of Taiwan would result in Apple's operations grinding "to a halt," says a former product designer at the tech giant. "There are incentives for China not to do that," they add. "But at the same time, that mere possibility—I'm sure it keeps Tim Cook up at night."

Mark Liu, TSMC's chairman at the time, tried to comfort investors in 2022 by minimizing the threat of a China invasion—explaining that unlike, say, oil fields, chip factories aren't some prize to be won. "Nobody can control TSMC by force," he told CNN. "If you [launch an] invasion, you will render TSMC factor[ies] non-operable." In the event Liu is wrong, some US officials have speculated that the American military would rather destroy the foundries than allow China to control them. "The US and its allies are never going to let those factories fall into Chinese hands," former US national security advisor Robert O'Brien told *Semafor* in April 2023.

But Taiwan's political vulnerabilities may not even be TSMC's biggest risk. The island nation is situated on what is known as "the world's greatest earthquake belt," where 81 percent of such tremors occur. Taiwan experiences thousands of small earthquakes per year. Only a fraction are large enough to be felt, but this amounts to hundreds per year. A single large earthquake could disrupt production for days, weeks, or months, depending on the location and magnitude. Yet Apple, TSMC's biggest client for more than a decade, relies on this location for the most important chips undergirding every one of its biggest products. "It's borderline malpractice," says an executive at a rival semiconductor group in the United States. "If I were on their board, I'd be nervous as shit."

There are signs that Warren Buffett, Apple's biggest single investor, *is* nervous. In early 2023 he sold his stake in TSMC, worth nearly $5 billion, citing geopolitical risks. Buffett called the Taiwanese chipmaker "one of the best managed and important companies in the world," but added: "I don't like its location, and I reevaluated that." Then, between August and November 2024, Buffett slashed his stake in Apple from $178 billion to $69.9 billion, a reduction of nearly two-thirds. The moves went unexplained, but the logic behind his sale of TSMC stock is just as valid for Apple.

These challenges are unlikely to dissipate with time. In the first Cold War, the United States could rely on its superior economic growth, knowing that if it ramped up military spending, the Soviet Union was likely to follow suit, hurting its economy and accelerating its own demise. The same logic doesn't apply to China, a country with four times the US population and a GDP that has been growing much faster for four straight decades. China, under an autocratic ruler who can dictate policy at will, is growing economically larger and militarily stronger, narrowing the GDP gap each year with the United States, which is beset by political polarization. And unlike the first Cold War, the two country's economies are, as Elon Musk has phrased it, as intertwined as conjoined twins. Indeed, Apple exports more products from China to the United States each year than the Soviet Union exported to America during the entire Cold War.

A year before resigning as Singapore's prime minister, Lee Hsien Loong warned in April 2023: "The risks of a miscalculation or mishap are growing." That same year General Mike Minihan, head of the US Air Mobility Command, said he believed a US-China war could be fought as early as 2025. In such an event, Apple is by far the most exposed Western company. Among Big Tech rivals, Meta and Alphabet depend on digital advertising for the bulk of their business; Amazon has no real presence in the region; and Microsoft's share of sales from hardware is roughly 6 percent. Even Korean giant Samsung, the only company that sells more phones than Apple, is much less vulnerable. Samsung runs its own chip foundries, which are second only to TSMC, in Korea and Texas, and in 2023 the company pledged to invest $230 billion to build five new fabrication plants over the next two decades. Indeed, Samsung is likely to be the biggest winner in the event of an earthquake in Taiwan, be it political or natural. Disruption to supply chains in Taiwan would hinder Samsung's ability to import certain components, but the impact would be far less than for Apple.

As Cupertino attempts to diversify to India for manufacturing, TSMC is in the process of diversifying chip fabrication to the United

States, with direct aid from Washington. In May 2020, TSMC announced a major investment to build an advanced semiconductor fabrication facility, or fab, in Phoenix, Arizona, and by 2024 the plans had expanded to include three new fabs for a total cost of more than $65 billion, underscoring pressure from its customers and the seriousness of Washington's efforts. The three fabs will be the "largest foreign direct investments in a greenfield project in US history," TSMC says. However, amid reports of culture clashes and a shortage of American talent to fill 6,000 planned roles, the start of production was delayed by a year to early 2025.

Even if TSMC does produce its cutting-edge chips for Apple at the site, some reporting suggests that the chips will first have to be shipped to Taiwan for advanced packaging, a complex process to shield silicon and enhance the electrical connectivity of the chip circuitry. As the chief analyst at SemiAnalysis, a semiconductor research firm, has said: "The TSMC Arizona fab is effectively a paperweight in any geopolitical tension or war [with China over Taiwan] due to the fact that it still requires sending the chips back to Taiwan for packaging."

Long-term, the Arizona fabs may prove to be a critical factor delivering resilience to Apple's supply chain. But advanced chip fabrication is the most complex and expensive form of manufacturing humankind has ever devised, and Taiwan had reason to keep its best export capabilities at home. No less than Morris Chang, the now retired founder of TSMC, has cast serious doubt on the efforts: "It's not going to be enough," he said in 2022. "I think it will be a very expensive exercise in futility." In addition, the reelection of Donald Trump could hamper or even implode TSMC's efforts, given that Trump has accused Taiwan of stealing America's semiconductor industry and has threatened to cancel the CHIPS and Science Act. The future is deeply uncertain.

CONCLUSION: UNWRITTEN LEGACY

There are five reasons to predict Apple's relationship with China will face major risks this decade:

(1) The Chinese company that poses the biggest threat to Apple, Huawei, is back with a vengeance. Just four years after the first Trump administration imposed sanctions depriving the tech giant of US-designed chips, software, and 5G antennas, Huawei began shipping phones with chipsets so fast that the Biden White House sought to investigate how it was even possible. To be clear, the chips don't match the bleeding-edge capabilities of those manufactured by TSMC, but they've demonstrated far more capability than most experts had predicted. Moreover, Huawei phones now run HarmonyOS, a novel operating system that, in early 2024, overtook iOS in Chinese market share. The latest version for Chinese users is completely divorced from Android and might, within a few years, become the preferred OS for multiple Chinese brands at home and abroad. Huawei also now trumpets what it calls "Super Device," an Apple-esque ability for its phones, tablets, computers, and earbuds to work seamlessly together.

Hours after the launch of the iPhone 16 in September 2024, Huawei held an event for the world's first trifold smartphone, the Mate XT. The phone appears to be a marvel of industrial engineering. When folded, it's 12.8 millimeters thin, thicker than an average smartphone but skinnier than standard foldables from Samsung and Motorola. Unfolded—it displays a 10.2-inch screen, equivalent to a standard iPad—its thickness is just 4.8 millimeters, *thinner* than the 5.1-millimeter iPad Pro, which

Cupertino has billed as "the thinnest Apple product ever." In the Western press, critics have derided the new Huawei handset for its $2,800 price tag. But in so doing they've missed the wider point. It was only in 2014 that Jony Ive complained of cheap Chinese phones and their brazen "theft" of his designs; it was 2018 when Cupertino expressed shock at Chinese brands' ability to match the newest features; now, a Chinese brand is designing, manufacturing, and shipping more expensive phones with alluring features that, according to analysts, Apple isn't expected to match until 2027. No wonder the most liked comment on a YouTube unboxing video of the Mate XT is, "Now you know why USA banned Huawei."

In late 2018, the threat of Huawei sowed something close to panic in Apple's executive ranks as the California company confronted its worst quarter since the advent of the iPhone. From a technology standpoint, Huawei may be an even *larger* threat now, a problem that could be exacerbated in the future by Washington-Beijing tension and Chinese nationalism.

(2) The more Apple de-risks iPhone assembly and other operations from China to India, the more it could face a backlash from Chinese consumers and Beijing. In September 2023, when iPhones were made in India on launch day for the first time, some Chinese netizens took to social media to denounce their quality, spread rumors, indulge in racist commentary, and even advocate a boycott. Chinese consumers have long thought of the iPhone as an indigenous product; if it's instead seen as a symbol for how Western companies will "decouple" from China, that carries unknown risks. The Chinese government is in a position to make Apple's diversification efforts painful. "They can lower the boom on you in a million different ways," says Brady MacKay, the former US special agent who has witnessed Beijing deploy a number of tactics against other companies to make its point. "Like, raw materials—they can shut that off in a heartbeat," he says. "Electricity—all of a sudden it's only available four hours a day."

(3) Then there is Apple's push into "services," the company's fastest-growing and, on a margin basis, most lucrative division. Services becoming

part and parcel of Apple products have varying consequences. On the one hand, they are a source of recurring revenue that, unlike hardware, are largely outside the control of China. Apple's push into services has likely played a far larger role in diversifying its revenue than any shifts in the supply chain. But this push also causes Apple to be sensitive. When in 2019 the company rolled out Apple TV+, its Netflix-style streaming service, software and services head Eddy Cue issued just two directives to Apple's content partners: no hard-core nudity and "avoid portraying China in a poor light." A few years later, political comedian Jon Stewart canceled his show on the platform, citing disagreements over upcoming episodes—including one on China.

Apple TV+ isn't even available in China, but Cupertino understands the country well enough to know when and how to self-censor.

(4) Apple's push into artificial intelligence represents another unknown. With the launch of the iPhone 16 in late 2024, Apple revenues stand to be supercharged by Apple Intelligence—a host of potentially groundbreaking AI features inaccessible to the vast bulk of iPhone users unless they upgrade. The potential to bring forward a mass of hardware purchases is huge; so is the opportunity to charge users recurring fees for new services. Apple isn't exactly leading the charge when it comes to AI, but its ownership of the hardware, chips, and software puts it in a unique position. For privacy reasons, Apple simply won't allow external developers to access content within different apps on a user's iPhone. But Siri, the Apple voice assistant, can and does do that. So while rival AI platforms such as ChatGPT can be launched from the iPhone and will prove useful for general content, Apple has a monopoly on mining data from the iPhone owner's emails, texts, and photos to produce more personal answers.

AI's usefulness as a driver of marketing efforts aside, Apple's push into the technology is constrained by its dependence on China. A hyperintelligent Siri that directly answers sensitive questions about Tiananmen Square, regardless of where the user is asking such questions, is a major no-no. Apple has thus established a relationship with ChatGPT, which can answer those questions without Cupertino looking or feeling liable. Using ChatGPT might be a way to wriggle out of the tight spot they're in, but for the fact that the technology isn't allowed in China. As a result, Apple is searching for a local partner—which is resulting in delays and a diminished user experience. Apple's struggles with AI in China have helped homegrown rivals look more attractive. No surprise, then, that both Xiaomi and Huawei outsold Apple in 2024, while iPhone shipments dropped by 13 percent, including an 18 percent decline in the all-important holiday quarter, according to Counterpoint Research.

(5) The comeback of Donald Trump all but ensures that trade wars, tariffs, and the threat of China as a high-tech rival will be consistent themes until 2030 and beyond. The "secret sauce" of how Apple trains America's biggest rival with cutting-edge expertise could very well be in jeopardy. That Tim Cook personally donated $1 million to Trump's inauguration suggests he's well aware of the threat.

The Cook Era

Two years after the death of Steve Jobs, Oracle CEO Larry Ellison claimed it was inevitable Apple would struggle under Tim Cook. You only had to look, he said, at what happened to the company in the period after Jobs was ousted in 1985. "We already know. We saw. We conducted the experiment," Ellison told talk show host Charlie Rose in 2013. His finger tracing an upwards curve, he said Apple had been an extraordinary success during Jobs's first spell at the company, only to slump—his finger dropped—when he left. "We saw Apple with Steve Jobs" when he returned in 1997—up went his finger. "Now, we're gonna see Apple without Steve Jobs"—another drop. "He is irreplaceable. They will not be nearly so successful."

Few predictions have ever been so wrong. From a shareholders' perspective, Tim Cook's triumph as Jobs's successor has been so unparalleled that, when Apple first hit the $3 trillion valuation in January 2022, it meant Apple's market value had grown by more than $700 million *a day* from when Cook took over in August 2011. Questions abound regarding Apple's ability to lead efforts in artificial intelligence or build a next-generation device that replaces the iPhone, but Cook's reputation has already achieved a sort of mythical status.

That legacy is far more tenuous than it appears, though—and it's not fanciful to think that it could crumble, owing to uncertainties related to China. Consider the case of Jack Welch, the CEO of General Electric from 1981 to 2001. Welch had inherited a $14 billion company best known as a manufacturer of light bulbs, toasters, and industrial equipment. By the time he retired, revenues had quintupled and GE had expanded into finance, healthcare, and energy, in the process acquiring hundreds of companies. The breadth of GE's operations was stunning: The company owned NBC Universal, made jet engines, and funded infrastructure projects around the world. GE's share price soared 21 percent a year for two decades, and by 2001 the company was worth nearly $600 billion—making it the most valuable in the world. In 1999, *Fortune* gave Welch a title that would be hard for anyone to beat: "manager of the century." His tenure had been so influential that *60 Minutes* reported some observers were calling the prior two decades the "Welch Era."

By the time Welch died in 2020, his reputation had become far more complicated. The gains of the Welch Era had been superb for GE shareholders, but a temporary win for the select few waned in importance as it became clearer that the company's vast offshoring efforts were partly responsible for the creation of America's Rust Belt. GE had inspired the deindustrialization of America. Good manufacturing jobs had been shipped overseas, and noncore jobs such as janitorial work had been outsourced. Both trends exacerbated inequality. As recently as the 1950s, the president of General Motors could credibly say, "What's good for General Motors is good for America." But the Welch Era had ushered in a new corporate religion—the worship of shareholder-first capitalism, which received academic respectability when the economist Milton Friedman proclaimed that a business had "one and only one social responsibility . . . to increase its profits."

The problem was, shareholder-first capitalism enabled—indeed, even encouraged—corporations to ignore, if not undermine, the national interest. Executives found that they could focus on actions to reap short-term benefits—gambits such as cutting costs and outsourcing jobs to Asia—and ignore wider societal impact. As this book has demonstrated, Cupertino's interests have significantly diverged from Washington's since the death of Steve Jobs; the wider implications could end up tarnishing Cook's legacy.

The other thing that shook Welch's reputation is that GE's finances and stock price began to wither. Just four days after he stepped down, terrorists flew planes into the World Trade Center. GE's insurance arm was a major insurer of both office space in the Twin Towers and all four of the hijacked planes. The US economy soon entered a recession, disrupting a wide swath of GE's businesses. Later, when the global financial crisis erupted in 2008, GE Capital wasn't some bystander; rather, it was revealed to be among the country's largest and most leveraged lenders, with significant exposure to the subprime mortgages that caused the crash. Under Welch, GE had used its triple-A credit rating to borrow on the cheap, lend to riskier borrowers at higher interest rates, and pocket the difference. "I thought it was easier than bending metal," Welch once said. The world's most valuable corporation at the start of the millennium was soon needing government-backed infusions of cash. At its worst point in 2009, GE's market value fell below $90 billion, a loss of around 85 percent.

The first major revisionist books on Welch's legacy pulled no punches. *New York Times* writer David Gelles titled his *The Man Who Broke Capitalism.* In *Power Failure,* investment banker William D. Cohan presents Welch as ruthlessly determined to hit quarterly financial goals, deceiving himself about the health of the business as industrial innovation waned. Cohan also critiques corporate America's tendency to think narrowly and in the short term. Neither book portrays Welch as a failure per se. But they make clear that Welch introduced great risks to the company while setting an example to rivals that had decidedly mixed implications for America's competitiveness.

In the next two decades, could Tim Cook's fortunes similarly suffer? Apple has been spectacularly successful, and in early 2025 its business looks solid. But as hedge fund investor Jay Newman warns: "Apple's scramble to reduce dependence on China won't beat the CCP's power to erase most of its value with the stroke of a pen." External risks—like China annexing Taiwan, or China and the United States becoming more estranged, or Beijing feeling the country has learned all it can from Apple—are far more existential than any product launch. The risk that Chinese nationalism presents to Apple is, for the foreseeable future, permanent.

Even if things go smoothly, China's economy is likely to overtake America's as the world's largest, which will surely prompt more people to ask: *How did they do it? How did China advance so quickly, particularly in such complex areas as advanced electronics?* Some portion of the disquieting answer is that Apple taught them. Year in, year out, Apple took the most cutting-edge designs, processes, and technical understandings from around the world and scaled them in China. One supply chain expert even adopts the language of a crime scene as he considers the whodunit at the heart of China's advances in electronics. Look around, he says, "There's Apple DNA everywhere."

"Real Danger"

For the 1984 Super Bowl, Apple released the most iconic computer TV spot ever. It featured a mass of gray, brainwashed citizens, listening intently to an Orwellian Big Brother extolling the virtues of conformity on a movie screen:

> We have created for the first time in all history a garden of pure ideology—where each worker may bloom, secure from the pests purveying contradictory thoughts.
>
> Our Unification of Thoughts is more powerful a weapon than any fleet or army on earth.

> We are one people, with one will, one resolve, one cause.
>
> Our enemies shall talk themselves to death, and we will bury them with their own confusion.
>
> We *shall* prevail!

Then came running into the scene a lone, athletic woman in bright colors, representing Apple. She hurled a sledgehammer against the movie screen, breaking the spell. Back then Apple was rebellious. It was innovative. It actively positioned Macintosh as the destroyer of lockstep ideology. That spirit was lost the first time Steve Jobs departed Apple, in 1985. When he returned twelve years later, his first major action wasn't a product; it was an advertisement. As internal meeting notes from that summer indicate, Jobs told colleagues: "We are in real danger." He'd diagnosed that Apple had lost its identity or was about to. He sought to avert crisis with major action. And that undertaking began with a few words: "Here's to the crazy ones. The misfits. The rebels. The troublemakers."

Apple is in real danger again. Financially, it's the most successful company ever. But the Big Brother on the screen isn't a work of fiction anymore. Rather, it's incarnated in the leadership of a country that has, in important ways, *captured* Apple—becoming so world-leading in manufacturing that Apple's efforts to escape are likely to prove fanciful. If Apple continues to spur Chinese development of cutting-edge processes, Americans may soon look up and see that China has become self-sufficient in advanced electronics, robotics, and chip fabrication. And from there it may be only a short leap to Xi Jinping's goal of bringing about "the ultimate demise of capitalism," as he pledged in 2013.

The relationship Apple enjoys with China "could blow up at any time," a former Apple senior director says. The company's executives have tried to demonstrate to Apple's board of directors that the firm isn't overly dependent on China, but a person familiar with the presentation calls it a "con job." They add: "There's no way that they could diversify from China in any meaningful way within the next five years. It's just impossible."

ACKNOWLEDGMENTS

This book was primarily written during an eighteen-month break from my daily reporting, following a decade of work for the *Financial Times* in Hong Kong, Germany, and San Francisco. In the most recent four years I covered Apple, gaining great respect for the company while slowly coming to realize it had sleepwalked into a major geopolitical dilemma. This book was an independent project. The *FT* has not seen or endorsed its contents.

Apple is a famously secretive company—more so than the US military, according to some sources with experience at both. To the more than 200 people I interviewed who took great risk to speak with me: I'm forever grateful for your trust, time, patience and honesty—without that, quite simply, there'd be no book. Not being able to mention you all is frustrating; I hope you're proud of what came out of our conversations.

More than 90 percent of my sources worked at Apple, from the earliest hires through today. Very few of them spent fewer than three years at Apple; many logged more than ten, fifteen, twenty, and even twenty-five years there. Often they served in senior roles, but as much as possible the anecdotes, experiences, and perspectives making up this narrative stem from sources on the ground and in the weeds. Apple's public relations team was not informed of my research or given a manuscript prior to publication.

The bulk of the research for this book was interview-based, but it was supplemented by academic articles and book-length histories of Apple,

IBM, the PC industry, Modern China, and Southeast Asia. The most important works can be found in the notes, but I'll highlight two that were pivotal in my understanding of China's economy: *Rival Partners: How Taiwanese Entrepreneurs and Guangdong Officials Forged the China Development Model,* by Jiehmin Wu, and *The Making of an Economic Superpower: Unlocking China's Secret of Rapid Industrialization,* by Yi Wen. Special thanks to the Computer History Museum, whose Oral History Collection served as a unique, invaluable source early in my research.

Chapter 36, "5 Alarm Fire," is exclusively sourced from more than 1,000 pages of documents including emails among Apple's top executives; internal studies of China, India, and Huawei; and depositions of key figures including Tim Cook. This material was made public in December 2023, several months before Apple settled the case, but through some miracle it hadn't been noticed or reported on. I spent more than thirty hours sifting through the documents and the resulting narrative is, I believe, the first presentation of the material outside of a courtroom. Other chapters were supplemented by original material derived from unnamed sources. These include notes from a series of Steve Jobs–led meetings in the summer of 1997; internal surveys of Chinese consumer sentiment in 2010; internal presentations on labor demand and churn in Chinese factories; and other material discussing Apple/supplier relationships and its dilemmas with China from after 2015.

To the reporters who've previously gone deep on Apple in China: your groundbreaking work has been tremendously helpful. I'm thinking especially of Wayne Ma from *The Information*; a variety of reporters from *The New York Times*—David Barboza, Jack Nicas, Charles Duhigg, and Tripp Mickle—and the team at *Nikkei Asia,* notably Lauly Li and Cheng Ting-Fang. The trio of China supply chain essays from James Fallows in *The Atlantic* are best in class. Aside from the tedium of working in China factories, the subject of Apple in China has not really been written about in books. That said, two consistent companions on my desk were *The One Device* by Brian Merchant and *Haunted Empire* by Yukari Kane—informative works that certainly included material on China.

As authoritative as I hope this work is, the Apple-China relationship alone is worth several more books. There is also far more to be researched and written about Foxconn, contract manufacturing, tech supply chains, the global history of manufacturing since World War II, and the intersection of technology and geopolitics. Much of this history is frustratingly under-covered. I look forward to reading and learning so much more about these topics from the many talented journalists working today.

Huge thanks to my editor, Rick Horgan, and the whole team at Scribner. You all championed this first-time author from the get-go. I had several great meetings with publishers, but only Scribner had five people join the call. Rick, your eye for the "big ideas" made you a perfect fit. Additional thanks to Kris Doyle, Paul Samuelson, Mark Galarrita, Brianna Yamashita, and Sophie Guimaraes.

I'm forever grateful to Chris Miller, the author of *Chip War,* which served as a template for my pitch after Chris introduced me to his agent, Toby Mundy, at Aevitas Creative. Toby: You asked all the right questions and handled the early process so, so expertly. When I asked, in January 2023, "When would you like the pitch by?" your answer—"yesterday"—filled me with confidence.

The *Financial Times* has been a superb home for me, on three continents. I can still recall arriving in Hong Kong in 2013 and staring up at the Centre, the skyscraper housing the *FT* bureau, feeling the weight of my move from New York and wondering if I could really understand Asia. To Megan Murphy, who recruited me to the *FT* and was my first editor: You believed in me far earlier than I did. I'll always be grateful for your enthusiasm and support. In Frankfurt, special thanks to bureau chief Claire Jones and my UK-based editors Andrew Parker and David Oakley. You all helped me up the learning curve.

In San Francisco, it's been a pleasure working with Richard Waters, a walking encyclopedia of all things tech, who dealt with my wide-eyed naïveté for years. Tim Bradshaw: I appreciate you getting me up to speed after your six years on the Apple beat. Shout-out to my SF colleagues past and present Hannah Murphy, Elaine Moore, Tabby Kinder, Dave Lee, Shannon Bond, Miles Kruppa, George Hammond, Camilla Hodgson, Cristina Criddle, Michael Acton, and Stephen Morris. Special thanks to my London-based tech editors, Malcolm Moore and Murad Ahmed, for handling my stubbornness and unshakable tendency to write beyond the word limit.

To Roula Khalaf and Lionel Barber, editors in chief of the *FT* during my twelve years: you've made the *FT* the best business paper in the world, every day. Just to play a small role in that is extremely gratifying.

My favorite thing at the *FT* has always been writing for The Big Read desk. Its editors Geoff Dyer, Dan Stewart, and Tom O'Sullivan have published my best work, including the two-part series that formed the basis of this book. Geoff and Dan: without your support publishing that back-to-back series, this book wouldn't exist.

Two amazing professors at the University of Toronto shaped my undergraduate years. Sam Solecki opened my eyes to Joyce and Proust; Gillian Gillison captured my whole being through Freud, Malinowski, and Spiro. I may have graduated with few practical skills beyond insatiable curiosity, but your classes, discussions, and feedback to my essays has reverberated for two decades.

Shout-out to Vik Saini for a lifetime of friendship. Without you and Nance offering me a place to stay in 2006, I might not have become a journalist. Hope this book brings back memories of your time in Beijing.

To some of my colleagues turned friends in journalism: Jordan Michael Smith, Michelle Donahue, Dan Seymour, Katy Burne, Peter Campbell, and Jemima Kelly, it was a pleasure learning the ropes from you and spitballing ideas. Special nod to Laura Noonan: I'll bring back Fit Hacks whenever you're ready.

Huge thanks to my older brothers, who offered encouragement and editing help and served as role models for many years before. Hope I've come a long way since you edited my first undergraduate paper by telling me: "Okay, highlight the entire text. Now . . . press any key." The manuscript would've been weeks late without your unbidden trip to San

Francisco. And to my sister-in-law Katina: I hope that fortune cookie of a mug you bought me comes true.

To my parents: I bet you never thought buying that tangerine iMac would play such an influential role in my life! My mom read an early draft of the book, providing the sort of encouragement only a mom can give—just when I needed it most. Thank you both for raising us in a household of questions, ideas, books, and—through my dad—gadgets.

To my wife: you're marvelous. Your edits were over-the-top helpful, but were nothing next to your strengths as a spouse, best friend, and mom. Here's to a lifetime of making up for missed dates and too many late nights when I lived a nocturnal existence at WeWork. Finally, to my daughters, who write several "books" per week and can't understand what took me so long—watching you grow up is the best thing in my life.

Patrick McGee
January 2025, San Francisco

NOTES

v *Building on a*: David Landes, "The Creation of Knowledge and Technique: Today's Task and Yesterday's Experience," *Daedalus*, 109, no. 1, Modern Technology: Problem or Opportunity? (Winter, 1980), pp. 111–20, https://www.jstor.org/stable/20024651.

Prologue: "Incomparable" Arrogance

2 *"low wages, low welfare"*: As quoted in Jiehmin Wu, *Rival Partners: How Taiwanese Entrepreneurs and Guangdong Officials Forged the China Development Model*. Translated by Stacy Mosher. Cambridge, MA: Harvard University Asia Center, 2022.

3 *"likely influenced"*: The internal study is called "Consumption in the Age of Xi: Understanding China's Evolving Consumer Markets."

4 *a new replacement policy*: Rebecca Greenfield, "China Has a Way Better iPhone Warranty Than America To Go with Its Apology from Apple," *The Atlantic*, April 1, 2013.

4 *"bow its arrogant head"*: Helen Gao, "How the Apple Confrontation Divides China," *The Atlantic* (online), April 8, 2013, https://www.theatlantic.com/china/archive/2013/04/how-the-apple-confrontation-divides-china/274764/.

5 *more than Apple's US buildings*: Independently corroborated in Apple's financial filings but first found here: Horace Dediu, "How Much Do Apple's Factories Cost?" Asymco (blog), October 16, 201, https://www.asymco.com/2011/10/16/how-much-do-apples-factories-cost/.

6 *exploited Chinese workers*: Reports of factory workers in Apple's supply chain laboring beyond Apple's 60-hour maximum date back to 2006, spurring the creation of a Supplier Responsibility team. When Apple audited "hundreds

of records" from multiple suppliers, it found "that employees on average had worked more than 60 hours per week 38% of the time, and 29% of employees had worked more than six consecutive days without a day off." See Apple, "Final Assembly Supplier Audit Report," February 2007, https://www.apple.com.cn/supplier-responsibility/pdf/Apple_SR_2007_Progress_Report.pdf. Later, independent reports from China Labor Watch, the Fair Labor Association, and others would find other problems. They are well documented here: Jenny Chan, Mark Selden, and Pun Ngai, *Dying for an iPhone: Apple, Foxconn, and the Lives of China's Workers*. London: Pluto Press, 2020.

7 *Even Xi Jinping*: Jiehmin Wu, *Rival Partners*.

7 *Taipei calculates*: See "Cross-Strait Relations: Fact Focus," Government Portal of the Republic of China (Taiwan), 2024, https://www.taiwan.gov.tw/content_6.php.

8 *between 1 million and 2.6 million jobs*: I'm citing two estimates. For 1 million, see "US Exports to China 2023," the US-China Business Council, 2024, https://www.uschina.org/reports/us-exports-china-2023-0; for 2.6 million, see Keith Belton, John Graham, and Suri Xia, "'Made in China 2025' and the Limitations of U.S. Trade Policy," July 30, 2020, https://ssrn.com/abstract=3664347 or http://dx.doi.org/10.2139/ssrn.3664347.

8 *$2 trillion in sales*: As calculated by Counterpoint Research; expected revenues for 2025 are analyst estimates compiled by S&P Global Market Intelligence.

8 *supports 5 million jobs*: Zhang Erchi and Yang Ge, "Exclusive: Apple Setting Down Deep Roots in China, CEO Says," Caixin Global, March 21, 2017, https://www.caixinglobal.com/2017-03-21/exclusive-apple-setting-down-deep-roots-in-china-ceo-says-101068558.html.

8 *estimated the new policy*: Meghan Bobrowsky, "Facebook Feels $10 Billion Sting from Apple's Privacy Push," *Wall Street Journal*, February 3, 2022, https://www.wsj.com/articles/facebook-feels-10-billion-sting-from-apples-privacy-push-11643898139.

9 *"playing in the minor leagues"*: Patrick McGee, "Apple's Privacy Changes Create Windfall for Its Own Advertising Business," *Financial Times*, October 16, 2021, https://www.ft.com/content/074b881f-a931-4986-888e-2ac53e286b9d.

11 *Only a dozen multinationals*: As calculated by *The Economist*: "Multinational Firms Are Finding it Hard to Let Go of China," November 24, 2022.

Chapter 1: The Brink of Bankruptcy

17 *sought bankruptcy counsel*: Far as I can tell, this has never been reported. My sources are confidential and have direct knowledge.

17 *"death spiral"*: Steven Levy, "Steve Jobs Unveils the iMac," *Newsweek,* May 18, 1998, https://www.newsweek.com/steve-jobs-unveils-imac-169734.

17 *"out of money somewhere around May"*: Gil Amelio and William L. Simon, *On the Firing Line: My 500 Days at Apple*. New York: HarperBusiness, 1998, 34.

17 *reserves had shrunk to $500 million*: Michael Malone, *Infinite Loop: How Apple, the World's Most Insanely Great Computer Company, Went Insane.* New York: Doubleday, 1999, 481.

17 *cut prices by as much as 30 percent*: Malone, *Infinite Loop,* 480.

18 *McNealy's "best offer"*: John Markoff, "Sun's Bid for Apple Computer Placed Below Stock's Price," *New York Times,* January 25, 1996, https://www.nytimes.com/1996/01/25/business/sun-s-bid-for-apple-computer-placed-below-stock-s-price.html.

18 *"Fall of an American Icon"*: Peter Burrows, "The Fall of an American Icon," *BusinessWeek,* February 4, 1996, https://www.bloomberg.com/news/articles/1996-02-04/the-fall-of-an-american-icon.

20 *"tried for war crimes"*: The venture capitalist was John Doerr, now the chairman of Kleiner, Perkins (Malone, *Infinite Loop,* 486–87).

20 *forty times larger*: Malone, *Infinite Loop,* 226.

20 *"the sun, the moon, the stars"*: David Rosenthal and Ben Gilbert, "Microsoft, Volume 1," *Acquired* (podcast), season 14, episode 4, April 21, 2024, https://www.acquired.fm/episodes/microsoft.

20 *His fear was that IBM*: Malone, *Infinite Loop,* 225.

22 *"killer app"*: Malone, *Infinite Loop,* 223.

22 *"Apple's robust system"*: Laine Nooney, *The Apple II Age: How the Computer Became Personal.* Chicago: University of Chicago Press, 2023.

23 *third-party developers as freeloaders*: Malone, *Infinite Loop,* 197.

23 *a dollar for every board she assembled*: Malone, *Infinite Loop,* 80.

25 *"thrown out of a lot of places"*: Claire Serant, "CEM Pioneer, Olin King, to Retire from SCI Systems," *EE Times,* May 1, 2000, https://www.eetimes.com/cem-pioner-olin-king-to-retire-from-sci-systems/.

25 *SCI sales jumped from $45 million*: Ellin Sterne Jimmerson, "SCI Systems, Inc." Encyclopedia of Alabama, October 5, 2009 (last updated October 14, 2024), https://encyclopediaofalabama.org/article/sci-systems-inc/.

Chapter 2: Adventures in Outsourcing—Japan and Taiwan

28 *every twenty-seven seconds*: Leander Kahney, "A Brief History of Apple's Misadventures in Manufacturing: Part 1," Cult of Mac (blog), April 6, 2019, https://www.cultofmac.com/news/a-brief-history-of-apples-misadventures-in-manufacturing-part-1-cook-book-leftovers.

28 *80,000 Macs per month*: Frank Rose, *West of Eden: The End of Innocence at Apple Computer*. New York: Penguin, 1989, 200.

28 *petered out to as low as 5,000*: Alan Deutschman, *The Second Coming of Steve Jobs*. New York: Broadway Books, 2000, 18

28 *was furious*: Rose, *West of Eden*, 239–40.

31 *"rafts of engineers"*: Rose, *West of Eden, 67.*

32 *half-page document of Apple specifications*: Brenton R. Schlender, "Apple's Japanese Ally: Its New Notebook Computer—Made by Sony—Shows Why Alliances Are Hot in the PC Business," *Fortune Magazine,* November 4, 1991, https://money.cnn.com/magazines/fortune/fortune_archive/1991/11/04/75695/index.htm.

35 *his tombstone*: Max Chafkin, *Design Crazy: Good Looks, Hot Tempers, and True Genius at Apple*. Fast Company/Byliner, 2013 (ebook), 17.

Chapter 3: An "Outrageous" Acquisition

36 *boarding the* Titanic: Gil Amelio and William L. Simon, *On the Firing Line: My 500 Days at Apple*. New York: HarperBusiness, 1998, 35.

37 *"ten years out of date"*: Amelio, *On the Firing Line*, 7.

37 *"the Apple Messiah"*: Malone, *Infinite Loop*, 494.

38 *orchestrated two deals*: Amelio, *On the Firing Line,* 84, 144.

39 *owed Japanese lenders $150 million*: Amelio, *On the Firing Line,* 35.

39 *"the first computer of the 1990s"*: KPIX, "KPIX Archive: Steve Jobs unveils the NeXT computer in S.F.," October 12, 1988 (uploaded December 21, 2023), https://www.youtube.com/watch?v=Zs3NwqW4d48.

39 *"full, unfortunate blooming"*: Brent Schlender and Rick Tetzeli, *Becoming Steve Jobs: The Evolution of a Reckless Upstart into a Visionary Leader.* New York: Crown Business, 2015, 95.

39 *conspicuous flop*: Deutschman, *The Second Coming of Steve Jobs,* 130.

40 *120 computers and was burning through $10 million*: Deutschman. *The Second Coming of Steve Jobs,* 121.

40 *cut staff by two-thirds*: Schlender and Tetzeli, *Becoming Steve Jobs,* 144.

41 *price tag to be "outrageous"*: Amelio, *On the Firing Line,* 200.

41 *"between five and seven years"*: John Markoff, "Why Apple Sees Next as a Match Made in Heaven," *New York Times*, December 23, 1996, https://www.nytimes.com/1996/12/23/business/why-apple-sees-next-as-a-match-made-in-heaven.html.

41 *"the presentation from Hell"*: mickeleh (Michael Markman), "Worst. Apple. Keynote. Ever." YouTube, April 7, 2013, https://www.youtube.com/watch?v=PsBVyUDs-84.

42 *Q&A with developers*: Steve Jobs, "Complete Apple WWDC | Steve Jobs talk and answer developers questions | 1997," YouTube, TheAppleFanBoy, uploaded January 28, 2015, https://www.youtube.com/watch?v=yQ16_YxLbB8.

Chapter 4: Columbus—A New World of Computing

45 *resignation letter already tucked*: Ian Parker, "The Shape of Things to Come" (profile of Jony Ive), *The New Yorker*, February 16, 2015, https://www.newyorker.com/magazine/2015/02/23/shape-things-come.

45 *"The products suck!"*: Leander Kahney, *Jony Ive: The Genius Behind Apple's Greatest Products*. New York: Portfolio, 2013, 101–105.

47 *"tight green spandex"*: Anonymous, "Apple eMate 300," *ancientelectronics* (blog), February 10, 2020, https://ancientelectronics.wordpress.com/2020/02/10/apple-emate-300/.

47 *collaborating that day*: Parker, "The Shape of Things to Come."

50 *"conspicuously absent"*: Mark Landler, "Apple Removes the Dalai Lama from Its Ads in Hong Kong," *New York Times*, April 17, 1998, https://www.nytimes.com/1998/04/17/world/apple-removes-the-dalai-lama-from-its-ads-in-hong-kong.html.

50 *wasn't well known enough*: "Apple: Dalai Lama Not Big Enough in Asia," *Wired*, April 13, 1998, https://www.wired.com/1998/04/apple-dalai-lama-not-big-enough-in-asia/.

Chapter 5: "Unmanufacturable"—The iMac

51 *"Make it lickable"*: Ian Parker, "The Shape of Things to Come" (profile of Jony Ive), *The New Yorker*, February 16, 2015, https://www.newyorker.com/magazine/2015/02/23/shape-things-come.

52 *a shortage of billiard balls*: Bill Hammack, "Plastic Injection Molding" (video), Youtube, November 14, 2015, https://www.youtube.com/watch?v=RMjtmsr3CqA.

55 *"I naïvely didn't fully understand"*: Ken Werner, "Brian Berkeley Reflects on His Career at Apple, Samsung, and SID," *ID* (magazine from the Society for Information Display) 37, no. 2 (March/April 2021): 52–57, https://sid.onlinelibrary.wiley.com/doi/10.1002/msid.1202.

56 *In Isaacson's telling*: Walter Isaacson, *Steve Jobs*. New York: Simon & Schuster, 2011, 461.

Chapter 6: Out of the Asian Financial Crisis—South Korea

63 *"not made in Osaka"*: Kahney, "A Brief History of Apple's Misadventures in Manufacturing: Part 1."

67 *"u-u-gly"*: Steve Jobs, "Steve Jobs Introduces the iMac—1998," YouTube, pil.com, uploaded May 4, 2015, https://www.youtube.com/watch?v=BiWd8ujtK5k.

67 *"giddiness of a pardoned prisoner"*: Parker, "The Shape of Things to Come." (profile of Jony Ive), *The New Yorker*, February 16, 2015, https://www.newyorker.com/magazine/2015/02/23/shape-things-come.

68 *stock had hit $39*: Doug Bartholomew, "What's Really Driving Apple's Recovery," *IndustryWeek*, March 1999: https://www.industryweek.com/leadership/companies-executives/article/21960994/whats-really-driving-apples-recovery.

Chapter 7: LG Goes Global—Wales and Mexico

70 *remembered as a debacle*: Leon Gooberman, "Business Failure in an Age of Globalisation: Interpreting the Rise and Fall of the LG Project in Wales, 1995–2006," *Business History* 62, no. 2 (2020): 240–60, https://doi.org/10.1080/00076791.2018.1426748.

Chapter 8: The Taishang—Taiwanese on the Mainland

78 *"not in the PC business"*: "Dell, the Conqueror," *BusinessWeek*, September 24, 2001, https://www.bloomberg.com/news/articles/2001-09-23/dell-the-conqueror.

80 *"untouched by human hands!"*: Kahney, "A Brief History of Apple's Misadventures in Manufacturing: Part 1."

81 *"Guangdong Model"*: For a deep dive on the Guangdong Model and the role Taiwanese entrepreneurs played in China's growth, see Jiehmin Wu, *Rival Partners: How Taiwanese Entrepreneurs and Guangdong Officials*

Forged the China Development Model. Translated by Stacy Mosher. Cambridge, MA: Harvard University Asia Center, 2022.

82 *A photographer who visited*: Forbes Conrad, "Terry Gou at Hon Hai/Foxconn in Shenzhen," September 8, 2010, https://www.forbesconrad.com/blog/terry-gou-foxconn-shenzhen/.

83 *name translates to "Dirt City"*: Eva Dou, "Tracking Foxconn Chief's Rise from 'Dirt City' to iPhone King," *Wall Street Journal,* March 31, 2016, https://www.wsj.com/articles/behind-foxconns-sharp-deal-gou-left-little-to-chance-1459407097.

84 *menu at Denny's*: Jason Dean, "The Forbidden City of Terry Gou," *Wall Street Journal,* August 11, 2007, https://www.wsj.com/articles/SB118677584137994489.

84 *Gou wore a beaded bracelet*: Dean, "The Forbidden City of Terry Gou."

84 *sayings of Terry Gou*: Joshua B. Freeman, *Behemoth: A History of the Factory and the Making of the Modern World.* New York: W. W. Norton, 2018, 301.

85 *"$2 billion in nickels and dimes"*: Dean, "The Forbidden City of Terry Gou."

Chapter 9: The Silicon Valley of Hardware—"Foxconn isn't called 'Fox-con' for nothing"

87 *"Third World costs"*: Michael J. Enright, Edith E. Scott, and Ka-mun Chang, *Regional Powerhouse: The Greater Pearl River Delta and the Rise of China.* Singapore: Wiley, 2005.

The ODM/OEM difference has a blurry parallel to the world of semiconductors. An ODM is more like Nvidia and Qualcomm, whose prowess is in chip design, not manufacturing; an OEM is more like TSMC, which operates a foundry to produce, or "fabricate," a chip. But the parallel is blurry because, unlike the clean distinction in the world of chips, both ODMs and OEMs are involved in manufacturing; the difference is how they earn profit. The ODM earns profit through *design*; the OEM earns it from vertical integration—that is, by sourcing more of the parts itself.

Chapter 10: IBM West—The Rise of Tim Cook

92 *"Most Studious"*: Tripp Mickle, *After Steve: How Apple Became a Trillion-Dollar Company and Lost Its Soul.* New York: William Morrow, 2022.

94 *"Go west, young man"*: Sam Colt, "Tim Cook Gave His Most In-Depth Interview to Date—Here's What He Said," *Business Insider,* September 20,

2014, https://www.businessinsider.com/tim-cook-full-interview-with-charlie-rose-with-transcript-2014-9.

94 *"Here's to the sensible ones"*: Austin Carr and Mark Gurman, "Apple Is the $2.3 Trillion Fortress That Tim Cook Built," *Bloomberg Businessweek*, February 9, 2021, https://www.bloomberg.com/news/features/2021-02-09/this-is-how-tim-cook-transformed-apple-aapl-after-steve-jobs.

Chapter 11: Foxconn Goes Global—China, California, and the Czech Republic

101 *"it moves to manufacturing engineers"*: Much of the work of manufacturing design engineers was done by Product Design at this time. Later Apple hired supply base engineers who focused specifically on the tooling and machining of the products ID and PD had designed. Around 2010, the group was feeling underappreciated and clamored for financial bonuses and a two-letter abbreviation like ID and PD. Since then, they've been known as MD, or MDE; in the pyramid metaphor, they are an independent group, but organizationally MD is a part of Operations. There is no senior vice president of MD.

106 *In May 2000, Foxconn was able*: Marek Čaněk, "Chapter 4: Building the European Centre in Czechia: Foxconn's Local Integration in Regional and Global Labour Markets," in *Flexible Workforces and Low Profit Margins: Electronics Assembly Between Europe and China,* eds. Rutvica Andrijasevic, Jan Drahokoupil, and Davi Sacchetto. Brussels, Belgium: European Trade Union Institute, 2020, https://www.etui.org/publications/books/flexible-workforces-and-low-profit-margins-electronics-assembly-between-europe-and-china.

106 *a ten-year tax holiday*: Rutvica Andrijasevic and Davi Sacchetto, "Made in the EU: Foxconn in the Czech Republic," WorkingUSA 17, no. 3 (2014): 391–415, https://onlinelibrary.wiley.com/doi/10.1111/wusa.12121.

107 *10,000 PCs a day*: Čaněk, "Chapter 4: Building the European Centre in Czechia."

107 *they threatened a "strike emergency"*: Andrijasevic and Sacchetto, "Made in the EU: Foxconn in the Czech Republic."

Chapter 12: A Farewell to Mactories

109 *a single day in late September 2000*: Lawrence M. Fisher, "Apple Says Quarterly Profit Won't Meet Expectations," *New York Times,* September 29, 2000, https://www.nytimes.com/2000/09/29/business/apple

-says-quarterly-profit-won-t-meet-expectations.html; staff and wire reports, "Apple Bruises Tech Sector," CNN Money, September 29, 2000, https://money.cnn.com/2000/09/29/markets/techwrap/.

110 *"Apple R.I.P."*: Michael S. Malone, "Apple R.I.P.," *Forbes*, October 5, 2000 (updated June 6, 2013), https://www.forbes.com/2000/10/09/1005malone.html.

110 *"The shit hit the fan"*: Jon Rubinstein, "Oral History of Jon Rubinstein," interviewed by Dag Spicer, Computer History Museum, August 15, 2019, https://archive.computerhistory.org/resources/access/text/2020/02/102717908-05-01-acc.pdf.

110 *Apple posted a loss of $195 million*: Apple, "Apple Reports First Quarter Results," Apple press release, January 17, 2001: https://www.apple.com/newsroom/2001/01/17Apple-Reports-First-Quarter-Results/.

110 *"as inconsequential as Liechtenstein"*: Brent Schlender, "Steve Jobs: The Graying Prince of a Shrinking Kingdom. Older and Smarter, the CEO Whipped His Company Back into the Black," *Fortune*, May 14, 2001, https://money.cnn.com/magazines/fortune/fortune_archive/2001/05/14/302936/index.htm.

111 *most of its 1,100 employees*: Timothy J. Sturgeon, "Network-Led Development and the Rise of Turn-Key Production Networks: Technological Change and the Outsourcing of Electronics Manufacturing," in *Global Production and Local Jobs*, G. Gereffi, F. Palpacuer, and A. Parisotto, eds., Geneva: International Institute for Labour Studies, 1999, https://www.researchgate.net/publication/228538014_Network-Led_Development_and_the_Rise_of_Turn-key_Production_Networks_Technological_Change_and_the_Outsourcing_of_Electronics_Manufacturing.

111 *Solectron alone acquired some twenty companies*: James F. Peltz, "A Leader Behind the Scenes," Los Angeles Times, September 27, 1999.

111 *annual growth of 78 percent*: Timothy J. Sturgeon, "Exploring the Risks of Value Chain Modularity: Electronics Outsourcing During the Industry Cycle of 1992–2002," Massachusetts Institute of Technology IPC Working Paper Series, May 2003, https://www.files.ethz.ch/isn/29602/2003-002.pdf.

112 *"room for continued growth"*: Sturgeon, "Exploring the Risks of Value Chain Modularity."

112 *number one spot was taken by Foxconn*: Peter Clarke, "Top 50 Contract Manufacturers Ranked," *EE Times*, April 12, 2011, https://www.eetimes.com/top-50-contract-manufacturers-ranked. Revenue numbers

independently calculated using company reported numbers on S&P Capital IQ, a platform owned by S&P Global Market Intelligence.

112 *"a general undervaluing of manufacturing"*: Andy Grove, "How America Can Create Jobs," *Bloomberg Businessweek*, July 1, 2010, https://www.bloomberg.com/news/articles/2010-07-01/andy-grove-how-america can-create-jobs.

Chapter 13: 1,000 Songs—Making the iPod in Taiwan

117 *Tony Blevins walked into*: All biographical detail on Blevins in this chapter stems from three accounts of his life story: Tony Blevins, Deposition Transcript, Case 2:19-cv-00066-JRG, Document 495, August 6, 2020, *Optis v. Apple*; Tony Blevins, "Fired Apple Exec Tells the Real Story," *Medium*, December 17, 2022, https://medium.com/@fun_tonyb/fired-appe-exec-tells-the-real-story-79f3361450da; Helen Wang, "Mastering Negotiation: The Blevinator with Tony Blevins," *Oceanside Perspectives* (podcast), YouTube, uploaded on September 24, 2024, https://www.youtube.com/watch?v=uMj83Np46Os. Other details, including Blevins's negotiating tactics, were recounted and corroborated by multiple colleagues, subordinates, and rivals.

119 *"If you just stare"*: Wang, "Mastering Negotiation: The Blevinator with Tony Blevins."

123 *in Japan and stopped by Toshiba*: Jon Rubinstein, "Oral History of Jon Rubinstein," interviewed by Dag Spicer, Computer History Museum, August 15, 2019, https://archive.computerhistory.org/resources/access/text/2020/02/102717908-05-01-acc.pdf; Isaacson, *Steve Jobs*, 503–12.

123 *tied up on other projects*: Kahney, *Jony Ive*, 172–75.

123 *"In jail"*: Steven Levy, "The Perfect Thing," *Wired*, November 1, 2006, https://www.wired.com/2006/11/ipod/.

125 *He proposed "Pod"*: A version of Chieco's story was also published here: Leander Kahney, "Straight Dope on the iPod's Birth," *Wired*, October 17, 2006, https://www.wired.com/2006/10/straight-dope-on-the-ipods-birth/.

Chapter 14: Flat-Out Cool!—Making the iMac G4 Across Asia

127 *lines separating legitimacy from illegitimacy*: Ko-Lin Chin, *Heijin: Organized Crime, Business, and Politics in Taiwan*. Routledge, 2015 [originally published in 2003 by M. E. Sharpe], 19.

134 *all three models by $100*: Joe Wilcox, "iMac Price Hike Roils Apple Community," *ZDNET*, March 21, 2002.

135 *"miss our revenue projections"*: Steve Jobs quoted in CNET, "Apple Warns of Revenue, Earnings Shortfall," June 18, 2002.

Chapter 15: "You're Going to Give Us Your 'China Cost' for This"

138 *Seal, Moby, and Smash Mouth*: Apple iPod marketing video, 2001, JoshuaG, "The Very First iPod Promotional Video," YouTube, uploaded February 11, 2006, https://www.youtube.com/watch?v=e84SER_IkP4.

139 *nine quarters in a row*: Apple financial reports, accessed from Capital IQ, a platform from S&P Global Market Intelligence.

139 *"Screw it"*: Isaacson, *Steve Jobs*, 530.

141 *Shanghai-based factory in 1992*: James Fallows, "How the West Was Wired," *The Atlantic*, October 1, 2008, https://www.theatlantic.com/magazine/archive/2008/10/how-the-west-was-wired/306990/.

Chapter 16: The Replica—Making the iPod in China

151 *attributed his own cancer*: Isaacson, *Steve Jobs*, 591.

151 *long workweeks "shattering"*: Jon Rubinstein, "Oral History of Jon Rubinstein," interviewed by Dag Spicer, Computer History Museum, August 15, 2019, https://archive.computerhistory.org/resources/access/text/2020/02/102717908-05-01-acc.pdf.

Chapter 17: Project Purple in Asia

153 *82 percent in 2004*: Peter Cohen, "iPod US Marketshare Rises to 82 Percent," *MacWorld*, October 10, 2004, https://www.macworld.com/article/172751/ipodshare.html.

153 *"the new iPod Invisa"*: Fred Armisen, "Weekend Update: Tina Fey," *Saturday Night Live*, YouTube, uploaded October 25, 2013 (aired November 19, 2005), https://www.youtube.com/watch?v=plx69SIvgWI.

154 *"heavy, stomping footsteps"*: Lex Fridman, "Tony Fadell: iPhone, iPod, and Nest," episode 294, June 15, 2022, https://lexfridman.com/tony-fadell.

155 *had fled Chile*: Microsoft, "Rubén Caballero: Another Adventure and Loving It!" (corporate blog), March 24, 2021, https://blogs.microsoft.com/bayarea/2021/03/24/ruben-caballero-another-adventure-and-loving-it/.

156 *more of an enhanced iPod*: Markoff, as quoted in Fred Vogelstein, "Inside Apple's 6-Month Race to Make the First iPhone a Reality," *Wired,* June 28, 2017 (originally published in 2013), https://www.wired.com/story/iphone-history-dogfight/.

156 *"going through orifices"*: Brian Merchant, "The Secret Origin Story of the iPhone: An Exclusive Excerpt from *The One Device,*" *The Verge,* June 13, 2017, https://www.theverge.com/2017/6/13/15782200/one-device-secret-history-iphone-brian-merchant-book-excerpt. Note that Pegatron was at that time Asustek; it spun out of Asustek in 2009.

159 *"It filled the room"*: Fred Vogelstein, "And Then Steve Said, 'Let There Be an iPhone,'" *New York Times Magazine,* October 4, 2013, https://www.nytimes.com/2013/10/06/magazine/and-then-steve-said-let-there-be-an-iphone.html.

159 *"were exceedingly proud of it"*: Vogelstein, "And Then Steve Said, 'Let There Be an iPhone.'"

Chapter 18: The One Device

161 *"There we were in the fifth row"*: Fred Vogelstein, *Dogfight: How Apple and Google Went to War and Started a Revolution*. New York: Sarah Crichton Books/Farrar, Straus, and Giroux, 2013, 40.

162 *four months earlier*: Brian Merchant, *The One Device: The Secret History of the iPhone*. New York: Little, Brown, 2017.

163 *Zhou Qunfei*: David Barboza, "How a Chinese Billionaire Built Her Fortune," *New York Times,* July 30, 2015, https://www.nytimes.com/2015/08/02/business/international/how-zhou-qunfei-a-chinese-billionaire-built-her-fortune.html; Serena Lin, "The World's Richest Self-Made Woman Shares Her No. 1 Key to Success," CNBC, May 8, 2018, https://www.cnbc.com/2018/05/08/worlds-richest-self-made-woman-zhou-qunfei-shares-the-key-to-success.html.

163 *made $30 million sourcing monitors and then lost it all*: Russell Flannery, "Bobbing With Apple: Taiwan Touchscreen Champion TPK Faces Test Ahead," *Forbes,* May 24, 2012, https://www.forbes.com/sites/russellflannery/2012/05/23/bobbing-with-apple-taiwan-touchscreen-champion-tpk-faces-test-ahead/.

164 *"happens to be the last stop"*: Fred P. Hochberg, "The iPhone Isn't Made in China—It's Made Everywhere," *Wall Street Journal,* January 31, 2020, https://www.wsj.com/articles/the-iphone-isnt-made-in-chinaits-made-everywhere-11580485139.

164 *"Not Really 'Made in China'"*: Andrew Batson, "Not Really 'Made in China,'" *Wall Street Journal,* December 15, 2010, https://www.wsj.com/articles/SB10001424052748704828104576021142902413796.

165 *roused 8,000 workers*: Charles Duhigg and Keith Bradsher, "How the U.S. Lost Out on iPhone Work," *New York Times,* January 21, 2012, https://www.nytimes.com/2012/01/22/business/apple-america-and-a-squeezed-middle-class.html.

Chapter 19: The Apple Shock

170 *Years before Uber*: I'm riffing on a viral quote from Tom Goodwin, "The Battle Is for the Customer Interface," *TechCrunch,* March 3, 2015, https://techcrunch.com/2015/03/03/in-the-age-of-disintermediation-the-battle-is-all-for-the-customer-interface/.

171 *first major report was in the UK's* Daily Mail: "The Stark Reality of iPod's Chinese Factories," *Daily Mail,* August 18, 2006, https://www.dailymail.co.uk/news/article-401234/The-stark-reality-iPods-Chinese-factories.html.

171 *Supply Chain Top 25*: I told a shorter version of this story here: Patrick McGee, "How Apple Tied Its Fortunes to China," *Financial Times,* January 26, 2023, https://www.ft.com/content/d5a80891-b27d-4110-90c9-561b7836f11b; the original report is: Tony Friscia, Kevin O'Marah, and Joe Souza, "The AMR Research Supply Chain Top 25 for 2007," AMR Research Inc., May 2007.

172 *"fundamentally evil"*: Adam Lashinsky, "Tim Cook: The Genius Behind Steve," *Fortune,* November 23, 2008, https://fortune.com/2008/11/24/apple-the-genius-behind-steve/.

172 *"hours, not days"*: Doug Bartholomew, "What's Really Driving Apple's Recovery?" *IndustryWeek,* March 16, 1999, https://www.industryweek.com/leadership/companies-executives/article/21960994/whats-really-driving-apples-recovery.

173 *"machinery" that Apple owns*: Apple financial reports, via Capital IQ.

Chapter 20: The Missionary

181 *burst into tears on live TV*: Stephanie Strom, "A Sweetheart Becomes Suspect; Looking Behind Those Kathie Lee Labels," *New York Times,* June 27, 1996, https://www.nytimes.com/1996/06/27/business/a-sweetheart-becomes-suspect-looking-behind-those-kathie-lee-labels.html.

Chapter 21: The Sewing Machine Repair Shop

190 *Reports that September*: Associated Press, "Unauthorized iPhones on Sale in China," September 4, 2007.

190 *The average hourly wage of an urban worker*: The US Bureau of Labor Statistics estimates urban factory wages in China at $1.96 per hour in 2007. See Judith Banister, "China's Manufacturing Employment and Hourly Labor Compensation, 2002–2009," US Bureau of Labor Statistics, June 7, 2013, https://www.bls.gov/fls/china_method.htm.

191 *"third priority" market*: Dae-yub Nam, "Apple's Success Story in China," POSCO Research Institute: Summer 2012, https://www.posri.re.kr/dowload.do?fid=3886&pid=2613

192 *consumers were "anything but excited"*: Loretta Chao, "High Price for iPhone in China Will Test the Appetite for Apple," *Wall Street Journal*, October 29, 2009, https://www.wsj.com/articles/SB10001424052748703363704574503302512451942.

193 *"I BUY IPAD NO. 1"*: No Comment TV, "Apple iPad Debuts in Beijing," YouTube, September 17, 2010, https://www.youtube.com/watch?v=XlRLS95HrZs; Allison Jackson, "Crowds Turn Out for iPad's China Launch," Agence France-Presse, September 17, 2010, https://phys.org/news/2010-09-crowds-ipad-china.html.

194 *gang of scalpers*: Loretta Chao, "China iPhone Craze Breeds Scalpers," *Wall Street Journal*, September 30, 2010, https://www.wsj.com/articles/BL-CJB-10938.

Chapter 22: Yellow Cows in the Gray Market

195 *lucrative trade in train tickets*: Nicholas D. Kristof, "Beijing Journal: Counterfeit Train Ticket? No Problem. It's China," *New York Times*, November 24, 1992, https://www.nytimes.com/1992/11/24/world/beijing-journal-counterfeit-train-ticket-no-problem-it-s-china.html.

197 *"fastest-growing urban center"*: Pete Brook, "World's Fastest-Growing Megalopolis Hides in Fog," *Wired*, August 25, 2010, https://www.wired.com/2010/08/chongqing.

201 *"absolutely staggering"*: Tim Cook quoted in: Edmond Lococo, "Flocks of Customers Have Sent Apple's China Stores to the Top," Bloomberg News, January 26, 2011.

202 *study of college students in Wuhan*: "Apple Pursuit Lures Students into 'Usury,'" *Xinhua*, March 21, 2013, usa.chinadaily.com.cn/china/2013-03/21/content_16329739.htm.

202 *seventeen-year-old who underwent*: Melisa Goh, "Chinese Teen Sells Kidney for iPad and iPhone," NPR, April 7, 2012, https://www.npr.org/sections/thetwo-way/2012/04/07/150195037/chinese-teen-sells-kidney-for-ipad-and-iphone.

203 *bags down a zip line*: Leslie Horn, "Apple Products Smuggled into China Via Zipline, Crossbow," *PC Magazine,* August 9, 2011, https://www.yahoo.com/news/apple-products-smuggled-china-via-zipline-crossbow-155940033.html.

203 A *Chinese housewife was once caught*: Gregg Keizer, "Chinese Authorities Arrest iPad-smuggling 'Mules,'" ComputerWorld, December 8, 2010, https://www.computerworld.com/article/1438166/chinese-authorities-arrest-ipad-smuggling-mules.html.

Chapter 23: "Fire That Motherfucker!"

206 *Now reports from China*: Josh Ong, "China iPad 2, White iPhone 4 Frenzy Causes Apple Store Scuffle in Beijing," Apple Insider, May 7, 2011, https://appleinsider.com/articles/11/05/07/china_ipad_2_frenzy_causes_apple_store_scuffle_in_beijing; "Apple iPhone Triggers Fight in Chinese Shop," Associated Press, May 9, 2011, https://www.theguardian.com/technology/2011/may/09/apple-iphone-fight-chinese-shop.

Chapter 24: Twin Bets—Foxconn and TSMC

213 *"you were our teacher"*: Henry Paulson, "Oral History: Transcript," Presidential Oral Histories: George W. Bush Presidency, Miller Center, March 11, 2013, https://millercenter.org/the-presidency/presidential-oral-histories/henry-paulson-oral-history.

213 *$1.4 trillion of loans*: Geoff Dyer, "China Embarks on Infrastructure Spending Spree," *Financial Times,* June 7, 2010, https://www.ft.com/content/dc65a5c8-6fc2-11df-8fcf-00144feabdc0.

215 *"major ports serving the area"*: James Fallows, "China Makes, the World Takes," *The Atlantic,* July/August 2007, https://www.theatlantic.com/magazine/archive/2007/07/china-makes-the-world-takes/305987/.

215 *China remains 'a developing country"*: Wen Jiabao, "Premier Wen Jiabao Gives a Joint Interview to Journalists from Malaysia and Indonesia," International Press Center, April 26, 2011.

216 *"China compressed"*: Yi Wen, "The Making of an Economic

Superpower—Unlocking China's Secret of Rapid Industrialization," Federal Reserve of St. Louis Working Paper 2015-03-01, https://doi.org/10.20955/wp.2015.006.

216 *"no ancient wisdom"*: James McGregor, *No Ancient Wisdom, No Followers: The Challenges of Chinese Authoritarian Capitalism*. Westport, CT: Prospecta, 2012.

217 *One of the survivors*: Jenny Chan, Mark Selden, and Pun Ngai, *Dying for an iPhone: Apple, Foxconn, and The Lives of China's Workers*. London: Pluto Press, 2020.

217 *"There will be hospitals"*: Jason Dean and Peter Stein, "Inland China Beckons as Hon Hai Seeks Fresh, Cheaper Labor Force," *Wall Street Journal*, September 6, 2010, https://www.wsj.com/articles/SB10001424052748704392104575475591957325942.

218 *factory wages shot up*: Keith Bradsher, "Defying Global Slump, China Has Labor Shortage," *New York Times*, February 26, 2010, https://www.nytimes.com/2010/02/27/business/global/27yuan.html.

218 *"Rising wages suggest the re-emergence"*: Ibid.

218 *manufacturing labor costs rose by 15.6 percent*: As calculated by the Boston Consulting Group: "China's Next Leap in Manufacturing," December 13, 2018

220 *When workers protested*: Paul Mozur and John Liu, "The Chip Titan Whose Life's Work Is at the Center of a Tech Cold War," *New York Times*, August 4, 2023.

221 *through his wife, Sophie Chang*: Ibid.

221 *"The risk was very substantial"*: TSMC 30th Anniversary Forum 2017--Hosted by Morris Chang.

221 *Chang wouldn't commit*: "TSMC Founder Morris Chang," *Acquired* (podcast), Spring 2025, Episode 1, January 26, 2025, https://www.acquired.fm/episodes/tsmc-founder-morris-chang.

Chapter 25: "The Navy SEALs"

227 *a lawsuit emerged over its use of the term iPad*: "Apple 'Settles China iPad Trademark Dispute for $60m,'" BBC, July 2, 2012, https://www.bbc.com/news/business-18669394; Keith Bradsher, "Apple Settles an iPad Dispute in China," *New York Times*, July 2, 2012, https://www.nytimes.com/2012/07/02/business/global/apple-settles-an-ipad-trademark-dispute-in-china.html.

228 *"the square-foot equivalent of Rome"*: Evan Osnos, *Age of Ambition: Chasing*

Fortune, Truth, and Faith in the New China. New York: Farrar, Straux and Giroux, 2014, 25.

Chapter 26: The Despot

235 *"every reason to be proud"*: Edward Wong, "Ending Congress, China Presents New Leadership Headed by Xi Jinping," *New York Times,* November 14, 2012, https://www.nytimes.com/2012/11/15/world/asia/communists-conclude-party-congress-in-china.html.

236 *"What are you guys doing here?"*: Evan Osnos, "Born Red," *The New Yorker,* March 30, 2015, https://www.newyorker.com/magazine/2015/04/06/born-red.

236 *"the biggest Chinese political scandal"*: Jamil Anderlini, "Bo Xilai: Power, Death and Politics," *Financial Times,* July 20, 2012, https://www.ft.com/content/d67b90f0-d140-11e1-8957-00144feabdc0; Jamil Anderlini, *The Bo Xilai Scandal: Power, Death and Politics in China*. Penguin (ebook), 2012.

237 *"sooner than I used to suppose"*: Diamond quoted in Elizabeth Economy, "The World According to China with Elizabeth Economy," *Uncommon Knowledge with Peter Robinson,* October 23, 2013, https://www.hoover.org/research/world-according-china-elizabeth-economy.

237 *"collective presidency"*: Osnos, "Born Red."

237 *"impressive economic gains"*: Elizabeth Economy, "Excerpt: The Third Revolution," Council on Foreign Relations, 2018, https://www.cfr.org/excerpt-third-revolution.

237 *"Facts have repeatedly told us"*: Matt Pottinger, Matthew Johnson, and David Feith, "Xi Jinping in His Own Words," *Foreign Affairs,* November 30, 2022, https://www.foreignaffairs.com/china/xi-jinping-his-own-words.

239 *2,000 Foxconn staff in the city of Taiyuan rioted*: David Barboza and Keith Bradsher, "Foxconn Plant Closed After Riot, Company Says," *New York Times,* September 24, 2012, https://www.nytimes.com/2012/09/25/technology/foxconn-plant-in-china-closed-after-worker-riot.html; Evan Osnos: "What the Foxconn Riot Says About China," *New Yorker,* September 15, 2012, https://www.newyorker.com/news/evan-osnos/what-the-foxconn-riot-says-about-china.

240 *"As one Japanese executive"*: Jamil Anderlini and Mure Dickie, "China: A Future on Track," *Financial Times,* September 23, 2010.

243 *"largely backfired"*: Helen Gao, "How the Apple Confrontation Divides China," *The Atlantic,* April 8, 2013, https://www.theatlantic.com/china/archive/2013/04/how-the-apple-confrontation-divides-china/274764/.

243 *an obvious goof*: Gordon G. Chang, "Did China Just Declare War on Apple? Sure Looks Like It," *Forbes,* March 24, 2013, https://www.forbes.com/sites/gordonchang/2013/03/24/did-china-just-declare-war-on-apple-sure-looks-like-it/.

243 *"editorial in the* Global Times*"*: Sean Silbert, "China's Gray Market for iPhones, Even Amid Push for Local Handsets," *Los Angeles Times,* September 26, 2014.

Chapter 27: The Gang of Eight

244 *billions of dollars' worth*: David Barboza, "How China Built 'iPhone City' With Billions in Perks for Apple's Partner," *New York Times,* December 29, 2016, https://www.nytimes.com/2016/12/29/technology/apple-iphone-china-foxconn.html.

Chapter 28: The China Whisperer

251 *compensatory technique called audiographic memory*: *Audiographic memory* is the term Guthrie uses for it. Sometimes it is referred to as eidetic memory for sound.

256 *"regionally decentralized authoritarian regime"*: Chenggang Xu, "The Fundamental Institutions of China's Reforms and Development," *Journal of Economic Literature* 49, no. 4 (2011): 1076–151.

257 *"One of the great ironies"*: Doug Guthrie, "China's Success Story," YouTube, August 26, 2013, https://www.youtube.com/watch?v=2DLYhZnkeBI.

Chapter 29: Voluntary Is the New Mandatory

260 *"an aggressive by-hook-or-by-crook strategy"*: Louise Lucas and Emily Feng, "China's Push to Become a Tech Superpower Triggers Alarms Abroad," *Financial Times,* March 19, 2017, https://www.ft.com/content/1d815944-f1da-11e6-8758-6876151821a6.

260 *"Doing business in China"*: Doug Guthrie, "The Lesson of China's Market Economy," YouTube, August 26, 2013, https://www.youtube.com/watch?v=yCkkER_dWac.

261 *the professor's response only confused*: Jack Nicas, "He Warned Apple About the Risks in China. Then They Became Reality," *New York Times,* June 17, 2021, https://www.nytimes.com/2021/06/17/technology/apple-china-doug-guthrie.html.

261 *"Our 'surprise and delight' business model"*: Wayne Ma, "Apple Turned

Blind Eye to Supplier Breaches of Chinese Labor Laws," *The Information,* December 9, 2020, https://www.theinformation.com/articles/apple-turned-blind-eye-to-supplier-breaches-of-chinese-labor-laws?rc=ropvb4.

263 *"voluntary is the new mandatory"*: James McGregor, *No Ancient Wisdom, No Followers: The Challenges of Chinese Authoritarian Capitalism*. Westport, CT: Prospecta, 2012.

263 *"In the West, CSR is"*: Jiangyu Wang, "CSR as CPR: The Political Logic of Corporate Social Responsibility in China," *USALI East-West Studies* 2, no. 5 (2022), https://usali.org/s/CSR-as-CPR-The-Political-Logic-of-Corporate-Social-Responsibility-in-China.pdf.

264 *The Korean giant had dozens*: Michael J. Enright, "Samsung's Contribution to China through FDI," Hinrich Foundation, 2017, https://www.hinrichfoundation.com/media/s04iyovs/hinrich-foundation-fdi-in-china-samsung-case-study-9-5-17.pdf.

264 *"The Ministry of Finance asked Apple"*: Katie Kuehner-Hebert, "Apple Pays Chins $71 Million in Back Taxes," CFO, September 11, 2015, https://www.cfo.com/news/apple-pays-china-71-million-in-back-taxes/663299/.

265 *to brief senior executives*: Jack Nicas, Raymond Zhong, and Daisuke Wakabayashi, "Censorship, Surveillance and Profits: A Hard Bargain for Apple in China," *New York Times,* May 17, 2021, https://www.nytimes.com/2021/05/17/technology/apple-china-censorship-data.html.

265 *a senior Chinese official had threatened*: Michael Martina, "Exclusive: Tough-Talking China Pricing Regulator Sought Confessions from Foreign Firms," Reuters, August 22, 2013, https://www.reuters.com/article/breakingviews/exclusive-tough-talking-china-pricing-regulator-sought-confessions-from-foreign-idUSBRE97K051/.

265 *"a partial blueprint of its higher-end servers"*: Paul Mozur, "IBM Venture with China Stirs Concerns," *New York Times,* April 19, 2015, https://www.nytimes.com/2015/04/20/business/ibm-project-in-china-raises-us-concerns.html.

Chapter 30: The Apple Squeeze

269 *when iPhone margins were 33 percent*: All margin figures are from Counterpoint Research.

271 *$13.3 billion*: Figures are from Apple's 10-k annual filings with the SEC.

271 *"worst thing in the world"*: John Paczkowski, "Patent Wars Are 'Pain in the Ass,' Says Tim Cook (video)," All Things Digital, May 29, 2012,

https://allthingsd.com/20120529/patent-wars-are-pain-in-the-ass-says-tim-cook/.

271 *"it really is theft"*: Graydon Carter, "Apple's Jonathan Ive in Conversation with Vanity Fair's Graydon Carter," *Vanity Fair*, October 16, 2014, https://www.vanityfair.com/video/watch/the-new-establishment-summit-apples-jonathan-ive-in-conversation-with-vf-graydon-carter.

272 *"pain in the ass"*: Paczkowski, "Patent Wars Are 'Pain in the Ass,' Says Tim Cook."

272 *iPhone shipments* and *local market share of such Chinese brands*: Courtesy of CounterPoint Research.

277 *"machinery, equipment and internal-use software"*: Available in Apple 10-k filings with the SEC.

Chapter 31: A Marshall Plan for China

278 *met with vice premier Li Keqiang*: Loretta Chao, "Apple Bolsters Ties with China's Leadership," *Wall Street Journal*, March 28, 2012, https://www.wsj.com/articles/SB10001424052702303816504577309293480251760.

278 *mobilize the entire population of China*: Alexander Pantsov and Nikita Pivovarov, "The Secret Negotiations of N.S. Khrushchev and Mao Zedong, July-August 1958," February 2024, Cold War International History Project, February 2024, https://www.wilsoncenter.org/publication/secret-negotiations-ns-khrushchev-and-mao-zedong-july-august-1958.

279 *"Apple had not seen a downturn"*: The confidential study, "Consumption in the Age of Xi: Understanding China's Evolving Consumer Markets," was produced in court discovery. See the chapter "5 Alarm Fire."

279 *startling move with major significance* : Paul Mozur and Jane Perlez, "Apple Services Shut Down in China in Startling About-Face," *New York Times*, April 21, 2016, https://www.nytimes.com/2016/04/22/technology/apple-no-longer-immune-to-chinas-scrutiny-of-us-tech-firms.html.

279 *"grow almost unimpeded in China"*: Adam Satariano and Aleksandra Gjorgievska, "Closing of iTunes Movies Shows Apple Isn't Immune to Chinese Regulators," Bloomberg, April 21, 2016, https://www.bloomberg.com/news/articles/2016-04-22/apple-says-itunes-movies-book-services-closed-down-in-china.

280 *a pledge to invest $275 billion*: Independently corroborated for this book but first reported in *The Information*—possibly the greatest Apple scoop ever: Wayne Ma, "Inside Tim Cook's Secret $275 Billion Deal with Chinese Authorities," *The Information*, December 7, 2021, https://www

.theinformation.com/articles/facing-hostile-chinese-authorities-apple-ceo-signed-275-billion-deal-with-them.

280 *45 percent tariffs*: Maggie Haberman, "Donald Trump Says He Favors Big Tariffs on Chinese Exports," *New York Times*, January 7, 2016, https://archive.nytimes.com/www.nytimes.com/politics/first-draft/2016/01/07/donald-trump-says-he-favors-big-tariffs-on-chinese-exports/.

280 *"their damn computers"*: Issie Lapowsky, "Trump's Plan for American-Made iPhones Would Be Disastrous," *Wired*, March 30, 2016, https://www.wired.com/2016/03/trump-wont-get-apple-make-iphones-shouldnt/.

281 *Apple was promising*: Shannon O'Neil, *The Globalization Myth: Why Regions Matter*, New Haven, CT: Yale University Press, 2022, 107.

281 *"moving Europe from a dysfunctional system"*: Niall Ferguson, "Dollar Diplomacy," *The New Yorker*, August 20, 2007, https://www.newyorker.com/magazine/2007/08/27/dollar-diplomacy.

282 *"by far the most important"*: Ella Apostoaie, "Barry Naughton on the State of the Xi Jinping Economy," *The Wire China*, January 6, 2025.

285 *tacit knowledge*: Yi Wen, "The Making of an Economic Superpower—Unlocking China's Secret of Rapid Industrialization," Federal Reserve of St. Louis Working Paper 2015-03-01, https://doi.org/10.20955/wp.2015.006.

285 *"If the gains from trade"*: David Landes, *The Wealth and Poverty of Nation*. Norton, 1998, 136.

285 *"Apple's business is out of step"*: Tripp Mickle, "Apple Pledges New Centers in China as Cook Set to Address Major Government Conference," *Wall Street Journal*, March 17, 2017, https://www.wsj.com/articles/apple-pledges-new-development-centers-in-china-1489758033.

286 *"the formula of 'the first machine imported'"*: Chris Miller, *Chip War*. New York: Scribner, 2022, 176.

286 *"For all its manufacturing might"*: "How China Became a Car-Exporting Juggernaut," *The Economist*, August 10, 2023, https://www.economist.com/graphic-detail/2023/08/10/how-china-became-a-car-exporting-juggernaut#.

287 *17,000 electric buses*: Selina Xu, "This Chinese Province Has More EV Chargers Than All of the US," Bloomberg, October 21, 2022, https://www.bloomberg.com/news/articles/2022-10-22/this-chinese-province-has-three-times-more-ev-chargers-than-all-of-the-us.

287 *EVs and plug-in hybrids together*: Wenyi Zhang, "Market Share of Electric Vehicles (BEVs and PHEVs) in China from 2018 to 2021," EV-

Volumes.com (JD Power & Associates), republished by Statista, https://www.statista.com/statistics/1050111/china-electric-car-market-share/.

288 *share of EVs and plug-ins soared*: International Energy Agency, *Global EV Outlook 2024*, Paris, https://www.iea.org/reports/global-ev-outlook-2024.

Chapter 32: Bureaucratic Protection

289 *Jean Liu's meeting*: Charles Clover and Leslie Hook, "Jean Liu: Splashing the Cash," *Financial Times*, August 5, 2016, https://www.ft.com/content/4b0a0c56-5afb-11e6-9f70-badea1b336d4.

290 *"legal name is called 'little orange'"*: Mike Isaac and Vindu Goel, "Apple Puts $1 Billion in Didi, a Rival to Uber in China," *New York Times*, May 12, 2016, https://www.nytimes.com/2016/05/13/technology/apple-puts-1-billion-in-didi-a-rival-to-uber-in-china.html.

290 *"built a company"*: Tim Cook, "Jean Liu," the TIME 100, *Time*, 2017, https://time.com/collection/2017-time-100/4742753/jean-liu/.

291 *"like lightning"*: Maya Kosoff, "Apple Just Made a $1 Billion Bet Against Uber," *Vanity Fair*, May 13, 2016, https://www.vanityfair.com/news/2016/05/apple-just-made-a-billion-dollar-bet-against-uber; Jessica E. Lessin and Amir Efrati, "What Apple's Investment in Didi Means," *The Information*, May 12, 2016, https://www.theinformation.com/articles/what-apples-investment-in-didi-means?rc=ropvb4.

292 *variety of US government bodies*: Roslyn Layton, "New Pentagon Report Shows How Restricted Chinese IT Products Routinely Enter US Military Networks," American Enterprise Institute, August 12, 2019, https://www.aei.org/technology-and-innovation/new-pentagon-reports-shows-how-restricted-chinese-it-products-routinely-make-their-way-into-us-military-networks.

292 *"bigger than Google"*: Patrick McGee, "Robotaxis: Have Google and Amazon Backed the Wrong Technology?" *Financial Times*, July 18, 2021, https://www.ft.com/content/46ff4fe4-0ae6-4f68-902c-3fd14d294d72.

293 *bureaucratic protection*: Jiehmin Wu, *Rival Partners: How Taiwanese Entrepreneurs and Guangdong Officials Forged the China Development Model*. Translated by Stacy Mosher. Cambridge, MA: Harvard University Asia Center, 2022.

293 *"The thing I like"*: Ma Si, "Tim Cook Visits Apple Store in Beijing, with Didi President," *China Daily*, May 15, 2016, https://www.chinadaily.com.cn/business/tech/2016-05/16/content_25294753.htm.

293 *"Apple had no investment strategy"*: The analyst was Hu Yanping, an expert from the Data Center of China Internet. "Apple CEO Hails Didi Taxi to Meet Chinese Developers in Beijing," CCTV Video News Agency, May 17, 2016, https://www.youtube.com/watch?v=v4PwCfGcFzw&t=2s.

295 *6,857-mile flight*: Nancy Trejos, "United Starts Flights to China's Fourth Largest City," *USA Today*, June 12, 2014, https://www.usatoday.com/story/todayinthesky/2014/06/12/united-non-stop-service-san-francisco-chengdu/10390597/.

296 *"almost five million jobs"*: "Exclusive: Apple Setting Down Deep Roots in China, CEO Says," *Caixin Global*, March 21, 2017, https://www.caixinglobal.com/2017-03-21/exclusive-apple-setting-down-deep-roots-in-china-ceo-says-101068558.html.

296 *"We follow the law wherever we do business"*: Vindu Goel, "Apple Sales Exceed Expectations as Buyers Wait for New iPhones," *New York Times*, August 1, 2017, https://www.nytimes.com/2017/08/01/technology/apple-iphone-earnings.html.

297 *"the pretty lady who greets you"*: Patrick McGee, "Apple Engineer Likened App Store Security to 'Butter Knife in Gunfight,'" *Financial Times*, April 8, 2021, https://www.ft.com/content/914ce719-f538-4bd9-9fdf-42220d857d5e.

298 *674 VPN apps*: Tim Bradshaw, "Apple Drops Hundreds of VPN Apps at Beijing's Request," *Financial Times*, November 21, 2017, https://www.ft.com/content/ad42e536-cf36-11e7-b781-794ce08b24dc.

298 *"the most drastic measure"*: Keith Fong, "Apple Removes VPN Apps from China App Store," ExpressVPN (corporate blog), July 28, 2017, https://www.expressvpn.com/blog/china-ios-app-store-removes-vpns/#.

298 *Apple met with officials*: Wayne Ma, "Inside Tim Cook's Secret $275 Billion Deal with Chinese Authorities," *The Information*, December 7, 2021, https://www.theinformation.com/articles/facing-hostile-chinese-authorities-apple-ceo-signed-275-billion-deal-with-them.

299 *"Chinese government workers"*: Jack Nicas, "Apple's Compromises in China: 5 Takeaways," *New York Times*, May 17, 2021, https://www.nytimes.com/2021/05/17/technology/apple-china-privacy-censorship.html.

Chapter 33: Cognitive Dissonance—Supplier Responsibility

303 *"Apple has zero tolerance"*: "Apple's Unkept Promises: Investigation of Three Pegatron Group Factories Supplying to Apple," China Labor Watch,

July 29, 2013, https://chinalaborwatch.org/apples-unkept-promises-investigation-of-three-pegatron-group-factories-supplying-to-apple/.

307 *A senior executive at Foxconn*: Rob Schmitz, "The People Behind Your iPad: The Bosses," Marketplace, April 12, 2012, https://www.marketplace.org/2012/04/12/people-behind-your-ipad-bosses/.

309 *"regular rounds of repression"*: Eli Friedman, Aaron Halegua, and Jerome A. Cohen, "Cruel Irony: China's Communists Are Stamping Out Labor Activism," *Washington Post*, January 3, 2016: https://www.washingtonpost.com/opinions/cruel-irony-chinas-communists-are-stamping-out-labor-activism/2016/01/03/99e986f2-b0bb-11e5-b820-eea4d64be2a1_story.html.

309 *"restricting the work"*: Edward Wong, "Clampdown in China Restricts 7,000 Foreign Organizations," *New York Times*, April 28, 2016, https://www.nytimes.com/2016/04/29/world/asia/china-foreign-ngo-law.html.

309 *"The new rules placed responsibility"*: Gerry Shih, "China Tightens Control of Online News After Sensitive Gaffes," Associated Press, August 19, 2016, https://apnews.com/e8567f6879074fd09c311301467d45b0/China-tightens-control-of-online-news-after-sensitive-gaffes.

310 *"Your choice is"*: Dan Strumpf, "Apple's Tim Cook: No Point Yelling at China," *Wall Street Journal*, December 7, 2017, https://www.wsj.com/articles/apples-tim-cook-no-point-yelling-at-china-1512563332.

311 *"We are Marxists"*: Javier C. Hernández, "China's Leaders Confront an Unlikely Foe: Ardent Young Communists," *New York Times*, September 28, 2018, https://www.nytimes.com/2018/09/28/world/asia/china-maoists-xi-protests.html.

Chapter 34: The Figurehead—Isabel Mahe

316 *father was a college professor*: "SFU Outstanding Alumni Awards 2019," YogaPanda Studios, YouTube, https://www.youtube.com/watch?v=N4TNLJr6XUE.

317 *"bait and switch!"*: Claire Zillman, "Apple Is Counting on This Star Exec to Reboot its Sales in China," *Fortune*, September 25, 2017, https://fortune.com/2017/09/25/apple-china-iphone-features/.

318 *"'bad mess' occurs"*: Joel M. Podolny and Morten T. Hansen, "How Apple Is Organized for Innovation," *Harvard Business Review*, November/December 2020, https://hbr.org/2020/11/how-apple-is-organized-for-innovation.

319 *Apple formally announced*: Apple, "Isabel Ge Mahe Named Apple's Managing Director of Greater China," Apple, July 18, 2017, https://www.apple.com/jo/newsroom/2017/07/isabel-ge-mahe-named-apple-managing-director-of-greater-china/.

321 *"write my own playbook"*: "SFU Outstanding Alumni Awards 2019."

321 *"When times are tough"*: Isabel Mahe, "CEIBS Executive Lounge: Isabel Ge Mahe (Apple)," China Europe International Business School (interview), YouTube, April 8, 2021, https://www.youtube.com/watch?v=cp3xB_6wWG8. Mahe's board positions verified in company annual reports and are also posted on her LinkedIn page: https://www.linkedin.com/in/isabel-mahe-7603301; her page for the American Chamber of Commerce is online: https://www.amchamchina.org/amcham_staff/isabel-ge-mahe-2/.

Chapter 35: The Red Supply Chain

323 *"an extraordinary example"*: "Tim Cook Visits the AirPods Plant: Apple Does Not Intend to Shift Production Capacity to Lower Cost Regions," *The Paper*, reprinted by Luxshare-ICT, December 5, 2017, https://www.luxshare-ict.com/en/news/release/103.html.

323 *even took to Weibo*: Wayne Ma, "How Apple Grew Closer to China by Turning 'Little Foxconn' Into a National Champion," *The Information*, December 30, 2021, https://www.theinformation.com/articles/how-apple-grew-closer-to-china-by-turning-little-foxconn-into-a-national-champion.

324 *39 percent of its shares*: According to Luxshare annual reports. Wang and her brother own Luxshare Limited, a holding company with 39 percent ownership of Luxshare Precision.

325 *task force to study*: Yimou Lee and Josh Horwitz, "Apple Supplier Luxshare Unnerves Foxconn as U.S.-China Feud Speeds Supply Chain Shift," Reuters, October 25, 2020, https://www.reuters.com/article/world/uk/apple-supplier-luxshare-unnerves-foxconn-as-us-china-feud-speeds-supply-chain-idUSKBN27B06M/.

325 *one of the first migrant workers*: Luxshare annual report, 2020, 84, https://www.luxshare-ict.com/Public/Uploads/uploadfile2/files/20231019/lixunjingmi2020nianniandubaogaoyingwenban.PDF.

325 *plastered to the walls* and *an entire month*: Wayne Ma, "How Apple Grew Closer to China." All numbers from company reports, derived from Capital IQ.

326 *"master core technologies"*: As quoted in Jiehmin Wu, *Rival Partners: How Taiwanese Entrepreneurs and Guangdong Officials Forged the China Development Model*. Translated by Stacy Mosher. Cambridge, MA: Harvard University Asia Center, 2022.

327 *"the number of mainland Chinese companies"*: Lauly Li and Cheng Ting-Fang, "Apple Moves Closer to China Despite Supply Chain Shifts," *Nikkei Asia*, April 26, 2024; Lauly Li and Cheng Ting-Fang, "Apple's Chinese Suppliers Overtake US for First Time," *Nikkei Asia*, March 18, 2019.

327 *151 of Apple's 200 major suppliers:* Ma Si, "Apple Pushes for 'Smart' Tie-ups with Local Manufacturers," *China Daily*, December 1, 2023, https://global.chinadaily.com.cn/a/202312/01/WS65693446a31090682a5f0e0d.html.

327 *"blood in the water"*: Yimou Lee and Josh Horwitz, "Apple Supplier Luxshare Unnerves Foxconn as U.S.-China Feud Speeds Supply Chain Shift," Reuters, October 25, 2020, https://www.reuters.com/article/world/uk/apple-supplier-luxshare-unnerves-foxconn-as-us-china-feud-speeds-supply-chain-idUSKBN27B06M/.

328 *"Apple is happy"*: Ma Si, "Apple to Enhance Suppliers' Potential," *China Daily*, August 19, 2023, https://www.chinadaily.com.cn/a/202308/19/WS64dff5e2a31035260b81d04b.html. Note: the English edition of China Daily refers to "intelligent manufacturing," but I've amended to "smart manufacturing" to align with common English usage.

329 *operating margins for the iPhone jumped*: Estimates provided by Counterpoint Research.

330 *The "underpoliticized" narrative*: Jiehmin Wu, *Rival Partners*, 57.

330 *buying two China-based subsidiaries of Wistron*: Kathrin Hille and Qianer Liu, "Luxshare Rises as China's Homegrown iPhone Manufacturer," *Financial Times*, August 9, 2020, https://www.ft.com/content/5a9afb09-a9f2-483a-bd90-c30cee996480.

330 *BYD Electronic spent*: Data courtesy of PitchBook; confirmed by company press releases.

331 *"hired away more than half"*: Ma, "How Apple Grew Closer to China."

331 *the practice became so brazen*: "Taiwan Accuses Chinese Apple Supplier of Trying to Illegally Poach Tech Talent," Reuters, May 30, 2024, https://www.reuters.com/technology/taiwan-accuses-chinese-apple-supplier-trying-illegally-poach-tech-talent-2024-05-31/.

Chapter 36: "5 Alarm Fire"

332 *official sales launch of the iPhone XR*: The X in XR is rendered as *ten*. In emails, executives often write "Xr."

332 *made public in court discovery*: The case was brought by investors representing Norfolk County Council in the US District Court, Northern District of California. It's known as Securities Litigation No. 4:19-cv-02033-YGR.

337 *The news Cook and Maestri concealed*: Lauly Li and Cheng Ting-Fang, "Apple Cancels Production Boost for Budget iPhone XR: Sources," *Nikkei Asia*, November 5, 2018.

338 *"has stoked fears over the health"*: Robin Wigglesworth, Tim Bradshaw, and Richard Waters, "Apple Warning Bell Triggers Fears for Global Economy," *Financial Times*, January 3, 2019, https://www.ft.com/content/2abeab48-0f79-11e9-a3aa-118c761d2745.

338 *"Cook said two months ago"*: Shira Ovide, "As Stock Plummets, Apple Can No Longer Deny the Truth About Its iPhone Business," Bloomberg, January 3, 2019. Republished in *Time*, https://time.com/5492878/apple-stock-iphone-sales/.

Chapter 37: The Huawei Threat

340 *investors, led by the UK's Norfolk County council*: The legal battle took more than five years, concluding in September 2024. Apple didn't admit wrongdoing but agreed to pay $490 million, saying it settled to avoid an "overly burdensome" legal battle.

342 *onslaught from Huawei*: All market share numbers courtesy of Counterpoint Research.

344 *Trump told his supporters*: Jeremy Diamond, "Trump Calls for Apple Boycott," CNN, February 19, 2016, https://www.cnn.com/2016/02/19/politics/donald-trump-apple-boycott/index.html.

344 *"Tim, unless you start"*: Tripp Mickle and Peter Nicholas, "Trump Says Apple CEO Has Promised to Build Three Manufacturing Plants in U.S." *Wall Street Journal*, July 25, 2017: https://www.wsj.com/articles/trump-says-apple-ceo-has-promised-to-build-three-manufacturing-plants-in-u-s-1501012372.

344 *The tweet was patently false*: Jack Nicas, "No, That Mac Factory in Texas Is Not New," *New York Times*, November 20, 2019, https://www.nytimes.com/2019/11/20/us/politics/trump-texas-apple-factory.html.

347 *to the point of ideating suicide*: Episodes 121 and 122, *Courage to Leap & Lead with Doug Guthrie* (podcast), April 18, 2023.

348 *"cost of doing business in China"*: Doug Guthrie, "The Age of Cooptation: The Cost of Doing Business in Xi's China," On Global Leadership, January 1, 2020, https://ongloballeadership.com/f/the-age-of-cooptation-the-cost-of-doing-business-in-xis-china.

Chapter 38: Global Pandemic

350 *issued a revenue warning*: "Investor Update on Quarterly Guidance," Apple press release, February 17, 2020, https://www.apple.com/newsroom/2020/02/investor-update-on-quarterly-guidance/.

350 *"50 business class seats daily"*: Nick Statt, "Apple Pays United So Much for Corporate Travel It May Help Upgrade Its SFO Terminal," *The Verge*, October 25, 2019, https://www.theverge.com/2019/10/25/20932487/apple-united-airlines-sfo-terminal-upgrades.

352 *nickname "White Guards"*: Rita Cheng, Qiao Long, and Ching-man for RFA Mandarin, "China's 'White Guards' Gain Reputation for Brutal Enforcement of Shanghai Lockdown," Radio Free Asia, May 29, 2022, https://www.rfa.org/english/news/china/shanghai-whiteguards-05292022070418.html.

353 *reduced Apple revenue by $30 billion*: Krish Sankar et al., "The Apple Supply Chain's Great Reshoring," TD Cowen, January 4, 2024.

354 *Ma critiqued Beijing governance*: James Kynge, Henry Sender, and Sun Yu, "'The Party Is Pushing Back': Why Beijing Reined in Jack Ma and Ant," *Financial Times*, November 4, 2020, https://www.ft.com/content/3d2f174d-aa73-44fc-8c90-45c2a554e97b.

354 *wrote two China scholars*: Christopher Marquis and Kunyuan Qiao, *Mao and Markets: The Communist Roots of Chinese Enterprise*. New Haven, CT: Yale University Press, 2022, 2.

354 *the sell-off had wiped out*: Jeanny Yu, "China's New Crackdown Shows $1.5 Trillion Tech Rout Not Over Yet," Bloomberg, February 18, 2022, https://www.bloomberg.com/news/articles/2022-02-19/china-s-new-crackdown-shows-1-5-trillion-tech-rout-not-over-yet,

355 *"basically stagnant"*: Lauly Li and Cheng Ting-Fang, "Half of Apple Suppliers Operating in China's Lockdown-Hit Areas," *Nikkei Asia*, April 20, 2022.

355 *"massive losses"*: Cheng Ting-Fang and Lauly Li, "Huawei Exec: Supply Chains at Risk If Shanghai Lockdown Persists," *Nikkei Asia*, April 15, 2022.

355 *more than half of its 200 primary suppliers*: Li and Cheng, "Half of Apple Suppliers Operating in China's Lockdown-Hit Areas."

356 *"Apple is playing with fire"*: Demetri Sevastopulo and Patrick McGee, "US Lawmakers Warn Apple on Using Chinese Group's Chips in New iPhone," *Financial Times,* September 8, 2022, https://www.ft.com/content/099a409a-49c2-4ed3-a630-87bf6dc8ce15.

Chapter 39: "An Unprecedented Nightmare for Apple"

357 "As *Hu was hustled"*: James Kynge, "China, Xi Jinping and the Making of 'One People, One Ideology,'" *Financial Times,* February 29, 2024, https://www.ft.com/content/3ae0d3a0-85fa-4d1f-93e9-f3f084147517.

359 *introduced a "closed-loop" system* and *false rumors spread that 20,000 people:* Zen Soo, "Workers Leave iPhone Factory in Zhengzhou Amid COVID Curbs," Associated Press, October 30, 2022, https://apnews.com/article/health-china-business-hong-kong-covid-61692fa2d76eeeb8c68b706d0e649de7.

359 *walk more than sixty miles back*: Jing Xuan Teng, "'We Were Scared': Workers at Foxconn iPhone Factory in China Recount Covid Chaos," AFP, November 5, 2022, https://hongkongfp.com/2022/11/05/we-were-scared-workers-at-foxconn-iphone-factory-in-china-recount-covid-chaos/.

359 *food and medical shortages*: Viola Zhou, "As Covid-19 Surges in China, Sick Foxconn Workers Are Still Making iPhones," Rest of World, December 19, 2022, https://restofworld.org/2022/covid-foxconn-iphone-factory/.

359 *workers protested*: FT reporters, "Inside the Covid Revolt at the Zhengzhou 'iPhone City' Plant," *Financial Times,* December 1, 2022, https://www.ft.com/content/083e038c-9b10-45d1-85e2-3eb339313a38.

359 *riot police beat them with batons*: Selina Cheng and Wenxin Fan, "iPhone Factory Workers Clash With Police at Covid-Hit Plant in China," *Wall Street Journal,* November 23, 2022, https://www.wsj.com/articles/iphone-factory-workers-clash-with-police-at-covid-hit-plant-in-china-11669193001.

359 *"Zhengzhou debacle"*: FT Reporters, "Inside the Covid Revolt at the Zhengzhou 'iPhone City' Plant," *Financial Times,* December 1, 2022, https://www.ft.com/content/083e038c-9b10-45d1-85e2-3eb339313a38

359 *"If you look at the shock"*: Anna Akins, "Apple Faces Hurdles Amid Renewed Calls to Trim Reliance on Chinese Production," S&P Global, May 14, 2020, https://www.spglobal.com/marketintelligence/en/news

-insights/latest-news-headlines/apple-faces-hurdles-amid-renewed-calls-to-trim-reliance-on-chinese-production-58610617.

360 *"everything we want to say"*: Martin Quin Pollard and Brenda Goh, "Blank Sheets of Paper Become Symbol of Defiance in China Protests," Reuters, November 27, 2022, https://www.reuters.com/world/china/blank-sheets-paper-become-symbol-defiance-china-protests-2022-11-27/.

360 *use of its file-sharing tool AirDrop*: Steven Jiang and Juliana Liu, "Apple Curbs AirDrop File Sharing on Devices in China," CNN, November 11, 2022, https://www.cnn.com/2022/11/11/business/china-apple-airdrop-function-restricted-hnk-intl/index.html.

360 *confronted by a reporter*: Patrick McGee, "What It Would Take for Apple to Disentangle Itself from China," *Financial Times*, January 17, 2023, https://www.ft.com/content/74f7e284-c047-4cc4-9b7a-408d40611bfa.

361 *"silence is the ultimate consent"*: "Tim Cook Talks Global Leadership," YouTube, uploaded by Mike Bloomberg, September 20, 2017, https://www.youtube.com/watch?v=osGvoS130J8&t=1071s.

Chapter 40: Plan B—Assembled in India?

363 *these four groups spent $16 billion*: Krish Sankar et al., "The Apple Supply Chain's Great Reshoring," TD Cowen, January 4, 2024.

364 *As an internal memo prepared for Tim Cook*: The document was produced in court discovery. See chapter 36, "5 Alarm Fire."

367 *Average monthly manufacturing wages*: Torsten Sløk, "US Wages vs Wages in China and India," Apollo Academy, September 16, 2024, https://www.apolloacademy.com/us-wages-vs-wages-in-china-and-india/.

368 *landmark bill in the Indian state*: John Reed and Kathrin Hille, "Apple and Foxconn Win Labour Reforms to Advance Indian Production Plans," *The Financial Times*, March 9, 2023, https://www.ft.com/content/86bf4c20-e95a-4f8e-bd8d-b7bdee3bc3ba.

368 *"lowest rate of internal migration"*: Supriyo De, "Internal Migration in India Grows, But Inter-State Movements Remain Low," World Bank: Blogs, December 18, 2019, https://blogs.worldbank.org/en/peoplemove/internal-migration-india-grows-inter-state-movements-remain-low.

368 *"a class of its own"*: Robert D. Atkinson, "Chinese Manufacturers Use 12 Times More Robots Than U.S. Manufacturers When Controlling for Wages," Information Technology and Innovation Foundation, September 5, 2023, https://itif.org/publications/2023/09/05/chinese-man

ufacturers-use-12-times-more-robots-than-us-manufacturers-when-controlling-for-wages/.

369 *1,500 Samsung workers*: Cherylann Mollan, "Why Hundreds of Samsung Workers Are Protesting in India," BBC, September 19, 2024, https://www.bbc.com/news/articles/c7488w85n00o.

370 *around fourteen suppliers*: Saritha Rai and Sankalp Phartiyal, "Apple Gets a Boost in India as Chinese Suppliers Given Clearance," Bloomberg, January 17, 2023, https://www.bloomberg.com/news/articles/2023-01-18/apple-gets-boost-in-india-as-chinese-suppliers-luxshare-ningbo-given-clearance?embedded-checkout=true&sref=jnL7D1QX.

371 *Tata said it would hire* and *Tata acquired a majority stake:* Shine Jacob, "Tata Electronics to Hire 20K More Employees at Hosur Unit: Chandrasekaran," Business Standard, September 30, 2024, https://www.business-standard.com/companies/news/tata-electronics-to-hire-20k-more-employees-at-hosur-unit-chandrasekaran-124092800322_1.html; "Tata Seals Deal with Pegatron for iPhone Plant in Tamil Nadu, Sources Say," Reuters, November 17, 2024, https://economictimes.indiatimes.com/industry/cons-products/electronics/tata-seals-deal-with-pegatron-for-iphone-plant-in-indias-tamil-nadu-sources-say/articleshow/115380573.cms?from=mdr.

Chapter 41: A Staggering Vulnerability—TSMC

373 *reiterated his desire to "reunify"*: Nectar Gan, "Xi Vows 'Reunification' with Taiwan on Eve of Communist China's 75th Birthday," CNN, October 1, 2024, https://www.cnn.com/2024/10/01/china/china-xi-reunification-taiwan-national-day-intl-hnk/index.html.

373 *"out of business on day one"*: "Chip War" (interview with Chris Miller), *Slate*, January 28, 2023, https://slate.com/transcripts/RUZlS0o3UHYydVBib1BqWEV1Q1lMN0puTnFOemRpRVBzVmZ6N3dkT0hmQT0=.

373 *Avril Haines:* "United States Senate: Hearing to Receive Testimony on Worldwide Threats," May 4, 2023, 86, https://www.armed-services.senate.gov/imo/media/doc/23-44_05-04-2023.pdf.

373 *"the only corporation in history"*: Nicholas Kristof, "Visiting the Most Important Company in the World," *New York Times*, January 24, 2024.

374 *"Nobody can control"*: Kif Leswing, "Apple Chipmaker TSMC Warns Taiwan-China War Would Make Everybody Losers," CNBC, August 2, 2022, https://www.cnbc.com/2022/08/02/apple-chipmaker-tsmc-warns-taiwan-china-war-would-make-everybody-losers.html.

374 *"never going to let"*: Steve Clemons, "The U.S. Would Destroy Taiwan's Chip Plants if China Invades, Says Former Trump Official," *Semafor,* March 13, 2023, https://www.semafor.com/article/03/13/2023/the-us-would-destroy-taiwans-chip-plants-if-china-invades-says-former-trump-official.

374 *"the world's greatest earthquake belt"*: "Where Do Earthquakes Occur?" US Geological Survey, https://www.usgs.gov/faqs/where-do-earthquakes-occur.

374 *sold his stake in TSMC*: Michelle Toh, "Warren Buffett's Berkshire Hathaway Sells Entire Stake in TSMC," CNN, May 16, 2023, https://www.cnn.com/2023/05/16/investing/berkshire-hathaway-taiwan-tsmc-stock-exit-hnk-intl/index.html.

374 *slashed his stake in Apple*: Eric Platt, "Warren Buffett's Berkshire Hathaway Halves Stake in Apple," *Financial Times,* August 3, 2024, https://www.ft.com/content/2aa3b542-d4e4-4afb-8d81-89bb734d7b17; Eric Platt, "Warren Buffett Slashes Apple Stake as He Boosts Cash to Record High," *Financial Times,* November 2, 2024, https://www.ft.com/content/61a7e376-5ad4-4d58-bbbb-1b443ab69591.

375 *"risks of a miscalculation"*: Lee Hsien Loong, "PM Lee Hsien Loong at the Debate on the Motion of Thanks to the President 2023," Prime Minister's Office Singapore, April 19, 2023, https://www.pmo.gov.sg/Newsroom/PM-Lee-Hsien-Loong-at-the-Debate-on-the-Motion-of-Thanks-to-the-President.

375 *fought as early as 2025*: Courtney Kobe and Mosheh Gains, "Air Force General Predicts War with China in 2025, Tells Officers to Prep by Firing 'a Clip' at a Target, and 'Aim for the Head,'" NBC News, January 27, 2023, https://www.nbcnews.com/politics/national-security/us-air-force-general-predicts-war-china-2025-memo-rcna67967.

376 *shipped to Taiwan for advanced packaging* : Wayne Ma, "The Flaw in Apple's Plan to Make Chips in Arizona," *The Information*, September 11, 2023, https://www.theinformation.com/articles/apples-plan-to-make-chips-in-arizona-tsmc-nvidia-amd-tesla?rc=ropvb4.

376 *"It's not going"*: Chang's comments, quoted in the Kristof column, were first made here: Morris Chang, Jude Blanchette, and Ryan Hass, "Can Semiconductor Manufacturing Return to the US?" *Vying for Talent* (podcast), The Brookings Institution, April 14, 2022, https://www.brookings.edu/articles/can-semiconductor-manufacturing-return-to-the-us/.

376 *accused Taiwan of stealing*: Seema Mody, "Trump Accuses Taiwan of

Stealing U.S. Chip Industry. Here's What the Election Could Bring," CNN, October 28, 2024, https://www.cnbc.com/2024/10/28/trump-accuses-taiwan-of-stealing-us-chip-business-on-joe-rogan-podcast.html.

Conclusion: Unwritten Legacy

377 *White House sought to investigate*: Eleanor Olcott, "US to Check on Chips Used in Huawei's 'Made in China' Smartphone," *Financial Times*, September 6, 2023, https://www.ft.com/content/44f833a0-dc74-47be-833c-cb94a9d9e856.

378 *unboxing video*: Sami Luo Tech, "Hands-On with the $3000 Huawei Mate XT: A Triple-Fold Masterpiece?!" (English), YouTube, September 11, 2024, https://www.youtube.com/watch?v=7etrsiaoMMU.

379 *Eddy Cue issued just two directives*: Originally from BuzzFeed News, but cited here: Ben Smith, "Apple TV Was Making a Show About Gawker. Then Tim Cook Found Out," *New York Times*, December 13, 2020, https://www.nytimes.com/2020/12/13/business/media/apple-gawker-tim-cook.html#:~:text=Then%2C%20an%20Apple%20executive%20got,back%20in%202008%2C%20as%20gay.

380 *while iPhone shipments dropped*: Counterpoint Research, "China Smartphone Sales Fall 3.2% YoY in Q4, Only Quarter With YoY Decline in 2024," January 21, 2025, https://www.counterpointresearch.com/insight/post-insight-research-notes-blogs-china-smartphone-sales-fall-32-yoy-in-q4-only-quarter-with-yoy-decline-in-2024.

381 *"manager of the century"*: Steve Lohr, "Jack Welch, G.E. Chief Who Became a Business Superstar, Dies at 84," *New York Times*, March 2, 2020, https://www.nytimes.com/2020/03/02/business/jack-welch-died.html.

382 *"easier than bending metal"*: Hettie O'Brien, "Power Failure by William D. 384 Review—Pulling the Plug," *The Guardian*, November 17, 2022, https://www.theguardian.com/books/2022/nov/17/power-failure-by-william-d-cohan-review-pulling-the-plug.

383 *"Apple's scramble to reduce dependence"*: Jay Newman, "Apple Is a Chinese Company," *FT Alphaville*, May 2, 2023.

383 *most iconic computer TV spot ever*: "1984 (advertisement)," Wikipedia, https://en.m.wikipedia.org/wiki/1984_(advertisement).

INDEX